NOW IT CAN BE TOLD

NOW IT CAN BE TOLD

BY

PHILIP GIBBS

ISBN: 978-93-5128-969-2(HB)

First Published in 1920
Indian Reprint in 2017

Published by

Kalpaz Publications
C-30, Satyawati Nagar,
Delhi – 110052
E-mail: kalpaz@hotmail.com
Website: kalpazpublications.com
Ph.: +91-9212142040

CONTENTS

PREFACE

In this book I have written about some aspects of the war which, I believe, the world must know and remember, not only as a memorial of men's courage in tragic years, but as a warning of what will happen again—surely—if a heritage of evil and of folly is not cut out of the hearts of peoples. Here it is the reality of modern warfare not only as it appears to British soldiers, of whom I can tell, but to soldiers on all the fronts where conditions were the same.

What I have written here does not cancel, nor alter, nor deny anything in my daily narratives of events on the western front as they are now published in book form. They stand, I may claim sincerely and humbly, as a truthful, accurate, and tragic record of the battles in France and Belgium during the years of war, broadly pictured out as far as I could see and know. My duty, then, was that of a chronicler, not arguing why things should have happened so nor giving reasons why they should not happen so, but describing faithfully many of the things I saw, and narrating the facts as I found them, as far as the censorship would allow. After early, hostile days it allowed nearly all but criticism, protest, and of the figures of loss.

The purpose of this book is to get deeper into the truth of this war and of all war—not by a more detailed narrative of events, but rather as the truth was revealed to the minds of men, in many aspects, out of their experience; and by a plain statement of realities, however painful, to add something to the world's knowledge out of which men of good-will may try to shape some new system of relationship between one people and another, some new code of international morality, preventing or at least postponing another massacre of youth like that five years' sacrifice of boys of which I was a witness.

PART ONE

OBSERVERS AND COMMANDERS

I

When Germany threw down her challenge to Russia and France, and England knew that her Imperial power would be one of the prizes of German victory (the common people did not think this, at first, but saw only the outrage to Belgium, a brutal attack on civilization, and a glorious adventure), some newspaper correspondents were sent out from London to report the proceedings, and I was one of them.

We went in civilian clothes without military passports—the War Office was not giving any—with bags of money which might be necessary for the hire of motor-cars, hotel life, and the bribery of doorkeepers in the antechambers of war, as some of us had gone to the Balkan War, and others. The Old Guard of war correspondents besieged the War Office for official recognition and were insulted day after day by junior staff-officers who knew that "K" hated these men and thought the press ought to be throttled in time of war; or they were beguiled into false hopes by officials who hoped to go in charge of them and were told to buy horses and sleeping-bags and be ready to start at a moment's notice for the front.

The moment's notice was postponed for months....

The younger ones did not wait for it. They took their chance of "seeing something," without authority, and made wild, desperate efforts to break through the barrier that had been put up against them by French and British staffs in the zone of war. Many of them were arrested, put into prison, let out, caught again in forbidden places, rearrested, and expelled from France. That was after fantastic adventures in which they saw what war meant in civilized countries where vast populations were made fugitives of fear, where millions of women and children and old people became wanderers along the roads in a tide of human misery, with the red flame of war behind them and following them, and where the first battalions of youth, so gay in their approach to war, so confident of victory, so careless of the dangers (which they did not know), came back maimed and mangled and blinded and wrecked, in the backwash of retreat, which presently became a spate through Belgium and the north of France, swamping over many cities and thousands of villages and many fields. Those young writing-men who had set out in a spirit of adventure went back to Fleet Street with a queer look in their eyes, unable to write the things they had seen, unable to tell them to people who had not seen and could not understand. Because there was no code of words which would convey the picture of that wild agony of peoples, that smashing of all civilized laws, to men and women who still thought of war in terms of heroic pageantry.

"Had a good time?" asked a colleague along the corridor, hardly waiting for an answer.

"A good time!"... God!... Did people think it was amusing to be an onlooker of world-tragedy?... One of them remembered a lady of France with a small boy who had fled from Charleville, which was in flames and smoke. She was weak with hunger, with dirty and bedraggled skirts on her flight, and she had heard that her husband was in the battle that was now being fought round their own town. She was brave—pointed out the line of the German advance on the map—and it was in a troop-train crowded with French soldiers—and then burst into wild weeping, clasping the hand of an English writing-man so that her nails dug into his flesh. I remember her still.

"Courage, maman! Courage, p'tite maman!" said the boy of eight.

Through Amiens at night had come a French army in retreat. There were dead and wounded on their wagons. Cuirassiers stumbled as they led their tired horses. Crowds of people with white faces, like ghosts in the darkness, stared at their men retreating like this through their city, and knew that the enemy was close behind.

"Nous sommes perdus!" whispered a woman, and gave a wailing cry.

People were fighting their way into railway trucks at every station for hundreds of miles across northern France. Women were beseeching a place for the sake of their babes. There was no food for them on journeys of nineteen hours or more; they fainted with heat and hunger. An old woman died, and her corpse blocked up the lavatory. At night they slept on the pavements in cities invaded by fugitives.

At Furnes in Belgium, and at Dunkirk on the coast of France, there were columns of ambulances bringing in an endless tide of wounded. They were laid out stretcher by stretcher in station-yards, five hundred at a time. Some of their faces were masks of clotted blood. Some of their bodies were horribly torn. They breathed with a hard snuffle. A foul smell came from them.

At Chartres they were swilling over the station hall with disinfecting fluid after getting through with one day's wounded. The French doctor in charge had received a telegram from the director of medical services: "Make ready for forty thousand wounded." It was during the first battle of the Marne.

"It is impossible!" said the French doctor....

Four hundred thousand people were in flight from Antwerp, into which big shells were falling, as English correspondents flattened themselves against the walls and said, "God in heaven!" Two hundred and fifty thousand people coming across the Scheldt in rowing-boats, sailing-craft, rafts, invaded one village in Holland. They had no food. Children were mad with fright. Young mothers had no milk in their breasts. It was cold at night and there were only a few canal-boats and fishermen's cottages, and in them were crowds of fugitives. The odor of human filth exuded from them, as I smell it now, and sicken in remembrance....

Then Dixmude was in flames, and Pervyse, and many other towns from the Belgian coast to Switzerland. In Dixmude young boys of France—fusiliers marins—lay dead about the Grande Place. In the Town Hall, falling to bits under shell-fire, a colonel stood dazed and waiting for death amid the dead bodies of his men—one so young, so handsome, lying there on his back, with a waxen face, staring steadily at the sky through the broken roof....

At Nieuport-les-Bains one dead soldier lay at the end of the esplanade, and a little group of living were huddled under the wall of a red-brick villa, watching other villas falling like card houses in a town that had been built for love and pretty women and the lucky people of the world. British monitors lying close into shore were answering the German bombardment, firing over Nieuport to the dunes by Ostend. From one monitor came a group of figures with white masks of cotton-wool tipped with wet blood. British seamen, and all blind, with the dead body of an officer tied up in a sack....

"O Jesu!... O maman!... O ma pauvre p'tite femme!... O Jesu! O Jesu!"

From thousands of French soldiers lying wounded or parched in the burning sun before the battle of the Marne these cries went up to the blue sky of France in August of '14. They were the cries of youth's agony in war. Afterward I went across the fields where they fought and saw their bodies and their graves, and the proof of the victory that saved France and us. The German dead had been gathered into heaps like autumn leaves. They were soaked in petrol and oily smoke was rising from them....

That was after the retreat from Mons, and the French retreat along all their line, and the thrust that drew very close to Paris, when I saw our little Regular Army, the "Old Contemptibles," on their way back, with the German hordes following close. Sir John French had his headquarters for the night in Creil. English, Irish, Scottish soldiers, stragglers from units still keeping some kind of order, were coming in, bronzed, dusty, parched with thirst, with light wounds tied round with rags, with blistered feet. French soldiers, bearded, dirty, thirsty as dogs, crowded the station platforms. They, too, had been retreating and retreating. A company of sappers had blown up forty bridges of France. Under a gas-lamp in a foul-smelling urinal I copied out the diary of their officer. Some spiritual faith upheld these men. "Wait," they said. "In a few days we shall give them a hard knock. They will never get Paris. *Jamais de la vie!"*...

In Beauvais there was hardly a living soul when three English correspondents went there, after escape from Amiens, now in German hands. A tall cuirassier stood by some bags of gunpowder, ready to blow up the bridge. The streets were strewn with barbed wire and broken bottles... In Paris there was a great fear and solitude, except where grief-stricken crowds stormed the railway stations for escape and where French and British soldiers—stragglers all—drank together, and sang above their broken glasses, and cursed the war and the Germans.

And down all the roads from the front, on every day in every month of that first six months of war—as afterward—came back the tide of wounded; wounded everywhere, maimed men at every junction; hospitals crowded with blind and dying and moaning men....

"Had an interesting time?" asked a man I wanted to kill because of his smug ignorance, his damnable indifference, his impregnable stupidity of cheerfulness in this world of agony. I had changed the clothes which were smeared with blood of French and Belgian soldiers whom I had helped, in a week of strange adventure, to carry to the surgeons. As an onlooker of war I hated the people who had not seen, because they could not understand. All these things I had seen in the first nine months I put down in a book called The Soul of the War, so that some might know; but it was only a few who understood....

II

In 1915 the War Office at last moved in the matter of war correspondents. Lord Kitchener, prejudiced against them, was being broken down a little by the pressure of public opinion (mentioned from time to time by members of the government), which demanded more news of their men in the field than was given by bald communiqués from General Headquarters and by an "eye-witness" who, as one paper had the audacity to say, wrote nothing but "eye-wash." Even the enormous, impregnable stupidity of our High Command on all matters of psychology was penetrated by a vague notion that a few "writing fellows" might be sent out with permission to follow the armies in the field, under the strictest censorship, in order to silence the popular clamor for more news. Dimly and nervously they apprehended that in order to stimulate the recruiting of the New Army now being called to the colors by vulgar appeals to sentiment and passion, it might be well to "write up" the glorious side of war as it could be seen at the base and in the organization of transport, without, of course, any allusion to dead or dying men, to the ghastly failures of distinguished generals, or to the filth and horror of the battlefields. They could not understand, nor did they ever understand (these soldiers of the old school) that a nation which was sending all its sons to the field of honor desired with a deep and poignant craving to know how those boys of theirs were living and how they were dying, and what suffering was theirs, and what chances they had against their enemy, and how it was going with the war which was absorbing all the energy and wealth of the people at home.

"Why don't they trust their leaders?" asked the army chiefs. "Why don't they leave it to us?"

"We do trust you—with some misgivings," thought the people, "and we do leave it to you—though you seem to be making a mess of things—but we want to know what we have a right to know, and that is the life and progress of this war in which our men are engaged. We want to know more about their heroism, so that it shall be remembered by their people and known by the world; about their agony, so that we may share it in our hearts; and about the way of their death, so that our grief may be softened by the thought of their courage. We will not stand for this anonymous war; and you are wasting time by keeping it secret, because the imagination of those who have not joined cannot be fired by cold lines which say, 'There is nothing to report on the western front.'"

In March of 1915 I went out with the first body of accredited war correspondents, and we saw some of the bad places where our men lived and died, and the traffic to the lines, and the mechanism of war in fixed positions as were then established after the battle of the Marne and the first battle of Ypres. Even then it was only an experimental visit. It was not until June of that year, after an adventure on the French front in the Champagne, that I received full credentials as a war correspondent with the British armies on the western front, and joined four other men who had been selected for this service, and began that long innings as an authorized onlooker of war which ended, after long and dreadful years, with the Army of Occupation beyond the Rhine.

III

In the very early days we lived in a small old house, called by courtesy a chateau, in the village of Tatinghem, near General Headquarters at St.-Omer. (Afterward we shifted our quarters from time to time, according to the drift of battle and our convenience.) It was very peaceful there amid fields of standing corn, where peasant women worked while their men were fighting, but in the motor-cars supplied us by the army (with military drivers, all complete) it was a quick ride over Cassel Hill to the edge of the Ypres salient and the farthest point where any car could go without being seen by a watchful enemy and blown to bits at a signal to the guns. Then we walked, up sinister roads, or along communication trenches, to the fire-step in the front line, or into places like "Plug Street" wood and Kemmel village, and the ruins of Vermelles, and the lines by Neuve Chapelle—the training-schools of British armies—where always birds of death were on the wing, screaming with high and rising notes before coming to earth with the cough that killed... After hours in those hiding-places where boys of the New Army were learning the lessons of war in dugouts and ditches under the range of German guns, back again to the little white chateau at Tatinghem, with a sweet scent of flowers from the fields, and nightingales singing in the woods and a bell tinkling for Benediction in the old church tower beyond our gate.

"To-morrow," said the colonel—our first chief—before driving in for a late visit to G. H. Q., "we will go to Armentieres and see how the 'Kitchener' boys are shaping in the line up there. It ought to be interesting."

The colonel was profoundly interested in the technic of war, in its organization of supplies and transport, and methods of command. He was a Regular of the Indian Army, a soldier by blood and caste and training, and the noblest type of the old school of Imperial officer, with obedience to command as a religious instinct; of stainless honor, I think, in small things as well as great, with a deep love of England, and a belief and pride in her Imperial destiny to govern many peoples for their own good, and with the narrowness of such belief. His imagination was limited to the boundaries of his professional interests, though now and then his humanity made him realize in a perplexed way greater issues at stake in this war than the challenge to British Empiry.

One day, when we were walking through the desolation of a battlefield, with the smell of human corruption about us, and men crouched in chalky ditches below their breastworks of sand-bags, he turned to a colleague of mine and said in a startled way:

"This must never happen again! Never!"

It will never happen again for him, as for many others. He was too tall for the trenches, and one day a German sniper saw the red glint of his hat-band—he was on the staff of the 11th Corps—and thought, "a gay bird"! So he fell; and in our mess, when the news came, we were sad at his going, and one of our orderlies, who had been his body-servant, wept as he waited on us.

Late at night the colonel—that first chief of ours—used to come home from G. H. Q., as all men called General Headquarters with a sense of mystery, power, and inexplicable industry accomplishing—what?—in those initials. He came back with a cheery shout of, "Fine weather to-morrow!" or, "A starry night and all's well!" looking fine and soldierly as the glare of his headlights shone on his tall figure with red tabs and a colored armlet. But that cheeriness covered secret worries. Night after night, in those early weeks of our service, he sat in his little office, talking earnestly with the press officers—our censors. They seemed to be arguing, debating, protesting, about secret influences and hostilities surrounding us and them. I could only guess what it was all about. It all seemed to make no difference to me when I sat down before pieces of blank paper to get down some kind of picture, some kind of impression, of a long day in place where I had been scared awhile because death was on the prowl in a noisy way and I had seen it pounce on human bodies. I knew that tomorrow I was going to another little peep-show of war, where I should hear the same noises. That talk downstairs, that worry about some mystery at G. H. Q. would make no difference to the life or death of men, nor get rid of that coldness which came to me when men were being killed nearby. Why all that argument?

It seemed that G. H. Q.—mysterious people in a mysterious place—were drawing up rules for war correspondence and censorship; altering rules made the day before, formulating new rules for to-morrow, establishing precedents, writing minutes, initialing reports with, "Passed to you," or, "I agree," written on the margin. The censors who lived with us and traveled with us and were our friends, and read what we wrote before the ink was dry, had to examine our screeds with microscopic eyes and with infinite remembrance of the thousand and one rules. Was it safe to mention the weather? Would that give any information to the enemy? Was it permissible to describe the smell of chloride-of-lime in the trenches, or would that discourage recruiting? That description of the traffic on the roads of war, with transport wagons, gun-limbers, lorries, mules—how did that conflict with Rule No. 17a (or whatever it was) prohibiting all mention of movements of troops?

One of the censors working late at night, with lines of worry on his forehead and little puckers about his eyes, turned to me with a queer laugh, one night in the early days. He was an Indian Civil Servant, and therefore, by every rule, a gentleman and a charming fellow.

"You don't know what I am risking in passing your despatch! It's too good to spoil, but G. H. Q. will probably find that it conveys accurate information to the enemy about the offensive in 1925. I shall get the sack—and oh, the difference to me!"

It appeared that G. H. Q. was nervous of us. They suggested that our private letters should be tested for writing in invisible ink between the lines. They were afraid that, either deliberately for some journalistic advantage, or in sheer ignorance as "outsiders," we might hand information to the enemy about important secrets. Belonging to the old caste of army mind, they believed that war was the special prerogative of professional soldiers, of which politicians and people should have no knowledge. Therefore as civilians in khaki we were hardly better than spies.

The Indian Civil Servant went for a stroll with me in the moonlight, after a day up the line, where young men were living and dying in dirty ditches. I could see that he was worried, even angry.

"Those people!" he said.

"What people?"

"G. H. Q."

"Oh, Lord!" I groaned. "Again?" and looked across the fields of corn to the dark outline of a convent on the hill where young officers were learning the gentle art of killing by machine-guns before their turn came to be killed or crippled. I thought of a dead boy I had seen that day—or yesterday was it?—kneeling on the fire-step of a trench, with his forehead against the parapet as though in prayer... How sweet was the scent of the clover to-night! And how that star twinkled above the low flashes of gun-fire away there in the salient.

"They want us to waste your time," said the officer. "Those were the very words used by the Chief of Intelligence—in writing which I have kept. 'Waste their time!'... I'll be damned if I consider my work is to waste the time of war correspondents. Don't those good fools see that this is not a professional adventure, like their other little wars; that the whole nation is in it, and that the nation demands to know what its men are doing? They have a right to know."

IV

Just at first—though not for long—there was a touch of hostility against us among divisional and brigade staffs, of the Regulars, but not of the New Army. They, too, suspected our motive in going to their quarters, wondered why we should come "spying around," trying to "see things." I was faintly conscious of this one day in those very early times, when with the officer who had been a ruler in India I went to a brigade headquarters of the 1st Division near Vermelles. It was not easy nor pleasant to get there, though it was a summer day with fleecy clouds in a blue sky. There was a long straight road leading to the village of Vermelles, with a crisscross of communication trenches on one side, and, on the other, fields where corn and grass grew rankly in abandoned fields. Some lean sheep were browsing there as though this were Arcady in days of peace. It was not. The red ruins of Vermelles, a mile or so away, were sharply defined, as through stereoscopic lenses, in the quiver of sunlight, and had the sinister look of a death-haunted place. It was where the French had fought their way through gardens, walls, and houses in murderous battle, before leaving it for British troops to hold. Across it now came the whine of shells, and I saw that shrapnel bullets were kicking up the dust of a thousand yards down the straight road, following a small body of brown men whose tramp of feet raised another cloud of dust, like smoke. They were the only representatives of human life—besides ourselves—in this loneliness, though many men must have been in hiding somewhere. Then heavy "crumps" burst in the fields where the sheep were browsing, across the way we had to go to the brigade headquarters.

"How about it?" asked the captain with me. "I don't like crossing that field, in spite of the buttercups and daisies and the little frisky lambs."

"I hate the idea of it," I said.

Then we looked down the road at the little body of brown men. They were nearer now, and I could see the face of the officer leading them—a boy subaltern, rather pale though the sun was hot. He halted and saluted my companion.

"The enemy seems to have sighted our dust, sir. His shrapnel is following up pretty closely. Would you advise me to put my men under cover, or carry on?"

The captain hesitated. This was rather outside his sphere of influence. But the boyishness of the other officer asked for help.

"My advice is to put your men into that ditch and keep them there until the strafe is over." Some shrapnel bullets whipped the sun-baked road as he spoke.

"Very good, sir."

The men sat in the ditch, with their packs against the bank, and wiped the sweat off their faces. They looked tired and dispirited, but not alarmed.

In the fields behind them—our way—the 4.2's (four—point-twos) were busy plugging holes in the grass and flowers, rather deep holes, from which white smoke-clouds rose after explosive noises.

"With a little careful strategy we might get through," said the captain. "There's a general waiting for us, and I have noticed that generals are impatient fellows. Let's try our luck."

We walked across the wild flowers, past the sheep, who only raised their heads in meek surprise when shells came with a shrill, intensifying snarl and burrowed up the earth about them. I noticed how loudly and sweetly the larks were singing up in the blue. Several horses lay dead, newly killed, with blood oozing about them, and their entrails smoking. We made a half-loop around them and then struck straight for the chateau which was the brigade headquarters. Neither of us spoke now. We were thoughtful, calculating the chance of getting to that red-brick house between the shells. It was just dependent on the coincidence of time and place.

Three men jumped up from a ditch below a brown wall round the chateau garden and ran hard for the gateway. A shell had pitched quite close to them. One man laughed as though at a grotesque joke, and fell as he reached the courtyard. Smoke was rising from the outhouses, and there was a clatter of tiles and timbers, after an explosive crash.

"It rather looks," said my companion, "as though the Germans knew there is a party on in that charming house."

It was as good to go on as to go back, and it was never good to go back before reaching one's objective. That was bad for the discipline of the courage that is just beyond fear.

Two gunners were killed in the back yard of the chateau, and as we went in through the gateway a sergeant made a quick jump for a barn as a shell burst somewhere close. As visitors we hesitated between two ways into the chateau, and chose the easier; and it was then that I became dimly aware of hostility against me on the part of a number of officers in the front hall. The brigade staff was there, grouped under the banisters. I wondered why, and guessed (rightly, as I found) that the center of the house might have a better chance of escape than the rooms on either side, in case of direct hits from those things falling outside.

It was the brigade major who asked our business. He was a tall, handsome young man of something over thirty, with the arrogance of a Christ Church blood.

"Oh, he has come out to see something in Vermelles? A pleasant place for sightseeing! Meanwhile the Hun is ranging on this house, so he may see more than he wants."

He turned on his heel and rejoined his group. They all stared in my direction as though at a curious animal. A very young gentleman—the general's A. D. C.—made a funny remark at my expense and the others laughed. Then they ignored me, and I was glad, and made a little study in the psychology of men awaiting a close call of death. I was perfectly conscious myself that in a moment or two some of us, perhaps all of us, might be in a pulp of mangled flesh beneath the ruins of a red-brick villa—the shells were crashing among the outhouses and in the courtyard, and the enemy was making good shooting—and the idea did not please me at all. At the back of my brain was Fear, and there was a cold sweat in the palms of my hands; but I was master of myself, and I remember having a sense of satisfaction because I had answered the brigade major in a level voice, with a touch of his own arrogance. I saw that these officers were afraid; that they, too, had Fear at the back of the brain, and that their conversation and laughter were the camouflage of the soul. The face of the young A. D. C. was flushed and he laughed too much at his own jokes, and his laughter was just a tone too shrill. An officer came into the hall, carrying two Mills bombs—new toys in those days—and the others fell back from him, and one said:

"For Christ's sake don't bring them here—in the middle of a bombardment!"

"Where's the general?" asked the newcomer.

"Down in the cellar with the other brigadier. They don't ask us down to tea, I notice."

Those last words caused all the officers to laugh—almost excessively. But their laughter ended sharply, and they listened intently as there was a heavy crash outside.

Another officer came up the steps and made a rapid entry into the hall.

"I understand there is to be a conference of battalion commanders," he said, with a queer catch in his breath. "In view of this—er—bombardment, I had better come in later, perhaps?"

"You had better wait," said the brigade major, rather grimly.

"Oh, certainly."

A sergeant-major was pacing up and down the passage by the back door. He was calm and stolid. I liked the look of him and found something comforting in his presence, so that I went to have a few words with him.

"How long is this likely to last, Sergeant-major"

"There's no saying, sir. They may be searching for the chateau to pass the time, so to speak, or they may go on till they get it. I'm sorry they caught those gunners. Nice lads, both of them."

He did not seem to be worrying about his own chance.

Then suddenly there was silence. The German guns had switched off. I heard the larks singing through the open doorway, and all the little sounds of a summer day. The group of officers in the hall started chatting more quietly. There was no more need of finding jokes and laughter. They had been reprieved, and could be serious.

"We'd better get forward to Vermelles," said my companion.

As we walked away from the chateau, the brigade major passed us on his horse. He leaned over his saddle toward me and said, "Good day to you, and I hope you'll like Vermelles."

The words were civil, but there was an underlying meaning in them.

"I hope to do so, sir."

We walked down the long straight road toward the ruins of Vermelles with a young soldier-guide who on the outskirts of the village remarked in a casual way:

"No one is allowed along this road in daylight, as a rule. It's under hobservation of the henemy."

"Then why the devil did you come this way?" asked my companion.

"I thought you might prefer the short cut, sir."

We explored the ruins of Vermelles, where many young Frenchmen had fallen in fighting through the walls and gardens. One could see the track of their strife, in trampled bushes and broken walls. Bits of red rag—the red pantaloons of the first French soldiers—were still fastened to brambles and barbed wire. Broken rifles, cartouches, water-bottles, torn letters, twisted bayonets, and German stick-bombs littered the ditches which had been dug as trenches across streets of burned-out houses.

V

A young gunner officer whom we met was very civil, and stopped in front of the chateau of Vermelles, a big red villa with the outer walls still standing, and told us the story of its capture.

"It was a wild scrap. I was told all about it by a French sergeant who was in it. They were under the cover of that wall over there, about a hundred yards away, and fixing up a charge of high explosives to knock a breach in the wall. The chateau was a machine-gun fortress, with the Germans on the top floor, the ground floor, and in the basement, protected by sand-bags, through which they fired. A German officer made a bad mistake. He opened the front door and came out with some of his machine-gunners from the ground floor to hold a trench across the square in front of the house. Instantly a French lieutenant called to his men. They climbed over the wall and made a dash for the chateau, bayoneting the Germans who tried to stop them. Then they swarmed into the chateau—a platoon of them with the lieutenant. They were in the drawing-room, quite an elegant place, you know, with the usual gilt furniture and long mirrors. In one corner was a pedestal, with a statue of Venus standing on it. Rather charming, I expect. A few Germans were killed in the room, easily. But upstairs there was a mob who fired down through the ceiling when they found what had happened. The French soldiers prodded the ceiling with their bayonets, and all the plaster broke, falling on them. A German, fat and heavy, fell half-way through the rafters, and a bayonet was poked into him as he stuck there. The whole ceiling gave way, and the Germans upstairs came downstairs, in a heap. They fought like wolves—wild beasts—with fear and rage. French and Germans clawed at one another's throats, grabbed hold of noses, rolled over each other. The French sergeant told me he had his teeth into a German's neck. The man was all over him, pinning his arms, trying to choke him. It was the French lieutenant who did most damage. He fired his last shot and smashed a German's face with his empty revolver. Then he caught hold of the marble Venus by the legs and swung it above his head, in the old Berserker style, and laid out Germans like ninepins... The fellows in the basement surrendered."

VI

The chateau of Vermelles, where that had happened, was an empty ruin, and there was no sign of the gilt furniture, or the long mirrors, or the marble Venus when I looked through the charred window-frames upon piles of bricks and timber churned up by shell-fire. The gunner officer took us to the cemetery, to meet some friends of his who had their battery nearby. We stumbled over broken walls and pushed through undergrowth to get to the graveyard, where some broken crosses and wire frames with immortelles remained as relics of that garden where the people of Vermelles had laid their dead to rest. New dead had followed old dead. I stumbled over something soft, like a ball of clay, and saw that it was the head of a faceless man, in a battered kepi. From a ditch close by came a sickly stench of half-buried flesh.

"The whole place is a pest-house," said the gunner.

Another voice spoke from some hiding-place.

"Salvo!"

The earth shook and there was a flash of red flame, and a shock of noise which hurt one's ear-drums.

"That's my battery," said the gunner officer. "It's the very devil when one doesn't expect it."

I was introduced to the gentleman who had said "Salvo!" He was the gunner-major, and a charming fellow, recently from civil life. All the battery was made up of New Army men learning their job, and learning it very well, I should say. There was no arrogance about them.

"It's sporting of you to come along to a spot like this," said one of them. "I wouldn't unless I had to. Of course you'll take tea in our mess?"

I was glad to take tea—in a little house at the end of the ruined high-street of Vermelles which had by some miracle escaped destruction, though a shell had pierced through the brick wall of the parlor and had failed to burst. It was there still, firmly wedged, like a huge nail. The tea was good, in tin mugs. Better still was the company of the gunner officers. They told me how often they were "scared stiff." They had been very frightened an hour before I came, when the German gunners had ranged up and down the street, smashing up ruined houses into greater ruin.

"They're so methodical!" said one of the officers.

"Wonderful shooting!" said another.

"I will say they're topping gunners," said the major. "But we're learning; my men are very keen. Put in a good word for the new artillery. It would buck them up no end."

We went back before sunset, down the long straight road, and past the chateau which we had visited in the afternoon. It looked very peaceful there among the trees.

It is curious that I remember the details of that day so vividly, as though they happened yesterday. On hundreds of other days I had adventures like that, which I remember more dimly.

"That brigade major was a trifle haughty, don't you think?" said my companion. "And the others didn't seem very friendly. Not like those gunner boys."

"We called at an awkward time. They were rather fussed."

"One expects good manners. Especially from Regulars who pride themselves on being different in that way from the New Army."

"It's the difference between the professional and the amateur soldier. The Regular crowd think the war belongs to them... But I liked their pluck. They're arrogant to Death himself when he comes knocking at the door."

VII

It was not long before we broke down the prejudice against us among the fighting units. The new armies were our friends from the first, and liked us to visit them in their trenches and their dugouts, their camps and their billets. Every young officer was keen to show us his particular "peep-show" or to tell us his latest "stunt." We made many friends among them, and it was our grief that as the war went on so many of them disappeared from their battalions, and old faces were replaced by new faces, and those again by others when they had become familiar. Again and again, after battle, twenty-two officers in a battalion mess were reduced to two or three, and the gaps were filled up from the reserve depots. I was afraid to ask, "Where is So-and-so?" because I knew that the best answer would be, "A Blighty wound," and the worst was more likely.

It was the duration of all the drama of death that seared one's soul as an onlooker; the frightful sum of sacrifice that we were recording day by day. There were times when it became intolerable and agonizing, and when I at least desired peace-at-almost-any-price, peace by negotiation, by compromise, that the river of blood might cease to flow. The men looked so splendid as they marched up to the lines, singing, whistling, with an easy swing. They looked so different when thousands came down again, to field dressing-stations—the walking wounded and the stretcher cases, the blind and the gassed—as we saw them on the mornings of battle, month after month, year after year.

Our work as chroniclers of their acts was not altogether "soft," though we did not go "over the top" or live in the dirty ditches with them. We had to travel prodigiously to cover the ground between one division and another along a hundred miles of front, with long walks often at the journey's end and a wet way back. Sometimes we were soaked to the skin on the journey home. Often we were so cold and numbed in those long wild drives up desolate roads that our limbs lost consciousness and the wind cut into us like knives. We were working against time, always against time, and another tire-burst would mean that no despatch could be written of a great battle on the British front, or only a short record written in the wildest haste when there was so much to tell, so much to describe, such unforgetable pictures in one's brain of another day's impressions in the fields and on the roads.

There were five English correspondents and, two years later, two Americans. On mornings of big battle we divided up the line of front and drew lots for the particular section which each man would cover. Then before the dawn, or in the murk of winter mornings, or the first glimmer of a summer day, our cars would pull out and we would go off separately to the part of the line allotted to us by the number drawn, to see the preliminary bombardment, to walk over newly captured ground, to get into the backwash of prisoners and walking wounded, amid batteries firing a new barrage, guns moving forward on days of good advance, artillery transport bringing up new stores of ammunition, troops in support marching to repel a counter-attack or follow through the new objectives, ambulances threading their way back through the traffic, with loads of prostrate men, mules, gunhorses, lorries churning up the mud in Flanders.

So we gained a personal view of all this activity of strife, and from many men in its whirlpool details of their own adventure and of general progress or disaster on one sector of the battle-front. Then in divisional headquarters we saw the reports of the battle as they came in by telephone, or aircraft, or pigeon-post, from half-hour to half-hour, or ten minutes by ten minutes. Three divisions widely separated provided all the work one war correspondent could do on one day of action, and later news on a broader scale, could be obtained from corps headquarters farther back. Tired, hungry, nerve-racked, splashed to the eyes in mud, or covered in a mask of dust, we started for the journey back to our own quarters, which we shifted from time to time in order to get as near as we could to the latest battle-front without getting beyond reach of the telegraph instruments—by relays of despatch-riders—at "Signals," G. H. Q., which remained immovably fixed in the rear.

There was a rendezvous in one of our rooms, and each man outlined the historical narrative of the day upon the front he had covered, reserving for himself his own adventures, impressions, and emotions.

Time slipped away, and time was short, while the despatch-riders waited for our unwritten despatches, and censors who had been our fellow-travelers washed themselves cleaner and kept an eye on the clock.

Time was short while the world waited for our tales of tragedy or victory... and tempers were frayed, and nerves on edge, among five men who hated one another, sometimes, with a murderous hatred (though, otherwise, good comrades) and desired one another's death by slow torture or poison-gas when they fumbled over notes, written in a jolting car, or on a battlefield walk, and went into past history in order to explain present happenings, or became tangled in the numbers of battalions and divisions.

Percival Phillips turned pink-and-white under the hideous strain of nervous control, with an hour and a half for two columns in The Morning Post. A little pulse throbbed in his forehead. His lips were tightly pressed. His oaths and his anguish were in his soul, but unuttered. Beach Thomas, the most amiable of men, the Peter Pan who went a bird-nesting on battlefields, a lover of beauty and games and old poems and Greek and Latin tags, and all joy in life—what had he to do with war?—looked bored with an infinite boredom, irritable with a scornful impatience of unnecessary detail, gazed through his gold-rimmed spectacles with an air of extreme detachment (when Percy Robinson rebuilt the map with dabs and dashes on a blank sheet of paper), and said, "I've got more than I can write, and The Daily Mail goes early to press."

"Thanks very much... It's very kind of you."

We gathered up our note-books and were punctiliously polite. (Afterward we were the best of friends.) Thomas was first out of the room, with short, quick little steps in spite of his long legs. His door banged. Phillips was first at his typewriter, working it like a machine-gun, in short, furious spasms of word-fire. I sat down to my typewriter—a new instrument of torture to me—and coaxed its evil genius with conciliatory prayers.

"For dear God's sake," I said, "don't go twisting that blasted ribbon of yours to-day. I must write this despatch, and I've just an hour when I want five."

Sometimes that Corona was a mechanism of singular sweetness, and I blessed it with a benediction. But often there was a devil in it which mocked at me. After the first sentence or two it twisted the ribbon; at the end of twenty sentences the ribbon was like an angry snake, writhing and coiling hideously.

I shouted for Mackenzie, the American, a master of these things.

He came in and saw my blanched face, my sweat of anguish, my crise de nerfs. I could see by his eyes that he understood my stress and had pity on me.

"That's all right," he said. "A little patience—"

By a touch or two he exorcised the devil, laughed, and said: "Go easy. You've just about reached breaking—point."

I wrote, as we all wrote, fast and furiously, to get down something of enormous history, word-pictures of things seen, heroic anecdotes, the underlying meaning of this new slaughter. There was never time to think out a sentence or a phrase, to touch up a clumsy paragraph, to go back on a false start, to annihilate a vulgar adjective, to put a touch of style into one's narrative. One wrote instinctively, blindly, feverishly... And downstairs were the censors, sending up messages by orderlies to say "half-time," or "ten minutes more," and cutting out sometimes the things one wanted most to say, modifying a direct statement of fact into a vague surmise, taking away the honor due to the heroic men who had fought and died to-day... Who would be a war correspondent, or a censor?

So it happened day by day, for five months at a stretch, when big battles were in progress. It was not an easy life. There were times when I was so physically and mentally exhausted that I could hardly rouse myself to a new day's effort. There were times when I was faint and sick and weak; and my colleagues were like me. But we struggled on to tell the daily history of the war and the public cursed us because we did not tell more, or sneered at us because they thought we were "spoon-fed" by G. H. Q.—who never gave us any news and who were far from our way of life, except when they thwarted us, by petty restrictions and foolish rules.

VIII

The Commander-in-Chief—Sir John French—received us when we were first attached to the British armies in the field—a lifetime ago, as it seems to me now. It was a formal ceremony in the chateau near St.-Omer, which he used as his own headquarters, with his A. D. C.'s in attendance, though the main general headquarters were in the town. Our first colonel gathered us like a shepherd with his flock, counting us twice over before we passed in. A tall, dark young man, whom I knew afterward to be Sir Philip Sassoon, received us and chatted pleasantly in a French salon with folding-doors which shut off an inner room. There were a few portraits of ladies and gentlemen of France in the days before the Revolution, like those belonging to that old aristocracy which still existed, in poverty and pride, in other chateaus in this French Flanders. There was a bouquet of flowers on the table, giving a sweet scent to the room, and sunlight streamed through the shutters... I thought for a moment of the men living in ditches in the salient, under harassing fire by day and night. Their actions and their encounters with death were being arranged, without their knowledge, in this sunny little chateau....

The folding-doors opened and Sir John French came in. He wore top-boots and spurs, and after saying, "Good day, gentlemen," stood with his legs apart, a stocky, soldierly figure, with a square head and heavy jaw. I wondered whether there were any light of genius in him—any inspiration, any force which would break the awful strength of the enemy against us, any cunning in modern warfare.

He coughed a little, and made us a speech. I forget his words, but remember the gist of them. He was pleased to welcome us within his army, and trusted to our honor and loyalty. He made an allusion to the power of the press, and promised us facilities for seeing and writing, within the bounds of censorship. I noticed that he pronounced St.-Omer, St.-Omar, as though Omar Khayyam had been canonized. He said, "Good day, gentlemen," again, and coughed huskily again to clear his throat, and then went back through the folding-doors.

I saw him later, during the battle of Loos, after its ghastly failure. He was riding a white horse in the villages of Heuchin and Houdain, through which lightly wounded Scots of the 1st and 15th Divisions were making their way back. He leaned over his saddle, questioning the men and thanking them for their gallantry. I thought he looked grayer and older than when he had addressed us.

"Who mun that old geezer be, Jock?" asked a Highlander when he had passed.

"I dinna ken," said the other Scot. "An' I dinna care."

"It's the Commander-in-Chief," I said. "Sir John French."

"Eh?" said the younger man, of the 8th Gordons. He did not seem thrilled by the knowledge I had given him, but turned his head and stared after the figure on the white horse. Then he said: "Well, he's made a mess o' the battle. We could've held Hill 70 against all the di'els o' hell if there had bin supports behind us."

"Ay," said his comrade, "an' there's few o' the laddies'll come back fra Cite St.-Auguste."

IX

It was another commander-in-chief who received us some months after the battle of Loos, in a chateau near Montreuil, to which G. H. Q. had then removed. Our only knowledge of Sir Douglas Haig before that day was of a hostile influence against us in the First Army, which he commanded. He had drawn a line through his area beyond which we might not pass. He did not desire our presence among his troops nor in his neighborhood. That line had been broken by the protests of our commandant, and now as Commander-in-Chief, Sir Douglas Haig had realized dimly that he might be helped by our services.

It was in another French salon that we waited for the man who controlled the British armies in the field—those armies which we now knew in some intimacy, whom we had seen in the front-line trenches and rest-camps and billets, hearing their point of view, knowing their suffering and their patience, and their impatience—and their deadly hatred of G. H. Q.

He was very handsome as he sat behind a Louis XIV table, with General Charteris—his Chief of Intelligence, who was our chief, too—behind him at one side, for prompting and advice. He received us with fine courtesy and said:

"Pray be seated, gentlemen."

There had been many troubles over censorship, of which he knew but vaguely through General Charteris, who looked upon us as his special "cross." We had fought hard for liberty in mentioning units, to give the honor to the troops, and for other concessions which would free our pens.

The Commander-in-Chief was sympathetic, but his sympathy was expressed in words which revealed a complete misunderstanding of our purpose and of our work, and was indeed no less than an insult, unconscious but very hurtful.

"I think I understand fairly well what you gentlemen want," he said. "You want to get hold of little stories of heroism, and so forth, and to write them up in a bright way to make good reading for Mary Ann in the kitchen, and the Man in the Street." The quiet passion with which those words were resented by us, the quick repudiation of this slur upon our purpose by a charming man perfectly ignorant at that time of the new psychology of nations in a war which was no longer a professional adventure, surprised him. We took occasion to point out to him that the British Empire, which had sent its men into this war, yearned to know what they were doing and how they were doing, and that their patience and loyalty depended upon closer knowledge of what was happening than was told them in the communiques issued by the Commander-in-Chief himself. We urged him to let us mention more frequently the names of the troops engaged—especially English troops—for the sake of the soldiers themselves, who were discouraged by this lack of recognition, and for the sake of the people behind them... It was to the pressure of the war correspondents, very largely, that the troops owed the mention and world-wide honor which came to them, more generously, in the later phases of the war.

The Commander-in-Chief made a note of our grievances, turning now and again to General Charteris, who was extremely nervous at our frankness of speech, and telling him to relax the rules of censorship as far as possible. That was done, and in later stages of the war I personally had no great complaint against the censorship, and wrote all that was possible to write of the actions day by day, though I had to leave out something of the underlying horror of them all, in spite of my continual emphasis, by temperament and by conviction, on the tragedy of all this sacrifice of youth. The only alternative to what we wrote would have been a passionate denunciation of all this ghastly slaughter and violent attacks on British generalship. Even now I do not think that would have been justified. As Bernard Shaw told me, "while the war lasts one must put one's own soul under censorship."

After many bloody battles had been fought we were received again by the Commander-in-Chief, and this time his cordiality was not marred by any slighting touch.

"Gentlemen," he said, "you have played the game like men!"

When victory came at last—at last!—after the years of slaughter, it was the little band of war correspondents on the British front, our foreign comrades included, whom the Field-Marshal addressed on his first visit to the Rhine. We stood on the Hohenzollern Bridge in Cologne, watched by groups of Germans peering through the escort of Lancers. It was a dank and foul day, but to us beautiful, because this was the end of the long journey—four-and—a-half years long, which had been filled with slaughter all the way, so that we were tired of its backwash of agony, which had overwhelmed our souls—mine, certainly. The Commander-in-Chief read out a speech to us, thanking us for our services, which, he said, had helped him to victory, because we had heartened the troops and the people by our work. It was a recognition by the leader of our armies that, as chroniclers of war, we had been a spiritual force behind his arms. It was a reward for many mournful days, for much agony of spirit, for hours of danger—some of us had walked often in the ways of death—and for exhausting labors which we did so that the world might know what British soldiers had been doing and suffering.

X

I came to know General Headquarters more closely when it removed, for fresher air, to Montreuil, a fine old walled town, once within sight of the sea, which ebbed over the low-lying ground below its hill, but now looking across a wide vista of richly cultivated fields where many hamlets are scattered among clumps of trees. One came to G. H. Q. from journeys over the wild desert of the battlefields, where men lived in ditches and "pill-boxes," muddy, miserable in all things but spirit, as to a place where the pageantry of war still maintained its old and dead tradition. It was like one of those pageants which used to be played in England before the war—picturesque, romantic, utterly unreal. It was as though men were playing at war here, while others sixty miles away were fighting and dying, in mud and gas-waves and explosive barrages.

An "open sesame," by means of a special pass, was needed to enter this City of Beautiful Nonsense. Below the gateway, up the steep hillside, sentries stood at a white post across the road, which lifted up on pulleys when the pass had been examined by a military policeman in a red cap. Then the sentries slapped their hands on their rifles to the occupants of any motor-car, sure that more staff-officers were going in to perform those duties which no private soldier could attempt to understand, believing they belonged to such mysteries as those of God. Through the narrow streets walked elderly generals, middle-aged colonels and majors, youthful subalterns all wearing red hat-bands, red tabs, and the blue-and-red armlet of G. H. Q., so that color went with them on their way.

Often one saw the Commander-in-Chief starting for an afternoon ride, a fine figure, nobly mounted, with two A. D. C.'s and an escort of Lancers. A pretty sight, with fluttering pennons on all their lances, and horses groomed to the last hair. It was prettier than the real thing up in the salient or beyond the Somme, where dead bodies lay in upheaved earth among ruins and slaughtered trees. War at Montreuil was quite a pleasant occupation for elderly generals who liked their little stroll after lunch, and for young Regular officers, released from the painful necessity of dying for their country, who were glad to get a game of tennis, down below the walls there, after strenuous office-work in which they had written "Passed to you" on many "minutes," or had drawn the most comical caricatures of their immediate chief, and of his immediate chief, on blotting-pads and writing-blocks.

It seemed, at a mere glance, that all these military inhabitants of G. H. Q. were great and glorious soldiers. Some of the youngest of them had a row of decorations from Montenegro, Serbia, Italy, Rumania, and other states, as recognition of gallant service in translating German letters (found in dugouts by the fighting-men), or arranging for visits of political personages to the back areas of war, or initialing requisitions for pink, blue, green, and yellow forms, which in due course would find their way to battalion adjutants for immediate filling-up in the middle of an action. The oldest of them, those white-haired, bronze-faced, gray-eyed generals in the administrative side of war, had started their third row of ribbons well before the end of the Somme battles, and had flower-borders on their breasts by the time the massacres had been accomplished in the fields of Flanders. I know an officer who was awarded the D. S. O. because he had hindered the work of war correspondents with the zeal of a hedge-sparrow in search of worms, and another who was the best-decorated man in the army because he had presided over a visitors' chateau and entertained Royalties, Members of Parliament, Mrs. Humphry Ward, miners, Japanese, Russian revolutionaries, Portuguese ministers, Harry Lauder, Swedes, Danes, Norwegians, clergymen, Montenegrins, and the Editor of John Bull, at the government's expense—and I am bound to say he deserved them all, being a man of infinite tact, many languages, and a devastating sense of humor. There was always a Charlie Chaplin film between moving pictures of the battles of the Somme. He brought the actualities of war to the visitors' chateau by sentry-boxes outside the door, a toy "tank" in the front garden, and a collection of war trophies in the hall. He spoke to High Personages with less deference than he showed to miners from Durham and Wales, and was master of them always, ordering them sternly to bed at ten o'clock (when he sat down to bridge with his junior officers), and with strict military discipline insisting upon their inspection of the bakeries at Boulogne, and boot-mending factories at Calais, as part of the glory of war which they had come out for to see.

So it was that there were brilliant colors in the streets of Montreuil, and at every doorway a sentry slapped his hand to his rifle, with smart and untiring iteration, as the "brains" of the army, under "brass hats" and red bands, went hither and thither in the town, looking stern, as soldiers of grave responsibility, answering salutes absent—mindedly, staring haughtily at young battalion officers who passed through Montreuil and looked meekly for a chance of a lorry-ride to Boulogne, on seven days' leave from the lines.

The smart society of G. H. Q. was best seen at the Officers' Club in Montreuil, at dinner-time. It was as much like musical comedy as any stage setting of war at the Gaiety. A band played ragtime and light music while the warriors fed, and all these generals and staff officers, with their decorations and arm-bands and polished buttons and crossed swords, were waited upon by little W. A. A. C.'s with the G. H. Q. colors tied up in bows on their hair, and khaki stockings under their short skirts and fancy aprons. Such a chatter! Such bursts of light-hearted laughter! Such whisperings of secrets and intrigues and scandals in high places! Such careless—hearted courage when British soldiers were being blown to bits, gassed, blinded, maimed, and shell-shocked in places that were far—so very far—from G. H. Q.!

XI

There were shrill voices one morning outside the gate of our quarters—women's voices, excited, angry, passionate. An orderly came into the mess—we were at breakfast—and explained the meaning of the clamor, which by some intuition and a quick ear for French he had gathered from all this confusion of tongues.

"There's a soldier up the road, drunk or mad. He has been attacking a girl. The villagers want an officer to arrest him."

The colonel sliced off the top of his egg and then rose. "Tell three orderlies to follow me."

We went into the roadway, and twenty women crowded round us with a story of attempted violence against an innocent girl. The man had been drinking last night at the estaminet up there. Then he had followed the girl, trying to make love to her. She had barricaded herself in the room, when he tried to climb through the window.

"If you don't come out I'll get in and kill you," he said, according to the women.

But she had kept him out, though he prowled round all night. Now he was hiding in an outhouse. The brute! The pig!

When we went up the road the man was standing in the center of it, with a sullen look.

"What's the trouble?" he asked. "It looks as if all France were out to grab me."

He glanced sideways over the field, as though reckoning his chance of escape. There was no chance.

The colonel placed him under arrest and he marched back between the orderlies, with an old soldier of the Contemptibles behind him.

Later in the day he was lined up for identification by the girl, among a crowd of other men.

The girl looked down the line, and we watched her curiously—a slim creature with dark hair neatly coiled.

She stretched out her right hand with a pointing finger.

"Le voila!... c'est l'homme."

There was no mistake about it, and the man looked sheepishly at her, not denying. He was sent off under escort to the military prison in St. Omer for court-martial.

"What's the punishment—if guilty?" I asked.

"Death," said the colonel, resuming his egg.

He was a fine-looking fellow, the prisoner. He had answered the call for king and country without delay. In the estaminet, after coming down from the salient for a machine-gun course, he had drunk more beer than was good for him, and the face of a pretty girl had bewitched him, stirring up desire. He wanted to kiss her lips... There were no women in the Ypres salient. Nothing pretty or soft. It was hell up there, and this girl was a pretty witch, bringing back thoughts of the other side—for life, womanhood, love, caresses which were good for the souls and bodies of men. It was a starved life up there in the salient... Why shouldn't she give him her lips? Wasn't he fighting for France? Wasn't he a tall and proper lad? Curse the girl for being so sulky to an English soldier!... And now, if those other women, those old hags, were to swear against him things he had never said, things he had never done, unless drink had made him forget—by God! supposing drink had made him forget? He would be shot against a white wall. Shot dead, disgracefully, shamefully, by his own comrades! O Christ! and the little mother in a Sussex cottage!...

XII

Going up to Kemmel one day I had to wait in battalion headquarters for the officer I had gone to see. He was attending a court martial. Presently he came into the wooden hut, with a flushed face.

"Sorry I had to keep you," he said. "Tomorrow there will be one swine less in the world."

"A death sentence?"

He nodded.

"A damned coward. Said he didn't mind rifle-fire, but couldn't stand shells. Admitted he left his post. He doesn't mind rifle-fire!... Well, tomorrow morning."

The officer laughed grimly, and then listened for a second.

There were some heavy crumps falling over Kemmel Hill, rather close, it seemed, to our wooden hut.

"Damn those German gunners" said the officer. "Why can't they give us a little peace?"

He turned to his papers, but several times while I talked with him he jerked his head up and listened to a heavy crash.

On the way back I saw a man on foot, walking in front of a mounted man, past the old hill of the Scherpenberg, toward the village of Locre. There was something in the way he walked, in his attitude—the head hunched forward a little, and his arms behind his back—which made me turn to look at him. He was manacled, and tied by a rope to the mounted man. I caught one glimpse of his face, and then turned away, cold and sick. There was doom written on his face, and in his eyes a captured look. He was walking to his wall.

XIII

There were other men who could not stand shell-fire. It filled them with an animal terror and took all will-power out of them. One young officer was like that man who "did not mind rifle-fire." He, by some strange freak of psychology, was brave under machine-gun fire. He had done several gallant things, and was bright and cheerful in the trenches until the enemy barraged them with high explosive. Then he was seen wandering back to the support trenches in a dazed way. It happened three times, and he was sentenced to death. Before going out at dawn to face the firing-squad he was calm. There was a lighted candle on the table, and he sorted out his personal belongings and made small packages of them as keepsakes for his family and friends. His hand did not tremble. When his time came he put out the candle, between thumb and finger, raised his hand, and said, "Right O!"

Another man, shot for cowardice in face of the enemy, was sullen and silent to one who hoped to comfort him in the last hour. The chaplain asked him whether he had any message for his relatives. He said, "I have no relatives." He was asked whether he would like to say any prayers, and he said, "I don't believe in them." The chaplain talked to him, but could get no answer—and time was creeping on. There were two guards in the room, sitting motionless, with loaded rifles between their knees. Outside it was silent in the courtyard, except for little noises of the night and the wind. The chaplain suffered, and was torn with pity for that sullen man whose life was almost at an end. He took out his hymn—book and said: "I will sing to you. It will pass the time." He sang a hymn, and once or twice his voice broke a little, but he steadied it. Then the man said, "I will sing with you." He knew all the hymns, words and music. It was an unusual, astonishing knowledge, and he went on singing, hymn after hymn, with the chaplain by his side. It was the chaplain who tired first. His voice cracked and his throat became parched. Sweat broke out on his forehead, because of the nervous strain. But the man who was going to die sang on in a clear, hard voice. A faint glimmer of coming dawn lightened the cottage window. There were not many minutes more. The two guards shifted their feet. "Now," said the man, "we'll sing 'God Save the King.'" The two guards rose and stood at attention, and the chaplain sang the national anthem with the man who was to be shot for cowardice. Then the tramp of the firing-party came across the cobblestones in the courtyard. It was dawn.

XIV

Shell-shock was the worst thing to see. There were generals who said: "There is no such thing as shell-shock. It is cowardice. I would court-martial in every case." Doctors said: "It is difficult to draw the line between shell-shock and blue funk. Both are physical as well as mental. Often it is the destruction of the nerve tissues by concussion, or actual physical damage to the brain; sometimes it is a shock of horror unbalancing the mind, but that is more rare. It is not generally the slight, nervous men who suffer worst from shell-shock. It is often the stolid fellow, one of those we describe as being utterly without nerves, who goes down badly. Something snaps in him. He has no resilience in his nervous system. He has never trained himself in nerve-control, being so stolid and self-reliant. Now, the nervous man, the cockney, for example, is always training himself in the control of his nerves, on 'buses which lurch round corners, in the traffic that bears down on him, in a thousand and one situations which demand self-control in a 'nervy' man. That helps him in war; whereas the yokel, or the sergeant—major type, is splendid until the shock comes. Then he may crack. But there is no law. Imagination—apprehension—are the devil, too, and they go with 'nerves.'"

It was a sergeant-major whom I saw stricken badly with shell-shock in Aveluy Wood near Thiepval. He was convulsed with a dreadful rigor like a man in epilepsy, and clawed at his mouth, moaning horribly, with livid terror in his eyes. He had to be strapped to a stretcher before he could be carried away. He had been a tall and splendid man, this poor, terror-stricken lunatic.

Nearer to Thiepval, during the fighting there, other men were brought down with shell-shock. I remember one of them now, though I saw many others. He was a Wiltshire lad, very young, with an apple-cheeked face and blue-gray eyes. He stood outside a dugout, shaking in every limb, in a palsied way. His steel hat was at the back of his head and his mouth slobbered, and two comrades could not hold him still.

These badly shell-shocked boys clawed their mouths ceaselessly. It was a common, dreadful action. Others sat in the field hospitals in a state of coma, dazed, as though deaf, and actually dumb. I hated to see them, turned my eyes away from them, and yet wished that they might be seen by bloody-minded men and women who, far behind the lines, still spoke of war lightly, as a kind of sport, or heroic game, which brave boys liked or ought to like, and said, "We'll fight on to the last man rather than accept anything less than absolute victory," and when victory came said: "We stopped too soon. We ought to have gone on for another three months." It was for fighting-men to say those things, because they knew the things they suffered and risked. That word "we" was not to be used by gentlemen in government offices scared of air raids, nor by women dancing in scanty frocks at war-bazaars for the "poor dear wounded," nor even by generals at G. H. Q., enjoying the thrill of war without its dirt and danger.

Seeing these shell-shock cases month after month, during years of fighting, I, as an onlooker, hated the people who had not seen, and were callous of this misery; the laughing girls in the Strand greeting the boys on seven days' leave; the newspaper editors and leader-writers whose articles on war were always "cheery"; the bishops and clergy who praised God as the Commander-in-Chief of the Allied armies, and had never said a word before the war to make it less inevitable; the schoolmasters who gloried in the lengthening "Roll of Honor" and said, "We're doing very well," when more boys died; the pretty woman-faces ogling in the picture-papers, as "well—known war-workers"; the munition-workers who were getting good wages out of the war; the working-women who were buying gramophones and furs while their men were in the stinking trenches; the dreadful, callous, cheerful spirit of England at war.

Often I was unfair, bitter, unbalanced, wrong. The spirit of England, taking it broad and large—with dreadful exceptions—was wonderful in its courage and patience, and ached with sympathy for its fighting sons, and was stricken with the tragedy of all this slaughter. There were many tears in English homes; many sad and lonely women. But, as an onlooker, I could not be just or fair, and hated the non-combatants who did not reveal its wound in their souls, but were placid in their belief that we should win, and pleased with themselves because of their easy optimism. So easy for those who did not see!

XV

As war correspondents we were supposed to have honorary rank as captains, by custom and tradition—but it amounted to nothing, here or there. We were civilians in khaki, with green bands round our right arms, and uncertain status. It was better so, because we were in the peculiar and privileged position of being able to speak to Tommies and sergeants as human beings, to be on terms of comradeship with junior subalterns and battalion commanders, and to sit at the right hand of generals without embarrassment to them or to ourselves.

Physically, many of our generals were curiously alike. They were men turned fifty, with square jaws, tanned, ruddy faces, searching and rather stern gray eyes, closely cropped hair growing white, with a little white mustache, neatly trimmed, on the upper lip.

Mentally they had similar qualities. They had unfailing physical courage—though courage is not put to the test much in modern generalship, which, above the rank of brigadier, works far from the actual line of battle, unless it "slips" in the wrong direction. They were stern disciplinarians, and tested the quality of troops by their smartness in saluting and on parade, which did not account for the fighting merit of the Australians. Most of them were conservative by political tradition and hereditary instinct, and conservative also in military ideas and methods. They distrusted the "brilliant" fellow, and were inclined to think him unsafe; and they were not quick to allow young men to gain high command at the expense of their gray hair and experience. They were industrious, able, conscientious men, never sparing themselves long hours of work for a life of ease, and because they were willing to sacrifice their own lives, if need be, for their country's sake, they demanded equal willingness of sacrifice from every officer and man under their authority, having no mercy whatever for the slacker or the weakling.

Among them there was not one whose personality had that mysterious but essential quality of great generalship—inspiring large bodies of men with exalted enthusiasm, devotion, and faith. It did not matter to the men whether an army commander, a corps commander, or a divisional commander stood in the roadside to watch them march past on their way to battle or on their way back. They saw one of these sturdy men in his brass hat, with his ruddy face and white mustache, but no thrill passed down their ranks, no hoarse cheers broke from them because he was there, as when Wellington sat on his white horse in the Peninsular War, or as when Napoleon saluted his Old Guard, or even as when Lord Roberts, "Our Bob," came perched like a little old falcon on his big charger.

Nine men out of ten in the ranks did not even know the name of their army general or of the corps commander. It meant nothing to them. They did not face death with more passionate courage to win the approval of a military idol. That was due partly to the conditions of modern warfare, which make it difficult for generals of high rank to get into direct personal touch with their troops, and to the masses of men engaged. But those difficulties could have been overcome by a general of impressive personality, able to stir the imaginations of men by words of fire spoken at the right time, by deep, human sympathy, and by the luck of victory seized by daring adventure against great odds.

No such man appeared on the western front until Foch obtained the supreme command. On the British front there was no general with the gift of speech—a gift too much despised by our British men of action—or with a character and prestige which could raise him to the highest rank in popular imagination. During the retreat from Mona, Sir John French had a touch of that personal power—his presence meant something to the men because of his reputation in South Africa; but afterward, when trench warfare began, and the daily routine of slaughter under German gun-fire, when our artillery was weak, and when our infantry was ordered to attack fixed positions of terrible strength without adequate support, and not a dog's chance of luck against such odds, the prestige of the Commander-in-Chief faded from men's minds and he lost place in their admiration. It was washed out in blood and mud.

Sir Douglas Haig, who followed Sir John French, inherited the disillusionment of armies who saw now that war on the western front was to be a long struggle, with enormous slaughter, and no visible sign of the end beyond a vista of dreadful years. Sir Douglas Haig, in his general headquarters at St.-Omer, and afterward at Montreuil, near the coast, had the affection and loyalty of the staff—officers. A man of remarkably good looks, with fine, delicate features, strengthened by the firm line of his jaw, and of singular sweetness, courtesy, and simplicity in his manner toward all who approached him, he had qualities which might have raised him to the supreme height of personal influence among his armies but for lack of the magic touch and the tragic condition of his command.

He was intensely shy and reserved, shrinking from publicity and holding himself aloof from the human side of war. He was constitutionally unable to make a dramatic gesture before a multitude, or to say easy, stirring things to officers and men whom he reviewed. His shyness and reserve prevented him also from knowing as much as he ought to have known about the opinions of officers and men, and getting direct information from them. He held the supreme command of the British armies on the western front when, in the battlefields of the Somme and Flanders, of Picardy and Artois, there was not much chance for daring strategy, but only for hammer-strokes by the flesh and blood of men against fortress positions—the German trench systems, twenty-five miles deep in tunneled earthworks and machine-gun dugouts—when the immensity of casualties among British troops was out of all proportion to their gains of ground, so that our men's spirits revolted against these massacres of their youth and they were embittered against the generalship and staff-work which directed these sacrificial actions.

This sense of bitterness became intense, to the point of fury, so that a young staff officer, in his red tabs, with a jaunty manner, was like a red rag to a bull among battalion officers and men, and they desired his death exceedingly, exalting his little personality, dressed in a well-cut tunic and fawn-colored riding-breeches and highly polished top-boots, into the supreme folly of "the Staff" which made men attack impossible positions, send down conflicting orders, issued a litter of documents—called by an ugly name—containing impracticable instructions, to the torment of the adjutants and to the scorn of the troops. This hatred of the Staff was stoked high by the fires of passion and despair. Some of it was unjust, and even the jaunty young staff-officer—a G. S. O. 3, with red tabs and polished boots—was often not quite such a fool as he looked, but a fellow who had proved his pluck in the early days of the war and was now doing his duty—about equal to the work of a boy clerk—with real industry and an exaggerated sense of its importance.

Personally I can pay high tribute to some of our staff—officers at divisional, corps, and army headquarters, because of their industry, efficiency, and devotion to duty. And during the progress of battle I have seen them, hundreds of times, working desperately for long hours without much rest or sleep, so that the fighting-men should get their food and munitions, so that the artillery should support their actions, and the troops in reserve move up to their relief at the proper time and place.

Owing largely to new army brains the administrative side of our war became efficient in its method and organization, and the armies were worked like clockwork machines. The transport was good beyond all words of praise, and there was one thing which seldom failed to reach poor old Tommy Atkins, unless he was cut off by shell-fire, and that was his food. The motor-supply columns and ammunition-dumps were organized to the last item. Our map department was magnificent, and the admiration of the French. Our Intelligence branch became valuable (apart from a frequent insanity of optimism) and was sometimes uncanny in the accuracy of its information about the enemy's disposition and plans. So that the Staff was not altogether hopeless in its effect, as the young battalion officers, with sharp tongues and a sense of injustice in their hearts, made out, with pardonable blasphemy, in their dugouts.

Nevertheless the system was bad and British generalship made many mistakes, some of them, no doubt, unavoidable, because it is human to err, and some of them due to sheer, simple, impregnable stupidity.

In the early days the outstanding fault of our generals was their desire to gain ground which was utterly worthless when gained. They organized small attacks against strong positions, dreadfully costly to take, and after the desperate valor of men had seized a few yards of mangled earth, found that they had made another small salient, jutting out from their front in a V-shaped wedge, so that it was a death-trap for the men who had to hold it. This was done again and again, and I remember one distinguished officer saying, with bitter irony, remembering how many of his men had died, "Our generals must have their little V's at any price, to justify themselves at G. H. Q."

In the battles of the Somme they attacked isolated objectives on narrow fronts, so that the enemy swept our men with fire by artillery concentrated from all points, instead of having to disperse his fire during a general attack on a wide front. In the days of trench warfare, when the enemy artillery was much stronger than ours, and when his infantry strength was enormously greater, our generals insisted upon the British troops maintaining an "aggressive" attitude, with the result that they were shot to pieces, instead of adopting, like the French, a quiet and waiting attitude until the time came for a sharp and terrible blow. The battles of Neuve Chapelle, Fertubert, and Loos, in 1915, cost us thousands of dead and gave us no gain of any account; and both generalship and staff-work were, in the opinion of most officers who know anything of those battles, ghastly.

After all, our generals had to learn their lesson, like the private soldier, and the young battalion officer, in conditions of warfare which had never been seen before—and it was bad for the private soldier and the young battalion officer, who died so they might learn. As time went on staff-work improved, and British generalship was less rash in optimism and less rigid in ideas.

XVI

General Haldane was friendly to the war correspondents—he had been something of the kind himself in earlier days—and we were welcomed at his headquarters, both when he commanded the 3d Division and afterward when he became commander of the 6th Corps. I thought during the war, and I think now, that he had more intellect and "quality" than many of our other generals. A tall, strongly built man, with a distinction of movement and gesture, not "stocky" or rigid, but nervous and restless, he gave one a sense of power and intensity of purpose. There was a kind of slow-burning fire in him—a hatred of the enemy which was not weakened in him by any mercy, and a consuming rage, as it appeared to me, against inefficiency in high places, injustice of which he may have felt himself to be the victim, and restrictions upon his liberty of command. A bitter irony was often in his laughter when discussing politicians at home, and the wider strategy of war apart from that on his own front. He was intolerant of stupidity, which he found widespread, and there was no tenderness or emotion in his attitude toward life. The officers and men under his command accused him of ruthlessness. But they admitted that he took more personal risk than he need have done as a divisional general, and was constantly in the trenches examining his line. They also acknowledged that he was generous in his praise of their good service, though merciless if he found fault with them. He held himself aloof—too much, I am sure—from his battalion officers, and had an extreme haughtiness of bearing which was partly due to reserve and that shyness which is in many Englishmen and a few Scots.

In the old salient warfare he often demanded service in the way of raids and the holding of death-traps, and the execution of minor attacks which caused many casualties, and filled men with rage and horror at what they believed to be unnecessary waste of life—their life, and their comrades'—that did not make for popularity in the ranks of the battalion messes. Privately, in his own mess, he was gracious to visitors, and revealed not only a wide range of knowledge outside as well as inside his profession, but a curious, unexpected sympathy for ideas, not belonging as a rule to generals of the old caste. I liked him, though I was always conscious of that flame and steel in his nature which made his psychology a world away from mine. He was hit hard—in what I think was the softest spot in his heart—by the death of one of his A. D. C.'s—young Congreve, who was the beau ideal of knighthood, wonderfully handsome, elegant even when covered from head to foot in wet mud (as I saw him one day), fearless, or at least scornful of danger, to the verge of recklessness. General Haldane had marked him out as the most promising young soldier in the whole army. A bit of shell, a senseless bit of steel, spoiled that promise—as it spoiled the promise of a million boys—and the general was saddened more than by the death of other gallant officers.

I have one memory of General Haldane which shows him in a different light. It was during the great German offensive in the north, when Arras was hard beset and the enemy had come back over Monchy Hill and was shelling villages on the western side of Arras, which until then had been undamaged. It was in one of these villages—near Avesnes-le-Compte—to which the general had come back with his corps headquarters, established there for many months in earlier days, so that the peasants and their children knew him well by sight and had talked with him, because he liked to speak French with them. When I went to see him one day during that bad time in April of '18, he was surrounded by a group of children who were asking anxiously whether Arras would be taken. He drew a map for them in the dust of the roadway, and showed them where the enemy was attacking and the general strategy. He spoke simply and gravely, as though to a group of staff-officers, and the children followed his diagram in the dust and understood him perfectly.

"They will not take Arras if I can help it," he said. "You will be all right here."

XVII

Gen. Sir Neville Macready was adjutant-general in the days of Sir John French, and I dined at his mess once or twice, and he came to ours on return visits. The son of Macready, the actor, he had a subtlety of mind not common among British generals, to whom "subtlety" in any form is repulsive. His sense of humor was developed upon lines of irony and he had a sly twinkle in his eyes before telling one of his innumerable anecdotes. They were good stories, and I remember one of them, which had to do with the retreat from Mons. It was not, to tell the truth, that "orderly" retreat which is described in second-hand accounts. There were times when it was a wild stampede from the tightening loop of a German advance, with lorries and motor-cycles and transport wagons going helter-skelter among civilian refugees and mixed battalions and stragglers from every unit walking, footsore, in small groups. Even General Headquarters was flurried at times, far in advance of this procession backward. One night Sir Neville Macready, with the judge advocate and an officer named Colonel Childs (a hot-headed fellow!), took up their quarters in a French chateau somewhere, I think, in the neighborhood of Creil. The Commander-in-Chief was in another chateau some distance away. Other branches of G. H. Q. were billeted in private houses, widely scattered about a straggling village.

Colonel Childs was writing opposite the adjutant-general, who was working silently. Presently Childs looked up, listened, and said:

"It's rather quiet, sir, outside."

"So much the better," growled General Macready. "Get on with your job."

A quarter of an hour passed. No rumble of traffic passed by the windows. No gun-wagons were jolting over French *pave.*

Colonel Childs looked up again and listened.

"It's damned quiet outside, sir."

"Well, don't go making a noise," said the general, "Can't you see I'm busy?"

"I think I'll just take a turn round," said Colonel Childs.

He felt uneasy. Something in the silence of the village scared him. He went out into the roadway and walked toward Sir John French's quarters. There was no challenge from a sentry. The British Expeditionary Force seemed to be sleeping. They needed sleep—poor beggars!—but the Germans did not let them take much.

Colonel Childs went into the Commander-in-Chief's chateau and found a soldier in the front hall, licking out a jam-pot.

"Where's the Commander-in-Chief?" asked the officer.

"Gone hours ago, sir," said the soldier. "I was left behind for lack of transport. From what I hear the Germans ought to be here by now. I rather fancy I heard some shots pretty close awhile ago."

Colonel Childs walked back to his own quarters quickly. He made no apology for interrupting the work of the adjutant-general.

"General, the whole box of tricks has gone. We've been left behind. Forgotten!"

"The dirty dogs!" said General Macready.

There was not much time for packing up, and only one motor-car, and only one rifle. The general said he would look after the rifle, but Colonel Childs said if that were so he would rather stay behind and take his chance of being captured. It would be safer for him. So the adjutant-general, the judge advocate, the deputy assistant judge advocate (Colonel Childs), and an orderly or two packed into the car and set out to find G.H.Q. Before they found it they had to run the gantlet of Germans, and were sniped all the way through a wood, and took flying shots at moving figures. Then, miles away, they found G.H.Q.

"And weren't they sorry to see me again!" said General Macready, who told me the tale. "They thought they had lost me forever."

The day's casualty list was brought into the adjutant—general one evening when I was dining in his mess. The orderly put it down by the side of his plate, and he interrupted a funny story to glance down the columns of names.

"Du Maurier has been killed... I'm sorry."

He put down the paper beside his plate again and continued his story, and we all laughed heartily at the end of the anecdote. It was the only way, and the soldier's way. There was no hugging of grief when our best friend fell. A sigh, another ghost in one's life, and then, "Carry on!"

XVIII

Scores of times, hundreds of times, during the battles of the Somme, I passed the headquarters of Gen. Sir Henry Rawlinson, commanding the Fourth Army, and several times I met the army commander there and elsewhere. One of my first meetings with him was extraordinarily embarrassing to me for a moment or two. While he was organizing his army, which was to be called, with unconscious irony, "The Army of Pursuit"—the battles of the Somme were a siege rather than a pursuit—he desired to take over the chateau at

Tilques, in which the war correspondents were then quartered. As we were paying for it and liked it, we put up an opposition which was most annoying to his A.D.C.'s, especially to one young gentleman of enormous wealth, haughty manners, and a boyish intolerance of other people's interests, who had looked over our rooms without troubling to knock at the doors, and then said, "This will suit us down to the ground." On my way back from the salient one evening I walked up the drive in the flickering light of summer eve, and saw two officers coming in my direction, one of whom I thought I recognized as an old friend.

"Hullo!" I said, cheerily. "You here again?"

Then I saw that I was face to face with Sir Henry Rawlinson. He must have been surprised, but dug me in the ribs in a genial way, and said, "Hullo, young feller!"

He made no further attempt to "pinch" our quarters, but my familiar method of address could not have produced that result.

His headquarters at Querrieux were in another old chateau on the Amiens-Albert road, surrounded by pleasant fields through which a stream wound its way. Everywhere the sign-boards were red, and a military policeman, authorized to secure obedience to the rules thereon, slowed down every motor-car on its way through the village, as though Sir Henry Rawlinson lay sick of a fever, so anxious were his gestures and his expression of "Hush! do be careful!"

The army commander seemed to me to have a roguish eye. He seemed to be thinking to himself, "This war is a rare old joke!" He spoke habitually of the enemy as "the old Hun" or "old Fritz," in an affectionate, contemptuous way, as a fellow who was trying his best but getting the worst of it every time. Before the battles of the Somme I had a talk with him among his maps, and found that I had been to many places in his line which he did not seem to know. He could not find there very quickly on his large-sized maps, or pretended not to, though I concluded that this was "camouflage," in case I might tell "old Fritz" that such places existed. Like most of our generals, he had amazing, overweening optimism. He had always got the enemy "nearly beat," and he arranged attacks during the Somme fighting with the jovial sense of striking another blow which would lead this time to stupendous results. In the early days, in command of the 7th Division, he had done well, and he was a gallant soldier, with initiative and courage of decision and a quick intelligence in open warfare. His trouble on the Somme was that the enemy did not permit open warfare, but made a siege of it, with defensive lines all the way back to Bapaume, and every hillock a machine-gun fortress and every wood a death-trap. We were always preparing for a "break-through" for cavalry pursuit, and the cavalry were always being massed behind the lines and then turned back again, after futile waiting, encumbering the roads. "The bloodbath of the

Somme," as the Germans called it, was ours as well as theirs, and scores of times when I saw the dead bodies of our men lying strewn over those dreadful fields, after desperate and, in the end, successful attacks through the woods of death—Mametz Wood, Delville Wood, Trones Wood, Bernafay Wood, High Wood, and over the Pozieres ridge to Courcellette and Martinpuich—I thought of Rawlinson in his chateau in Querrieux, scheming out the battles and ordering up new masses of troops to the great assault over the bodies of their dead... Well, it is not for generals to sit down with their heads in their hands, bemoaning slaughter, or to shed tears over their maps when directing battle. It is their job to be cheerful, to harden their hearts against the casualty lists, to keep out of the danger-zone unless their presence is strictly necessary. But it is inevitable that the men who risk death daily, the fighting-men who carry out the plans of the High Command and see no sense in them, should be savage in their irony when they pass a peaceful house where their doom is being planned, and green-eyed when they see an army general taking a stroll in buttercup fields, with a jaunty young A.D.C. slashing the flowers with his cane and telling the latest joke from London to his laughing chief. As onlookers of sacrifice some of us—I, for one—adopted the point of view of the men who were to die, finding some reason in their hatred of the staffs, though they were doing their job with a sense of duty, and with as much intelligence as God had given them. Gen. Sir Henry Rawlinson was one of our best generals, as may be seen by the ribbons on his breast, and in the last phase commanded a real "Army of Pursuit," which had the enemy on the run, and broke through to Victory. It was in that last phase of open warfare that Rawlinson showed his qualities of generalship and once again that driving purpose which was his in the Somme battles, but achieved only by prodigious cost of life.

XIX

Of General Allenby, commanding the Third Army before he was succeeded by Gen. Sir Julian Byng and went to his triumph in Palestine, I knew very little except by hearsay. He went by the name of "The Bull," because of his burly size and deep voice. The costly fighting that followed the battle of Arras on April 9th along the glacis of the Scarpe did not reveal high generalship. There were many young officers—and some divisional generals who complained bitterly of attacks ordered without sufficient forethought, and the stream of casualties which poured back, day by day, with tales of tragic happenings did not inspire one with a sense of some high purpose behind it all, or some presiding genius.

General Byng, "Bungo Byng," as he was called by his troops, won the admiration of the Canadian Corps which he commanded, and afterward, in the Cambrai advance of November, '17, he showed daring of conception and gained the first striking surprise in the war by novel methods of attack—spoiled by the quick come-back of the enemy under Von Marwitz and our withdrawal from Bourlon Wood, Masnieres, and Marcoing, and other places, after desperate fighting.

His chief of staff, Gen. Louis Vaughan, was a charming, gentle-mannered man, with a scientific outlook on the problems of war, and so kind in his expression and character that it seemed impossible that he could devise methods of killing Germans in a wholesale way. He was like an Oxford professor of history discoursing on the Marlborough wars, though when I saw him many times outside the Third Army headquarters, in a railway carriage, somewhere near Villers Carbonnel on the Somme battlefields, he was explaining his preparations and strategy for actions to be fought next day which would be of bloody consequence to our men and the enemy.

General Birdwood, commanding the Australian Corps, and afterward the Fifth Army in succession to General Gough, was always known as "Birdie" by high and low, and this dapper man, so neat, so bright, so brisk, had a human touch with him which won him the affection of all his troops.

Gen. Hunter Weston, of the 8th Corps, was another man of character in high command. He spoke of himself in the House of Commons one day as "a plain, blunt soldier," and the army roared with laughter from end to end. There was nothing plain or blunt about him. He was a man of airy imagination and a wide range of knowledge, and theories on life and war which he put forward with dramatic eloquence.

It was of Gen. Hunter Weston that the story was told about the drunken soldier put onto a stretcher and covered with a blanket, to get him out of the way when the army commander made a visit to the lines.

"What's this?" said the general.

"Casualty, sir," said the quaking platoon commander.

"Not bad, I hope?"

"Dead, sir," said the subaltern. He meant dead drunk.

The general drew himself up, and said, in his dramatic way, "The army commander salutes the honored dead!"

And the drunken private put his head from under the blanket and asked, "What's the old geezer a-sayin' of?"

That story may have been invented in a battalion mess, but it went through the army affixed to the name of Hunter Weston, and seemed to fit him.

The 8th Corps was on the left in the first attack on the Somme, when many of our divisions were cut to pieces in the attempt to break the German line at Gommecourt. It was a ghastly tragedy, which spoiled the success on the right at Fricourt and Montauban. But Gen. Hunter Weston was not *degomme,* as the French would say, and continued to air his theories on life and warfare until the day of Victory, when once again we had "muddled through," not by great generalship, but by the courage of common men.

Among the divisional generals with whom I came in contact—I met most of them at one time or another—were General Hull of the 56th (London) Division, General Hickey of the 16th (Irish) Division, General Harper of the 51st (Highland) Division, General Nugent of the 36th (Ulster) Division, and General Pinnie of the 35th (Bantams) Division, afterward of the 33d.

General Hull was a handsome, straight-speaking, straight-thinking man, and I should say an able general. "Ruthless," his men said, but this was a war of ruthlessness, because life was cheap. Bitter he was at times, because he had to order his men to do things which he knew were folly. I remember sitting on the window-sill of his bedroom, in an old house of Arras, while he gave me an account of "the battle in the dark," in which the Londoners and other English troops lost their direction and found themselves at dawn with the enemy behind them. General Hull made no secret of the tragedy or the stupidity... On another day I met him somewhere on the other side of Peronne, before March 21st, when he was commanding the 16th (Irish) Division in the absence of General Hickey, who was ill. He talked a good deal about the belief in a great German offensive, and gave many reasons for thinking it was all "bluff." A few days later the enemy had rolled over his lines... Out of thirteen generals I met at that time, there were only three who believed that the enemy would make his great assault in a final effort to gain decisive victory, though our Intelligence had amassed innumerable proofs and were utterly convinced of the approaching menace.

"They will never risk it!" said General Gorringe of the 47th (London) Division. "Our lines are too strong. We should mow them down."

I was standing with him on a wagon, watching the sports of the London men. We could see the German lines, south of St.-Quentin, very quiet over there, without any sign of coming trouble. A few days later the place where we were standing was under waves of German storm-troops.

I liked the love of General Hickey for his Irish division. An Irishman himself, with a touch of the old Irish soldier as drawn by Charles Lever, gay-hearted, proud of his boys, he was always pleased to see me because he knew I had a warm spot in my heart for the Irish troops. He had a good story to tell every time, and passed me on to "the boys" to get at the heart of them. It was long before he lost hope of keeping the division together, though it was hard to get recruits and losses were high at Guillemont and Ginchy. For the first time he lost heart and was very sad when the division was cut to pieces in a Flanders battle. It lost 2,000 men and 162 officers before the battle began—they were shelled to death in the trenches—and 2,000 men and 170 officers more during the progress of the battle. It was murderous and ghastly.

General Harper of the 51st (Highland) Division, afterward commanding the 4th Corps, had the respect of his troops, though they called him "Uncle" because of his shock of white hair. The Highland division, under his command, fought many battles and gained great honor, even from the enemy, who feared them and called the kilted men "the ladies from hell." It was to them the Germans sent their message in a small balloon during the retreat from the Somme: "Poor old 51st. Still sticking it! Cheery-oh!"

"Uncle" Harper invited me to lunch in his mess, and was ironical with war correspondents, and censors, and the British public, and new theories of training, and many things in which he saw no sense. There was a smoldering passion in him which glowed in his dark eyes.

He was against bayonet-training, which took the field against rifle-fire for a time.

"No man in this war," he said, with a sweeping assertion, "has ever been killed by the bayonet unless he had his hands up first." And, broadly speaking, I think he was right, in spite of the Director of Training, who was extremely annoyed with me when I quoted this authority.

XX

I met many other generals who were men of ability, energy, high sense of duty, and strong personality. I found them intellectually, with few exceptions, narrowly molded to the same type, strangely limited in their range of ideas and qualities of character.

"One has to leave many gaps in one's conversation with generals," said a friend of mine, after lunching with an army commander.

That was true. One had to talk to them on the lines of leading articles in *The Morning Post.* Their patriotism, their knowledge of human nature, their idealism, and their imagination were restricted to the traditional views of English country gentlemen of the Tory school. Anything outside that range of thought was to them heresy, treason, or wishy-washy sentiment.

What mainly was wrong with our generalship was the system which put the High Command into the hands of a group of men belonging to the old school of war, unable, by reason of their age and traditions, to get away from rigid methods and to become elastic in face of new conditions.

Our Staff College had been hopelessly inefficient in its system of training, if I am justified in forming such an opinion from specimens produced by it, who had the brains of canaries and the manners of Potsdam. There was also a close corporation among the officers of the Regular Army, so that they took the lion's share of staff appointments, thus keeping out brilliant young men of the new armies, whose brain-power, to say the least of it, was on a higher level than that of the Sandhurst standard. Here and there, where the unprofessional soldier obtained a chance of high command or staff authority, he proved the value of the business mind applied to war, and this was seen very clearly—blindingly—in the able generalship of the Australian Corps, in which most of the commanders, like Generals Hobbs, Monash, and others, were men in civil life before the war. The same thing was observed in the Canadian Corps, General Currie, the corps commander, having been an estate agent, and many of his high officers having had no military training of any scientific importance before they handled their own men in France and Flanders.

XXI

As there are exceptions to every rule, so harsh criticism must be modified in favor of the generalship and organization of the Second Army-of rare efficiency under the restrictions and authority of the General Staff. I often used to wonder what qualities belonged to Sir Herbert Plumer, the army commander. In appearance he was almost a caricature of an old-time British general, with his ruddy, pippin-cheeked face, with white hair, and a fierce little white mustache, and blue, watery eyes, and a little pot-belly and short legs. He puffed and panted when he walked, and after two minutes in his company Cyril Maude would have played him to perfection. The staff-work of his army was as good in detail as any machinery of war may be, and the tactical direction of the Second Army battles was not slipshod nor haphazard, as so many others, but prepared with minute attention to detail and after thoughtful planning of the general scheme. The battle of Wytschaete and Messines was a model in organization and method, and worked in its frightful destructiveness like the clockwork of a death machine. Even the battles of Flanders in the autumn of '17, ghastly as they were in the losses of our men in the state of the ground through which they had to fight, and in futile results, were well organized by the Second Army headquarters, compared with the abominable mismanagement of other troops, the contrast being visible to every battalion officer and even to the private soldier. How much share of this was due to Sir Herbert Plumer it is impossible for me to tell, though it is fair to give him credit for soundness of judgment in general ideas and in the choice of men.

He had for his chief of staff Sir John Harington, and beyond all doubt this general was the organizing brain of to Second Army, though with punctilious chivalry he gave, always, the credit of all his work to the army commander. A thin, nervous, highly strung man, with extreme simplicity of manner and clarity of intelligence, he impressed me as a brain of the highest temper and quality in staff-work. His memory for detail was like a card-index system, yet his mind was not clogged with detail, but saw the wood as well as the trees, and the whole broad sweep of the problem which confronted him. There was something fascinating as well as terrible in his exposition of a battle that he was planning. For the first time in his presence and over his maps, I saw that after all there was such a thing as the science of war, and that it was not always a fetish of elementary ideas raised to the nth degree of pomposity, as I had been led to believe by contact with other generals and staff-officers. Here at least was a man who dealt with it as a scientific business, according to the methods of science—calculating the weight and effect of gun-fire, the strength of the enemy's defenses and man-power, the psychology of German generalship and of German units, the pressure which could be put on British troops before the breaking-point of courage, the relative or cumulative effects of poison-gas, mines, heavy and light artillery, tanks, the disposition of German guns and the probability of their movement in this direction or that, the amount of their wastage under our counter-battery work, the advantages of attacks in depth—one body of troops "leap-frogging," another in an advance to further objectives—the time-table of transport, the supply of food and water and ammunition, the comfort of troops before action, and a thousand other factors of success.

Before every battle fought by the Second Army, and of the eve of it, Sir John Harington sent for the war correspondents and devoted an hour or more to a detailed explanation of his plans. He put down all his cards on the table with perfect candor, hiding nothing, neither minimizing nor exaggerating the difficulties and dangers of the attack, pointing out the tactical obstacles which must be overcome before any chance of success, and exposing the general strategy in the simplest and clearest speech.

I used to study him at those times, and marveled at him. After intense and prolonged work at all this detail involving the lives of thousands of men, he was highly wrought, with every nerve in his body and brain at full tension, but he was never flurried, never irritable, never depressed or elated by false pessimism or false optimism. He was a chemist explaining the factors of a great experiment of which the result was still uncertain. He could only hope for certain results after careful analysis and synthesis. Yet he was not dehumanized. He laughed sometimes at surprises he had caused the enemy, or was likely to cause them—surprises which would lead to a massacre of their men. He warmed to the glory of the courage of the troops who were carrying out his plans.

"It depends on these fellows," he would say. "I am setting them a difficult job. If they can do it, as I hope and believe, it will be a fine achievement. They have been very much tried, poor fellows, but their spirit is still high, as I know from their commanding officers."

One of his ambitions was to break down the prejudice between the fighting units and the Staff. "We want them to know that we are all working together, for the same purpose and with the same zeal. They cannot do without us, as we cannot do without them, and I want them to feel that the work done here is to help them to do theirs more easily, with lighter losses, in better physical conditions, with organization behind them at every stage."

Many times the Second Army would not order an attack or decide the time of it before consulting the divisional generals and brigadiers, and obtaining their consensus of opinion. The officers and men in the Second Army did actually come to acknowledge the value of the staff-work behind them, and felt a confidence in its devotion to their interests which was rare on the western front.

At the end of one of his expositions Sir John Harington would rise and gather up his maps and papers, and say:

"Well, there you are, gentlemen. You know as much as I do about the plans for to-morrow's battle. At the end of the day you will be able to see the result of all our work and tell me things I do not know."

Those conferences took place in the Second Army headquarters on Cassel Hill, in a big building which was a casino before the war, with a far-reaching view across Flanders, so that one could see in the distance the whole sweep of the Ypres salient, and southward the country below Notre Dame de Lorette, with Merville and Hazebrouck in the foreground. Often we assembled in a glass house, furnished with trestle tables on which maps were spread, and, thinking back to these scenes, I remember now, as I write, the noise of rain beating on that glass roof, and the clammy touch of fog on the window-panes stealing through the cracks and creeping into the room. The meteorologist of the Second Army was often a gloomy prophet, and his prophecies were right. How it rained on nights when hundreds of thousands of British soldiers were waiting in their trenches to attack in a murky dawn!... We said good night to General Harington, each one of us, I think, excited by the thought of the drama of human life and death which we had heard in advance in that glass house on the hill; to be played out by flesh and blood before many hours had passed. A kind of sickness took possession of my soul when I stumbled down the rock path from those headquarters in pitch darkness, over slabs of stones designed by a casino architect to break one's neck, with the rain dribbling down one's collar, and, far away, watery lights in the sky, of gun-flashes and ammunition-dumps afire, and the noise of artillery thudding in dull, crumbling shocks. We were starting early to see the opening of the battle and its backwash. There would be more streams of bloody, muddy men, more crowds of miserable prisoners, more dead bodies lying in the muck of captured ground, more shells plunging into the wet earth and throwing up columns of smoke and mud, more dead horses, disemboweled, and another victory at fearful cost, over one of the Flanders ridges.

Curses and prayers surged up in my heart. How long was this to go on—this massacre of youth, this agony of men? Was there no sanity left in the world that could settle the argument by other means than this? When we had taken that ridge to-morrow there would be another to take, and another. And what then? Had we such endless reserves of men that we could go on gaining ground at such a price? Was it to be extermination on both sides? The end of civilization itself? General Harington had said: "The enemy is still very strong. He has plenty of reserves on hand and he is fighting hard. It won't be a walk-over to-morrow."

As an onlooker I was overwhelmed by the full measure of all this tragic drama. The vastness and the duration of its horror appalled me. I went to my billet in an old monastery, and sat there in the darkness, my window glimmering with the faint glow of distant shell-flashes, and said, "O God, give us victory to-morrow, if that may help us to the end." Then to bed, without undressing. There was an early start before the dawn. Major Lytton would be with me. He had a gallant look along the duckboards... Or Montague—white-haired Montague, who liked to gain a far objective, whatever the risk, and gave one a little courage by his apparent fearlessness. I had no courage on those early mornings of battle. All that I had, which was little, oozed out of me when we came to the first dead horses and the first dead men, and passed the tumult of our guns firing out of the mud, and heard the scream of shells. I hated it all with a cold hatred; and I went on hating it for years that seem a lifetime. I was not alone in that hatred, and other men had greater cause, though it was for their sake that I suffered most, as an observer of their drama of death... As observers we saw most of the grisly game.

PART TWO

THE SCHOOL OF COURAGE EARLY DAYS WITH THE NEW ARMY

I

By the time stationary warfare had been established on the western front in trench lines from the sea to Switzerland, the British Regular Army had withered away. That was after the retreat from Mons, the victory of the Marne, the early battles round Ypres, and the slaughter at Neuve Chapelle. The "Old Contemptibles" were an army of ghosts whose dead clay was under earth in many fields of France, but whose spirit still "carried on" as an heroic tradition to those who came after them into those same fields, to the same fate. The only survivors were Regular officers taken out of the fighting-lines to form the staffs of new divisions and to train the army of volunteers now being raised at home, and men who were recovering from wounds or serving behind the lines: those, and non-commissioned officers who were the best schoolmasters of the new boys, the best friends and guides of the new officers, stubborn in their courage, hard and ruthless in their discipline, foul-mouthed according to their own traditions, until they, too, fell in the shambles. It was in March of 1915 that a lieutenant-colonel in the trenches said to me: "I am one out of 150 Regular officers still serving with their battalions. That is to say, there are 150 of us left in the fighting-lines out of 1,500."

That little Regular Army of ours had justified its pride in a long history of fighting courage. It had helped to save England and France by its own death. Those boys of ours whom I had seen in the first August of the war, landing at Boulogne and marching, as though to a festival, toward the enemy, with French girls kissing them and loading them with fruit and flowers, had proved the quality of their spirit and training. As riflemen they had stupefied the enemy, brought to a sudden check by forces they had despised. They held their fire until the German ranks were within eight hundred yards of them, and then mowed them down as though by machine-gun fire—before we had machine-guns, except as rare specimens, here and there. Our horse artillery was beyond any doubt the best in the world at that time. Even before peace came German generals paid ungrudging tributes to the efficiency of our Regular Army, writing down in their histories of war that this was the model of all armies, the most perfectly trained... It was spent by the spring of '15. Its memory remains as the last epic of those professional soldiers who, through centuries of English history, took "the King's shilling" and fought when they were told to fight, and left their bones in far places of the world and in many fields in Europe, and won for the British soldier universal fame as a terrible warrior. There will never be a Regular Army like that. Modern warfare has opened the arena to the multitude. They may no longer sit in the Coliseum watching the paid gladiators. If there be war they must take their share of its sacrifice. They must be victims as well as victors. They must pay for the luxury of conquest, hatred, and revenge by their own bodies, and for their safety against aggression by national service.

After the first quick phases of the war this need of national soldiers to replace the professional forces became clear to the military leaders. The Territorials who had been raised for home defense were sent out to fill up the gaps, and their elementary training was shown to be good enough, as a beginning, in the fighting-lines. The courage of those Territorial divisions who came out first to France was quickly proved, and soon put to the supreme test, in which they did not fail. From the beginning to the end these men, who had made a game of soldiering in days of peace, yet a serious game to which they had devoted much of their spare time after working-hours, were splendid beyond all words of praise, and from the beginning to the end the Territorial officers—men of good standing in their counties, men of brain and business training—were handicapped by lack of promotion and treated with contempt by the High Command, who gave preference always to the Regular officers in every staff appointment.

This was natural and inevitable in armies controlled by the old Regular school of service and tradition. As a close corporation in command of the machine, it was not within their nature or philosophy to make way for the new type. The Staff College was jealous of its own. Sandhurst and Woolwich were still the only schools of soldiering recognized as giving the right "tone" to officers and gentlemen fit for high appointment. The cavalry, above all, held the power of supreme command in a war of machines and chemistry and national psychology....

I should hate to attack the Regular officer. His caste belonged to the best of our blood. He was the heir to fine old traditions of courage and leadership in battle. He was a gentleman whose touch of arrogance was subject to a rigid code of honor which made him look to the comfort of his men first, to the health of his horse second, to his own physical needs last. He had the stern sense of justice of a Roman Centurian, and his men knew that though he would not spare them punishment if guilty, he would give them always a fair hearing, with a point in their favor, if possible. It was in their code to take the greatest risk in time of danger, to be scornful of death in the face of their men whatever secret fear they had, and to be proud and jealous of the honor of the regiment. In action men found them good to follow—better than some of the young officers of the New Army, who had not the same traditional pride nor the same instinct for command nor the same consideration for their men, though more easy-going and human in sympathy.

So I salute in spirit those battalion officers of the Old Army who fulfilled their heritage until it was overwhelmed by new forces, and I find extenuating circumstances even in remembrance of the high stupidities, the narrow imagination, the deep, impregnable, intolerant ignorance of Staff College men who with their red tape and their general orders were the inquisitors and torturers of the new armies. *Tout comprendre c'est tout pardonner.* They were molded in an old system, and could not change their *cliche.*

II

The New Army was called into being by Lord Kitchener and his advisers, who adopted modern advertising methods to stir the sluggish imagination of the masses, so that every wall in London and great cities, every fence in rural places, was placarded with picture-posters.

... "What did you do in the Great War, Daddy?"... "What will your best girl say if you're not in khaki?"

Those were vulgar appeals which, no doubt, stirred many simple souls, and so were good enough. It would have been better to let the people know more of the truth of what was happening in France and Flanders—the truth of tragedy, instead of carefully camouflaged communiques, hiding the losses, ignoring the deeds of famous regiments, veiling all the drama of that early fighting by a deliberate screen of mystery, though all was known to the enemy. It was fear of their own people, not of the enemy, which guided the rules of censorship then and later.

For some little time the British people did not understand what was happening. How could they know? It appeared that all was going well. Then why worry? Soon there would be the joy-bells of peace, and the boys would come marching home again, as in earlier wars. It was only very slowly—because of the conspiracy of silence—that there crept into the consciousness of our people the dim realization of a desperate struggle ahead, in which all their young manhood would be needed to save France and Belgium, and—dear God!—England herself. It was as that thought touched one mind and another that the recruiting offices were crowded with young men. Some of them offered their bodies because of the promise of a great adventure—and life had been rather dull in office and factory and on the farm. Something stirred in their blood—an old call to youth. Some instinct of a primitive, savage kind, for open-air life, fighting, killing, the comradeship of hunters, violent emotions, the chance of death, surged up into the brains of quiet boys, clerks, mechanics, miners, factory hands. It was the call of the wild—the hark-back of the mind to the old barbarities of the world's dawn, which is in the embryo of modern man. The shock of anger at frightful tales from Belgium—little children with their hands cut off (no evidence for that one); women foully outraged; civilians shot in cold blood—sent many men at a quick pace to the recruiting agents. Others were sent there by the taunt of a girl, or the sneer of a comrade in khaki, or the straight, steady look in the eyes of a father who said, "What about it, Dick?... The old country is up against it." It was that last thought which worked in the brain of England's manhood. That was his real call, which whispered to men at the plow—quiet, ruminating lads, the peasant type, the yeoman—and excited undergraduates in their rooms at Oxford and Cambridge, and the masters of public schools, and all manner of young men, and some, as I know, old in years but young in heart. "The old country is in danger!" The shadow of a menace was creeping over some little patch of England—or of Scotland.

"I's best be going," said the village boy.

"'Dulce et decorum est—'" said the undergraduate.

"I hate the idea, but it's got to be done," said the city—bred man.

So they disappeared from their familiar haunts—more and more of them as the months passed. They were put into training-camps, "pigged" it on dirty straw in dirty barns, were ill-fed and ill-equipped, and trained by hard—mouthed sergeants—tyrants and bullies in a good cause—until they became automata at the word of command, lost their souls, as it seemed, in that grinding-machine of military training, and cursed their fate. Only comradeship helped them—not always jolly, if they happened to be a class above their fellows, a moral peg above foul-mouthed slum-dwellers and men of filthy habits, but splendid if they were in their own crowd of decent, laughter-loving, companionable lads. Eleven months' training! Were they ever going to the front? The war would be over before they landed in France... Then, at last, they came.

III

It was not until July of 1915 that the Commander-in-Chief announced that a part of the New Army was in France, and lifted the veil from the secret which had mystified people at home whose boys had gone from them, but who could not get a word of their doings in France.

I saw the first of the "Kitchener men," as we called them then. The tramp of their feet in a steady scrunch, scrunch, along a gritty road of France, passed the window of my billet very early in the mornings, and I poked my head out to get another glimpse of those lads marching forward to the firing-line. For as long as history lasts the imagination of our people will strive to conjure up the vision of those boys who, in the year of 1915, went out to Flanders, not as conscript soldiers, but as volunteers, for the old country's sake, to take their risks and "do their bit" in the world's bloodiest war. I saw those fellows day by day, touched hands with them, went into the trenches with them, heard their first tales, and strolled into their billets when they had shaken down for a night or two within sound of the guns. History will envy me that, this living touch with the men who, beyond any doubt, did in their simple way act and suffer things before the war ended which revealed new wonders of human courage and endurance. Some people envied me then—those people at home to whom those boys belonged, and who in country towns and villages and suburban houses would have given their hearts to get one look at them there in Flanders and to see the way of their life... How were they living? How did they like it? How were they sleeping? What did the Regulars think of the New Army?

"Oh, a very cheerful lot," said a sergeant-major of the old Regular type, who was having a quiet pipe over a half-penny paper in a shed at the back of some farm buildings in the neighborhood of Armentieres, which had been plugged by two hundred German shells that time the day before. (One never knew when the fellows on the other side would take it into their heads to empty their guns that way. They had already killed a lot of civilians thereabouts, but the others stayed on.)

"Not a bit of trouble with them," said the sergeant-major, "and all as keen as when they grinned into a recruiting office and said, 'I'm going.' They're glad to be out. Over-trained, some of 'em. For ten months we've been working 'em pretty hard. Had to, but they were willing enough. Now you couldn't find a better battalion, though some more famous... Till we get our chance, you know."

He pointed with the stem of his pipe to the open door of an old barn, where a party of his men were resting.

"You'll find plenty of hot heads among them, but no cold feet. I'll bet on that."

The men were lying on a stone floor with haversacks for pillows, or squatting tailor-wise, writing letters home. From a far corner came a whistling trio, harmonized in a tune which for some reason made me think of hayfields in southern England.

They belonged to a Sussex battalion, and I said, "Any one here from Burpham?"

One of the boys sat up, stared, flushed to the roots of his yellow hair, and said, "Yes."

I spoke to him of people I knew there, and he was astonished that I should know them. Distressed also in a queer way. Those memories of a Sussex village seemed to break down some of the hardness in which he had cased himself. I could see a frightful homesickness in his blue eyes.

"P'raps I've seed the last o' Burpham," he said in a kind of whisper, so that the other men should not hear.

The other men were from Arundel, Littlehampton, and Sussex villages. They were of Saxon breed. There was hardly a difference between them and some German prisoners I saw, yellow-haired as they were, with fair, freckled, sun-baked skins. They told me they were glad to be out in France. Anything was better than training at home.

"I like Germans more'n sergeant-majors," said one young yokel, and the others shouted with laughter at his jest.

"Perhaps you haven't met the German sergeants," I said.

"I've met our'n," said the Sussex boy. "A man's a fool to be a soldier. Eh, lads?"

They agreed heartily, though they were all volunteers.

"Not that we're skeered," said one of them. "We'll be glad when the fighting begins."

"Speak for yourself, Dick Meekcombe, and don't forget the shells last night."

There was another roar of laughter. Those boys of the South Saxons were full of spirit. In their yokel way they were disguising their real thoughts—their fear of being afraid, their hatred of the thought of death—very close to them now—and their sense of strangeness in this scene on the edge of Armentieres, a world away from their old life.

The colonel sat in a little room at headquarters, a bronzed man with a grizzled mustache and light-blue eyes, with a fine tenderness in his smile.

"These boys of mine are all right," he said. "They're dear fellows, and ready for anything. Of course, it was anxious work at first, but my N. C. O.'s are a first-class lot, and we're ready for business."

He spoke of the recruiting task which had begun the business eleven months ago. It had not been easy, among all those scattered villages of the southern county. He had gone hunting among the farms and cottages for likely young fellows. They were of good class, and he had picked the lads of intelligence, and weeded out the others. They came from a good stock—the yeoman breed. One could not ask for better stuff. The officers were men of old county families, and they knew their men. That was a great thing. So far they had been very lucky with regard to casualties, though it was unfortunate that a company commander, a fine fellow who had been a schoolmaster and a parson, should have been picked off by a sniper on his first day out.

The New Army had received its baptism of fire, though nothing very fierce as yet. They were led on in easy stages to the danger-zone. It was not fair to plunge them straight away into the bad places. But the test of steadiness was good enough on a dark night behind the reserve trenches, when the reliefs had gone up, and there was a bit of digging to do in the open.

"Quiet there, boys," said the sergeant-major. "And no larks."

It was not a larky kind of place or time. There was no moon, and a light drizzle of rain fell. The enemy's trenches were about a thousand yards away, and their guns were busy in the night, so that the shells came overhead, and lads who had heard the owls hoot in English woods now heard stranger night-birds crying through the air, with the noise of rushing wings, ending in a thunderclap.

"And my old mother thinks I'm enjoying myself!" said the heir to a seaside lodging-house.

"Thirsty work, this grave-digging job," said a lad who used to skate on rollers between the bath-chairs of Brighton promenade.

"Can't see much in those shells," said a young man who once sold ladies' blouses in an emporium of a south coast village. "How those newspaper chaps do try to frighten us!"

He put his head on one side with a sudden jerk.

"What's that? Wasps?"

A number of insects were flying overhead with a queer, sibilant noise. Somewhere in the darkness there was a steady rattle in the throat of a beast.

"What's that, Sergeant?"

"Machine-gums, my child. Keep your head down, or you'll lose hold of it... Steady, there. Don't get jumpy, now!"

The machine-gun was firing too high to do any serious damage. It was probably a ricochet from a broken tree which made one of the boys suddenly drop his spade and fall over it in a crumpled way.

"Get up, Charlie," said the comrade next to him; and then, in a scared voice, "Oh, Sergeant!"

"That's all right," said the sergeant-major. "We're getting off very lightly. New remember what I've been telling you... Stretcher this way."

They were very steady through the night, this first company of the New Army.

"Like old soldiers, sir," said the sergeant-major, when he stood chatting with the colonel after breakfast.

It was a bit of bad luck, though not very bad, after all—which made the Germans shell a hamlet into which I went just as some of the New Army were marching through to their quarters. These men had already seen what shellfire could do to knock the beauty out of old houses and quiet streets. They had gone tramping through one or two villages to which the enemy's guns had turned their attention, and had received that unforgetable sensation of one's first sight of roofless cottages, and great gaps in garden walls, and tall houses which have tumbled inside themselves. But now they saw this destruction in the process, and stood very still, listening to the infernal clatter as shells burst at the other end of the street, tumbling down huge masses of masonry and plugging holes into neat cottages, and tearing great gashes out of red-brick walls.

"Funny business!" said one of the boys.

"Regular Drury Lane melodrama," said another.

"Looks as if some of us wouldn't be home in time for lunch," was another comment, greeted by a guffaw along the line.

They tried to see the humor of it, though there was a false note in some of the jokes. But it was the heroic falsity of boys whose pride is stronger than their fear, that inevitable fear which chills one when this beastliness is being done.

"Not a single casualty," said one of the officers when the storm of shells ended with a few last concussions and a rumble of falling bricks. "Anything wrong with our luck?"

Everything was all right with the luck of this battalion of the New Army in its first experience of war on the first night in the danger-zone. No damage was done even when two shells came into one of their billets, where a number of men were sleeping after a hard day and a long march.

"I woke up pretty quick," said one of them, "and thought the house had fallen in. I was out of it before the second came. Then I laughed. I'm a heavy sleeper, you know. [He spoke as if I knew his weakness.] My mother bought me an alarm-clock last birthday. 'Perhaps you'll be down for breakfast now,' she said. But a shell is better—as a knocker-up. I didn't stop to dress."

Death had missed him by a foot or two, but he laughed at the fluke of his escape.

"K.'s men" had not forgotten how to laugh after those eleven months of hard training, and they found a joke in grisly things which do not appeal humorously to sensitive men.

"Any room for us there?" asked one of these bronzed fellows as he marched with his battalion past a cemetery where the fantastic devices of French graves rose above the churchyard wall.

"Oh, we'll do all right in the open air, all along of the German trenches," was the answer he had from the lad at his side. They grinned at their own wit.

IV

I did not find any self-conscious patriotism among the rank and file of the New Army. The word itself meant nothing to them. Unlike the French soldier, to whom patriotism is a religion and who has the name of France on his lips at the moment of peril, our men were silent about the reasons for their coming out and the cause for which they risked their lives. It was not for imperial power. Any illusion to "The Empire" left them stone—cold unless they confused it with the Empire Music Hall, when their hearts warmed to the name. It was not because they hated Germans, because after a few turns in the trenches many of them had a fellow-feeling for the poor devils over the way, and to the end of the war treated any prisoners they took (after the killing in hot blood) like pet monkeys or tame bears. But for stringent regulations they would have fraternized with the enemy at the slightest excuse, and did so in the winter of 1914, to the great scandal of G. H. Q. "What's patriotism?" asked a boy of me, in Ypres, and there was hard scorn in his voice. Yet the love of the old country was deep down in the roots of their hearts, and, as with a boy who came from the village where I lived for a time, the name of some such place held all the meaning of life to many of them. The simple minds of country boys clung fast to that, went back in waking dreams to dwell in a cottage parlor where their parents sat, and an old clock ticked, and a dog slept with its head on its paws. The smell of the fields and the barns, the friendship of familiar trees, the heritage that was in their blood from old yeoman ancestry, touched them with the spirit of England, and it was because of that they fought.

The London lad was more self-conscious, had a more glib way of expressing his convictions, but even he hid his purpose in the war under a covering of irony and cynical jests. It was the spirit of the old city and the pride of it which helped him to suffer, and in his daydreams was the clanging of 'buses from Charing Cross to the Bank, the lights of the embankment reflected in the dark river, the back yard where he had kept his bicycle, or the suburban garden where he had watered his mother's plants... London! Good old London!... His heart ached for it sometimes when, as sentry, he stared across the parapet to the barbed wire in No Man's Land.

One night, strolling outside my own billet and wandering down the lane a way, I heard the sound of singing coming from a big brick barn on the roadside. I stood close under the blank wall at the back of the building, and listened. The men were singing "Auld Lang Syne" to the accompaniment of a concertina and a mouth-organ. They were taking parts, and the old tune—so strange to hear out in a village of France, in the war zone—sounded very well, with deep-throated harmonies. Presently the concertina changed its tune, and the men of the New Army sang "God Save the King." I heard it sung a thousand times or more on royal festivals and tours, but listening to it then from that dark old barn in Flanders, where a number of "K.'s men" lay on the straw a night or two away from the ordeal of advanced trenches, in which they had to take their turn, I heard it with more emotion than ever before. In that anthem, chanted by these boys in the darkness, was the spirit of England. If I had been king, like that Harry who wandered round the camp of Agincourt, where his men lay sleeping, I should have been glad to stand and listen outside that barn and hear those words:

Send him victorious,
Happy and glorious.

As the chief of the British tribes, the fifth George received his tribute from those warrior boys who had come out to fight for the flag that meant to them some old village on the Sussex Downs, where a mother and a sweetheart waited, or some town in the Midlands where the walls were placarded with posters which made the Germans gibe, or old London, where the 'buses went clanging down the Strand.

As I went back up the lane a dark figure loomed out, and I heard the click of a rifle-bolt. It was one of K.'s men, standing sentry outside the camp.

"Who goes there?"

It was a cockney voice.

"Friends."

"Pass, friends. All's well."

Yes, all was well then, as far as human courage and the spirit of a splendid youthfulness counted in that war of high explosives and destructive chemistry. The fighting in front of these lads of the New Army decided the fate of the world, and it was the valor of those young soldiers who, in a little while, were flung into hell-fires and killed in great numbers, which made all things different in the philosophy of modern life. That concertina in the barn was playing the music of an epic which will make those who sang it seem like heroes of mythology to the future race which will read of this death-struggle in Europe. Yet it was a cockney, perhaps from Clapham junction or Peckham Rye, who said, like a voice of Fate, "All's well."

V

When the New Army first came out to learn their lessons in the trenches in the long days before open warfare, the enemy had the best of it in every way. In gunpowder and in supplies of ammunition he was our master all along the line, and made use of his mastery by flinging over large numbers of shells, of all sizes and types, which caused a heavy toll in casualties to us; while our gunners were strictly limited to a few rounds a day, and cursed bitterly because they could not "answer back." In March of 1915 I saw the first fifteen-inch howitzer open fire. We called this monster "grandma," and there was a little group of generals on the Scherpenberg, near Kemmel, to see the effect of the first shell. Its target was on the lower slope of the Wytschaete Ridge, where some trenches were to be attacked for reasons only known by our generals and by God. Preliminary to the attack our field-guns opened fire with shrapnel, which scattered over the German trenches—their formidable earthworks with deep, shell-proof dugouts—like the glitter of confetti, and had no more effect than that before the infantry made a rush for the enemy's line and were mown down by machine-gun fire—the Germans were very strong in machine-guns, and we were very weak—in the usual way of those early days. The first shell fired by our monster howitzer was heralded by a low reverberation, as of thunder, from the field below us. Then, several seconds later, there rose from the Wytschaete Ridge a tall, black column of smoke which stood steady until the breeze clawed at it and tore it to tatters.

"Some shell!" said an officer. "Now we ought to win the war—I don't think!"

Later there arrived the first 9.2 (nine-point-two)—"aunty," as we called it.

Well, that was something in the way of heavy artillery, and gradually our gun-power grew and grew, until we could "answer back," and give more than came to us; but meanwhile the New Army had to stand the racket, as the Old Army had done, being strafed by harassing fire, having their trenches blown in, and their billets smashed, and their bodies broken, at all times and in all places within range of German guns.

Everywhere the enemy was on high ground and had observation of our position. From the Westhook Ridge and the Pilkem Ridge his observers watched every movement of our men round Ypres, and along the main road to Hooge, signaling back to their guns if anybody of them were visible. From the Wytschaete Ridge (White-sheet, as we called it) and Messines they could see for miles across our territory, not only the trenches, but the ways up to the trenches, and the villages behind them and the roads through the villages. They looked straight into Kemmel village and turned their guns on to it when our men crouched among its ruins and opened the graves in the cemetery and lay old bones bare. Clear and vivid to them were the red roofs of Dickebusch village and the gaunt ribs of its broken houses. (I knew a boy from Fleet Street who was cobbler there in a room between the ruins.) Those Germans gazed down the roads to Vierstraat and Vormizeele, and watched for the rising of white dust which would tell them when men were marching by—more cannon fodder. Southward they saw Neuve Eglise, with its rag of a tower, and Plug Street wood. In cheerful mood, on sunny days, German gunners with shells to spare ranged upon separate farm-houses and isolated barns until they became bits of oddly standing brick about great holes. They shelled the roads down which our transport wagons went at night, and the communication trenches to which our men moved up to the front lines, and gun-positions revealed by every flash, and dugouts foolishly frail against their 5.9's, which in those early days we could only answer by a few pip-squeaks. They made fixed targets of crossroads and points our men were bound to pass, so that to our men those places became sinister with remembered horror and present fear: Dead Horse Corner and Dead Cow Farm, and the farm beyond Plug Street; Dead Dog Farm and the Moated Grange on the way to St.-Eloi; Stinking Farm and Suicide Corner and Shell-trap Barn, out by Ypres.

All the fighting youth of our race took their turn in those places, searched along those roads, lived in ditches and dugouts there, under constant fire. In wet holes along the Yser Canal by Ypres, young officers who had known the decencies of home life tried to camouflage their beastliness by giving a touch of decoration to the clammy walls. They bought Kirchner prints of little ladies too lightly clad for the climate of Flanders, and pinned them up as a reminder of the dainty feminine side of life which here was banished. They brought broken chairs and mirrors from the ruins of Ypres, and said, "It's quite cozy, after all!"

And they sat there chatting, as in St. James's Street clubs, in the same tone of voice, with the same courtesy and sense of humor—while they listened to noises without, and wondered whether it would be to-day or to-morrow, or in the middle of the sentence they were speaking, that bits of steel would smash through that mud above their heads and tear them to bits and make a mess of things.

There was an officer of the Coldstream Guards who sat in one of these holes, like many others. A nice, gentle fellow, fond of music, a fine judge of wine, a connoisseur of old furniture and good food. It was cruelty to put such a man into a hole in the earth, like the ape-houses of Hagenbeck's Zoo. He had been used to comfort, the little luxuries of court life. There, on the canal-bank, he refused to sink into the squalor. He put on pajamas at night before sleeping in his bunk—silk pajamas—and while waiting for his breakfast smoked his own brand of gold-tipped cigarettes, until one morning a big shell blew out the back of his dugout and hurled him under a heap of earth and timber. He crawled out, cursing loudly with a nice choice of language, and then lit another gold—tipped cigarette, and called to his servant for breakfast. His batman was a fine lad, brought up in the old traditions of service to an officer of the Guards, and he provided excellent little meals, done to a turn, until something else happened, and he was buried alive within a few yards of his master... Whenever I went to the canal-bank, and I went there many times (when still and always hungry high velocities came searching for a chance meal), I thought of my friend in the Guards, and of other men I knew who had lived there in the worst days, and some of whom had died there. They hated that canal-bank and dreaded it, but they jested in their dugouts, and there was the laughter of men who hid the fear in their hearts and were "game" until some bit of steel plugged them with a gaping wound or tore their flesh to tatters.

VI

Because the enemy was on the high ground and our men were in the low ground, many of our trenches were wet and waterlogged, even in summer, after heavy rain. In winter they were in bogs and swamps, up by St.-Eloi and southward this side of Gommecourt, and in many other evil places. The enemy drained his water into our ditches when he could, with the cunning and the science of his way of war, and that made our men savage.

I remember going to the line this side of Fricourt on an August day in '15. It was the seventeenth of August, as I have it in my diary, and the episode is vivid in my mind because I saw then the New Army lads learning one of the lessons of war in one of the foulest places. I also learned the sense of humor of a British general, and afterward, not enjoying the joke, the fatalistic valor of officers and men (in civil life a year before) who lived with the knowledge that the ground beneath them was mined and charged with high explosives, and might hurl them to eternity between the whiffs of a cigarette.

We were sitting in the garden of the general's headquarters, having a picnic meal before going into the trenches. In spite of the wasps, which attacked the sandwiches, it was a nice, quiet place in time of war. No shell same crashing in our neighborhood (though we were well within range of the enemy's guns), and the loudest noise was the drop of an over-ripe apple in the orchard. Later on a shrill whistle signaled a hostile airplane overhead, but it passed without throwing a bomb.

"You will have a moist time in some of the trenches," said the general (whose boots were finely polished). "The rain has made them rather damp... But you must get down as far as the mine craters. We're expecting the Germans to fire one at any moment, and some of our trenches are only six yards away from the enemy. It's an interesting place."

The interest of it seemed to me too much of a good thing, and I uttered a pious prayer that the enemy would not explode his beastly mine under me. It makes such a mess of a man.

A staff captain came out with a report, which he read: "The sound of picks has been heard close to our sap-head. The enemy will probably explode their mine in a few hours."

"That's the place I was telling you about," said the general. "It's well worth a visit... But you must make up your mind to get your feet wet."

As long as I could keep my head dry and firmly fixed to my shoulders, I was ready to brave the perils of wet feet with any man.

It had been raining heavily for a day or two. I remember thinking that in London—which seemed a long way off—people were going about under umbrellas and looking glum when their clothes were splashed by passing omnibuses. The women had their skirts tucked up and showed their pretty ankles. (Those things used to happen in the far-off days of peace.) But in the trenches, those that lay low, rain meant something different, and hideously uncomfortable for men who lived in holes. Our soldiers, who cursed the rain—as in the old days, "they swore terribly in Flanders"—did not tuck their clothes up above their ankles. They took off their trousers.

There was something ludicrous, yet pitiable, in the sight of those hefty men coming back through the communication trenches with the tails of their shirts flapping above their bare legs, which were plastered with a yellowish mud. Shouldering their rifles or their spades, they trudged on grimly through two feet of water, and the boots which they wore without socks squelched at every step with a loud, sucking noise—"like a German drinking soup," said an officer who preceded me.

"Why grouse?" he said, presently. "It's better than Brighton!"

It was a queer experience, this paddling through the long communication trenches, which wound in and out like the Hampton Court maze toward the front line, and the mine craters which made a salient to our right, by a place called the "Tambour." Shells came whining overhead and somewhere behind us iron doors were slamming in the sky, with metallic bangs, as though opening and shutting in a tempest. The sharp crack of rifle-shots showed that the snipers were busy on both sides, and once I stood in a deep pool, with the water up to my knees, listening to what sounded like the tap-tap-tap of invisible blacksmiths playing a tattoo on an anvil.

It was one of our machine-guns at work a few yards away from my head, which I ducked below the trench parapet. Splodge! went the officer in front of me, with a yell of dismay. The water was well above his top-boots. Splosh! went another man ahead, recovering from a side-slip in the oozy mud and clinging desperately to some bunches of yarrow growing up the side of the trench. Squelch! went a young gentleman whose puttees and breeches had lost their glory and were but swabs about his elegant legs.

"Clever fellows!" said the officer, as two of us climbed on to the fire-stand of the trench in order to avoid a specially deep water-hole, and with ducked heads and bodies bent double (the Germans were only two hundred yards on the other side of the parapet) walked on dry earth for at least ten paces. The officer's laughter was loud at the corner of the next traverse, when there was an abrupt descent into a slough of despond.

"And I hope they can swim!" said an ironical voice from a dugout, as the officers passed. They were lying in wet mud in those square burrows, the men who had been working all night under their platoon commanders, and were now sleeping and resting in their trench dwellings. As I paddled on I glanced at those men lying on straw which gave out a moist smell, mixed with the pungent vapors of chloride of lime. They were not interested in the German guns, which were giving their daily dose of "hate" to the village of Becourt-Becordel. The noise did not interrupt their heavy, slumbrous breathing. Some of those who were awake were reading novelettes, forgetting war in the eternal plot of cheap romance. Others sat at the entrance of their burrows with their knees tucked up, staring gloomily to the opposite wall of the trench in day-dreams of some places betwixt Aberdeen and Hackney Downs. I spoke to one of them, and said, "How are you getting on?" He answered, "I'm not getting on... I don't see the fun of this."

"Can you keep dry?"

"Dry?... I'm soaked to the skin."

"What's it like here?"

"It's hell... The devils blow up mines to make things worse."

Another boy spoke.

"Don't you mind what he says, sir. He's always a gloomy bastard. Doesn't believe in his luck."

There were mascots for luck, at the doorways of their dugouts—a woman's face carved in chalk, the name of a girl written in pebbles, a portrait of the King in a frame of withered wild flowers.

A company of our New Army boys had respected a memento of French troops who were once in this section of trenches. It was an altar built into the side of the trench, where mass was said each morning by a soldier—priest. It was decorated with vases and candlesticks, and above the altar-table was a statue, crudely modeled, upon the base of which I read the words Notre Dame des Tranchees ("Our Lady of the Trenches"). A tablet fastened in the earth-wall recorded in French the desire of those who worshiped here:

"This altar, dedicated to Our Lady of the Trenches, was blessed by the chaplain of the French regiment. The 9th Squadron of the 6th Company recommends its care and preservation to their successors. Please do not touch the fragile statue in trench-clay."

"Our Lady of the Trenches!" It was the first time I had heard of this new title of the Madonna, whose spirit, if she visited those ditches of death, must have wept with pity for all those poor children of mankind whose faith was so unlike the work they had to do.

From a dugout near the altar there came tinkling music. A young soldier was playing the mandolin to two comrades. "All the latest ragtime," said one of them with a grin.

So we paddled on our way, glimpsing every now and then over the parapets at the German lines a few hundred yards away, and at a village in which the enemy was intrenched, quiet and sinister there. The water through which we waded was alive with a multitude of swimming frogs. Red slugs crawled up the sides of the trenches, and queer beetles with dangerous-looking horns wriggled along dry ledges and invaded the dugouts in search of the vermin which infested them.

"Rats are the worst plague," said a colonel, coming out of the battalion headquarters, where he had a hole large enough for a bed and table. "There are thousands of rats in this part of the line, and they're audacious devils. In the dugout next door the straw at night writhes with them... I don't mind the mice so much. One of them comes to dinner on my table every evening, a friendly little beggar who is very pally with me."

We looked out above the mine-craters, a chaos of tumbled earth, where our trenches ran so close to the enemy's that it was forbidden to smoke or talk, and where our sappers listened with all their souls in their ears to any little tapping or picking which might signal approaching upheaval. The coats of some French soldiers, blown up long ago by some of these mines, looked like the blue of the chicory flower growing in the churned-up soil... The new mine was not fired that afternoon, up to the time of my going away. But it was fired next day, and I wondered whether the gloomy boy had gone up with it. There was a foreknowledge of death in his eyes.

One of the officers had spoken to me privately.

"I'm afraid of losing my nerve before the men. It haunts me, that thought. The shelling is bad enough, but it's the mining business that wears one's nerve to shreds. One never knows."

I hated to leave him there to his agony... The colonel himself was all nerves, and he loathed the rats as much as the shell-fire and the mining, those big, lean, hungry rats of the trenches, who invaded the dugouts and frisked over the bodies of sleeping men. One young subaltern was in terror of them.

He told me how he shot at one, seeing the glint of its eyes in the darkness. The bullet from his revolver ricocheted from wall to wall, and he was nearly court-martialed for having fired.

The rats, the lice that lived on the bodies of our men, the water-logged trenches, the shell-fire which broke down the parapets and buried men in wet mud, wetter for their blood, the German snipers waiting for English heads, and then the mines—oh, a cheery little school of courage for the sons of gentlemen! A gentle academy of war for the devil and General Squeers!

VII

The city of Ypres was the capital of our battlefields in Flanders from the beginning to the end of the war, and the ground on which it stands, whether a new city rises there or its remnants of ruin stay as a memorial of dreadful things, will be forever haunted by the spirit of those men of ours who passed through its gates to fight in the fields beyond or to fall within its ramparts.

I went through Ypres so many times in early days and late days of the war that I think I could find my way about it blindfold, even now. I saw it first in March of 1915, before the battle when the Germans first used poison-gas and bombarded its choking people, and French and British soldiers, until the city fell into a chaos of masonry. On that first visit I found it scarred by shell—fire, and its great Cloth Hall was roofless and licked out by the flame of burning timbers, but most of the buildings were still standing and the shops were busy with customers in khaki, and in the Grande Place were many small booths served by the women and girls who sold picture post-cards and Flemish lace and fancy cakes and soap to British soldiers sauntering about without a thought of what might happen here in this city, so close to the enemy's lines, so close to his guns. I had tea in a bun-shop, crowded with young officers, who were served by two Flemish girls, buxom, smiling, glad of all the English money they were making.

A few weeks later the devil came to Ypres. The first sign of his work was when a mass of French soldiers and colored troops, and English, Irish, Scottish, and Canadian soldiers came staggering through the Lille and Menin gates with panic in their look, and some foul spell upon them. They were gasping for breath, vomiting, falling into unconsciousness, and, as they lay, their lungs were struggling desperately against some stifling thing. A whitish cloud crept up to the gates of Ypres, with a sweet smell of violets, and women and girls smelled it and then gasped and lurched as they ran and fell. It was after that when shells came in hurricane flights over Ypres, smashing the houses and setting them on fire, until they toppled and fell inside themselves. Hundreds of civilians hid in their cellars, and many were buried there. Others crawled into a big drain-pipe—there were wounded women and children among them, and a young French interpreter, the Baron de Rosen, who tried to help them—and they stayed there three days and nights, in their vomit and excrement and blood, until the bombardment ceased. Ypres was a city of ruin, with a red fire in its heart where the Cloth Hall and cathedral smoldered below their broken arches and high ribs of masonry that had been their buttresses and towers.

When I went there two months later I saw Ypres as it stood through the years of the war that followed, changing only in the disintegration of its ruin as broken walls became more broken and fallen houses were raked into smaller fragments by new bombardments, for there was never a day for years in which Ypres was not shelled.

The approach to it was sinister after one had left Poperinghe and passed through the skeleton of Vlamertinghe church, beyond Goldfish Chateau... For a long time Poperinghe was the last link with a life in which men and women could move freely without hiding from the pursuit of death; and even there, from time to time, there were shells from long-range guns and, later, night-birds dropping high-explosive eggs. Round about Poperinghe, by Reninghelst and Locre, long convoys of motor-wagons, taking up a new day's rations from the rail-heads, raised clouds of dust which powdered the hedges white. Flemish cart-horses with huge fringes of knotted string wended their way between motor-lorries and gun-limbers. Often the sky was blue above the hop-gardens, with fleecy clouds over distant woodlands and the gray old towers of Flemish churches and the windmills on Mont Rouge and Mont Neir, whose sails have turned through centuries of peace and strife. It all comes back to me as I write—that way to Ypres, and the sounds and the smells of the roads and fields where the traffic of war went up, month after month, year after year.

That day when I saw it first, after the gas-attack, was strangely quiet, I remember. There was "nothing doing," as our men used to say. The German gunners seemed asleep in the noonday sun, and it was a charming day for a stroll and a talk about the raving madness of war under every old hedge.

"What about lunch in Dickebusch on the way up?" asked one of my companions. There were three of us.

It seemed a good idea, and we walked toward the village which then—they were early days!—looked a peaceful spot, with a shimmer of sunshine above its gray thatch and red-tiled roofs.

Suddenly one of us said, "Good God!"

An iron door had slammed down the corridors of the sky and the hamlet into which we were just going was blotted out by black smoke, which came up from its center as though its market-place had opened up and vomited out infernal vapors.

"A big shell that!" said one man, a tall, lean-limbed officer, who later in the war was sniper-in-chief of the British army. Something enraged him at the sight of that shelled village.

"Damn them!" he said. "Damn the war! Damn all dirty dogs who smash up life!"

Four times the thing happened, and we were glad there had been a minute or so between us and Dickebusch. (In Dickebusch my young cobbler friend from Fleet Street was crouching low, expecting death.) The peace of the day was spoiled. There was seldom a real peace on the way to Ypres. The German gunners had wakened up again. They always did. They were getting busy, those house-wreckers. The long rush of shells tore great holes through the air. Under a hedge, with our feet in the ditch, we ate the luncheon we had carried in our pockets.

"A silly idea!" said the lanky man, with a fierce, sad look in his eyes. He was Norman-Irish, and a man of letters, and a crack shot, and all the boys he knew were being killed.

"What's silly?" I asked, wondering what particular foolishness he was thinking of, in a world of folly.

"Silly to die with a broken bit of sandwich in one's mouth, just because some German fellow, some fat, stupid man a few miles away, looses off a bit of steel in search of the bodies of men with whom he has no personal acquaintance."

"Damn silly," I said.

"That's all there is to it in modern warfare," said the lanky man. "It's not like the old way of fighting, body to body. Your strength against your enemy's, your cunning against his. Now it is mechanics and chemistry. What is the splendor of courage, the glory of youth, when guns kill at fifteen miles?"

Afterward this man went close to the enemy, devised tricks to make him show his head, and shot each head that showed.

The guns ceased fire. Their tumult died down, and all was quiet again. It was horribly quiet on our way into Ypres, across the railway, past the red-brick asylum, where a calvary hung unscathed on broken walls, past the gas-tank at the crossroads. This silence was not reassuring, as our heels clicked over bits of broken brick on our way into Ypres. The enemy had been shelling heavily for three-quarters of an hour in the morning. There was no reason why he should not begin again... I remember now the intense silence of the Grande Place that day after the gas-attack, when we three men stood there looking up at the charred ruins of the Cloth Hall. It was a great solitude of ruin. No living figure stirred among the piles of masonry which were tombstones above many dead. We three were like travelers who had come to some capital of an old and buried civilization, staring with awe and uncanny fear at this burial-place of ancient splendor, with broken traces of peoples who once had lived here in security. I looked up at the blue sky above those white ruins, and had an idea that death hovered there like a hawk ready to pounce. Even as one of us (not I) spoke the thought, the signal came. It was a humming drone high up in the sky.

"Look out!" said the lanky man. "Germans!"

It was certain that two birds hovering over the Grande Place were hostile things, because suddenly white puffballs burst all round them, as the shrapnel of our own guns scattered about them. But they flew round steadily in a half-circle until they were poised above our heads.

It was time to seek cover, which was not easy to find just there, where masses of stonework were piled high. At any moment things might drop. I ducked my head behind a curtain of bricks as I heard a shrill "coo-ee!" from a shell. It burst close with a scatter, and a tin cup was flung against a bit of wall close to where the lanky man sat in a shell-hole. He picked it up and said, "Queer!" and then smelled it, and said "Queer!" again. It was not an ordinary bomb. It had held some poisonous liquid from a German chemist's shop. Other bombs were dropping round as the two hostile airmen circled overhead, untouched still by the following shell-bursts. Then they passed toward their own lines, and my friend in the shell-hole called to me and said, "Let's be going."

It was time to go.

When we reached the edge of the town our guns away back started shelling, and we knew the Germans would answer. So we sat in a field nearby to watch the bombardment. The air moved with the rushing waves which tracked the carry of each shell from our batteries, and over Ypres came the high singsong of the enemies' answering voice.

As the dusk fell there was a movement out from Vlamertinghe, a movement of transport wagons and marching men. They were going up in the darkness through Ypres—rations and reliefs. They were the New Army men of the West Riding.

"Carry on there," said a young officer at the head of his company. Something in his eyes startled me. Was it fear, or an act of sacrifice? I wondered if he would be killed that night. Men were killed most nights on the way through Ypres, sometimes a few and sometimes many. One shell killed thirty one night, and their bodies lay strewn, headless and limbless, at the corner of the Grande Place. Transport wagons galloped their way through, between bursts of shell-fire, hoping to dodge them, and sometimes not dodging them. I saw the litter of their wheels and shafts, and the bodies of the drivers, and the raw flesh of the dead horses that had not dodged them. Many men were buried alive in Ypres, under masses of masonry when they had been sleeping in cellars, and were wakened by the avalanche above them. Comrades tried to dig them out, to pull away great stones, to get down to those vaults below from which voices were calling; and while they worked other shells came and laid dead bodies above the stones which had entombed their living comrades. That happened, not once or twice, but many times in Ypres.

There was a Town Major of Ypres. Men said it was a sentence of death to any officer appointed to that job. I think one of them I met had had eleven predecessors. He sat in a cellar of the old prison, with walls of sandbags on each side of him, but he could not sit there very long at a stretch, because it was his duty to regulate the traffic according to the shell-fire. He kept a visitors' book as a hobby, until it was buried under piles of prison, and was a hearty, cheerful soul, in spite of the menace of death always about him.

VIII

My memory goes back to a strange night in Ypres in those early days. It was Gullett, the Australian eyewitness, afterward in Palestine, who had the idea.

"It would be a great adventure," he said, as we stood listening to the gun-fire over there.

"It would be damn silly," said a staff officer. "Only a stern sense of duty would make me do it."

It was Gullett who was the brave man.

We took a bottle of Cointreau and a sweet cake as a gift to any battalion mess we might find in the ramparts, and were sorry for ourselves when we failed to find it, nor, for a long time, any living soul.

Our own footsteps were the noisiest sounds as we stumbled over the broken stones. No other footstep paced down any of those streets of shattered houses through which we wandered with tightened nerves. There was no movement among all those rubbish heaps of fallen masonry and twisted iron. We were in the loneliness of a sepulcher which had been once a fair city.

For a little while my friend and I stood in the Grande Place, not speaking. In the deepening twilight, beneath the last flame-feathers of the sinking sun and the first stars that glimmered in a pale sky, the frightful beauty of the ruins put a spell upon us.

The tower of the cathedral rose high above the framework of broken arches and single pillars, like a white rock which had been split from end to end by a thunderbolt. A recent shell had torn out a slice so that the top of the tower was supported only upon broken buttresses, and the great pile was hollowed out like a decayed tooth. The Cloth Hall was but a skeleton in stone, with immense gaunt ribs about the dead carcass of its former majesty. Beyond, the tower of St. Mark's was a stark ruin, which gleamed white through the darkening twilight.

We felt as men who should stand gazing upon the ruins of Westminster Abbey, while the shadows of night crept into their dark caverns and into their yawning chasms of chaotic masonry, with a gleam of moon upon their riven towers and fingers of pale light touching the ribs of isolated arches. In the spaciousness of the Grande Place at Ypres my friend and I stood like the last men on earth in a city of buried life.

It was almost dark now as we made our way through other streets of rubbish heaps. Strangely enough, as I remember, many of the iron lamp-posts had been left standing, though bent and twisted in a drunken way, and here and there we caught the sweet whiff of flowers and plants still growing in gardens which had not been utterly destroyed by the daily tempest of shells, though the houses about them had been all wrecked.

The woods below the ramparts were slashed and torn by these storms, and in the darkness, lightened faintly by the crescent moon, we stumbled over broken branches and innumerable shell-holes. The silence was broken now by the roar of a gun, which sounded so loud that I jumped sideways with the sudden shock of it. It seemed to be the signal for our batteries, and shell after shell went rushing through the night, with that long, menacing hiss which ends in a dull blast.

The reports of the guns and the explosions of the shells followed each other, and mingled in an enormous tumult, echoed back by the ruins of Ypres in hollow, reverberating thunder-strokes. The enemy was answering back, not very fiercely yet, and from the center of the town, in or about the Grande Place, came the noise of falling houses or of huge blocks of stone splitting into fragments.

We groped along, scared with the sense of death around us. The first flares of the night were being lighted by both sides above their trenches on each side of the salient. The balls of light rose into the velvety darkness and a moment later suffused the sky with a white glare which faded away tremulously after half a minute.

Against the first vivid brightness of it the lines of trees along the roads to Hooge were silhouetted as black as ink, and the fields between Ypres and the trenches were flooded with a milky luminance. The whole shape of the salient was revealed to us in those flashes. We could see all those places for which our soldiers fought and died. We stared across the fields beyond the Menin road toward the Hooge crater, and those trenches which were battered to pieces but not abandoned in the first battle of Ypres and the second battle.

That salient was, even then, in 1915, a graveyard of British soldiers—there were years to follow when many more would lie there—and as between flash and flash the scene was revealed, I seemed to see a great army of ghosts, the spirits of all those boys who had died on this ground. It was the darkness, and the tumult of guns, and our loneliness here on the ramparts, which put an edge to my nerves and made me see unnatural things.

No wonder a sentry was startled when he saw our two figures approaching him through a clump of trees. His words rang out like pistol-shots.

"Halt! Who goes there?"

"Friends!" we shouted, seeing the gleam of light on a shaking bayonet.

"Come close to be recognized!" he said, and his voice was harsh.

We went close, and I for one was afraid. Young sentries sometimes shot too soon.

"Who are you?" he asked, in a more natural voice, and when we explained he laughed gruffly. "I never saw two strangers pass this way before!"

He was an old soldier, "back to the army again," with Kitchener's men. He had been in the Chitral campaign and South Africa—"Little wars compared to this," as he said. A fine, simple man, and although a bricklayer's laborer in private life, with a knowledge of the right word. I was struck when he said that the German flares were more "luminous" than ours. I could hardly see his face in the darkness, except when he struck a match once, but his figure was black against the illumined sky, and I watched the motion of his arm as he pointed to the roads up which his comrades had gone to the support of another battalion at Hooge, who were hard pressed. "They went along under a lot of shrapnel and had many casualties."

He told the story of that night in a quiet, thoughtful way, with phrases of almost biblical beauty in their simple truth, and the soul of the man, the spirit of the whole army in which he was a private soldier, was revealed when he flashed out a sentence with his one note of fire, "But the enemy lost more than we did, sir, that night!"

We wandered away again into the darkness, with the din of the bombardment all about us. There was not a square yard of ground unplowed by shells and we did not nourish any false illusions as to finding a safe spot for a bivouac.

There was no spot within the ramparts of Ypres where a man might say "No shells will fall here." But one place we found where there seemed some reasonable odds of safety. There also, if sleep assailed us, we might curl up in an abandoned dugout and hope that it would not be "crumped" before the dawn. There were several of these shelters there, but, peering into them by the light of a match, I shuddered at the idea of lying in one of them. They had been long out of use and there was a foul look about the damp bedding and rugs which had been left to rot there. They were inhabited already by half-wild cats—the abandoned cats of Ypres, which hunted mice through the ruins of their old houses—and they spat at me and glared with green-eyed fear as I thrust a match into their lairs.

There were two kitchen chairs, with a deal table on which we put our cake and Cointreau, and here, through half a night, my friend and I sat watching and listening to that weird scene upon which the old moon looked down; and, as two men will at such a time, we talked over all the problems of life and death and the meaning of man's heritage.

Another sentry challenged us—all his nerves jangled at our apparition. He was a young fellow, one of "Kitchener's crowd," and told us frankly that he had the "jimjams" in this solitude of Ypres and "saw Germans" every time a rat jumped. He lingered near us—"for company.

It was becoming chilly. The dew made our clothes damp. Cake and sweet liquor were poor provisions for the night, and the thought of hot tea was infinitely seductive. Perhaps somewhere one might find a few soldiers round a kettle in some friendly dugout. We groped our way along, holding our breath at times as a shell came sweeping overhead or burst with a sputter of steel against the ramparts. It was profoundly dark, so that only the glowworms glittered like jewels on black velvet. The moon had gone down, and inside Ypres the light of the distant flares only glimmered faintly above the broken walls. In a tunnel of darkness voices were speaking and some one was whistling softly, and a gleam of red light made a bar across the grass. We walked toward a group of black figures, suddenly silent at our approach—obviously startled.

"Who's there?" said a voice.

We were just in time for tea—a stroke of luck—with a company of boys (all Kitchener lads from the Civil Service) who were spending the night here. They had made a fire behind a screen to give them a little comfort and frighten off the ghosts, and gossiped with a queer sense of humor, cynical and blasphemous, but even through their jokes there was a yearning for the end of a business which was too close to death.

I remember the gist of their conversation, which was partly devised for my benefit. One boy declared that he was sick of the whole business.

"I should like to cancel my contract," he remarked.

"Yes, send in your resignation, old lad," said another, with ironical laughter.

"They'd consider it, wouldn't they? P'raps offer a rise in wages—I don't think!"

Another boy said, "I am a citizen of no mean Empire, but what the hell is the Empire going to do for me when the next shell blows off both my bleeding legs?"

This remark was also received by a gust of subdued laughter, silenced for a moment by a roar and upheaval of masonry somewhere by the ruins of the Cloth Hall.

"Soldiers are prisoners," said a boy without any trace of humor. "You're lagged, and you can't escape. A 'blighty' is the best luck you can hope for."

"I don't want to kill Germans," said a fellow with a superior accent. "I've no personal quarrel against them; and, anyhow, I don't like butcher's work."

"Christian service, that's what the padre calls it. I wonder if Christ would have stuck a bayonet into a German stomach—a German with his hands up. That's what we're asked to do."

"Oh, Christianity is out of business, my child. Why mention it? This is war, and we're back to the primitive state—B.C. All the same, I say my little prayers when I'm in a blue funk.

"Gentle Jesus, meek and mild, Look upon a little child."

This last remark was the prize joke of the evening, received with much hilarity, not too loud, for fear of drawing fire—though really no Germans could have heard any laughter in Ypres.

Nearby, their officer was spending the night. We called on him, and found him sitting alone in a dugout furnished by odd bits from the wrecked houses, with waxen flowers in a glass case on the shelf, and an old cottage clock which ticked out the night, and a velvet armchair which had been the pride of a Flemish home. He was a Devonshire lad, with a pale, thoughtful face, and I was sorry for him in his loneliness, with a roof over his head which would be no proof against a fair-sized shell.

He expressed no surprise at seeing us. I think he would not have been surprised if the ghost of Edward the Black Prince had called on him. He would have greeted him with the same politeness and offered him his green armchair.

The night passed. The guns slackened down before the dawn. For a little while there was almost silence, even over the trenches. But as the first faint glow of dawn crept through the darkness the rifle-fire burst out again feverishly, and the machine-guns clucked with new spasms of ferocity. The boys of the New Army, and the Germans facing them, had an attack of the nerves, as always at that hour.

The flares were still rising, but had the debauched look of belated fireworks after a night of orgy.

In a distant field a cock crew.

The dawn lightened all the sky, and the shadows crept away from the ruins of Ypres, and all the ghastly wreckage of the city was revealed again nakedly. Then the guns ceased for a while, and there was quietude in the trenches, and out of Ypres, sneaking by side ways, went two tired figures, padding the hoof with a slouching swiftness to escape the early morning "hate" which was sure to come as soon as a clock in Vlamertinghe still working in a ruined tower chimed the hour of six.

I went through Ypres scores of times afterward, and during the battles of Flanders saw it day by day as columns of men and guns and pack-mules and transports went up toward the ridge which led at last to Passchendaele. We had big guns in the ruins of Ypres, and round about, and they fired with violent concussions which shook loose stones, and their flashes were red through the Flanders mist. Always this capital of the battlefields was sinister, with the sense of menace about.

"Steel helmets to be worn. Gas-masks at the alert."

So said the traffic man at the crossroads.

As one strapped on one's steel helmet and shortened the strap of one's gas-mask, the spirit of Ypres touched one's soul icily.

IX

The worst school of war for the sons of gentlemen was, in those early days, and for long afterward, Hooge. That was the devil's playground and his chamber of horrors, wherein he devised merry tortures for young Christian men. It was not far out of Ypres, to the left of the Menin road, and to the north of Zouave Wood and Sanctuary Wood. For a time there was a chateau there called the White Chateau, with excellent stables and good accommodation for one of our brigade staffs, until one of our generals was killed and others wounded by a shell, which broke up their conference. Afterward there was no chateau, but only a rubble of bricks banked up with sandbags and deep mine-craters filled with stinking water slopping over from the Bellewarde Lake and low-lying pools. Bodies, and bits of bodies, and clots of blood, and green metallic-looking slime, made by explosive gases, were floating on the surface of that water below the crater banks when I first passed that way, and so it was always. Our men lived there and died there within a few yards of the enemy, crouched below the sand-bags and burrowed in the sides of the crater. Lice crawled over them in legions. Human flesh, rotting and stinking, mere pulp, was pasted into the mud-banks. If they dug to get deeper cover their shovels went into the softness of dead bodies who had been their comrades. Scraps of flesh, booted legs, blackened hands, eyeless heads, came falling over them when the enemy trench-mortared their position or blew up a new mine-shaft.

I remember one young Irish officer who came down to bur quarters on a brief respite from commanding the garrison at Hooge. He was a handsome fellow, like young Philip of Spain by Velasquez, and he had a profound melancholy in his eyes in spite of a charming smile.

"Do you mind if I have a bath before I join you?" he asked.

He walked about in the open air until the bath was ready. Even there a strong, fetid smell came from him.

"Hooge," he said, in a thoughtful way, "is not a health resort."

He was more cheerful after his bath and did not feel quite such a leper. He told one or two stories about the things that happened at Hooge, and I wondered if hell could be so bad. After a short stay he went back again, and I could see that he expected to be killed. Before saying good-by he touched some flowers on the mess-table, and for a moment or two listened to birds twittering in the trees.

"Thanks very much," he said. "I've enjoyed this visit a good deal.. . Good-by."

He went back through Ypres on the way to Hooge, and the mine-crater where his Irish soldiers were lying in slime, in which vermin crawled.

Sometimes it was the enemy who mined under our position, blowing a few men to bits and scattering the sand-bags. Sometimes it was our men who upheaved the earth beyond them by mine charges and rushed the new crater.

It was in July of '15 that the devils of Hooge became merry and bright with increased activity. The Germans had taken possession of one of the mine-craters which formed the apex of a triangle across the Menin road, with trenches running down to it on either side, so that it was like the spear-head of their position. They had fortified it with sand-bags and crammed it with machine—guns which could sweep the ground on three sides, so making a direct attack by infantry a suicidal enterprise. Our trenches immediately faced this stronghold from the other side of a road at right angles with the Menin road, and our men—the New Army boys—were shelled day and night, so that many of them were torn to pieces, and others buried alive, and others sent mad by shell-shock. (They were learning their lessons in the school of courage.) It was decided by a conference of generals, not at Hooge, to clear out this hornets' nest, and the job was given to the sappers, who mined under the roadway toward the redoubt, while our heavy artillery shelled the enemy's position all around the neighborhood.

On July 22d the mine was exploded, while our men crouched low, horribly afraid after hours of suspense. The earth was rent asunder by a gust of flame, and vomited up a tumult of soil and stones and human limbs and bodies. Our men still crouched while these things fell upon them.

"I thought I had been blown to bits," one of them told me. "I was a quaking fear, with my head in the earth. I kept saying, 'Christ!... Christ!'"

When the earth and smoke had settled again it was seen that the enemy's redoubt had ceased to exist. In its place, where there had been a crisscross of trenches and sand-bag shelters for their machine-guns and a network of barbed wire, there was now an enormous crater, hollowed deep with shelving sides surrounded by tumbled earth heaps which had blocked up the enemy's trenches on either side of the position, so that they could not rush into the cavern and take possession. It was our men who "rushed" the crater and lay there panting in its smoking soil.

Our generals had asked for trouble when they destroyed that redoubt, and our men had it. Infuriated by a massacre of their garrison in the mine-explosion and by the loss of their spear-head, the Germans kept up a furious bombardment on our trenches in that neighborhood in bursts of gun-fire which tossed our earthworks about and killed and wounded many men. Our line at Hooge at that time was held by the King's Royal Rifles of the 14th Division, young fellows, not far advanced in the training-school of war. They held on under the gunning of their positions, and each man among them wondered whether it was the shell screeching overhead or the next which would smash him into pulp like those bodies lying nearby in dugouts and upheaved earthworks.

On the morning of July 30th there was a strange lull of silence after a heavy bout of shells and mortars. Men of the K. R. R. raised their heads above broken parapets and crawled out of shell-holes and looked about. There were many dead bodies lying around, and wounded men were wailing. The unwounded, startled by the silence, became aware of some moisture falling on them; thick, oily drops of liquid.

"What in hell's name—?" said a subaltern.

One man smelled his clothes, which reeked of something like paraffin.

Coming across from the German trenches were men hunched up under some heavy weights. They were carrying cylinders with nozles like hose-pipes. Suddenly there was a rushing noise like an escape of air from some blast-furnace. Long tongues of flame licked across to the broken ground where the King's Royal Rifles lay.

Some of them were set on fire, their clothes burning on them, making them living torches, and in a second or two cinders.

It was a new horror of war—the *Flammenwerfer.*

Some of the men leaped to their feet, cursing, and fired repeatedly at the Germans carrying the flaming jets. Here and there the shots were true. A man hunched under a cylinder exploded like a fat moth caught in a candle-flame. But that advancing line of fire after the long bombardment was too much for the rank and file, whose clothes were smoking and whose bodies were scorched. In something like a panic they fell back, abandoning the cratered ground in which their dead lay.

The news of this disaster and of the new horror reached the troops in reserve, who had been resting in the rear after a long spell. They moved up at once to support their comrades and make a counter-attack. The ground they had to cover was swept by machine-guns, and many fell, but the others attacked again and again, regardless of their losses, and won back part of the lost ground, leaving only a depth of five hundred yards in the enemy's hands.

So the position remained until the morning of August 9th, when a new attack was begun by the Durham, Yorkshire, Lancashire, and Midland troops of the 6th Division, who had been long in the salient and had proved the quality of northern "grit" in the foul places and the foul weather of that region.

It was late on the night of August 8th that these battalions took up their position, ready for the assault. These men, who came mostly from mines and workshops, were hard and steady and did not show any outward sign of nervousness, though they knew well enough that before the light of another day came their numbers would have passed through the lottery of this game of death. Each man's life depended on no more than a fluke of luck by the throw of those dice which explode as they fall. They knew what their job was. It was to cross five hundred yards of open ground to capture and to hold a certain part of the German position near the Chateau of Hooge.

They were at the apex of the triangle which made a German salient after the ground was lost, on July 30th. On the left side of the triangle was Zouave Wood, and Sanctuary Wood ran up the right side to a strong fort held by the enemy and crammed with machine-guns and every kind of bomb. The base of the upturned triangle was made by the Menin road, to the north, beyond which lay the crater, the chateau, and the stables.

The way that lay between the regiment and their goal was not an easy one to pass. It was cut and crosscut by our old trenches, now held by the enemy, who had made tangles of barbed wire in front of their parapets, and had placed machine-guns at various points. The ground was littered with dead bodies belonging to the battle of July 30th, and pock-marked by deep shell-holes. To cross five hundred yards of such ground in the storm of the enemy's fire would be an ordeal greater than that of rushing from one trench to another. It would have to be done in regular attack formation, and with the best of luck would be a grim and costly progress.

The night was pitch dark. The men drawn up could only see one another as shadows blacker than the night. They were very quiet; each man was fighting down his fear in his soul, trying to get a grip on nerves hideously strained by the rack of this suspense. The words, "Steady, lads." were spoken down the ranks by young lieutenants and sergeants. The sounds of men whispering, a cough here and there, a word of command, the clink of bayonets, the cracking of twigs under heavy boots, the shuffle of troops getting into line, would not carry with any loudness to German ears.

The men deployed before dawn broke, waiting for the preliminary bombardment which would smash a way for them. The officers struck matches now and then to glance at their wrist-watches, set very carefully to those of the gunners. Then our artillery burst forth with an enormous violence of shell-fire, so that the night was shattered with the tumult of it. Guns of every caliber mingled their explosions, and the long screech of the shells rushed through the air as though thousands of engines were chasing one another madly through a vast junction in that black vault.

The men listened and waited. As soon as the guns lengthened their fuses the infantry advance would begin. Their nerves were getting jangled. It was just the torture of human animals. There was an indrawing of breath when suddenly the enemy began to fire rockets, sending up flares which made white waves of light. If they were seen! There would be a shambles.

But the smoke of all the bursting shells rolled up in a thick veil, hiding those mining lads who stared toward the illuminations above the black vapors and at the flashes which seemed to stab great rents in the pall of smoke. "It was a jumpy moment," said the colonel of the Durhams, and the moment lengthened into minutes.

Then the time came. The watch hands pointed to the second which had been given for the assault to begin, and instantly, to the tick, the guns lifted and made a curtain of fire round the Chateau of Hooge, beyond the Menin road, six hundred yards away.

"Time!"

The company officers blew their whistles, and there was a sudden clatter from trench-spades slung to rifle-barrels, and from men girdled with hand-grenades, as the advancing companies deployed and made their first rush forward. The ground had been churned up by our shells, and the trenches had been battered into shapelessness, strewn with broken wire and heaps of loose stones and fragments of steel.

It seemed impossible that any German should be left alive in this quagmire, but there was still a rattle of machine-guns from holes and hillocks. Not for long. The bombing-parties searched and found them, and silenced them. From the heaps of earth which had once been trenches German soldiers rose and staggered in a dazed, drunken way, stupefied by the bombardment beneath which they had crouched.

Our men spitted them on their bayonets or hurled hand-grenades, and swept the ground before them. Some Germans screeched like pigs in a slaughter-house.

The men went on in short rushes. They were across the Menin road now, and were first to the crater, though other troops were advancing quickly from the left. They went down into the crater, shouting hoarsely, and hurling bombs at Germans, who were caught like rats in a trap, and scurried up the steep sides beyond, firing before rolling down again, until at least two hundred bodies lay dead at the bottom of this pit of hell.

While some of the men dug themselves into the crater or held the dugouts already made by the enemy, others climbed up to the ridge beyond and with a final rush, almost winded and spent, reached the extreme limit of their line of assault and achieved the task which had been set them. They were mad now, not human in their senses. They saw red through bloodshot eyes. They were beasts of prey—these decent Yorkshire lads.

Round the stables themselves three hundred Germans were bayoneted, until not a single enemy lived on this ground, and the light of day on that 9th of August revealed a bloody and terrible scene, not decent for words to tell. Not decent, but a shambles of human flesh which had been a panic-stricken crowd of living men crying for mercy, with that dreadful screech of terror from German boys who saw the white gleam of steel at their stomachs before they were spitted. Not many of those Durham and Yorkshire lads remain alive now with that memory. The few who do must have thrust it out of their vision, unless at night it haunts them.

The assaulting battalion had lost many men during the assault, but their main ordeal came after the first advance, when the German guns belched out a large quantity of heavy shells from the direction of Hill 60. They raked the ground, and tried to make our men yield the position they had gained. But they would not go back or crawl away from their dead.

All through the day the bombardment continued, answered from our side by fourteen hours of concentrated fire, which I watched from our battery positions. In spite of the difficulties of getting up supplies through the "crumped" trenches, the men held on and consolidated their positions. One of the most astounding feats was done by the sappers, who put up barbed wire beyond the line under a devilish cannonade.

A telephone operator had had his apparatus smashed by a shell early in the action, and worked his way back to get another. He succeeded in reaching the advanced line again, but another shell knocked out his second instrument. It was then only possible to keep in touch with the battalion headquarters by means of messengers, and again and again officers and men made their way across the zone of fire or died in the attempt. Messages reached the colonel of the regiment that part of his front trenches had been blown away.

From other parts of the line reports came in that the enemy was preparing a counter-attack. For several hours now the colonel of the Durhams could not get into touch with his companies, isolated and hidden beneath the smoke of the shell-bursts. Flag-wagging and heliographing were out of the question. He could not tell even if a single man remained alive out there beneath all those shells. No word came from them now to let him know if the enemy were counter-attacking.

Early in the afternoon he decided to go out and make his own reconnaissance. The bombardment was still relentless, and it was only possible to go part of the way in an old communication trench. The ground about was littered with the dead, still being blown about by high explosives.

The soul of the colonel was heavy then with doubt and with the knowledge that most of the dead here were his own. When he told me this adventure his only comment was the soldier's phrase, "It was not what might be called a 'healthy' place." He could see no sign of a counter-attack, but, straining through the smoke-clouds, his eyes could detect no sign of life where his men had been holding the captured lines. Were they all dead out there?

On Monday night the colonel was told that his battalion would be relieved, and managed to send this order to a part of it. It was sent through by various routes, but some men who carried it came back with the news that it was still impossible to get into touch with the companies holding the advanced positions above the Menin road.

In trying to do so they had had astounding escapes. Several of them had been blown as far as ten yards by the air-pressure of exploding shells and had been buried in the scatter of earth.

"When at last my men came back—those of them who had received the order," said the colonel, "I knew the price of their achievement—its cost in officers and men." He spoke as a man resentful of that bloody sacrifice.

There were other men still alive and still holding on. With some of them were four young officers, who clung to their ground all through the next night, before being relieved. They were without a drop of water and suffered the extreme miseries of the battlefield.

There was no distinction in courage between those four men, but the greater share of suffering was borne by one. Early in the day he had had his jaw broken by a piece of shell, but still led his men. Later in the day he was wounded in the shoulder and leg, but kept his command, and he was still leading the survivors of his company when he came back on the morning of Tuesday, August 10th.

Another party of men had even a longer time of trial. They were under the command of a lance-corporal, who had gained possession of the stables above the Menin road and now defended their ruins. During the previous twenty-four hours he had managed to send through several messages, but they were not to report his exposed position nor to ask for supports nor to request relief. What he said each time was, "Send us more bombs." It was only at seven-thirty in the morning of Tuesday, after thirty hours under shell-fire, that the survivors came away from their rubbish heap in the lines of death.

So it was at Hooge on that day of August. I talked with these men, touched hands with them while the mud and blood of the business still fouled them. Even now, in remembrance, I wonder how men could go through such hours without having on their faces more traces of their hell, though some of them were still shaking with a kind of ague.

X

Here and there on the roadsides behind the lines queer sacks hung from wooden poles. They had round, red disks painted on them, and looked like the trunks of human bodies after Red Indians had been doing decorative work with their enemy's slain. At Flixecourt, near Amiens, I passed one on a Sunday when bells were ringing for high mass and a crowd of young soldiers were trooping into the field with fixed bayonets.

A friend of mine—an ironical fellow—nudged me, and said, "Sunday-school for young Christians!" and made a hideous face, very comical.

It was a bayonet-school of instruction, and "O. C. Bayonets"—Col. Ronald Campbell—was giving a little demonstration. It was a curiously interesting form of exercise. It was as though the primitive nature in man, which had been sleeping through the centuries, was suddenly awakened in the souls of these cockney soldier—boys. They made sudden jabs at one another fiercely and with savage grimaces, leaped at men standing with their backs turned, who wheeled round sharply, and crossed bayonets, and taunted the attackers. Then they lunged at the hanging sacks, stabbing them where the red circles were painted. These inanimate things became revoltingly lifelike as they jerked to and fro, and the bayonet men seemed enraged with them. One fell from the rope, and a boy sprang at it, dug his bayonet in, put his foot on the prostrate thing to get a purchase for the bayonet, which he lugged out again, and then kicked the sack.

"That's what I like to see," said an officer. "There's a fine fighting-spirit in that lad. He'll kill plenty of Germans before he's done."

Col. Ronald Campbell was a great lecturer on bayonet exercise. He curdled the blood of boys with his eloquence on the method of attack to pierce liver and lights and kidneys of the enemy. He made their eyes bulge out of their heads, fired them with blood-lust, stoked up hatred of Germans—all in a quiet, earnest, persuasive voice, and a sense of latent power and passion in him. He told funny stories—one, famous in the army, called "Where's 'Arry?"

It was the story of an attack on German trenches in which a crowd of Germans were captured in a dugout. The sergeant had been told to blood his men, and during the killing he turned round and asked, "Where's 'Arry?... 'Arry 'asn't 'ad a go yet."

'Arry was a timid boy, who shrank from butcher's work, but he was called up and given his man to kill. And after that 'Arry was like a man-eating tiger in his desire for German blood.

He used another illustration in his bayonet lectures. "You may meet a German who says, 'Mercy! I have ten children.'... Kill him! He might have ten more."

At those training-schools of British youth (when nature was averse to human slaughter until very scientifically trained) one might see every form of instruction in every kind of weapon and instrument of death—machine-guns, trench-mortars, bombs, torpedoes, gas, and, later on, tanks; and as the months passed, and the years, the youth of the British Empire graduated in these schools of war, and those who lived longest were experts in divers branches of technical education.

Col. Ronald Campbell retired from bayonet instruction and devoted his genius and his heart (which was bigger than the point of a bayonet) to the physical instruction of the army and the recuperation of battle-worn men. I liked him better in that job, and saw the real imagination of the man at work, and his amazing, self-taught knowledge of psychology. When men came down from the trenches, dazed, sullen, stupid, dismal, broken, he set to work to build up their vitality again, to get them interested in life again, and to make them keen and alert. As they had been dehumanized by war, so he rehumanized them by natural means. He had a farm, with flowers and vegetables, pigs, poultry, and queer beasts. A tame bear named Flanagan was the comic character of the camp. Colonel Campbell found a thousand qualities of character in this animal, and brought laughter back to gloomy boys by his description of them. He had names for many of his pets—the game-cocks and the mother-hens; and he taught the men to know each one, and to rear chicks, and tend flowers, and grow vegetables. Love, and not hate, was now his gospel. All his training was done by games, simple games arousing intelligence, leading up to elaborate games demanding skill of hand and eye. He challenged the whole army system of discipline imposed by authority by a new system of self-discipline based upon interest and instinct. His results were startling, and men who had been dumb, blear-eyed, dejected, shell-shocked wrecks of life were changed quite quickly into bright, cheery fellows, with laughter in their eyes.

"It's a pity," he said, "they have to go off again and be shot to pieces. I cure them only to be killed—but that's not my fault. It's the fault of war."

It was Colonel Campbell who discovered "Willie Woodbine," the fighting parson and soldier's poet, who was the leading member of a traveling troupe of thick-eared thugs. They gave pugilistic entertainments to tired men. Each of them had one thick ear. Willie Woodbine had two. They fought one another with science (as old professionals) and challenged any man in the crowd.

Then one of them played the violin and drew the soul out of soldiers who seemed mere animals, and after another fight Willie Woodbine stepped up and talked of God, and war, and the weakness of men, and the meaning of courage. He held all those fellows in his hand, put a spell on them, kept them excited by a new revelation, gave them, poor devils, an extra touch of courage to face the menace that was ahead of them when they went to the trenches again.

XI

Our men were not always in the trenches. As the New Army grew in numbers reliefs were more frequent than in the old days, when battalions held the line for long spells, until their souls as well as their bodies were sunk in squalor. Now in the summer of 1915 it was not usual for men to stay in the line for more than three weeks at a stretch, and they came back to camps and billets, where there was more sense of life, though still the chance of death from long-range guns. Farther back still, as far back as the coast, and all the way between the sea and the edge of war, there were new battalions quartered in French and Flemish villages, so that every cottage and farmstead, villa, and chateau was inhabited by men in khaki, who made themselves at home and established friendly relations with civilians there unless they were too flagrant in their robbery, or too sour in their temper, or too filthy in their habits. Generally the British troops were popular in Picardy and Artois, and when they left women kissed and cried, in spite of laughter, and joked in a queer jargon of English-French. In the *estaminets* of France and Flanders they danced with frowzy peasant girls to the tune of a penny-in-the-slot piano, or, failing the girls, danced with one another.

For many years to come, perhaps for centuries, those cottages and barns into which our men crowded will retain signs and memories of that British occupation in the great war. Boys who afterward went forward to the fighting-fields and stepped across the line to the world of ghosts carved their names on wooden beams, and on the whitewashed walls scribbled legends proclaiming that Private John Johnson was a bastard; or that a certain battalion was a rabble of ruffians; or that Kaiser Bill would die on the gallows, illustrating those remarks with portraits and allegorical devices, sketchily drawn, but vivid and significant.

The soldier in the house learned quite a lot of French, with which he made his needs understood by the elderly woman who cooked for his officers' mess. He could say, with a fine fluency, "Ou est le blooming couteau?" or "Donnez-moi le bally fourchette, s'il vous plait, madame." It was not beyond his vocabulary to explain that "Les pommes de terre frites are absolument all right if only madame will tenir ses cheveux on." In the courtyards of ancient farmhouses, so old in their timbers and gables that the Scottish bodyguard of Louis XI may have passed them on their way to Paris, modern Scots with khaki-covered kilts pumped up the water from old wells, and whistled "I Know a Lassie" to the girl who brought the cattle home, and munched their evening rations while Sandy played a "wee bit" on the pipes to the peasant—folk who gathered at the gate. Such good relations existed between the cottagers and their temporary guests that one day, for instance, when a young friend of mine came back from a long spell in the trenches (his conversation was of dead men, flies, bombs, lice, and hell), the old lady who had given him her best bedroom at the beginning of the war flung her arms about him and greeted him like a long-lost son. To a young Guardsman, with his undeveloped mustache on his upper lip, her demonstrations were embarrassing.

It was one of the paradoxes of the war that beauty lived but a mile or two away from hideous squalôr. While men in the lines lived in dugouts and marched down communicating trenches thigh-high, after rainy weather, in mud and water, and suffered the beastliness of the primitive earth-men, those who were out of the trenches, turn and turn about, came back to leafy villages and drilled in fields all golden with buttercups, and were not too uncomfortable in spite of overcrowding in dirty barns.

There was more than comfort in some of the headquarters where our officers were billeted in French chateaux. There was a splendor of surroundings which gave a graciousness and elegance to the daily life of that extraordinary war in which men fought as brutally as in prehistoric times. I knew scores of such places, and went through gilded gates emblazoned with noble coats of arms belonging to the days of the Sun King, or farther back to the Valois, and on my visits to generals and their staffs stood on long flights of steps which led up to old mansions, with many towers and turrets, surrounded by noble parks and ornamental waters and deep barns in which five centuries of harvests had been stored. From one of the archways here one might see in the mind's eye Mme. de Pompadour come out with a hawk on her wrist, or even Henri de Navarre with his gentlemen-at-arms, all their plumes alight in the sun as they mounted their horses for a morning's boar-hunt.

It was surprising at first when a young British officer came out and said, "Toppin' morning," or, "Any news from the Dardanelles?" There was something incongruous about this habitation of French chiteaux by British officers with their war-kit. The strangeness of it made me laugh in early days of first impressions, when I went through the rooms of one of those old historic houses, well within range of the German guns with a brigade major. It was the Chateau de Henencourt, near Albert.

"This is the general's bedroom," said the brigade major, opening a door which led off a gallery, in which many beautiful women of France and many great nobles of the old regime looked down from their gilt frames.

The general had a nice bed to sleep in. In such a bed Mme. du Barry might have stretched her arms and yawned, or the beautiful Duchesse de Mazarin might have held her morning levee. A British general, with his bronzed face and bristly mustache, would look a little strange under that blue-silk canopy, with rosy cherubs dancing overhead on the flowered ceiling. His top-boots and spurs stood next to a Louis Quinze toilet-table. His leather belts and field-glasses lay on the polished boards beneath the tapestry on which Venus wooed Adonis and Diana went a-hunting. In other rooms no less elegantly rose-tinted or darkly paneled other officers had made a litter of their bags, haversacks, rubber baths, trench—boots, and puttees. At night the staff sat down to dinner in a salon where the portraits of a great family of France, in silks and satins and Pompadour wigs, looked down upon their khaki. The owner of the chateau, in whose veins flowed the blood of those old aristocrats, was away with his regiment, in which he held the rank of corporal. His wife, the Comtesse de Henencourt, managed the estate, from which all the men-servants except the veterans had been mobilized. In her own chateau she kept one room for herself, and every morning came in from the dairies, where she had been working with her maids, to say, with her very gracious smile, to the invaders of her house: "Bon jour, messieurs! Ca va bien?"

She hid any fear she had under the courage of her smile. Poor chateaux of France! German shells came to knock down their painted turrets, to smash through the ceilings where the rosy Cupids played, and in one hour or two to ruin the beauty that had lived through centuries of pride.

Scores of them along the line of battle were but heaps of brick-dust and twisted iron.

I saw the ruins of the Chateau de Henencourt two years after my first visit there. The enemy's line had come closer to it and it was a target for their guns. Our guns—heavy and light—were firing from the back yard and neighboring fields, with deafening tumult. Shells had already broken the roofs and turrets of the chateau and torn away great chunks of wall. A colonel of artillery had his headquarters in the *petit salon*. His hand trembled as he greeted me.

"I'm not fond of this place," he said. "The whole damn thing will come down on my head at any time. I think I shall take to the cellars."

We walked out to the courtyard and he showed me the way down to the vault. A shell came over the chateau and burst in the outhouses.

"They knocked out a 9.2 a little while ago," said the colonel. "Made a mess of some heavy gunners."

There was a sense of imminent death about us, but it was not so sinister a place as farther on, where a brother of mine sat in a hole directing his battery... The Countess of Henencourt had gone. She went away with her dairymaids, driving her cattle down the roads.

XII

One of the most curious little schools of courage inhabited by British soldiers in early days was the village of Vaux-sur-Somme, which we took over from the French, who were our next-door neighbors at the village of Frise in the summer of '15. After the foul conditions of the salient it seemed unreal and fantastic, with a touch of romance not found in other places. Strange as it seemed, the village garrisoned by our men was in advance of our trench lines, with nothing dividing them from the enemy but a little undergrowth—and the queerest part of it all was the sense of safety, the ridiculously false security with which one could wander about the village and up the footpath beyond, with the knowledge that one's movements were being watched by German eyes and that the whole place could be blown off the face of the earth... but for the convenient fact that the Germans, who were living in the village of Curlu, beyond the footpath, were under our own observation and at the mercy of our own guns.

That sounded like a fairy-tale to men who, in other places, could not go over the parapet of the first-line trenches, or even put their heads up for a single second, without risking instant death.

I stood on a hill here, with a French interpreter and one of his men. A battalion of loyal North Lancashires was some distance away, but after an exchange of compliments in an idyllic glade, where a party of French soldiers lived in the friendliest juxtaposition with the British infantry surrounding them—it was a cheery bivouac among the trees, with the fragrance of a stew-pot mingling with the odor of burning wood—the lieutenant insisted upon leading the way to the top of the hill.

He made a slight detour to point out a German shell which had fallen there without exploding, and made laughing comments upon the harmless, futile character of those poor Germans in front of us. They did their best to kill us, but oh, so feebly!

Yet when I took a pace toward the shell he called out, sharply, "Ne touchez pas!" I would rather have touched a sleeping tiger than that conical piece of metal with its unexploded possibilities, but bent low to see the inscriptions on it, scratched by French gunners with wore recklessness of death. *Mort aux Boches* was scrawled upon it between the men's initials.

Then we came to the hill-crest and to the last of our trenches, and, standing there, looked down upon the villages of Vaux and Curlu, separated by a piece of marshy water. In the farthest village were the Germans, and in the nearest, just below us down the steep cliff, our own men. Between the two there was a narrow causeway across the marsh and a strip of woods half a rifle-shot in length.

Behind, in a sweeping semicircle round their village and ours, were the German trenches and the German guns. I looked into the streets of both villages as clearly as one may see into Clovelly village from the crest of the hill. In Vaux-sur-Somme a few British soldiers were strolling about. One was sitting on the window-sill of a cottage, kicking up his heels.

In the German village of Curlu the roadways were concealed by the perspective of the houses, with their gables and chimney-stacks, so that I could not see any passers—by. But at the top of the road, going out of the village and standing outside the last house on the road, was a solitary figure—a German sentry.

The French lieutenant pointed to a thin mast away from the village on the hillside.

"Do you see that? That is their flagstaff. They hoist their flag for victories. It wagged a good deal during the recent Russian fighting. But lately they have not had the cheek to put it up."

This interpreter—the Baron de Rosen—laughed very heartily at that naked pole on the hill.

Then I left him and joined our own men, and went down a steep hill into Vaux, well outside our line of trenches, and thrust forward as an outpost in the marsh. German eyes could see me as I walked. At any moment those little houses about me might have been smashed into rubbish heaps. But no shells came to disturb the waterfowl among the reeds around.

And so it was that the life in this place was utterly abnormal, and while the guns were silent except for long—range fire, an old-fashioned mode of war—what the adjutant of this little outpost called a "gentlemanly warfare," prevailed. Officers and men slept within a few hundred yards of the enemy, and the officers wore their pajamas at night. When a fight took place it was a chivalrous excursion, such as Sir Walter Manny would have liked, between thirty or forty men on one side against somewhat the same number on the other.

Our men used to steal out along the causeway which crossed the marsh—a pathway about four feet wide, broadening out in the middle, so that a little redoubt or blockhouse was established there, then across a narrow drawbridge, then along the path again until they came to the thicket which screened the German village of Curlu.

It sometimes happened that a party of Germans were creeping forward from the other direction, in just the same way, disguised in party-colored clothes splashed with greens and reds and browns to make them invisible between the trees, with brown masks over their faces. Then suddenly contact was made.

Into the silence of the wood came the sharp crack of rifles, the zip-zip of bullets, the shouts of men who had given up the game of invisibility. It was a sharp encounter one night when the Loyal North Lancashires held the village of Vaux, and our men brought back many German helmets and other trophies as proofs of victory. Then to bed in the village, and a good night's rest, as when English knights fought the French, not far from these fields, as chronicled in the pages of that early war correspondent, Sir John Froissart.

All was quiet when I went along the causeway and out into the wood, where the outposts stood listening for any crack of a twig which might betray a German footstep. I was startled when I came suddenly upon two men, almost invisible, against the tree-trunks. There they stood, motionless, with their rifles ready, peering through the brushwood. If I had followed the path on which they stood for just a little way I should have walked into the German village. But, on the other hand, I should not have walked back again....

When I left the village, and climbed up the hill to our own trenches again, I laughed aloud at the fantastic visit to that grim little outpost in the marsh. If all the war had been like this it would have been more endurable for men who had no need to hide in holes in the earth, nor crouch for three months below ground, until an hour or two of massacre below a storm of high explosives. In the village on the marsh men fought at least against other men, and not against invisible powers which belched forth death.

It was part of the French system of "keeping quiet" until the turn of big offensives; a good system, to my mind, if not carried too far. At Frise, next door to Vaux, in a loop of the Somme, it was carried a little too far, with relaxed vigilance.

It was a joke of our soldiers to crawl on and through the reeds and enter the French line and exchange souvenirs with the sentries.

"Souvenir!" said one of them one day. "Bullet—you know—*cartouche.* Comprenny?"

A French poilu of Territorials, who had been dozing, sat up with a grin and said, "Mais oui, mon vieux," and felt in his pouch for a cartridge, and then in his pockets, and then in the magazine of the rifle between his knees.

"Fini!" he said. "Tout fini, mon p'tit camarade."

The Germans one day made a pounce on Frise, that little village in the loop of the Somme, and "pinched" every man of the French garrison. There was the devil to pay, and I heard it being played to the tune of the French soixante-quinzes, slashing over the trees.

Vaux and Curlu went the way of all French villages in the zone of war, when the battles of the Somme began, and were blown off the map.

XIII

At a place called the Pont de Nieppe, beyond Armentieres—a most "unhealthy" place in later years of war—a bathing establishment was organized by officers who were as proud of their work as though they had brought a piece of paradise to Flanders. To be fair to them, they had done that. To any interested visitor, understanding the nobility of their work, they exhibited a curious relic. It was the Holy Shirt of Nieppe, which should be treasured as a memorial in our War Museum—an object-lesson of what the great war meant to clean-living men. It was not a saint's shirt, but had been worn by a British officer in the trenches, and was like tens of thousands of other shirts worn by our officers and men in the first winters of the war, neither better nor worse, but a fair average specimen. It had been framed in a glass case, and revealed, on its linen, the corpses of thousands of lice. That vermin swarmed upon the bodies of all our boys who went into the trenches and tortured them. After three days they were lousy from head to foot. After three weeks they were walking menageries. To English boys from clean homes, to young officers who had been brought up in the religion of the morning tub, this was one of the worst horrors of war. They were disgusted with themselves. Their own bodies were revolting to them. Scores of times I have seen battalions of men just out of battle stripping themselves and hunting in their shirts for the foul beast. They had a technical name for this hunter's job. They called it "chatting." They desired a bath as the hart panteth for the water—brooks, and baths were but a mirage of the brain to men in Flanders fields and beyond the Somme, until here and there, as at Nieppe, officers with human sympathy organized a system by which battalions of men could wash their bodies.

The place in Nieppe had been a jute-factory, and there were big tubs in the sheds, and nearby was the water of the Lys. Boilers were set going to heat the water. A battalion's shirts were put into an oven and the lice were baked and killed. It was a splendid thing to see scores of boys wallowing in those big tubs, six in a tub, with a bit of soap for each. They gave little grunts and shouts of joyous satisfaction. The cleansing water, the liquid heat, made their flesh tingle with exquisite delight, sensuous and spiritual. They were like children. They splashed one another, with gurgles of laughter. They put their heads under water and came up puffing and blowing like grampuses. Something broke in one's heart to see them, those splendid boys whose bodies might soon be torn to tatters by chunks of steel. One of them remembered a bit of Latin he had sung at Stonyhurst: "*Asperges me, Domine, hyssopo, et mundabor; lavabis me, et super nivem dealbabor.*" ("Thou shalt sprinkle me with hyssop, O Lord, and I shall be cleansed; thou shalt wash me, and I shall be made whiter than snow.")

On the other side of the lines the Germans were suffering in the same way, lousy also, and they, too, were organizing bath-houses. After their first retreat I saw a queer name on a wooden shed: Entlausunganstalt. I puzzled over it a moment, and then understood. It was a new word created out of the dirt of modern war—"Delousing station."

XIV

It was harvest-time in the summer of '15, and Death was not the only reaper who went about the fields, although he was busy and did not rest even when the sun had flamed down below the belt of trees on the far ridge, and left the world in darkness.

On a night in August two of us stood in a cornfield, silent, under the great dome, staring up at the startling splendor of it. The red ball just showed above the far line of single trees which were black as charcoal on the edge of a long, straight road two miles away, and from its furnace there were flung a million feathers of flame against the silk-blue canopy of the evening sky. The burning colors died out in a few minutes, and the fields darkened, and all the corn-shocks paled until they became quite white, like rows of tents, under the harvest moon. Another night had come in this year of war.

Up Ypres way the guns were busy, and at regular intervals the earth trembled, and the air vibrated with dull, thunderous shocks.

"The moon's face looks full of irony to-night," said the man by my side. "It seems to say, `What fools those creatures are down there, spoiling their harvest-time with such a mess of blood!'"

The stars were very bright in some of those Flemish nights. I saw the Milky Way clearly tracked across the dark desert. The Pleiades and Orion's belt were like diamonds on black velvet. But among all these worlds of light other stars, unknown to astronomers, appeared and disappeared. On the road back from a French town one night I looked Arras way, and saw what seemed a bursting planet. It fell with a scatter of burning pieces. Then suddenly the thick cloth of the night was rent with stabs of light, as though flashing swords were hacking it, and a moment later a finger of white fire was traced along the black edge of the far-off woods, so that the whole sky was brightened for a moment and then was blotted out by a deeper darkness... Arras was being shelled again, as I saw it many times in those long years of war.

The darkness of all the towns in the war zone was rather horrible. Their strange, intense quietude, when the guns were not at work, made them dead, as the very spirit of a town dies on the edge of war. One night, as on many others, I walked through one of them with a friend. Every house was shuttered, and hardly a gleam came through any crack. No footstep, save our own, told of life. The darkness was almost palpable. It seemed to press against one's eyeballs like a velvet mask. My nerves were so on edge with a sense of the uncanny silence and invisibility that I started violently at the sound of a quiet voice speaking three inches from my ear.

"Halte! Qui va la?"

It was a French sentry, who stood with his back to the wall of a house in such a gulf of blackness that not even his bayonet was revealed by a glint.

Another day of war came. The old beauty of the world was there, close to the lines of the bronzed cornfields splashed with the scarlet of poppies, and the pale yellow of the newly cut sheaves, stretching away and away, without the break of a hedge, to the last slopes which met the sky.

I stood in some of those harvest-fields, staring across to a slope of rising ground where there was no ripening wheat, and where the grass itself came to a sudden halt, as though afraid of something. I knew the reason of this, and of the long white lines of earth thrown up for miles each way. Those were the parapets of German trenches, and in the ditches below them were earth-men, armed with deadly weapons, staring out across the beauty of France and wondering, perhaps, why they should be there to mar it, and watching me, a little black dot in their range of vision, with an idle thought as to whether it were worth their while to let a bullet loose and end my walk. They could have done so easily, but did not bother. No shot or shell came to break through the hum of bees or to crash through the sigh of the wind, which was bending all the ears of corn to listen to the murmurous insect-life in these fields of France.

Close to me was a group of peasants—a study for a painter like Millet. One of them shouted out to me, "Voilà les Boches!" waving his arm to left and right, and then shaking a clenched fist at them.

A sturdy girl with a brown throat showing through an open bodice munched an apple, like Audrey in "As You Like It," and between her bites told me that she had had a brother killed in the war, and that she had been nearly killed herself, a week ago, by shells that came bursting all round her as she was tying up her sheaves (she pointed to great holes in the field), and described the coming of the Germans into her village over there, when she had lied to some Uhlans about the whereabouts of French soldiers and had given one of those fat Germans a blow on the face when he had tried to make love to her in her father's barn. Her mother had been raped.

In further fields out of view of the German trenches, but well within shell-range, the harvesting was being done by French soldiers. One of them was driving the reaping—machine and looked like a gunner on his limber, with his kepi thrust to the back of his head. The trousers of his comrades were as red as the poppies that grew on the edge of the wheat, and three of these poilus had ceased their work to drink out of a leather wine-bottle which had been replenished from a hand-cart. It was a pretty scene if one could forget the grim purpose which had put those harvesters in uniform.

The same thought was in the mind of a British officer.

"A beautiful country, this," he said. "It's a pity to cut it up with trenches and barbed wire."

Battalions of New Army men were being reviewed but a furlong or two away from that Invisible Man who was wielding a scythe which had no mercy for unripe wheat. Out of those lines of eyes stared the courage of men's souls, not shirking the next ordeal.

It was through red ears of corn, in that summer of '15, that one found one's way to many of the trenches that marked the boundary-lines of the year's harvesting, and in Belgium (by Kemmel Hill) the shells of our batteries, answered by German guns, came with their long-drawn howls of murder across the heads of peasant women who were gleaning, with bent backs.

In Plug Street Wood the trees had worn thin under showers of shrapnel, but the long avenues between the trenches were cool and pleasant in the heat of the day. It was one of the elementary schools where many of our soldiers learned the A B C of actual warfare after their training in camps behind the lines. Here one might sport with Amaryllis in the shade, but for the fact that country wenches were not allowed in the dugouts and trenches, where I found our soldiers killing flies in the intervals between pot-shots at German periscopes.

The enemy was engaged, presumably, in the same pursuit of killing time and life (with luck), and sniping was hot on both sides, so that the wood resounded with sharp reports as though hard filbert nuts were being cracked by giant teeth. Each time I went there one of our men was hit by a sniper, and his body was carried off for burial as I went toward the first line of trenches, hoping that my shadow would not fall across a German periscope. The sight of that dead body passing chilled one a little. There were many graves in the bosky arbors—eighteen under one mound—but some of those who had fallen six months before still lay where the gleaners could not reach them.

I used to peer through the leaves of Plug Street Wood at No Man's Land between the lines, where every creature had been killed by the sweeping flail of machine-guns and shrapnel. Along the harvest-fields there were many barren territories like that, and up by Hooge, along the edge of the fatal crater, and behind the stripped trees of Zouave Wood there was no other gleaning to be had but that of broken shells and shrapnel bullets and a litter of limbs.

XV

For some time the War Office would not allow military bands at the front, not understanding that music was like water to parched souls. By degrees divisional generals realized the utter need of entertainment among men dulled and dazed by the routine of war, and encouraged "variety" shows, organized by young officers who had been amateur actors before the war, who searched around for likely talent. There was plenty of it in the New Army, including professional "funny men," trick cyclists, conjurers, and singers of all kinds. So by the summer of '15 most of the divisions had their dramatic entertainments: "The Follies," "The Bow Bells," "The Jocks," "The Pip-Squeaks," "The Whizz-Bangs," "The Diamonds," "The Brass Hats," "The Verey Lights," and many others with fancy names.

I remember going to one of the first of them in the village of Acheux, a few miles from the German lines. It was held in an old sugar-factory, and I shall long remember the impressions of the place, with seven or eight hundred men sitting in the gloom of that big, broken, barn-like building, where strange bits of machinery looked through the darkness, and where through gashes in the walls stars twinkled.

There was a smell of clay and moist sugar and tarpaulins and damp khaki, and chloride of lime, very pungent in one's nostrils, and when the curtain went up on a well—fitted stage and "The Follies" began their performance, the squalor of the place did not matter. What mattered was the enormous whimsicality of the Bombardier at the piano, and the outrageous comicality of a tousle-haired soldier with a red nose, who described how he had run away from Mons "with the rest of you," and the light—heartedness of a performance which could have gone straight to a London music-hall and brought down the house with jokes and songs made up in dugouts and front—line trenches.

At first the audience sat silent, with glazed eyes. It was difficult to get a laugh out of them. The mud of the trenches was still on them. They stank of the trenches, and the stench was in their souls. Presently they began to brighten up. Life came back into their eyes. They laughed!... Later, from this audience of soldiers there were yells of laughter, though the effect of shells arriving at unexpected moments, in untoward circumstances, was a favorite theme of the jesters. Many of the men were going into the trenches that night again, and there would be no fun in the noise of the shells, but they went more gaily and with stronger hearts, I am sure, because of the laughter which had roared through the old sugar—factory.

A night or two later I went to another concert and heard the same gaiety of men who had been through a year of war. It was in an open field, under a velvety sky studded with innumerable stars. Nearly a thousand soldiers trooped through the gates and massed before the little canvas theater. In front a small crowd of Flemish children squatted on the grass, not understanding a word of the jokes, but laughing in shrill delight at the antics of soldier-Pierrots. The corner-man was a funny fellow, and his by-play with a stout Flemish woman round the flap of the canvas screen, to whom he made amorous advances while his comrades were singing sentimental ballads, was truly comic. The hit of the evening was when an Australian behind the stage gave an unexpected imitation of a laughing-jackass.

There was something indescribably weird and wild and grotesque in that prolonged cry of cackling, unnatural mirth. An Australian by my side said: "Well done! Exactly right!" and the Flemish children shrieked with joy, without understanding the meaning of the noise. Old, old songs belonging to the early Victorian age were given by the soldiers, who had great emotion and broke down sometimes in the middle of a verse. There were funny men dressed in the Widow Twankey style, or in burlesque uniforms, who were greeted with yells of laughter by their comrades. An Australian giant played some clever card tricks, and another Australian recited Kipling's "Gunga Din" with splendid fire. And between every "turn" the soldiers in the field roared out a chorus:

"Jolly good song,

Jolly well sung.

If you can think of a better you're welcome to try.

But don't forget the singer is dry;

Give the poor beggar some beer!"

A touring company of mouth-organ musicians was having a great success in the war zone. But, apart from all those organized methods of mirth, there was a funny man in every billet who played the part of court jester, and clowned it whatever the state of the weather or the risks of war. The British soldier would have his game of "house" or "crown and anchor" even on the edge of the shell-storm, and his little bit of sport wherever there was room to stretch his legs. It was a jesting army (though some of its jokes were very grim), and those who saw, as I did, the daily tragedy of war, never ceasing, always adding to the sum of human suffering, were not likely to discourage that sense of humor.

A successful concert with mouth-organs, combs, and tissue-paper and penny whistles was given by the Guards in the front-line trenches near Loos. They played old English melodies, harmonized with great emotion and technical skill. It attracted an unexpected audience. The Germans crowded into their front line—not far away—and applauded each number. Presently, in good English, a German voice shouted across:

"Play 'Annie Laurie' and I will sing it."

The Guards played "Annie Laurie," and a German officer stood up on the parapet—the evening sun was red behind him—and sang the old song admirably, with great tenderness. There was applause on both sides.

"Let's have another concert to-morrow!" shouted the Germans.

But there was a different kind of concert next day, and the music was played by trench-mortars, Mills bombs, rifle-grenades, and other instruments of death in possession of the Guards. There were cries of agony and terror from the German trenches, and young officers of the Guards told the story as an amusing anecdote, with loud laughter.

XVI

It was astonishing how loudly one laughed at tales of gruesome things, of war's brutality-I with the rest of them. I think at the bottom of it was a sense of the ironical contrast between the normal ways of civilian life and this hark-back to the caveman code. It made all our old philosophy of life monstrously ridiculous. It played the "hat trick" with the gentility of modern manners. Men who had been brought up to Christian virtues, who had prattled their little prayers at mothers' knees, who had grown up to a love of poetry, painting, music, the gentle arts, over-sensitized to the subtleties of half-tones, delicate scales of emotion, fastidious in their choice of words, in their sense of beauty, found themselves compelled to live and act like ape-men; and it was abominably funny. They laughed at the most frightful episodes, which revealed this contrast between civilized ethics and the old beast law. The more revolting it was the more, sometimes, they shouted with laughter, especially in reminiscence, when the tale was told in the gilded *salon* of a French chateau, or at a mess-table.

It was, I think, the laughter of mortals at the trick which had been played on them by an ironical fate. They had been taught to believe that the whole object of life was to reach out to beauty and love, and that mankind, in its progress to perfection, had killed the beast instinct, cruelty, blood-lust, the primitive, savage law of survival by tooth and claw and club and ax. All poetry, all art, all religion had preached this gospel and this promise.

Now that ideal had broken like a china vase dashed to hard ground. The contrast between That and This was devastating. It was, in an enormous world-shaking way, like a highly dignified man in a silk hat, morning coat, creased trousers, spats, and patent boots suddenly slipping on a piece of orange-peel and sitting, all of a heap, with silk hat flying, in a filthy gutter. The war-time humor of the soul roared with mirth at the sight of all that dignity and elegance despoiled.

So we laughed merrily, I remember, when a military chaplain (Eton, Christ Church, and Christian service) described how an English sergeant stood round the traverse of a German trench, in a night raid, and as the Germans came his way, thinking to escape, he cleft one skull after another with a steel-studded bludgeon—a weapon which he had made with loving craftsmanship on the model of Blunderbore's club in the pictures of a fairy-tale.

So we laughed at the adventures of a young barrister (a brilliant fellow in the Oxford "Union") whose pleasure it was to creep out o' nights into No Man's Land and lie doggo in a shell-hole close to the enemy's barbed wire, until presently, after an hour's waiting or two, a German soldier would crawl out to fetch in a corpse. The English barrister lay with his rifle ready. Where there had been one corpse there were two. Each night he made a notch on his rifle—three notches one night—to check the number of his victims. Then he came back to breakfast in his dugout with a hearty appetite.

In one section of trenches the men made a habit of betting upon those who would be wounded first. It had all the uncertainty of the roulette-table... One day, when the German gunners were putting over a special dose of hate, a sergeant kept coming to one dugout to inquire about a "new chum," who had come up with the drafts.

"Is Private Smith all right?" he asked.

"Yes, Sergeant, he's all right," answered the men crouching in the dark hole.

"Private Smith isn't wounded yet?" asked the, sergeant again, five minutes later.

"No, Sergeant."

Private Smith was touched by this interest in his well-being.

"That sergeant seems a very kind man," said the boy. "Seems to love me like a father!"

A yell of laughter answered him.

"You poor, bleeding fool!" said one of his comrades. "He's drawn you in a lottery! Stood to win if you'd been hit."

In digging new trenches and new dugouts, bodies and bits of bodies were unearthed, and put into sand-bags with the soil that was sent back down a line of men concealing their work from German eyes waiting for any new activity in our ditches.

"Bit of Bill," said the leading man, putting in a leg.

"Another bit of Bill," he said, unearthing a hand.

"Bill's ugly mug," he said at a later stage in the operations, when a head was found.

As told afterward, that little episode in the trenches seemed immensely comic. Generals chuckled over it. Chaplains treasured it.

How we used to guffaw at the answer of the cockney soldier who met a German soldier with his hands up, crying: "Kamerad! Kamerad! Mercy!"

"Not so much of your 'Mercy, Kamerad,'" said the cockney. "'And us over your bloody ticker!"

It was the man's watch he wanted, without sentiment.

One tale was most popular, most mirth-arousing in the early days of the war.

"Where's your prisoner?" asked an Intelligence officer waiting to receive a German sent down from the trenches under escort of an honest corporal.

"I lost him on the way, sir," said the corporal.

"Lost him?"

The corporal was embarrassed.

"Very sorry, sir. My feelings overcame me, sir. It was like this, sir. The man started talking on the way down. Said he was thinking of his poor wife. I'd been thinking of mine, and I felt sorry for him. Then he mentioned as how he had two kiddies at home. I 'ave two kiddies at 'ome, sir, and I couldn't 'elp feeling sorry for him. Then he said as how his old mother had died awhile ago and he'd never see her again. When he started cryin' I was so sorry for him I couldn't stand it any longer, sir. So I killed the poor blighter."

Our men in the trenches, and out of them, up to the waist in water sometimes, lying in slimy dugouts, lice—eaten, rat-haunted, on the edge of mine-craters, under harassing fire, with just the fluke of luck between life and death, seized upon any kind of joke as an excuse for laughter, and many a time in ruins and in trenches and in dugouts I have heard great laughter. It was the protective armor of men's souls. They knew that if they did not laugh their courage would go and nothing would stand between them and fear.

"You know, sir," said a sergeant-major, one day, when I walked with him down a communication trench so waterlogged that my top-boots were full of slime, "it doesn't do to take this war seriously."

And, as though in answer to him, a soldier without breeches and with his shirt tied between his legs looked at me and remarked, in a philosophical way, with just a glint of comedy in his eyes:

"That there Grand Fleet of ours don't seem to be very active, sir. It's a pity it don't come down these blinkin' trenches and do a bit of work!"

"Having a clean-up, my man?" said a brigadier to a soldier trying to wash in a basin about the size of a kitchen mug.

"Yes, sir," said the man, "and I wish I was a blasted canary."

One of the most remarkable battles on the front was fought by a battalion of Worcesters for the benefit of two English members of Parliament. It was not a very big battle, but most dramatic while it lasted. The colonel (who had a sense of humor) arranged it after a telephone message to his dugout telling him that two politicians were about to visit his battalion in the line, and asking him to show them something interesting.

"Interesting?" said the colonel. "Do they think this war is a peep-show for politicians? Do they want me to arrange a massacre to make a London holiday?" Then his voice changed and he laughed. "Show them something interesting? Oh, all right; I dare say I can do that."

He did. When the two M. P.'s arrived, apparently at the front-line trenches, they were informed by the colonel that, much to his regret, for their sake, the enemy was just attacking, and that his men were defending their position desperately.

"We hope for the best," he said, "and I think there is just a chance that you will escape with your lives if you stay here quite quietly."

"Great God!" said one of the M. P.'s, and the other was silent, but pale.

Certainly there was all the noise of a big attack. The Worcesters were standing-to on the fire-step, firing rifle—grenades and throwing bombs with terrific energy. Every now and then a man fell, and the stretcher-bearers pounced on him, tied him up in bandages, and carried him away to the field dressing-station, whistling as they went, "We won't go home till morning," in a most heroic way... The battle lasted twenty minutes, at the end of which time the colonel announced to his visitors:

"The attack is repulsed, and you, gentlemen, have nothing more to fear."

One of the M. P.'s was thrilled with excitement. "The valor of your men was marvelous," he said. "What impressed me most was the cheerfulness of the wounded. They were actually grinning as they came down on the stretchers."

The colonel grinned, too. In fact, he stifled a fit of coughing. "Funny devils!" he said. "They are so glad to be going home."

The members of Parliament went away enormously impressed, but they had not enjoyed themselves nearly as well as the Worcesters, who had fought a sham battle—not in the front-line trenches, but in the support trenches two miles back! They laughed for a week afterward.

XVII

On the hill at Wizerne, not far from the stately old town of St.-Omer (visited from time to time by monstrous nightbirds who dropped high-explosive eggs), was a large convent. There were no nuns there, but generally some hundreds of young officers and men from many different battalions, attending a machine-gun course under the direction of General Baker-Carr, who was the master machine-gunner of the British army (at a time when we were very weak in those weapons compared with the enemy's strength) and a cheery, vital man.

"This war has produced two great dugouts," said Lord Kitchener on a visit to the convent. "Me and Baker-Carr."

It was the boys who interested me more than the machines. (I was never much interested in the machinery of war.) They came down from the trenches to this school with a sense of escape from prison, and for the ten days of their course they were like "freshers" at Oxford and made the most of their minutes, organizing concerts and other entertainments in the evenings after their initiation into the mysteries of Vickers and Lewis. I was invited to dinner there one night, and sat between two young cavalry officers on long benches crowded with subalterns of many regiments. It was a merry meal and a good one—to this day I remember a potato pie, gloriously baked, and afterward, as it was the last night of the course, all the officers went wild and indulged in a "rag" of the public-school kind. They straddled across the benches and barged at each other in single tourneys and jousts, riding their hobby-horses with violent rearings and plungings and bruising one another without grievous hurt and with yells of laughter. Glasses broke, crockery crashed upon the polished boards. One boy danced the Highland fling on the tables, others were waltzing down the corridors. There was a Rugby scrum in the refectory, and hunting-men cried the "View halloo!" and shouted "Yoicks! yoicks!" ... General Baker-Carr was a human soul, and kept to his own room that night and let discipline go hang....

When the battles of the Somme began it was those young officers who led their machine-gun sections into the woods of death—Belville Wood, Mametz Wood, High Wood, and the others. It was they who afterward held the outpost lines in Flanders. Some of them were still alive on March 21, 1918, when they were surrounded by a sea of Germans and fought until the last, in isolated redoubts north and south of St.-Quentin. Two of them are still alive, those between whom I sat at dinner that night, and who escaped many close calls of death before the armistice. Of the others who charged one another with wooden benches, their laughter ringing out, some were blown to bits, and some were buried alive, and some were blinded and gassed, and some went "missing" for evermore.

XVIII

In those long days of trench warfare and stationary lines it was boredom that was the worst malady of the mind; a large, overwhelming boredom to thousands of men who were in exile from the normal interests of life and from the activities of brain-work; an intolerable, abominable boredom, sapping the will-power, the moral code, the intellect; a boredom from which there seemed no escape except by death, no relief except by vice, no probable or possible change in its dreary routine. It was bad enough in the trenches, where men looked across the parapet to the same corner of hell day by day, to the same dead bodies rotting by the edge of the same mine-crater, to the same old sand-bags in the enemy's line, to the blasted tree sliced by shell-fire, the upturned railway—truck of which only the metal remained, the distant fringe of trees like gallows on the sky-line, the broken spire of a church which could be seen in the round O of the telescope when the weather was not too misty. In "quiet" sections of the line the only variation to the routine was the number of casualties day by day, by casual shell-fire or snipers' bullets, and that became part of the boredom. "What casualties?" asked the adjutant in his dugout.

"Two killed, three wounded, sir."

"Very well... You can go."

A salute in the doorway of the dugout, a groan from the adjutant lighting another cigarette, leaning with his elbow on the deal table, staring at the guttering of the candle by his side, at the pile of forms in front of him, at the glint of light on the steel helmet hanging by its strap on a nail near the shelf where he kept his safety-razor, flash—lamp, love-letters (in an old cigar-box), soap, whisky—bottle (almost empty now), and an unread novel.

"Hell!... What a life!"

But there was always work to do, and odd incidents, and frights, and responsibilities.

It was worse—this boredom—for men behind the lines; in lorry columns which went from rail-head to dump every damned morning, and back again by the middle of the morning, and then nothing else to do for all the day, in a cramped little billet with a sulky woman in the kitchen, and squealing children in the yard, and a stench of manure through the small window. A dull life for an actor who had toured in England and America (like one I met dazed and stupefied by years of boredom—paying too much for safety), or for a barrister who had many briefs before the war and now found his memory going, though a young man, because of the narrow limits of his life between one Flemish village and another, which was the length of his lorry column and of his adventure of war. Nothing ever happened to break the monotony—not even shell-fire. So it was also in small towns like Hesdin, St.-Pol, Bruay, Lillers—a hundred others where officers stayed for years in charge of motor-repair shops, ordnance-stores, labor battalions, administration offices, claim commissions, graves' registration, agriculture for soldiers, all kinds of jobs connected with that life of war, but not exciting.

Not exciting. So frightful in boredom that men were tempted to take to drink, to look around for unattached women, to gamble at cards with any poor devil like themselves. Those were most bored who were most virtuous. For them, with an ideal in their souls, there was no possibility of relief (for virtue is not its own reward), unless they were mystics, as some became, who found

God good company and needed no other help. They had rare luck, those fellows with an astounding faith which rose above the irony and the brutality of that business being done in the trenches, but there were few of them.

Even with hours of leisure, men who had been "bookish" could not read. That was a common phenomenon. I could read hardly at all, for years, and thousands were like me. The most "exciting" novel was dull stuff up against that world convulsion. What did the romance of love mean, the little tortures of one man's heart, or one woman's, troubled in their mating, when thousands of men were being killed and vast populations were in agony? History—Greek or Roman or medieval—what was the use of reading that old stuff, now that world history was being made with a rush? Poetry—poor poets with their love of beauty! What did beauty matter, now that it lay dead in the soul of the world, under the filth of battlefields, and the dirt of hate and cruelty, and the law of the apelike man? No—we could not read; but talked and talked about the old philosophy of life, and the structure of society, and Democracy and Liberty and Patriotism and Internationalism, and Brotherhood of Men, and God, and Christian ethics; and then talked no more, because all words were futile, and just brooded and brooded, after searching the daily paper (two days old) for any kind of hope and light, not finding either.

XIX

At first, in the beginning of the war, our officers and men believed that it would have a quick ending. Our first Expeditionary Force came out to France with the cheerful shout of "Now we sha'n't be long!" before they fell back from an advancing tide of Germans from Mons to the Marne, and fell in their youth like autumn leaves. The New Army boys who followed them were desperate to get out to "the great adventure." They cursed the length of their training in English camps. "We sha'n't get out till it's too late!" they said. Too late, O God! Even when they had had their first spell in the trenches and came up against German strength they kept a queer faith, for a time, that "something" would happen to bring peace as quickly as war had come. Peace was always coming three months ahead. Generals and staff-officers, as well as sergeants and privates, had that strong optimism, not based on any kind of reason; but gradually it died out, and in its place came the awful conviction which settled upon the hearts of the fighting-men, that this war would go on forever, that it was their doom always to live in ditches and dugouts, and that their only way of escape was by a "Blighty" wound or by death.

A chaplain I knew used to try to cheer up despondent boys by pretending to have special knowledge of inside politics.

"I have it on good authority," he said, "that peace is near at hand. There have been negotiations in Paris—"

Or:

"I don't mind telling you lads that if you get through the next scrap you will have peace before you know where you are."

They were not believing, now. He had played that game too often.

"Old stuff, padre!" they said.

That particular crowd did not get through the next scrap. But the padre's authority was good. They had peace long before the armistice.

It was worst of all for boys of sensitive minds who were lucky enough to get a "cushie" wound, and so went on and on, or who were patched up again quickly after one, two, or three wounds, and came back again. It was a boy like that who revealed his bitterness to me one day as we stood together in the salient.

"It's the length of the war," he said, "which does one down. At first it seemed like a big adventure, and the excitement of it, horrible though it was, kept one going. Even the first time I went over the top wasn't so bad as I thought it would be. I was dazed and drunk with all sorts of emotions, including fear, that were worse before going over. I had what we call 'the needle.' They all have it. Afterward one didn't know what one was doing—even the killing part of the business—until one reached the objective and lay down and had time to think and to count the dead about... Now the excitement has gone out of it, and the war looks as though it would go on forever. At first we all searched the papers for some hope that the end was near. We don't do that now. We know that whenever the war ends, this year or next, this little crowd will be mostly wiped out. Bound to be. And why are we going to die? That's what all of us want to know. What's it all about? Oh yes, I know the usual answers: 'In defense of liberty,' 'To save the Empire.' But we've all lost our liberty. We're slaves under shell-fire. And as for the Empire—I don't give a curse for it. I'm thinking only of my little home at Streatham Hill. The horrible Hun? I've no quarrel with the poor blighters over there by Hooge. They are in the same bloody mess as we are. They hate it just as much. We're all under a spell together, which some devils have put on us. I wonder if there's a God anywhere."

This sense of being under a black spell I found expressed by other men, and by German prisoners who used the same phrase. I remember one of them in the battles of the Somme, who said, in good English: "This war was not made in any sense by mankind. We are under a spell." This belief was due, I think, to the impersonal character of modern warfare, in which gun-fire is at so long a range that shell-fire has the quality of natural and elemental powers of death—like thunderbolts—and men killed twenty miles behind the lines while walking over sunny fields or in busy villages had no thought of a human enemy desiring their individual death.

God and Christianity raised perplexities in the minds of simple lads desiring life and not death. They could not reconcile the Christian precepts of the chaplain with the bayoneting of Germans and the shambles of the battlefields. All this blood and mangled flesh in the fields of France and Flanders seemed to them—to many of them, I know—a certain proof that God did not exist, or if He did exist was not, as they were told, a God of Love, but a monster glad of the agonies of men. That at least was the thought expressed to me by some London lads who argued the matter with me one day, and that was the thought which our army chaplains had to meet from men who would not be put off by conventional words. It was not good enough to tell them that the Germans were guilty of all this crime and that unless the Germans were beaten the world would lose its liberty and life. "Yes, we know all that," they said, "but why did God allow the Germans, or the statesmen who arranged the world by force, or the clergy who christened British warships? And how is it that both sides pray to the same God for victory? There must be something wrong somewhere."

It was not often men talked like that, except to some chaplain who was a human, comradely soul, some Catholic "padre" who devoted himself fearlessly to their bodily and spiritual needs, risking his life with them, or to some Presbyterian minister who brought them hot cocoa under shell-fire, with a cheery word or two, as I once heard, of "Keep your hearts up, my lads, and your heads down."

Most of the men became fatalists, with odd superstitions in the place of faith. "It's no good worrying," they said.

"If your name is written on a German shell you can't escape it, and if it isn't written, nothing can touch you."

Officers as well as men had this fatalistic belief and superstitions which amused them and helped them. "Have the Huns found you out yet?" I asked some gunner officers in a ruined farmhouse near Kemmel Hill. "Not yet," said one of them, and then they all left the table at which we were at lunch and, making a rush for some oak beams, embraced them ardently. They were touching wood.

"Take this with you," said an Irish officer on a night I went to Ypres. "It will help you as it has helped me. It's my lucky charm." He gave me a little bit of coal which he carried in his tunic, and he was so earnest about it that I took it without a smile and felt the safer for it.

Once in a while the men went home on seven days' leave, or four, and then came back again, gloomily, with a curious kind of hatred of England because the people there seemed so callous to their suffering, so utterly without understanding, so "damned cheerful." They hated the smiling women in the streets. They loathed the old men who said, "If I had six sons I would sacrifice them all in the Sacred Cause." They desired that profiteers should die by poison-gas. They prayed God to get the Germans to send Zeppelins to England—to make the people know what war meant. Their leave had done them no good at all.

From a week-end at home I stood among a number of soldiers who were going back to the front, after one of those leaves. The boat warped away from the pier, the M. T. O. and a small group of officers, detectives, and Red Cross men disappeared behind an empty train, and the "revenants" on deck stared back at the cliffs of England across a widening strip of sea.

"Back to the bloody old trenches," said a voice, and the words ended with a hard laugh. They were spoken by a young officer of the Guards, whom I had seen on the platform of Victoria saying good-by to a pretty woman, who had put her hand on his shoulder for a moment, and said, "Do be careful, Desmond, for my sake!" Afterward he had sat in the corner of his carriage, staring with a fixed gaze at the rushing countryside, but seeing nothing of it, perhaps, as his thoughts traveled backward. (A few days later he was blown to bits by a bomb—an accident of war.)

A little man on deck came up to me and said, in a melancholy way, "You know who I am, don't you, sir?"

I hadn't the least idea who he was—this little ginger—haired soldier with a wizened and wistful face. But I saw that he wore the claret-colored ribbon of the V. C. on his khaki tunic. He gave me his name, and said the papers had "done him proud," and that they had made a lot of him at home—presentations, receptions, speeches, Lord Mayor's addresses, cheering crowds, and all that. He was one of our Heroes, though one couldn't tell it by the look of him.

"Now I'm going back to the trenches," he said, gloomily. "Same old business and one of the crowd again." He was suffering from the reaction of popular idolatry. He felt hipped because no one made a fuss of him now or bothered about his claret-colored ribbon. The staff-officers, chaplains, brigade majors, regimental officers, and army nurses were more interested in an airship, a silver fish with shining gills and a humming song in its stomach.

France... and the beginning of what the little V. C. had called "the same old business." There was the long fleet of motor-ambulances as a reminder of the ultimate business of all those young men in khaki whom I had seen drilling in the Embankment gardens and shouldering their way down the Strand.

Some stretchers were being carried to the lift which goes down to the deck of the hospital-ship, on which an officer was ticking off each wounded body after a glance at the label tied to the man's tunic. Several young officers lay under the blankets on those stretchers and one of them caught my eye and smiled as I looked down upon him. The same old business and the same old pluck.

I motored down the long, straight roads of France eastward, toward that network of lines which are the end of all journeys after a few days' leave, home and back again. The same old sights and sounds and smells which, as long as memory lasts, to men who had the luck to live through the war, will haunt them for the rest of life, and speak of Flanders.

The harvest was nearly gathered in, and where, a week or two before, there had been fields of high, bronzed corn there were now long stretches of stubbled ground waiting for the plow. The wheat-sheaves had been piled into stacks or, from many great fields, carted away to the red-roofed barns below the black old windmills whose sails were motionless because no breath of air stirred on this September afternoon. The smell of Flemish villages—a mingled odor of sun-baked thatch and bakeries and manure heaps and cows and ancient vapors stored up through the centuries—was overborne by a new and more pungent aroma which crept over the fields with the evening haze.

It was a sad, melancholy smell, telling of corruption and death. It was the first breath of autumn, and I shivered a little. Must there be another winter of war? The old misery of darkness and dampness was creeping up through the splendor of September sunshine.

Those soldiers did not seem to smell it, or, if their nostrils were keen, to mind its menace—those soldiers who came marching down the road, with tanned faces. How fine they looked, and how hard, and how cheerful, with their lot! Speak to them separately and every man would "grouse" at the duration of the war and swear that he was "fed up" with it. Homesickness assailed them at times with a deadly nostalgia. The hammering of shell-fire, which takes its daily toll, spoiled their temper and shook their nerves, as far as a British soldier had any nerves, which I used to sometimes doubt, until I saw again the shell-shock cases.

But again I heard their laughter and an old song whistled vilely out of tune, but cheerful to the tramp of their feet. They were going back to the trenches after a spell in a rest-camp, to the same old business of whizz-bangs and pip-squeaks, and dugouts, and the smell of wet clay and chloride of lime, and the life of earth-men who once belonged to a civilization which had passed. And they went whistling on their way, because it was the very best thing to do.

One picked up the old landmarks again, and got back into the "feel" of the war zone. There were the five old windmills of Cassel that wave their arms up the hill road, and the *estaminets* by which one found one's way down country lanes—"The Veritable Cuckoo" and "The Lost Corner" and "The Flower of the Fields"—and the first smashed roofs and broken barns which led to the area of constant shell-fire. Ugh!

So it was still going on, this bloody murder! There were some more cottages down in the village, where we had tea a month before. And in the market-place of a sleepy old town the windows were mostly broken and some shops had gone into dust and ashes. That was new since we last passed this way.

London was only seven hours away, but the hours on leave there seemed a year ago already. The men who had come back, after sleeping in civilization with a blessed sense of safety, had a few minutes of queer surprise that, after all, this business of war was something more real than a fantastic nightmare, and then put on their moral cloaks against the chill and grim reality, for another long spell of it. Very quickly the familiarity of it all came back to them and became the normal instead of the abnormal. They were back again to the settled state of war, as boys go back to public schools after the wrench from home, and find that the holiday is only the incident and school the more enduring experience.

There were no new impressions, only the repetition of old impressions. So I found when I heard the guns again and watched the shells bursting about Ypres and over Kemmel Ridge and Messines church tower.

Two German airplanes passed overhead, and the hum of their engines was loud in my ears as I lay in the grass. Our shrapnel burst about them, but did not touch their wings. All around there was the slamming of great guns, and I sat chewing a bit of straw by the side of a shell-hole, thinking in the same old way of the utter senselessness of all this noise and hate and sudden death which encircled me for miles. No amount of meditation would screw a new meaning out of it all. It was just the commonplace of life out here.

The routine of it went on. The officer who came back from home stepped into his old place, and after the first greeting of, "Hullo, old man! Had a good time?" found his old job waiting for him. So there was a new brigadier-general? Quick promotion, by Jove!

Four men had got knocked out that morning at D4, and it was rotten bad luck that the sergeant-major should have been among them. A real good fellow. However, there's that court martial for this afternoon, and, by the by, when is that timber coming up? Can't build the new dugout if there's no decent wood to be got by stealing or otherwise. You heard how the men got *strafed* in their billets the other day? Dirty work!

The man who had come back went into the trenches and had a word or two with the N.C.O.'s. Then he went into his own dugout. The mice had been getting at his papers. Oh yes, that's where he left his pipe! It was lying under the trestle-table, just where he dropped it before going on leave. The clay walls were a bit wet after the rains. He stood with a chilled feeling in this little hole of his, staring at every familiar thing in it.

Tacked to the wall was the portrait of a woman. He said good-by to her at Victoria Station. How long ago? Surely more than seven hours, or seven years...

Outside there were the old noises. The guns were at it again. That was a trench-mortar. The enemy's eight-inch howitzers were plugging away. What a beastly row that machine-gun was making! Playing on the same old spot. Why couldn't they leave it alone, the asses?... Anyhow, there was no doubt about it—he had come back again. Back to the trenches and the same old business.

There was a mine to be blown up that night and it would make a pretty mess in the enemy's lines. The colonel was very cheerful about it, and explained that a good deal of sapping had been done. "We've got the bulge on 'em," he said, referring to the enemy's failures in this class of work. In the mess all the officers were carrying on as usual, making the same old jokes.

The man who had come back got back also the spirit of the thing with astonishing rapidity. That other life of his, away there in old London, was shut up in the cupboard of his heart.

So it went on and on until the torture of its boredom was broken by the crash of big battles, and the New Armies, which had been learning lessons in the School of Courage, went forward to the great test, and passed, with honor.

PART THREE

THE NATURE OF A BATTLE

I

In September of 1915 the Commander-in-Chief and his staff were busy with preparations for a battle, in conjunction with the French, which had ambitious objects. These have never been stated because they were not gained (and it was the habit of our High Command to conceal its objectives and minimize their importance if their hopes were unfulfilled), but beyond doubt the purpose of the battle was to gain possession of Lens and its coal-fields, and by striking through Hulluch and Haisnes to menace the German occupation of Lille. On the British front the key of the enemy's position was Hill 70, to the north of Lens, beyond the village of Loos, and the capture of that village and that hill was the first essential of success.

The assault on these positions was to be made by two New Army divisions of the 4th Corps: the 47th (London) Division, and the 15th (Scottish) Division. They were to be supported by the 11th Corps, consisting of the Guards and two new and untried divisions, the 21st and the 24th. The Cavalry Corps (less the 3d Cavalry Division under General Fanshawe) was in reserve far back at St.-Pol and Pernes; and the Indian Cavalry Corps under General Remington was at Doullens; "to be in readiness," wrote Sir John French, "to co-operate with the French cavalry in exploiting any success which might be attained by the French and British forces."... Oh, wonderful optimism! In that Black Country of France, scattered with mining villages in which every house was a machine-gun fort, with slag heaps and pit-heads which were formidable redoubts, with trenches and barbed wire and brick-stacks, and quarries, organized for defense in siege-warfare, cavalry might as well have ridden through hell with hope of "exploiting" success... "Plans for effective co-operation were fully arranged between the cavalry commanders of both armies," wrote our Commander-in-Chief in his despatch. I can imagine those gallant old gentlemen devising their plans, with grave courtesy, over large maps, and A. D. C.'s clicking heels in attendance, and an air of immense wisdom and most cheerful assurance governing the proceedings in the salon of a French chateau. .. The 3d Cavalry Division, less one brigade, was assigned to the First Army as a reserve, and moved into the area of the 4th Corps on the 2lst and 22d of September.

II

The movements of troops and the preparations for big events revealed to every British soldier in France the "secret" of the coming battle. Casualty clearing-stations were ordered to make ready for big numbers of wounded. That was always one of the first signs of approaching massacre. Vast quantities of shells were being brought up to the rail-heads and stacked in the "dumps." They were the first-fruit of the speeding up of munition-factories at home after the public outcry against shell shortage and the lack of high explosives. Well, at last the guns would not be starved. There was enough high-explosive force available to blast the German trenches off the map. So it seemed to our innocence—though years afterward we knew that no bombardment would destroy all earthworks such as Germans made, and that always machine-guns would slash our infantry advancing over the chaos of mangled ground.

Behind our lines in France, in scores of villages where our men were quartered, there was a sense of impending fate. Soldiers of the New Army knew that in a little while the lessons they had learned in the School of Courage would be put to a more frightful test than that of holding trenches in stationary warfare. Their boredom, the intolerable monotony of that routine life, would be broken by more sensational drama, and some of them were glad of that, and said: "Let's get on with it. Anything rather than that deadly stagnation." And others, who guessed they were chosen for the coming battle, and had a clear vision of what kind of things would happen (they knew something about the losses at Neuve Chapelle and Festubert), became more thoughtful than usual, deeply introspective, wondering how many days of life they had left to them.

Life was good out of the line in that September of '15. The land of France was full of beauty, with bronzed corn-stooks in the fields, and scarlet poppies in the grass, and a golden sunlight on old barns and on little white churches and in orchards heavy with fruit. It was good to go into the garden of a French chateau and pluck a rose and smell its sweetness, and think back to England, where other roses were blooming. England!... And in a few days—who could say?—perhaps eternal sleep somewhere near Lens.

Some officers of the Guards came into the garden of the little house where I lived at that time with other onlookers. It was an untidy garden, with a stretch of grass-plot too rough to be called a lawn, but with pleasant shade under the trees, and a *potager* with raspberries and currants on the bushes, and flower-beds where red and white roses dropped their petals.

Two officers of the Scots Guards, inseparable friends, came to gossip with us, and read the papers, and drink a little whisky in the evenings, and pick the raspberries. They were not professional soldiers. One of them had been a stock-broker, the other "something in the city." They disliked the army system with an undisguised hatred and contempt. They hated war with a ferocity which was only a little "camouflaged" by the irony and the brutality of their anecdotes of war's little comedies. They took a grim delight in the humor of corpses, lice, bayonet—work, and the sniping of fair-haired German boys. They laughed, almost excessively, at these attributes of warfare, and one of them used to remark, after some such anecdote, "And once I was a little gentleman!"

He was a gentleman still, with a love of nature in his heart—I saw him touch the petals of living roses with a caress in his finger-tips—and with a spiritual revolt against the beastliness of this new job of his, although he was a strong, hard fellow, without weakness of sentiment. His close comrade was of more delicate fiber, a gentle soul, not made for soldiering at all, but rather for domestic life, with children about him, and books. As the evenings passed in this French village, drawing him closer to Loos by the flight of time, I saw the trouble in his eyes which he tried to hide by smiling and by courteous conversation. He was being drawn closer to Loos and farther away from the wife who knew nothing of what that name meant to her and to him.

Other officers of the Guards came into the garden—Grenadiers. There were two young brothers of an old family who had always sent their sons to war. They looked absurdly young when they took off their tunics and played a game of cricket, with a club for a bat, and a tennis-ball. They were just schoolboys, but with the gravity of men who knew that life is short. I watched their young athletic figures, so clean-limbed, so full of grace, as they threw the ball, and had a vision of them lying mangled.

An Indian prince came into the garden. It was "Ranjitsinji," who had carried his bat to many a pavilion where English men and women had clapped their hands to him, on glorious days when there was sunlight on English lawns. He took the club and stood at the wicket and was bowled third ball by a man who had only played cricket after ye manner of Stratford-atte-Bow. But then he found himself, handled the club like a sword, watched the ball with a falcon's eye, played with it. He was on the staff of the Indian Cavalry Corps, which was "to co-operate in exploiting any success."

"To-morrow we move," said one of the Scots Guards officers. The colonel of the battalion came to dinner at our mess, sitting down to a white tablecloth for the last time in his life. They played a game of cards, and went away earlier than usual.

Two of them lingered after the colonel had gone. They drank more whisky.

"We must be going," they said, but did not go.

The delicate-looking man could not hide the trouble in his eyes.

"I sha'n't be killed this time," he said to a friend of mine. "I shall be badly wounded."

The hard man, who loved flowers, drank his fourth glass of whisky.

"It's going to be damned uncomfortable," he said. "I wish the filthy thing were over. Our generals will probably arrange some glorious little massacres. I know 'em!... Well, good night, all."

They went out into the darkness of the village lane. Battalions were already on the move, in the night. Their steady tramp of feet beat on the hard road. Their dark figures looked like an army of ghosts. Sparks were spluttering out of the funnels of army cookers. A British soldier in full field kit was kissing a woman in the shadow-world of an *estaminet.* I passed close to them, almost touching them before I was aware of their presence.

"Bonne chance!" said the woman. "Quand to reviens—"

"One more kiss, lassie," said the man.

"Mans comme to es gourmand, toi!"

He kissed her savagely, hungrily. Then he lurched off the sidewalk and formed up with other men in the darkness.

The Scots Guards moved next morning. I stood by the side of the colonel, who was in a gruff mood.

"It looks like rain," he said, sniffing the air. "It will probably rain like hell when the battle begins."

I think he was killed somewhere by Fosse 8. The two comrades in the Scots Guards were badly wounded. One of the young brothers was killed and the other maimed. I found their names in the casualty lists which filled columns of *The Times* for a long time after Loos.

III

The town of Bethune was the capital of our army in the Black Country of the French coal-fields. It was not much shelled in those days, though afterward—years afterward—it was badly damaged by long-range guns, so that its people fled, at last, after living so long on the edge of war.

Its people were friendly to our men, and did not raise their prices exorbitantly. There were good shops in the town—"as good as Paris," said soldiers who had never been to Paris, but found these plate-glass windows dazzling, after trench life, and loved to see the "mamzelles" behind the counters and walking out smartly, with little high-heeled shoes. There were tea-shops, crowded always with officers on their way to the line or just out of it, and they liked to speak French with the girls who served them. Those girls saw the hunger in those men's eyes, who watched every movement they made, who tried to touch their hands and their frocks in passing. They knew they were desired, as daughters of Eve, by boys who were starved of love. They took that as part of their business, distributing cakes and buns without favor, with laughter in their eyes, and a merry word or two. Now and then, when they had leisure, they retired to inner rooms, divided by curtains from the shop, and sat on the knees of young British officers, while others played ragtime or sentimental ballads on untuned pianos. There was champagne as well as tea to be had in these bun—shops, but the A. P. M. was down on disorder or riotous gaiety, and there were no orgies. "Pas d'orgies," said the young ladies severely when things were getting a little too lively. They had to think of their business.

Down side-streets here and there were houses where other women lived, not so severe in their point of view. Their business, indeed, did not permit of severity, and they catered for the hunger of men exiled year after year from their own home-life and from decent womanhood. They gave the base counterfeit of love in return for a few francs, and there were long lines of men—English, Irish, and Scottish soldiers—who waited their turn to get that vile imitation of life's romance from women who were bought and paid for. Our men paid a higher price than a few francs for the Circe's cup of pleasure, which changed them into swine for a while, until the spell passed, and would have blasted their souls if God were not understanding of human weakness and of war. They paid in their bodies, if not in their souls, those boys of ours who loved life and beauty and gentle things, and lived in filth and shell-fire, and were trained to kill, and knew that death was hunting for them and had all the odds of luck. Their children and their children's children will pay also for the sins of their fathers, by rickety limbs and water—on-the-brain, and madness, and tuberculosis, and other evils which are the wages of sin, which flourished most rankly behind the fields of war.

The inhabitants of Bethune—the shopkeepers, and brave little families of France, and bright-eyed girls, and frowzy women, and heroines, and harlots—came out into the streets before the battle of Loos, and watched the British army pouring through—battalions of Londoners and Scots, in full fighting-kit, with hot sweat on their faces, and grim eyes, and endless columns of field-guns and limbers, drawn by hard-mouthed mules cursed and thrashed by their drivers, and ambulances, empty now, and wagons, and motor-lorries, hour after hour, day after day.

"Bonne chance!" cried the women, waving hands and handkerchiefs.

"Les pauvres enfants!" said the old women, wiping their eyes on dirty aprons. "We know how it is. They will be shot to pieces. It is always like that, in this sacred war. Oh, those sacred pigs of Germans! Those dirty Boches! Those sacred bandits!"

"They are going to give the Boches a hard knock," said grizzled men, who remembered in their boyhood another war. "The English army is ready. How splendid they are, those boys! And ours are on the right of them. This time—!"

"Mother of God, hark at the guns!"

At night, as dark fell, the people of Bethune gathered in the great square by the Hotel de Ville, which afterward was smashed, and listened to the laboring of the guns over there by Vermelles and Noeux-les-Mines, and Grenay, and beyond Notre Dame de Lorette, where the French guns were at work. There were loud, earth—shaking rumblings, and now and then enormous concussions. In the night sky lights rose in long, spreading bars of ruddy luminance, in single flashes, in sudden torches of scarlet flame rising to the clouds and touching them with rosy feathers.

"'Cre nom de Dieu!" said French peasants, on the edge of all that, in villages like Gouy, Servins, Heuchin, Houdain, Grenay, Bruay, and Pernes. "The caldron is boiling up... There will be a fine *pot-au-feu.*"

They wondered if their own sons would be in the broth. Some of them knew, and crossed themselves by wayside shrines for the sake of their sons' souls, or in their estaminets cursed the Germans with the same old curses for having brought all this woe into the world.

IV

In those villages—Heuchin, Houdain, Lillers, and others—on the edge of the Black Country the Scottish troops of the 15th Division were in training for the arena, practising attacks on trenches and villages, getting a fine edge of efficiency on to bayonet-work and bombing, and having their morale heightened by addresses from brigadiers and divisional commanders on the glorious privilege which was about to be theirs of leading the assault, and on the joys as well as the duty of killing Germans.

In one battalion of Scots—the 10th Gordons, who were afterward the 8/10th—there were conferences of company commanders and whispered consultations of subalterns. They were "Kitchener" men, from Edinburgh and Aberdeen and other towns in the North. I came to know them all after this battle, and gave them fancy names in my despatches: the Georgian gentleman, as handsome as Beau Brummell, and a gallant soldier, who was several times wounded, but came back to command his old battalion, and then was wounded again nigh unto death, but came back again; and Honest John, slow of speech, with a twinkle in his eyes, careless of shell splinters flying around his bullet head, hard and tough and cunning in war; and little Ginger, with his whimsical face and freckles, and love of pretty girls and all children, until he was killed in Flanders; and the Permanent Temporary Lieutenant who fell on the Somme; and the Giant who had a splinter through his brain beyond Arras; and many other Highland gentlemen, and one English padre who went with them always to the trenches, until a shell took his head off at the crossroads.

It was the first big attack of the 15th Division. They were determined to go fast and go far. Their pride of race was stronger than the strain on their nerves. Many of them, I am certain, had no sense of fear, no apprehension of death or wounds. Excitement, the comradeship of courage, the rivalry of battalions, lifted them above anxiety before the battle began, though here and there men like Ginger, of more delicate fiber, of imagination as well as courage, must have stared in great moments at the grisly specter toward whom they would soon be walking.

In other villages were battalions of the 47th London Division. They, too, were to be in the first line of attack, on the right of the Scots. They, too, had to win honor for the New Army and old London. They were a different crowd from the Scots, not so hard, not so steel—nerved, with more sensibility to suffering, more imagination, more instinctive revolt against the butchery that was to come. But they, too, had been "doped" for morale, their nervous tension had been tightened up by speeches addressed to their spirit and tradition. It was to be London's day out. They were to fight for the glory of the old town... the old town where they had lived in little suburban houses with flower-gardens, where they had gone up by the early morning trains to city offices and government offices and warehouses and shops, in days before they ever guessed they would go a-soldiering, and crouch in shell-holes under high explosives, and thrust sharp steel into German bowels. But they would do their best. They would go through with it. They would keep their sense of humor and make cockney jokes at death. They would show the stuff of London pride.

"Domine, dirige nos!"

I knew many of those young Londoners. I had sat in tea-shops with them when they were playing dominoes, before the war, as though that were the most important game in life. I had met one of them at a fancy-dress ball in the Albert Hall, when he was Sir Walter Raleigh and I was Richard Sheridan. Then we were both onlookers of life—chroniclers of passing history. I remained the onlooker, even in war, but my friend went into the arena. He was a Royal Fusilier, and the old way of life became a dream to him when he walked toward Loos, and afterward sat in shell-craters in the Somme fields, and knew that death would find him, as it did, in Flanders. I had played chess with one man whom afterward I met as a gunner officer at Heninel, near Arras, on an afternoon when a shell had killed three of his men bathing in a tank, and other shells made a mess of blood and flesh in his wagon-lines. We both wore steel hats, and he was the first to recognize a face from the world of peace. After his greeting he swore frightful oaths, cursing the war and the Staff. His nerves were all jangled. There was another officer in the 47th London Division whom I had known as a boy. He was only nineteen when he enlisted, not twenty when he had fought through several battles. He and hundreds like him had been playing at red Indians in Kensington Gardens a few years before an August in 1914... The 47th London Division, going forward to the battle of Loos, was made up of men whose souls had been shaped by all the influences of environment, habit, and tradition in which I had been born and bred. Their cradle had been rocked to the murmurous roar of London traffic. Their first adventures had been on London Commons. The lights along the Embankment, the excitement of the streets, the faces of London crowds, royal pageantry—marriages, crownings, burials—on the way to Westminster, the little dramas of London life, had been woven into the fiber of their thoughts, and it was the spirit of London which went with them wherever they walked in France or Flanders, more sensitive than country men to the things they saw. Some of them had to fight against their nerves on the way to Loos. But their spirit was exalted by a nervous stimulus before that battle, so that they did freakish and fantastic things of courage.

V

I watched the preliminary bombardment of the Loos battlefields from a black slag heap beyond Noeux-les-Mines, and afterward went on the battleground up to the Loos redoubt, when our guns and the enemy's were hard at work; and later still, in years that followed, when there was never a silence of guns in those fields, came to know the ground from many points of view. It was a hideous territory, this Black Country between Lens and Hulluch. From the flat country below the distant ridges of Notre Dame de Lorette and Vimy there rose a number of high black cones made by the refuse of the coal-mines, which were called Fosses. Around those black mounds there was great slaughter, as at Fosse 8 and Fosse 10 and Puits 14bis, and the Double Crassier near Loos, because they gave observation and were important to capture or hold. Near them were the pit-heads, with winding-gear in elevated towers of steel which were smashed and twisted by gun-fire; and in Loos itself were two of those towers joined by steel girders and gantries, called the "Tower Bridge" by men of London. Rows of red cottages where the French miners had lived were called corons, and where they were grouped into large units they were called cites, like the Cite St.-Auguste, the Cite St.-Pierre, and the Cite St.-Laurent, beyond Hill 70, on the outskirts of Lens. All those places were abandoned now by black-grimed men who had fled down mine-shafts and galleries with their women and children, and had come up on our side of the lines at Noeux-les-Mines or Bruay or Bully-Grenay, where they still lived close to the war. Shells pierced the roof of the church in that squalid village of Noeux—les-Mines and smashed some of the cottages and killed some of the people now and then. Later in the war, when aircraft dropped bombs at night, a new peril over—shadowed them with terror, and they lived in their cellars after dusk, and sometimes were buried there. But they would not retreat farther back—not many of them—and on days of battle I saw groups of French miners and dirty-bloused girls excited by the passage of our troops and by the walking wounded who came stumbling back, and by stretcher cases unloaded from ambulances to the floors of their dirty cottages. High velocities fell in some of the streets, shrapnel-shells whined overhead and burst like thunderclaps. Young hooligans of France slouched around with their hands in their pockets, talking to our men in a queer lingua franca, grimacing at those noises if they did not come too near. I saw lightly wounded girls among them, with bandaged heads and hands, but they did not think that a reason for escape. With smoothly braided hair they gathered round British soldiers in steel hats and clasped their arms or leaned against their shoulders. They had known many of those men before. They were their sweethearts. In those foul little mining towns the British troops had liked their billets, because of the girls there. London boys and Scots "kept company" with pretty slatterns, who stole their badges for keepsakes, and taught them a base patois of French, and had a smudge of tears on their cheeks when the boys went away for a spell in the ditches of death. They were kind-hearted little sluts with astounding courage.

"Aren't you afraid of this place?" I asked one of them in Bully-Grenay when it was "unhealthy" there. "You might be killed here any minute."

She shrugged her shoulders.

"Je m'en fiche de la mort!" ("I don't care a damn about death.")

I had the same answer from other girls in other places.

That was the *mise-en-scene* of the battle of Loos—those mining towns behind the lines, then a maze of communication trenches entered from a place called Philosophe, leading up to the trench-lines beyond Vermelles, and running northward to Cambrin and Givenchy, opposite Hulluch, Haisnes, and La Bassee, where the enemy had his trenches and earthworks among the slag heaps, the pit-heads, the *corons* and the *cites,* all broken by gun-fire, and nowhere a sign of human life aboveground, in which many men were hidden.

Storms of gun-fire broke loose from our batteries a week before the battle. It was our first demonstration of those stores of high-explosive shells which had been made by the speeding up of munition-work in England, and of a gun-power which had been growing steadily since the coming out of the New Army. The weather was heavy with mist and a drizzle of rain. Banks of smoke made a pall over all the arena of war, and it was stabbed and torn by the incessant flash of bursting shells. I stood on the slag heap, staring at this curtain of smoke, hour after hour, dazed by the tumult of noise and by that impenetrable veil which hid all human drama. There was no movement of men to be seen, no slaughter, no heroic episode—only through rifts in the smoke the blurred edges of slag heaps and pit-heads, and smoking ruins. German trenches were being battered in, German dugouts made into the tombs of living men, German bodies tossed up with earth and stones—all that was certain but invisible.

"Very boring," said an officer by my side. "Not a damn thing to be seen."

"Our men ought to have a walk-over," said an optimist. "Any living German must be a gibbering idiot with shell-shock."

"I expect they're playing cards in their dugouts," said the officer who was bored. "Even high explosives don't go down very deep."

"It's stupendous, all the same. By God! hark at that! It seems more than human. It's like some convulsion of nature."

"There's no adventure in modern war," said the bored man. "It's a dirty scientific business. I'd kill all chemists and explosive experts."

"Our men will have adventure enough when they go over the top at dawn. Hell must be a game compared with that."

The guns went on pounding away, day after day, laboring, pummeling, hammering, like Thor with his thunderbolts. It was the preparation for battle. No men were out of the trenches yet, though some were being killed there and elsewhere, at the crossroads by Philosophe, and outside the village of Masingarbe, and in the ruins of Vermelles, and away up at Cambrin and Givenchy. The German guns were answering back intermittently, but holding most of their fire until human flesh came out into the open. The battle began at dawn on September 25th.

VI

In order to distract the enemy's attention and hold his troops away from the main battle-front, "subsidiary attacks" were made upon the German lines as far north as Bellewarde Farm, to the east of Ypres, and southward to La Bassee Canal at Givenchy, by the troops of the Second and Third Armies. This object, wrote Sir John French, in his despatch, "was most effectively achieved." It was achieved by the bloody sacrifice of many brave battalions in the 3d and 14th Divisions (Yorkshire, Royal Scots, King's Royal Rifles, and others), and by the Meerut Division of the Indian Corps, who set out to attack terrible lines without sufficient artillery support, and without reserves behind them, and without any chance of holding the ground they might capture. It was part of the system of war. They were the pawns of "strategy," serving a high purpose in a way that seemed to them without reason. Not for them was the glory of a victorious assault. Their job was to "demonstrate" by exposing their bodies to devouring fire, and by attacking earthworks which they were not expected to hold. Here and there men of ours, after their rush over No Man's Land under a deadly sweep of machine-gun fire, flung themselves into the enemy's trenches, bayoneting the Germans and capturing the greater part of their first line. There they lay panting among wounded and dead, and after that shoveled up earth and burrowed to get cover from the shelling which was soon to fall on them. Quickly the enemy discovered their whereabouts and laid down a barrage fire which, with deadly accuracy, plowed up their old front line and tossed it about on the pitchforks of bursting shells. Our men's bodies were mangled in that earth. High explosives plunged into the midst of little groups crouching in holes and caverns of the ground, and scattered their limbs. Living, unwounded men lay under those screaming shells with the panting hearts of toads under the beat of flails. Wounded men crawled back over No Man's Land, and some were blown to bits as they crawled, and others got back. Before nightfall, in the dark, a general retirement was ordered to our original line in that northern sector, owing to the increasing casualties under the relentless work of the German guns. Like ants on the move, thousands of men rose from the upheaved earth, and with their stomachs close to it, crouching, came back, dragging their wounded. The dead were left.

"On the front of the Third Army," wrote Sir John French, "subsidiary operations of a similar nature were successfully carried out."

From the point of view of high generalship those holding attacks had served their purpose pretty well. From the point of view of mothers' sons they had been a bloody shambles without any gain. The point of view depends on the angle of vision.

VII

Let me now tell the story of the main battle of Loos as I was able to piece it together from the accounts of men in different parts of the field—no man could see more than his immediate neighborhood—and from the officers who survived. It is a story full of the psychology of battle, with many strange incidents which happened to men when their spirit was uplifted by that mingling of exultation and fear which is heroism, and with queer episodes almost verging on comedy in the midst of death and agony, at the end of a day of victory, most ghastly failure.

The three attacking divisions from left to right on the line opposite the villages of Hulluch and Loos were the 1st, the 15th (Scottish), and the 47th (London). Higher up, opposite Hulluch and Haisnes, the 9th (Scottish) Division and the 7th Division were in front of the Hohenzollern redoubt (chalky earthworks thrust out beyond the German front-line trenches, on rising ground) and some chalk-quarries.

The men of those divisions were lined up during the night in the communication trenches, which had been dug by the sappers and laid with miles of telephone wire. They were silent, except for the chink of shovels and side arms, the shuffle of men's feet, their hard breathing, and occasional words of command. At five-thirty, when the guns in all our batteries were firing at full blast, with a constant scream of shells over the heads of the waiting men, and when the first faint light of day stole into the sky, there was a slight rain falling, and the wind blew lightly from the southwest.

In the front-line trenches a number of men were busy with some long, narrow cylinders, which had been carried up a day before. They were arranging them in the mud of the parapets with their nozles facing the enemy lines.

"That's the stuff to give them!"

"What is it?"

"Poison-gas. Worse than they used at Ypres."

"Christ!... supposing we have to walk through it?"

"We shall walk behind it. The wind will carry it down the throat of the Fritzes. We shall find 'em dead."

So men I met had talked of that new weapon which most of them hated.

It was at five-thirty when the men busy with the cylinders turned on little taps. There was a faint hissing noise, the escape of gas from many pipes. A heavy, whitish cloud came out of the cylinders and traveled aboveground as it was lifted and carried forward by the breeze.

"How's the gas working?" asked a Scottish officer.

"Going fine!" said an English officer. But he looked anxious, and wetted a finger and held it up, to get the direction of the wind.

Some of the communication trenches were crowded with the Black Watch of the 1st Division, hard, bronzed fellows, with the red heckle in their bonnets. (It was before the time of steel hats.) They were leaning up against the walls of the trenches, waiting. They were strung round with spades, bombs, and sacks.

"A queer kind o' stink!" said one of them, sniffing.

Some of the men began coughing. Others were rubbing their eyes, as though they smarted.

The poison-gas... The wind had carried it half way across No Man's Land, then a swirl changed its course, and flicked it down a gully, and swept it right round to the Black Watch in the narrow trenches. Some German shell-fire was coming, too. In one small bunch eight men fell in a mush of blood and raw flesh. But the gas was worse. There was a movement in the trenches, the huddling together of frightened men who had been very brave. They were coughing, spitting, gasping. Some of them fell limp against their fellows, with pallid cheeks which blackened. Others tied handkerchiefs about their mouths and noses, but choked inside those bandages, and dropped to earth with a clatter of shovels. Officers and men were cursing and groaning. An hour later, when the whistles blew, there were gaps in the line of the 1st Division which went over the top. In the trenches lay gassed men. In No Man's Land others fell, swept by machine-gun bullets, shrapnel, and high explosives. The 1st Division was "checked."...

"We caught it badly," said some of them I met later in the day, bandaged and bloody, and plastered in wet chalk, while gassed men lay on stretchers about them, unconscious, with laboring lungs.

VIII

Farther south the front-lines of the 15th (Scottish) Division climbed over their parapets at six-thirty, and saw the open ground before them, and the dusky, paling sky above them, and broken wire in front of the enemy's churned-up trenches; and through the smoke, faintly, and far away, three and a half miles away, the ghostly outline of the "Tower Bridge" of Loos, which was their goal. For an hour there were steady tides of men all streaming slowly up those narrow communication ways, cut through the chalk to get into the light also, where death was in ambush for many of them somewhere in the shadows of that dawn.

By seven-forty the two assaulting brigades of the 15th Division had left the trenches and were in the open. Shriller than the scream of shells above them was the skirl of pipes, going with them. The Pipe Major of the 8th Gordons was badly wounded, but refused to be touched until the other men were tended. He was a giant, too big for a stretcher, and had to be carried back on a tarpaulin. At the dressing-station his leg was amputated, but he died after two operations, and the Gordons mourned him.

While the Highlanders went forward with their pipes, two brigades of the Londoners, on their right, were advancing in the direction of the long, double slag heap, southwest of Loos, called the Double Crassier. Some of them were blowing mouth-organs, playing the music-hall song of "Hullo, hullo, it's a different girl again!" and the "Robert E. Lee," until one after another a musician fell in a crumpled heap. Shrapnel burst over them, and here and there shells plowed up the earth where they were trudging. On the right of the Londoners the French still stayed in their trenches—their own attack was postponed until midday—and they cheered the London men, as they went forward, with cries of, *"Vivent les Angdais!" "A mort—les Boches!"* It was they who saw one man kicking a football in advance of the others.

"He is mad!" they said. "The poor boy is a lunatic!"

"He is not mad," said a French officer who had lived in England. "It is a beau geste. He is a sportsman scornful of death. That is the British sport."

It was a London Irishman dribbling a football toward the goal, and he held it for fourteen hundred yards—the best-kicked goal in history.

Many men fell in the five hundred yards of No Man's Land. But they were not missed then by those who went on in waves—rather, like molecules, separating, collecting, splitting up into smaller groups, bunching together again, on the way to the first line of German trenches. A glint of bayonets made a quickset hedge along the line of churned-up earth which had been the Germans' front—line trench. Our guns had cut the wire or torn gaps into it. Through the broken strands went the Londoners on the right, the Scots on the left, shouting hoarsely now. They saw red. They were hunters of human flesh. They swarmed down into the first long ditch, trampling over dead bodies, falling over them, clawing the earth and scrambling up the parados, all broken and crumbled, then on again to another ditch. Boys dropped with bullets in their brains, throats, and bodies. German machine-guns were at work at close range.

"Give'em hell!" said an officer of the Londoners—a boy of nineteen. There were a lot of living Germans in the second ditch, and in holes about. Some of them stood still, as though turned to clay, until they fell with half the length of a bayonet through their stomachs. Others shrieked and ran a little way before they died. Others sat behind hillocks of earth, spraying our men with machine-gun bullets until bombs were hurled on them and they were scattered into lumps of flesh.

Three lines of trench were taken, and the Londoners and the Scots went forward again in a spate toward Loos. All the way from our old lines men were streaming up, with shells bursting among them or near them.

On the way to Loos a company of Scots came face to face with a tall German. He was stone-dead, with a bullet in his brain, his face all blackened with the grime of battle; but he stood erect in the path, wedged somehow in a bit of trench. The Scots stared at this figure, and their line parted and swept each side of him, as though some obscene specter barred the way. Rank after rank streamed up, and then a big tide of men poured through the German trench systems and rushed forward. Three—quarters of a mile more to Loos. Some of them were panting, out of breath, speechless. Others talked to the men about them in stray sentences. Most of them were silent, staring ahead of them and licking their lips with swollen tongues. They were parched with thirst, some of them told me. Many stopped to drink the last drop out of their water-bottles. As one man drank he spun round and fell with a thud on his face. Machine-gun bullets were whipping up the earth. From Loos came a loud and constant rattle of machine-guns. Machine-guns were firing out of the broken windows of the houses and from the top of the "Tower Bridge," those steel girders which rose three hundred feet high from the center of the village, and from slit trenches across the narrow streets. There were one hundred machine-guns in the cemetery to the southwest of the town, pouring out lead upon the Londoners who had to pass that place.

Scots and London men were mixed up, and mingled in crowds which encircled Loos, and forced their way into the village; but roughly still, and in the mass, they were Scots who assaulted Loos itself, and London men who went south of it to the chalk-pits and the Double Crassier.

It was eight o'clock in the morning when the first crowds reached the village, and for nearly two hours afterward there was street-fighting.

It was the fighting of men in the open, armed with bayonets, rifles, and bombs, against men invisible and in hiding, with machine-guns. Small groups of Scots, like packs of wolves, prowled around the houses, where the lower rooms and cellars were crammed with Germans, trapped and terrified, but still defending themselves. In some of the houses they would not surrender, afraid of certain death, anyhow, and kept the Scots at bay awhile until those kilted men flung themselves in and killed their enemy to the last man. Outside those red-brick houses lay dead and wounded Scots. Inside there were the curses and screams of a bloody vengeance. In other houses the machine-gun garrisons ceased fire and put white rags through the broken windows, and surrendered like sheep. So it was in one house entered by a little kilted signaler, who shot down three men who tried to kill him. Thirty others held their hands up and said, in a chorus of fear, "Kamerad! Kamerad!"

A company of the 8th Gordons were among the first into Loos, led by some of those Highland officers I have mentioned on another page. It was "Honest John" who led one crowd of them, and he claims now, with a laugh, that he gained his Military Cross for saving the lives of two hundred Germans. "I ought to have got the Royal Humane Society's medal," he said. Those Germans—Poles, really, from Silesia—came swarming out of a house with their hands up. But the Gordons had tasted blood. They were hungry for it. They were panting and shouting, with red bayonets, behind their officer.

That young man thought deeply and quickly. If there were "no quarter" it might be ugly for the Gordons later in the day, and the day was young, and Loos was still untaken.

He stood facing his own men, ordered them sternly to keep steady. These men were to be taken prisoners and sent back under escort. He had his revolver handy, and, anyhow, the men knew him. They obeyed, grumbling sullenly.

There was the noise of fire in other parts of the village, and the tap-tap-tap of machine-guns from many cellars. Bombing-parties of Scots silenced those machine-gunners at last by going to the head of the stairways and flinging down their hand-grenades. The cellars of Loos were full of dead.

In one of them, hours after the fighting had ceased among the ruins of the village, and the line of fire was forward of Hill 70, a living man still hid and carried on his work. The colonel of one of our forward battalions came into Loos with his signalers and runners, and established his headquarters in a house almost untouched by shell-fire. At the time there was very little shelling, as the artillery officers on either side were afraid of killing their own men, and the house seemed fairly safe for the purpose of a temporary signal-station.

But the colonel noticed that shortly after his arrival heavy shells began to fall very close and the Germans obviously were aiming directly for this building. He ordered the cellars to be searched, and three Germans were found. It was only after he had been in the house for forty minutes that in a deeper cellar, which had not been seen before, the discovery was made of a German officer who was telephoning to his own batteries and directing their fire. Suspecting that the colonel and his companions were important officers directing general operations, he had caused the shells to fall upon the house knowing that a lucky shot would mean his own death as well as theirs.

As our searchers came into the cellar, he rose and stood there, waiting, with a cold dignity, for the fate which he knew would come to him, as it did. He was a very brave man.

Another German officer remained hiding in the church, which was so heavily mined that it would have blown half the village into dust and ashes if he had touched off the charges. He was fumbling at the job when our men found and killed him.

In the southern outskirts of Loos, and in the cemetery, the Londoners had a bloody fight among the tombstones, where nests of German machine-guns had been built into the vaults. New corpses, still bleeding, lay among old dead torn from their coffins by shell-fire. Londoners and Siiesian Germans lay together across one another's bodies. The London men routed out most of the machine-gunners and bayoneted some and took prisoners of others. They were not so fierce as the Scots, but in those hours forgot the flower-gardens in Streatham and Tooting Bec and the manners of suburban drawing rooms.. . It is strange that one German machine-gun, served by four men, remained hidden behind a gravestone all through that day, and Saturday, and Sunday, and sniped stray men of ours until routed at last by moppers-up of the Guards brigade.

As the Londoners came down the slope to the southern edge of Loos village, through a thick haze of smoke from shell-fire and burning houses, they were astounded to meet a crowd of civilians, mostly women and children, who came streaming across the open in panic-stricken groups. Some of them fell under machine-gun fire snapping from the houses or under shrapnel bursting overhead. The women were haggard and gaunt, with wild eyes and wild hair, like witches. They held their children in tight claws until they were near our soldiers, when they all set up a shrill crying and wailing. The children were dazed with terror. Other civilians crawled up from their cellars in Loos, spattered with German blood, and wandered about among soldiers of many British battalions who crowded amid the scarred and shattered houses, and among the wounded men who came staggering through the streets, where army doctors were giving first aid in the roadway, while shells were bursting overhead and all the roar of the battle filled the air for miles around with infernal tumult.

Isolated Germans still kept sniping from secret places, and some of them fired at a dressing-station in the market-place, until a French girl, afterward decorated for valor—she was called the Lady of Loos by Londoners and Scots—borrowed a revolver and shot two of them dead in a neighboring house. Then she came back to the soup she was making for wounded men.

Some of the German prisoners were impressed as stretcher-bearers, and one, "Jock," had compelled four Germans to carry him in, while he lay talking to them in broadest Scots, grinning despite his blood and wounds.

A London lieutenant called out to a stretcher-bearer helping to carry down a German officer, and was astounded to be greeted by the wounded man.

"Hullo, Leslie!... I knew we should meet one day."

Looking at the man's face, the Londoner saw it was his own cousin... There was all the drama of war in that dirty village of Loos, which reeked with the smell of death then, and years later, when I went walking through it on another day of war, after another battle on Hill 70, beyond.

IX

While the village of Loos was crowded with hunters of men, wounded, dead, batches of panic-stricken prisoners, women, doctors, Highlanders and Lowlanders "fey" with the intoxication of blood, London soldiers with tattered uniforms and muddy rifles and stained bayonets, mixed brigades were moving forward to new objectives. The orders of the Scottish troops, which I saw, were to go "all out," and to press on as far as they could, with the absolute assurance that all the ground they gained would be held behind them by supporting troops; and having that promise, they trudged on to Hill 70. The Londoners had been ordered to make a defensive flank on the right of the Scots by capturing the chalk-pit south of Loos and digging in. They did this after savage fighting in the pit, where they bayoneted many Germans, though raked by machine-gun bullets from a neighboring copse, which was a fringe of gashed and tattered trees. But some of the London boys were mixed up with the advancing Scots and went on with them, and a battalion of Scots Fusiliers who had been in the supporting brigade of the 15th Division, which was intended to follow the advance, joined the first assault, either through eagerness or a wrong order, and, unknown to their brigadier, were among the leaders in the bloody struggle in Loos, and labored on to Hill 70, where Camerons, Gordons, Black Watch, Seaforths, Argyll, and Sutherland men and Londoners were now up the slopes, stabbing stray Germans who were trying to retreat to a redoubt on the reverse side of the hill.

For a time there was a kind of Bank Holiday crowd on Hill 70. The German gunners, knowing that the redoubt on the crest was still held by their men, dared not fire; and many German batteries were on the move, out of Lens and from their secret lairs in the country thereabouts, in a state of panic. On our right the French were fighting desperately at Souchez and Neuville St.-Vaast and up the lower slopes of Vimy, suffering horrible casualties and failing to gain the heights in spite of the reckless valor of their men, but alarming the German staffs, who for a time had lost touch with the situation—their telephones had been destroyed by gun-fire—and were filled with gloomy apprehensions. So Hill 70 was quiet, except for spasms of machine-gun fire from the redoubt on the German side of the slope and the bombing of German dugouts, or the bayoneting of single men routed out from holes in the earth.

One of our men came face to face with four Germans, two of whom were armed with rifles and two with bombs. They were standing in the wreckage of a trench, pallid, and with the fear of death in their eyes. The rifles clattered to the earth, the bombs fell at their feet, and their hands went up when the young Scot appeared before them with his bayonet down. He was alone, and they could have killed him, but surrendered, and were glad of the life he granted them. As more men came up the slope there were greetings between comrades, of:

"Hullo, Jock!"

"Is that you, Alf?"

They were rummaging about for souvenirs in half-destroyed dugouts where dead bodies lay. They were "swapping" souvenirs—taken from prisoners—silver watches, tobacco-boxes, revolvers, compasses. Many of them put on German field-caps, like schoolboys with paper caps from Christmas crackers, shouting with laughter because of their German look. They thought the battle was won. After the first wild rush the shell-fire, the killing, the sight of dead comrades, the smell of blood, the nightmare of that hour after dawn, they were beginning to get normal again, to be conscious of themselves, to rejoice in their luck at having got so far with whole skins. It had been a fine victory. The enemy was nowhere. He had "mizzled off."

Some of the Scots, with the hunter's instinct still strong, decided to go on still farther to a new objective. They straggled away in batches to one of the suburbs of Lens—the Cite St.-Auguste. Very few of them came back with the tale of their comrades' slaughter by sudden bursts of machine-gun fire which cut off all chance of retreat....

The quietude of Hill 70 was broken by the beginning of a new bombardment from German guns.

"Dig in," said the officers. "We must hold on at all costs until the supports come up."

Where were the supporting troops which had been promised? There was no sign of them coming forward from Loos. The Scots were strangely isolated on the slopes of Hill 70. At night the sky above them was lit up by the red glow of fires in Lens, and at twelve-thirty that night, under that ruddy sky, dark figures moved on the east of the hill and a storm of machine-gun bullets swept down on the Highlanders and Lowlanders, who crouched low in the mangled earth. It was a counter-attack by masses of men crawling up to the crest from the reverse side and trying to get the Scots out of the slopes below. But the men of the 15th Division answered by volleys of rifle-fire, machine-gun fire, and bombs. They held on in spite of dead and wounded men thinning out their fighting strength. At five-thirty in the morning there was another strong counter-attack, repulsed also, but at another price of life in those holes and ditches on the hillside.

Scottish officers stared anxiously back toward their old lines. Where were the supports? Why did they get no help? Why were they left clinging like this to an isolated hill? The German artillery had reorganized. They were barraging the ground about Loos fiercely and continuously. They were covering a great stretch of country up to Hulluch, and north of it, with intense harassing fire. Later on that Saturday morning the 15th Division received orders to attack and capture the German earthwork redoubt on the crest of the hill. A brigade of the 21st Division was nominally in support of them, but only small groups of that brigade appeared on the scene, a few white-faced officers, savage with anger, almost mad with some despair in them, with batches of English lads who looked famished with hunger, weak after long marching, demoralized by some tragedy that had happened to them. They were Scots who did most of the work in trying to capture the redoubt, the same Scots who had fought through Loos. They tried to reach the crest. Again and again they crawled forward and up, but the blasts of machine-gun fire mowed them down, and many young Scots lay motionless on those chalky slopes, with their kilts riddled with bullets. Others, hit in the head, or arms, or legs, writhed like snakes back to the cover of broken trenches.

"Where are the supports?" asked the Scottish officers. "In God's name, where are the troops who were to follow on? Why did we do all this bloody fighting to be hung up in the air like this?"

The answer to their question has not been given in any official despatch. It is answered by the tragedy of the 21st and 24th Divisions, who will never forget the misery of that day, though not many are now alive who suffered it. Their part of the battle I will tell later.

X

To onlookers there were some of the signs of victory on that day of September 25th—of victory and its price. I met great numbers of the lightly wounded men, mostly "Jocks," and they were in exalted spirits because they had done well in this ordeal and had come through it, and out of it—alive. They came straggling back through the villages behind the lines to the casualty clearing—stations and ambulance-trains. Some of them had the sleeves of their tunics cut away and showed brown, brawny arms tightly bandaged and smeared with blood. Some of them were wounded in the legs and hobbled with their arms about their comrades' necks. Their kilts were torn and plastered with chalky mud. Nearly all of them had some "souvenir" of the fighting—German watches, caps, cartridges. They carried themselves with a warrior look, so hard, so lean, so clear-eyed, these young Scots of the Black Watch and Camerons and Gordons. They told tales of their own adventure in broad Scots, hard to understand, and laughed grimly at the killing they had done, though here and there a lad among them had a look of bad remembrance in his eyes, and older men spoke gravely of the scenes on the battlefield and called it "hellish." But their pride was high. They had done what they had been asked to do. The 15th Division had proved its quality. Their old battalions, famous in history, had gained new honor.

Thousands of those lightly wounded men swarmed about a long ambulance-train standing in a field near the village of Choques. They crowded the carriages, leaned out of the windows with their bandaged heads and arms, shouting at friends they saw in the other crowds. The spirit of victory, and of lucky escape, uplifted those lads, drugged them. And now they were going home for a spell. Home to bonny Scotland, with a wound that would take some time to heal.

There were other wounded men from whom no laughter came, nor any sound. They were carried to the train on stretchers, laid down awhile on the wooden platforms, covered with blankets up to their chins—unless they uncovered themselves with convulsive movements. I saw one young Londoner so smashed about the face that only his eyes were uncovered between layers of bandages, and they were glazed with the first film of death. Another had his jaw blown clean away, so the doctor told me, and the upper half of his face was livid and discolored by explosive gases. A splendid boy of the Black Watch was but a living trunk. Both his arms and both his legs were shattered. If he lived after butcher's work of surgery he would be one of those who go about in boxes on wheels, from whom men turn their eyes away, sick with a sense of horror. There were blind boys led to the train by wounded comrades, groping, very quiet, thinking of a life of darkness ahead of them—forever in the darkness which shut in their souls. For days and weeks that followed there was always a procession of ambulances on the way to the dirty little town of

Lillers, and going along the roads I used to look back at them and see the soles of muddy boots upturned below brown blankets. It was more human wreckage coming down from the salient of Loos, from the chalkpits of Hulluch and the tumbled earth of the Hohenzollern redoubt, which had been partly gained by the battle which did not succeed. Outside a square brick building, which was the Town Hall of Lillers, and for a time a casualty clearing-station, the "bad" cases were unloaded; men with chunks of steel in their lungs and bowels were vomiting great gobs of blood, men with arms and legs torn from their trunks, men without noses, and their brains throbbing through opened scalps, men without faces...

XI

To a field behind the railway station near the grimy village of Choques, on the edge of this Black Country of France, the prisoners were brought; and I went among them and talked with some of them, on a Sunday morning, when now the rain had stopped and there was a blue sky overhead and good visibility for German guns and ours.

There were fourteen hundred German prisoners awaiting entrainment, a mass of slate-gray men lying on the wet earth in huddled heaps of misery, while a few of our fresh-faced Tommies stood among them with fixed bayonets. They were the men who had surrendered from deep dugouts in the trenches between us and Loos and from the cellars of Loos itself. They had seen many of their comrades bayoneted. Some of them had shrieked for mercy. Others had not shrieked, having no power of sound in their throats, but had shrunk back at the sight of glinting bayonets, with an animal fear of death. Now, all that was a nightmare memory, and they were out of it all until the war should end, next year, the year after, the year after that—who could tell?

They had been soaked to the skin in the night and their gray uniforms were still soddened. Many of them were sleeping, in huddled, grotesque postures, like dead men, some lying on their stomachs, face downward. Others were awake, sitting hunched up, with drooping heads and a beaten, exhausted look. Others paced up and down, up and down, like caged animals, as they were, famished and parched, until we could distribute the rations. Many of them were dying, and a German ambulanceman went among them, injecting them with morphine to ease the agony which made them writhe and groan. Two men held their stomachs, moaning and whimpering with a pain that gnawed their bowels, caused by cold and damp. They cried out to me, asking for a doctor. A friend of mine carried a water jar to some of the wounded and held it to their lips. One of them refused. He was a tall, evil-looking fellow, with a bloody rag round his head—a typical "Hun," I thought. But he pointed to a comrade who lay gasping beside him and said, in German, "He needs it first."

This man had never heard of Sir Philip Sidney, who at Zutphen, when thirsty and near death, said, "His need is greater than mine," but he had the same chivalry in his soul.

The officer in charge of their escort could not speak German and had no means of explaining to the prisoners that they were to take their turn to get rations and water at a dump nearby. It was a war correspondent, young Valentine Williams, afterward a very gallant officer in the Irish Guards who gave the orders in fluent and incisive German. He began with a hoarse shout of "Achtung!" and that old word of command had an electrical effect on many of the men. Even those who had seemed asleep staggered to their feet and stood at attention. The habit of discipline was part of their very life, and men almost dead strove to obey.

The non-commissioned officers formed parties to draw and distribute the rations, and then those prisoners clutched at hunks of bread and ate in a famished way, like starved beasts. Some of them had been four days hungry, cut off from their supplies by our barrage fire, and intense hunger gave them a kind of vitality when food appeared. The sight of that mass of men reduced to such depths of human misery was horrible. One had no hate in one's heart for them then.

"Poor devils!" said an officer with me. "Poor beasts! Here we see the `glory' of war! the `romance' of war!"

I spoke to some of them in bad German, and understood their answer.

"It is better here than on the battlefield," said one of them. "We are glad to be prisoners."

One of them waved his hand toward the tumult of guns which were firing ceaselessly.

"I pity our poor people there," he said.

One of them, who spoke English, described all he had seen of the battle, which was not much, because no man at such a time sees more than what happens within a yard or two.

"The English caught us by surprise when the attack came at last," he said. "The bombardment had been going on for days, and we could not guess when the attack would begin. I was in a deep dugout, wondering how long it would be before a shell came through the roof and blow us to pieces. The earth shook above our heads. Wounded men crawled into the dugout, and some of them died down there. We sat looking at their bodies in the doorway and up the steps. I climbed over them when a lull came. A friend of mine was there, dead, and I stepped on his stomach to get upstairs. The first thing I saw was a crowd of your soldiers streaming past our trenches. We were surrounded on three sides, and our position was hopeless. Some of our men started firing, but it was only asking for death. Your men killed them with bayonets. I went back into my dugout and waited. Presently there was an explosion in the doorway and part of the dugout fell in. One of the men with me had his head blown off, and his blood spurted on me. I was dazed, but through the fumes I saw an English soldier in a petticoat standing at the doorway, making ready to throw another bomb.

"I shouted to him in English:

"'Don't kill us! We surrender!'

"He was silent for a second or two, and I thought he would throw his bomb. Then he said:

"'Come out, you swine.'

"So we went out, and saw many soldiers in petticoats, your Highlanders, with bayonets. They wanted to kill us, but one man argued with them in words I could not understand-a dialect-and we were told to go along a trench. Even then we expected death, but came to another group of prisoners, and joined them on their way back. Gott sei dank!"

He spoke gravely and simply, this dirty, bearded man, who had been a clerk in a London office. He had the truthfulness of a man who had just come from great horrors.

Many of the men around him were Silesians-more Polish than German. Some of them could not speak more than a few words of German, and were true Slavs in physical type, with flat cheek-bones.

A group of German artillery officers had been captured and they were behaving with studied arrogance and insolence as they smoked cigarettes apart from the men, and looked in a jeering way at our officers.

"Did you get any of our gas this morning?" I asked them, and one of them laughed and shrugged his shoulders.

"I smelled it a little. It was rather nice... The English always imitate the German war-methods, but without much success."

They grinned and imitated my way of saying "Guten Tag" when I left them. It took a year or more to tame the arrogance of the German officer. At the end of the Somme battles he changed his manner when captured, and was very polite.

In another place—a prison in St.-Omer—I had a conversation with two other officers of the German army who were more courteous than the gunners. They had been taken at Hooge and were both Prussians—one a stout captain, smiling behind horn spectacles, with a false, jovial manner, hiding the effect of the ordeal from which he had just escaped, and his hatred of us; the other a young, slim fellow, with clear-cut features, who was very nervous, but bowed repeatedly, with his heels together, as though in a cafe at Ehrenbreitstein, when high officers came in. A few hours before he had been buried alive. One of our mines had exploded under him, flinging a heap of earth over him. The fat man by his side—his captain—had been buried, too, in the dugout. They had scraped themselves out by clawing at the earth.

They were cautious about answering questions on the war, but the younger man said they were prepared down to the last gaiter for another winter campaign and—that seemed to me at the time a fine touch of audacity—for two more winter campaigns if need be. The winter of '16, after this autumn and winter of '15, and then after that the winter of '17! The words of that young Prussian seemed to me, the more I thought of them, idiotic and almost insane. Why, the world itself could not suffer two more years of war. It would end before then in general anarchy, the wild revolutions of armies on all fronts. Humanity of every nation would revolt against such prolonged slaughter... It was I who was mad, in the foolish faith that the war would end before another year had passed, because I thought that would be the limit of endurance of such mutual massacre.

In a room next to those two officers—a week before this battle, the captain had been rowing with his wife on the lake at Potsdam—was another prisoner, who wept and wept. He had escaped to our lines before the battle to save his skin, and now was conscience-stricken and thought he had lost his soul. What stabbed his conscience most was the thought that his wife and children would lose their allowances because of his treachery. He stared at us with wild, red eyes.

"Ach, mein armes Weib! Meine Kinder!... Ach, Gott in Himmel!"

He had no pride, no dignity, no courage.

This tall, bearded man, father of a family, put his hands against the wall and laid his head on his arm and wept.

XII

During the battle, for several days I went with other men to various points of view, trying to see something of the human conflict from slag heaps and rising ground, but could only see the swirl and flurry of gun-fire and the smoke of shells mixing with wet mist, and the backwash of wounded and prisoners, and the traffic of guns, and wagons, and supporting troops. Like an ant on the edge of a volcano I sat among the slag heaps with gunner observers, who were listening at telephones dumped down in the fields and connected with artillery brigades and field batteries.

"The Guards are fighting round Fosse 8," said one of these observers.

Through the mist I could see Fosse 8, a flat-topped hill of coal-dust. Little glinting lights were playing about it, like confetti shining in the sun. That was German shrapnel. Eruptions of red flame and black earth vomited out of the hill. That was German high explosive. For a time on Monday, September 27th, it was the storm-center of battle.

"What's that?" asked an artillery staff-officer, with his ear to the field telephone. "What's that?... Hullo!... Are you there?... The Guards have been kicked off Fosse 8... Oh, hell!"

From all parts of the field of battle such whispers came to listening men and were passed on to headquarters, where other men listened. This brigade was doing pretty well. That was hard pressed. The Germans were counter-attacking heavily. Their barrage was strong and our casualties heavy. "Oh, hell!" said other men. From behind the mist came the news of life and death, revealing things which no onlooker could see.

I went closer to see—into the center of the arc of battle, up by the Loos redoubt, where the German dead and ours still lay in heaps. John Buchan was my companion on that walk, and together we stood staring over the edge of a trench to where, grim and gaunt against the gray sky, loomed the high, steel columns of the "Tower Bridge," the mining-works which I had seen before the battle as an inaccessible landmark in the German lines. Now they were within our lines in the center of Loos, and no longer "leering" at us, as an officer once told me they used to do when he led his men into communication trenches under their observation.

Behind us now was the turmoil of war—thousands and scores of thousands of men moving in steady columns forward and backward in the queer, tangled way which during a great battle seems to have no purpose or meaning, except to the directing brains on the Headquarters Staff, and, sometimes in history, none to them.

Vast convoys of transports choked the roads, with teams of mules harnessed to wagons and gun-limbers, with trains of motor ambulances packed with wounded men, with infantry brigades plodding through the slush and slime, with divisional cavalry halted in the villages, and great bivouacs in the boggy fields.

The men, Londoners, and Scots, and Guards, and Yorkshires, and Leinsters, passed and repassed in dense masses, in small battalions, in scattered groups. One could tell them from those who were filling their places by the white chalk which covered them from head to foot, and sometimes by the blood which had splashed them.

Regiments which had lost many of their comrades and had fought in attack and counter-attack through those days and nights went very silently, and no man cheered them. Legions of tall lads, who a few months before marched smart and trim down English lanes, trudged toward the fighting-lines under the burden of their heavy packs, with all their smartness befouled by the business of war, but wonderful and pitiful to see because of the look of courage and the gravity in their eyes as they went up to dreadful places. Farther away within the zone of the enemy's fire the traffic ceased, and I came into the desolate lands of death, where there is but little movement, and the only noise is that of guns. I passed by ruined villages and towns.

To the left was Vermelles (two months before death nearly caught me there), and I stared at those broken houses and roofless farms and fallen churches which used to make one's soul shiver even when they stood clear in the daylight.

To the right, a few hundred yards away, was Masingarbe, from which many of our troops marched out to begin the great attack. Farther back were the great slag heaps of Noeux-les-Mines, and all around other black hills of this mining country which rise out of the flat plain. It was a long walk through narrow trenches toward that Loos redoubt where at last I stood. There was the smell of death in those narrow, winding ways. One boy, whom death had taken almost at the entrance-way, knelt on the fire-step, with his head bent and his forehead against the wet clay, as though in prayer. Farther on other bodies of London boys and Scots lay huddled up.

We were in the center of a wide field of fire, with the enemy's batteries on one side and ours on the other in sweeping semicircles. The shells of all these batteries went crying through the air with high, whining sighs, which ended in the cough of death. The roar of the guns was incessant and very close. The enemy was sweeping a road to my right, and his shells went overhead with a continual rush, passing our shells, which answered back. The whole sky was filled with these thunderbolts. Many of them were "Jack Johnsons," which raised a volume of black smoke where they fell. I wondered how it would feel to be caught by one of them, whether one would have any consciousness before being scattered. Fear, which had walked with me part of the way, left me for a time. I had a strange sense of exhilaration, an intoxicated interest in this foul scene and the activity of that shell-fire.

Peering over the parapet, we saw the whole panorama of the battleground. It was but an ugly, naked plain, rising up to Hulluch and Haisnes on the north, falling down to Loos on the east, from where we stood, and rising again to Hill 70 (now in German hands again), still farther east and a little south.

The villages of Haisnes and Hulluch fretted the skyline, and Fosse 8 was a black wart between them. The "Tower Bridge," close by in the town of Loos, was the one high landmark which broke the monotony of this desolation.

No men moved about this ground. Yet thousands of men were hidden about us in the ditches, waiting for another counter-attack behind storms of fire. The only moving things were the shells which vomited up earth and smoke and steel as they burst in all directions over the whole zone. We were shelling Hulluch and Haisnes and Fosse 8 with an intense, concentrated fire, and the enemy was retaliating by scattering shells over the town of Loos and our new line between Hill 70 and the chalk-pit, and the whole length of our line from north to south.

Only two men moved about above the trenches. They were two London boys carrying a gas-cylinder, and whistling as though it were a health resort under the autumn sun... It was not a health resort. It stank of death, from piles of corpses, all mangled and in a mush of flesh and bones lying around the Loos redoubt and all the ground in this neighborhood, and for a long distance north.

Through the streets of Bethune streamed a tide of war: the transport of divisions, gun-teams with their limber ambulance convoys, ammunition wagons, infantry moving up to the front, despatch riders, staff-officers, signalers, and a great host of men and mules and motor-cars. The rain lashed down upon the crowds; waterproofs and burberries and the tarpaulin covers of forage-carts streamed with water, and the bronzed faces of the soldiers were dripping wet. Mud splashed them to the thighs. Fountains of mud spurted up from the wheels of gun-carriages. The chill of winter made Highlanders as well as Indians—those poor, brave, wretched Indians who had been flung into the holding attack on the canal at La Bassee, and mown down in the inevitable way by shrapnel and machine-gun bullets—shiver in the wind.

Yet, in spite of rain and great death, there was a spirit of exultation among many fighting-men. At last there was a break in the months of stationary warfare. We were up and out of the trenches. The first proofs of victory were visible there in a long line of German guns captured at Loos, guarded on each side by British soldiers with fixed bayonets. Men moving up did not know the general failure that had swamped a partial success. They stared at the guns and said, “By God—we’ve got ‘em going this time!”

A group of French civilians gathered round them, excited at the sight. Artillery officers examined their broken breech-blocks and their inscriptions:

“Pro Gloria et Patria.”

“Ultima ratio regis.”

The irony of the words made some of the onlookers laugh. A French interpreter spoke to some English officers with a thrill of joy in his voice. Had they heard the last news from Champagne? The French had broken through the enemy’s line. The Germans were in full retreat.. . It was utterly untrue, because after the desperate valor of heroic youth and horrible casualties, the French attack had broken down. But the spirit of hope came down the cold wind and went with the men whom I saw marching to the fields of fate in the slanting rain, as the darkness and the mist came to end another day of battle.

Outside the headquarters of a British army corps stood another line of captured field-guns and several machine-guns, of which one had a strange history of adventure. It was a Russian machine-gun, taken by the Germans on the eastern front and retaken by us on the western front.

In General Rawlinson's headquarters I saw a queer piece of booty. It was a big bronze bell used by the Germans in their trenches to signal a British gas-attack.

General Rawlinson was taking tea in his chateau when I called on him, and was having an animated argument with Lord Cavan, commanding the Guards, as to the disposal of the captured artillery and other trophies. Lord Cavan claimed some for his own, with some violence of speech. But General Rawlinson was bright and breezy as usual. Our losses were not worrying him. As a great general he did not allow losses to worry him. He ate his tea with a hearty appetite, and chaffed his staff-officers. They were anticipating the real German counter-attack—a big affair. Away up the line there would be more dead piled up, more filth and stench of human slaughter, but the smell of it would not reach back to headquarters.

XIII

In a despatch by Sir John French, dated October 15, 1915, and issued by the War Office on November 1st of that year, the Commander-in-Chief stated that:

"In view of the great length of line along which the British troops were operating it was necessary to keep a strong reserve *in my own hand.* The 11th Corps, consisting of the Guards, the 21st and the 24th Divisions, were detailed for this purpose. This reserve was the more necessary owing to the fact that the Tenth French Army had to postpone its attack until one o'clock in the day; and further, that the corps operating on the French left had to be directed in a more or less southeasterly direction, involving, in case of our success, a considerable gap in our line. To insure, however, the speedy and effective support of the 1st and 4th Corps in the case of their success, the 21st and 24th Divisions passed the night of the 24th and 25th on the line Beuvry (to the east of Bethune)-Noeux-les-Mines. The Guards Division was in the neighborhood of Lillers on the same night."

By that statement, and by the facts that happened in accordance with it, the whole scheme of attack in the battle of Loos will stand challenged in history. Lord French admits in that despatch that he held his reserves "in his own hand," and later he states that it was not until nine-thirty on the morning of battle that "I placed the 21st and 24th Divisions at the disposal of the General Officer commanding First Army." He still held the Guards. He makes, as a defense of the decision to hold back the reserves, the extraordinary statement that there "would be a considerable gap in our line in case of our success." That is to say, he was actually envisaging a gap in the line if the attack succeeded according to his expectations, and risking the most frightful catastrophe that may befall any army in an assault upon a powerful enemy, provided with enormous reserves, as the Germans were at that time, and as our Commander-in-Chief ought to have known.

But apart from that the whole time-table of the battle was, as it now appears, fatally wrong. To move divisions along narrow roads requires an immense amount of time, even if the roads are clear, and those roads toward Loos were crowded with the transport and gun-limbers of the assaulting troops. To move them in daylight to the trenches meant inevitable loss of life and almost certain demoralization under the enemy's gun-fire.

"Between 11 A.M. and 12 noon the central brigade of these divisions filed past me at Bethune and Noeux-les-Mines, respectively," wrote Sir John French. It was not possible for them to reach our old trenches until 4 P.M. It was Gen. Sir Frederick Maurice, the Chief of Staff, who revealed that fact to me afterward in an official explanation, and it was confirmed by battalion officers of the 24th Division whom I met.

That time-table led to disaster. By eight o'clock in the morning there were Scots on Hill 70. They had been told to go "all out," with the promise that the ground they gained would be consolidated by following troops. Yet no supports were due to arrive until 4 P.M. at our original line of attack—still away back from Hill 70—by which time the enemy had recovered from his first surprise, had reorganized his guns, and was moving up his own supports. Tragedy befell the Scots on Hill 70 and in the Cite St.-Auguste, as I have told. Worse tragedy happened to the 21st and 24th Divisions. They became hopelessly checked and tangled in the traffic of the roads, and in their heavy kit were exhausted long before they reached the battlefield. They drank the water out of their bottles, and then were parched. They ate their iron rations, and then were hungry. Some of their transport moved too far forward in daylight, was seen by German observers, ranged on by German guns, and blown to bits on the road. The cookers were destroyed, and with them that night's food. None of the officers had been told that they were expected to attack on that day. All they anticipated was the duty of holding the old support trenches. In actual fact they arrived when the enemy was preparing a heavy counter-attack and flinging over storms of shell-fire. The officers had no maps and no orders. They were utterly bewildered with the situation, and had no knowledge as to the where-abouts of the enemy or their own objectives. Their men met heavy fire for the first time when their physical and moral condition was weakened by the long march, the lack of food and water, and the unexpected terror ahead of them. They crowded into broken trenches, where shells burst over them and into them. Young officers acting on their own initiative tried to lead their men forward, and isolated parties went forward, but uncertainly, not knowing the ground nor their purpose. Shrapnel lashed them, and high-explosive shells plowed up the earth about them and with them. Dusk came, and then darkness. Some officers were cursing, and some wept, fearing dishonor. The men were huddled together like sheep without shepherds when wolves are about, and saw by the bewilderment of the officers that they were without leadership. It is that which makes for demoralization, and these men, who afterward in the battle of the Somme in the following year fought with magnificent valor, were on that day at Loos demoralized in a tragic and complete way. Those who had gone forward came back to the crowded trenches and added to the panic and the rage and the anguish. Men smashed their rifles in a kind of madness. Boys were cursing and weeping at the same time. They were too hopelessly disordered and dismayed by the lack of guidance and by the shock to their sense of discipline to be of much use in that battle. Some bodies of them in both these unhappy divisions arrived in front of Hill 70 at the very time when the enemy launched his first counter-attack, and were driven back in disorder... Some days later I saw the 21st Division marching back behind the lines. Rain slashed them. They walked with bent heads. The young officers were blanched and had a beaten look. The sight of those dejected men was tragic and pitiful.

XIV

Meanwhile, at 6 P.M. on the evening of the first day of battle, the Guards arrived at Noeux-les-Mines. As I saw them march up, splendid in their height and strength and glory of youth, I looked out for the officers I knew, yet hoped I should not see them—that man who had given a farewell touch to the flowers in the garden of our billet, that other one who knew he would be wounded, those two young brothers who had played cricket on a sunny afternoon. I did not see them, but saw only columns of men, staring grimly ahead of them, with strange, unspeakable thoughts behind their masklike faces.

It was not until the morning of the 26th that the Commander-in-Chief "placed them at the disposal of the General Officer commanding First Army," and it was on the afternoon of Monday, the 27th, that they were ordered to attack.

By that time we had lost Fosse 8, one brigade of the 9th Scottish Division having been flung back to its own trenches after desperate fighting, at frightful cost, after the capture of the Hohenzollern redoubt by the 26th Brigade of that division. To the north of them the 7th Division was also suffering horrible losses after the capture of the quarries, near Hulluch, and the village of Haisnes, which afterward was lost. The commanding officers of both divisions, General Capper of the 7th, and General Thesiger of the 9th, were killed as they reconnoitered the ground, and wounded men were pouring down to the casualty clearing stations if they had the luck to get so far. Some of them had not that luck, but lay for nearly two days before they were rescued by the stretcher-bearers from Quality Street and Philosophe.

It was bad all along the line. The whole plan had gone astray from the beginning. With an optimism which was splendid in fighting-men and costly in the High Command, our men had attacked positions of enormous strength—held by an enemy in the full height of his power—without sufficient troops in reserve to follow up and support the initial attack, to consolidate the ground, and resist inevitable counter-attacks. What reserves the Commander-in-Chief had he held "in his own hand" too long and too far back.

The Guards went in when the enemy was reorganized to meet them. The 28th Division, afterward in support, was too late to be a decisive factor.

I do not blame Lord French. I have no right to blame him, as I am not a soldier nor a military expert. He did his best, with the highest motives. The blunders he made were due to ignorance of modern battles. Many other generals made many other blunders, and our men paid with their lives. Our High Command had to learn by mistakes, by ghastly mistakes, repeated often, until they became visible to the military mind and were paid for again by the slaughter of British youth. One does not blame. A writing-man, who was an observer and recorder, like myself, does not sit in judgment. He has no right to judge. He merely cries out, "O God!... O God!" in remembrance of all that agony and that waste of splendid boys who loved life, and died.

On Sunday, as I have told, the situation was full of danger. The Scots of the 15th Division, weakened by many losses and exhausted by their long fatigue, had been forced to abandon the important position of Puits 14—a mine-shaft half a mile north of Hill 70, linked up in defense with the enemy's redoubt on the northeast side of Hill 70. The Germans had been given time to bring up their reserves, to reorganize their broken lines, and to get their batteries into action again.

There was a consultation of anxious brigadiers in Loos when no man could find safe shelter owing to the heavy shelling which now ravaged among the houses. Rations were running short, and rain fell through the roofless ruins, and officers and men shivered in wet clothes. Dead bodies blown into bits, headless trunks, pools of blood, made a ghastly mess in the roadways and the houses. Badly wounded men were dragged down into the cellars, and lay there in the filth of Friday's fighting. The headquarters of one of the London brigades had put up in a roofless barn, but were shelled out, and settled down on some heaps of brick in the open. It was as cold as death in the night, and no fire could be lighted, and iron rations were the only food, until two chaplains, "R. C." and Church of England (no difference of dogma then), came up as volunteers in a perilous adventure, with bottles of hot soup in mackintoshes. They brought a touch of human warmth to the brigade staff, made those hours of the night more endurable, but the men farther forward had no such luck. They were famishing and soaked, in a cold hell where shells tossed up the earth about them and spattered them with the blood and flesh of their comrades.

On Monday morning the situation was still more critical, all along the line, and the Guards were ordered up to attack Hill 70, to which only a few Scots were clinging on the near slopes. The 6th Cavalry Brigade dismounted—no more dreams of exploiting success and galloping round Lens—were sent into Loos with orders to hold the village at all cost, with the men of the 15th Division, who had been left there.

The Londoners were still holding on to the chalk-pit south of Loos, under murderous fire.

It was a bad position for the troops sent into action at that stage. The result of the battle on September 25th had been to create a salient thrust like a wedge into the German position and enfiladed by their guns. The sides of the salient ran sharply back—from Hulluch in the north, past the chalk-quarries to Givenchy, and in the south from the lower slopes of Hill 70 past the Double Crassier to Grenay. The orders given to the Guards were to straighten out this salient on the north by capturing the whole of Hill 70, Puits 14, to the north of it, and the chalk-pit still farther north.

It was the 2d Brigade of Guards, including Grenadiers, Welsh and Scots Guards, which was to lead the assault, while the 1st Brigade on the left maintained a holding position and the 3d Brigade was in support, immediately behind.

As soon as the Guards started to attack they were met by a heavy storm of gas-shells. This checked them for a time, as smoke-helmets—the old fashioned things of flannel which were afterward changed for the masks with nozzles—had to be served out, and already men were choking and gasping in the poisonous fumes. Among them was the colonel of the Grenadiers, whose command was taken over by the major. Soon the men advanced again, looking like devils, as, in artillery formation (small separate groups), they groped their way through the poisoned clouds. Shrapnel and high explosives burst over them and among them, and many men fell as they came within close range of the enemy's positions running from Hill 70 northward to the chalk-pit.

The Irish Guards, supported by the Coldstreamers, advanced down the valley beyond Loos and gained the lower edge of Bois Hugo, near the chalk-pit, while the Scots Guards assaulted Puits 14 and the building in its group of houses known as the Keep. Another body of Guards, including Grenadiers and Welsh, attacked at the same time the lower slopes of Hill 70.

Puits 14 itself was won by a party of Scots Guards, led by an officer named Captain Cuthbert, which engaged in hand-to-hand fighting, routing out the enemy from the houses. Some companies of the Grenadiers came to the support of their comrades in the Scots Guards, but suffered heavy losses themselves. A platoon under a young lieutenant named Ayres Ritchie reached the Puits, and, storming their way into the Keep, knocked out a machine-gun, mounted on the second floor, by a desperate bombing attack. The officer held on in a most dauntless way to the position, until almost every man was either killed or wounded, unable to receive support, owing to the enfilade fire of the German machine-guns.

Night had now come on, the sky lightened by the bursting of shells and flares, and terrible in its tumult of battle. Some of the Coldstreamers had gained possession of the chalk-pit, which they were organizing into a strong defensive position, and various companies of the Guards divisions, after heroic assaults upon Hill 70, where they were shattered by the fire which met them on the crest from the enemy's redoubt on the northeast side, had dug themselves into the lower slopes.

There was a strange visitor that day at the headquarters of the Guards division, where Lord Cavan was directing operations. A young officer came in and said, quite calmly: "Sir, I have to report that my battalion has been cut to pieces. We have been utterly destroyed."

Lord Cavan questioned him, and then sent for another officer. "Look after that young man," he said, quietly. "He is mad. It is a case of shell-shock."

Reports came through of a mysterious officer going the round of the batteries, saying that the Germans had broken through and that they had better retire. Two batteries did actually move away.

Another unknown officer called out, "Retire! Retire!" until he was shot through the head. "German spies!" said some of our officers and men, but the Intelligence branch said, "Not spies... madmen... poor devils!"

Before the dawn came the Coldstreamers made another desperate attempt to attack and hold Puits 14, but the position was too deadly even for their height of valor, and although some men pushed on into this raging fire, the survivors had to fall back to the woods, where they strengthened their defensive works.

On the following day the position was the same, the sufferings of our men being still further increased by heavy shelling from 8-inch howitzers. Colonel Egerton of the Coldstream Guards and his adjutant were killed in the chalk-pit.

It was now seen by the headquarters staff of the Guards Division that Puits 14 was untenable, owing to its enfilading by heavy artillery, and the order was given for a retirement to the chalk-pit, which was a place of sanctuary owing to the wonderful work done throughout the night to strengthen its natural defensive features by sand—bags and barbed wire, in spite of machine-guns which raked it from the neighboring woods.

The retirement was done as though the men were on parade, slowly, and in perfect order, across the field of fire, each man bearing himself, so their officers told me, as though at the Trooping of the Colors, until now one and then another fell in a huddled heap. It was an astonishing tribute to the strength of tradition among troops. To safeguard the honor of a famous name these men showed such dignity in the presence of death that even the enemy must have been moved to admiration.

But they had failed, after suffering heavy losses, and the Commander-in-Chief had to call upon the French for help, realizing that without strong assistance the salient made by that battle of Loos would be a death-trap. The French Tenth Army had failed, too, at Vimy, thus failing to give the British troops protection on their right flank.

"On representing this to General Joffre," wrote Sir John French, "he was kind enough to ask the commander of the northern group of French armies to render us assistance. General Foch met those demands in the same friendly spirit which he has always displayed throughout the course of the whole campaign, and expressed his readiness to give me all the support he could. On the morning of the 28th we discussed the situation, and the general agreed to send the 9th French Corps to take over the ground occupied by us, extending from the French left up to and including that portion of Hill 70 which we were holding, and also the village of Loos. This relief was commenced on September 30th, and completed on the two following nights."

So ended the battle of Loos, except for a violent counter—attack delivered on October 8th all along the line from Fosse 8 on the north to the right of the French 9th Corps on the south, with twenty-eight battalions in the first line of assault. It was preceded by a stupendous bombardment which inflicted heavy casualties upon our 1st Division in the neighborhood of the chalk-pit, and upon the Guards holding the Hohenzollern redoubt near Hulluch. Once again those brigades, which had been sorely tried, had to crouch under a fury of fire, until the living were surrounded by dead, half buried or carved up into chunks of flesh in the chaos of broken trenches. The Germans had their own shambles, more frightful, we were told, than ours, and thousands of dead lay in front of our lines when the tide of their attack ebbed back and waves of living men were broken by the fire of our field-guns, rifles, and machine-guns. Sir John French's staff estimated the number of German dead as from eight to nine thousand. It was impossible to make any accurate sum in that arithmetic of slaughter, and always the enemy's losses were exaggerated because of the dreadful need of balancing accounts in new-made corpses in that Debit and Credit of war's bookkeeping.

What had we gained by great sacrifices of life? Not Lens, nor Lille, nor even Hill 70 (for our line had to be withdrawn from those bloody slopes where our men left many of their dead), but another sharp-edged salient enfiladed by German guns for two years more, and a foothold on one slag heap of the Double Crassier, where our men lived, if they could, a few yards from Germans on the other; and that part of the Hohenzollern redoubt which became another Hooge where English youth was blown up by mines, buried by trench-mortars, condemned to a living death in lousy caves dug into the chalk. Another V-shaped salient, narrower than that of Ypres, more dismal, and as deadly, among the pit-heads and the black dust hills and the broken mine-shafts of that foul country beyond Loos.

The battle which had been begun with such high hopes ended in ghastly failure by ourselves and by the French. Men who came back from it spoke in whispers of its generalship and staff work, and said things which were dangerous to speak aloud, cursing their fate as fighting-men, asking of God as well as of mortals why the courage of the soldiers they led should be thrown away in such a muck of slaughter, laughing with despairing mirth at the optimism of their leaders, who had been lured on by a strange, false, terrible belief in German weakness, and looking ahead at unending vistas of such massacre as this which would lead only to other salients, after desperate and futile endeavor.

PART FOUR

A WINTER OF DISCONTENT

I

The winter of 1915 was, I think, the worst of all. There was a settled hopelessness in it which was heavy in the hearts of men—ours and the enemy's. In 1914 there was the first battle of Ypres, when the bodies of British soldiers lay strewn in the fields beyond this city and their brown lines barred the way to Calais, but the war did not seem likely to go on forever. Most men believed, even then, that it would end quickly, and each side had faith in some miracle that might happen. In 1916-17 the winter was foul over the fields of the Somme after battles which had cut all our divisions to pieces and staggered the soul of the world by the immense martyrdom of boys—British, French, and German—on the western front. But the German retreat from the Somme to the shelter of their Hindenburg line gave some respite to our men, and theirs, from the long-drawn fury of attack and counter-attack, and from the intensity of gun-fire. There was at best the mirage of something like victory on our side, a faint flickering up of the old faith that the Germans had weakened and were nearly spent.

But for a time in those dark days of 1915 there was no hope ahead. No mental dope by which our fighting-men could drug themselves into seeing a vision of the war's end.

The battle of Loos and its aftermath of minor massacres in the ground we had gained—the new horror of that new salient—had sapped into the confidence of those battalion officers and men who had been assured of German weakness by cheery, optimistic, breezy-minded generals. It was no good some of those old gentlemen saying, "We've got 'em beat!" when from Hooge to the Hohenzollern redoubt our men sat in wet trenches under ceaseless bombardment of heavy guns, and when any small attack they made by the orders of a High Command which believed in small attacks, without much plan or purpose, was only "asking for trouble" from German counterattacks by mines, trench-mortars, bombing sorties, poison-gas, flame-throwers, and other forms of frightfulness which made a dirty mess of flesh and blood, without definite result on either side beyond piling up the lists of death.

"It keeps up the fighting spirit of the men," said the generals. "We must maintain an aggressive policy."

They searched their trench maps for good spots where another "small operation" might be organized. There was a competition among the corps and divisional generals as to the highest number of raids, mine explosions, trench-grabbings undertaken by their men.

"My corps," one old general told me over a cup of tea in his headquarters mess, "beats the record for raids." His casualties also beat the record, and many of his officers and men called him, just bluntly and simply, "Our old murderer." They disliked the necessity of dying so that he might add one more raid to his heroic competition with the corps commander of the sector on the left. When they waited for the explosion of a mine which afterward they had to "rush" in a race with the German bombing-parties, some of them saw no sense in the proceeding, but only the likelihood of having legs and arms torn off by German stick-bombs or shells. "What's the good of it?" they asked, and could find no answer except the satisfaction of an old man listening to the distant roar of the new tumult by which he had "raised hell" again.

II

The autumn of 1915 was wet in Flanders and Artois, where our men settled down—knee-deep where the trenches were worst—for the winter campaign. On rainy days, as I remember, a high wind hurtled over the Flemish fields, but it was moist, and swept gusts of rain into the faces of men marching through mud to the fighting-lines and of other men doing sentry on the fire-steps of trenches into which water came trickling down the slimy parapets.

When the wind dropped at dusk or dawn a whitish fog crept out of the ground, so that rifles were clammy to the touch and a blanket of moisture settled on every stick in the dugouts, and nothing could be seen through the veil of vapor to the enemy's lines, where he stayed invisible.

He was not likely to attack on a big scale while the battlefields were in that quagmire state. An advancing wave of men would have been clogged in the mud after the first jump over the slimy sand-bags, and to advance artillery was sheer impossibility. Nothing would be done on either side but stick-in-the-mud warfare and those trench-raids and minings which had no object except "to keep up the spirit of the men." There was always work to do in the trenches—draining them, strengthening their parapets, making their walls, tiling or boarding their floorways, timbering the dugouts, and after it was done another rainstorm or snowstorm undid most of it, and the parapets slid down, the water poured in, and spaces were opened for German machine-gun fire, and there was less head cover against shrapnel bullets which mixed with the raindrops, and high explosives which smashed through the mud. The working parties had a bad time and a wet one, in spite of waders and gum boots which were served out to lucky ones. Some of them wore a new kind of hat, seen for the first time, and greeted with guffaws—the "tin" hat which later became the headgear of all fighting-men. It saved many head wounds, but did not save body wounds, and every day the casualty lists grew longer in the routine of a warfare in which there was "Nothing to report."

Our men were never dry. They were wet in their trenches and wet in their dugouts. They slept in soaking clothes, with boots full of water, and they drank rain with their tea, and ate mud with their "bully," and endured it all with the philosophy of "grin and bear it!" and laughter, as I heard them laughing in those places between explosive curses.

On the other side of the barbed wire the Germans were more miserable, not because their plight was worse, but because I think they lacked the English sense of humor. In some places they had the advantage of our men in better trenches, with better drains and dugouts—due to an industry with which ours could never compete. Here and there, as in the ground to the north of Hooge, they were in a worse state, with such rivers in their trenches that they went to enormous trouble to drain the Bellewarde Lake which used to slop over in the rainy season. Those field-gray men had to wade through a Slough of Despond to get to their line, and at night by Hooge where the lines were close together—only a few yards apart—our men could hear their boots squelching in the mud with sucking, gurgling noises.

"They're drinking soup again!" said our humorists.

There, at Hooge, Germans and English talked to one another, out of their common misery.

"How deep is it with you?" shouted a German soldier.

His voice came from behind a pile of sand-bags which divided the enemy and ourselves in a communication trench between the main lines.

"Up to our blooming knees," said an English corporal, who was trying to keep his bombs dry under a tarpaulin.

"So?... You are lucky fellows. We are up to our belts in it."

It was so bad in parts of the line during November storms that whole sections of trench collapsed into a chaos of slime and ooze. It was the frost as well as the rain which caused this ruin, making the earthworks sink under their weight of sand-bags. German and English soldiers were exposed to one another like ants upturned from their nests by a minor landslide. They ignored one another. They pretended that the other fellows were not there. They had not been properly introduced. In another place, reckless because of their discomfort, the Germans crawled upon their slimy parapets and sat on top to dry their legs, and shouted: "Don't shoot! Don't shoot!"

Our men did not shoot. They, too, sat on the parapets drying their legs, and grinning at the gray ants yonder, until these incidents were reported back to G. H. Q.—where good fires were burning under dry roofs—and stringent orders came against "fraternization." Every German who showed himself was to be shot. Of course any Englishman who showed himself—owing to a parapet falling in—would be shot, too. It was six of one and half a dozen of the other, as always, in this trench warfare, but the dignity of G. H. Q. would not be outraged by the thought of such indecent spectacles as British and Germans refusing to kill each other on sight. Some of the men obeyed orders, and when a German sat up and said, "Don't shoot!" plugged him through the head. Others were extremely short-sighted... Now and again Germans crawled over to our trenches and asked meekly to be taken prisoner. I met a few of these men and spoke with them.

"There is no sense in this war," said one of them. "It is misery on both sides. There is no use in it."

That thought of war's futility inspired an episode which was narrated throughout the army in that winter of '15, and led to curious conversations in dugouts and billets. Above a German front-line trench appeared a plank on which, in big letters, was scrawled these words

"The English are fools."

"Not such bloody fools as all that!" said a sergeant, and in a few minutes the plank was smashed to splinters by rifle-fire.

Another plank appeared, with other words:

"The French are fools."

Loyalty to our allies caused the destruction of that board.

A third plank was put up:

"We're all fools. Let's all go home."

That board was also shot to pieces, but the message caused some laughter, and men repeating it said: "There's a deal of truth in those words. Why should this go on? What's it all about? Let the old men who made this war come and fight it out among themselves, at Hooge. The fighting-men have no real quarrel with one another. We all want to go home to our wives and our work."

But neither side was prepared to "go home" first. Each side was in a trap—a devil's trap from which there was no escape. Loyalty to their own side, discipline, with the death penalty behind it, spell words of old tradition, obedience to the laws of war or to the caste which ruled them, all the moral and spiritual propaganda handed out by pastors, newspapers, generals, staff-officers, old men at home, exalted women, female furies, a deep and simple love for England and Germany, pride of manhood, fear of cowardice—a thousand complexities of thought and sentiment prevented men, on both sides, from breaking the net of fate in which they were entangled, and revolting against that mutual, unceasing massacre, by a rising from the trenches with a shout of, "We're all fools!... Let's all go home!"

In Russia they did so, but the Germans did not go home, too. As an army and a nation they went on to the Peace of Brest-Litovsk and their doom. But many German soldiers were converted to that gospel of "We're all fools!" and would not fight again with any spirit, as we found at times, after August 8th, in the last year of war.

III

The men remained in the trenches, and suffered horribly. I have told about lice and rats and mine-shafts there. Another misery came to torture soldiers in the line, and it was called "trench-foot." Many men standing in slime for days and nights in field boots or puttees lost all sense of feeling in their feet. These feet of theirs, so cold and wet, began to swell, and then to go "dead," and then suddenly to burn as though touched by red-hot pokers. When the "reliefs" went up scores of men could not walk back from the trenches, but had to crawl, or be carried pick-a-back by their comrades, to the field dressing stations. So I saw hundreds of them, and, as the winter dragged on, thousands. The medical officers cut off their boots and their puttees, and the socks that had become part of their skins, exposing blackened and rotting feet. They put oil on them, and wrapped them round with cotton-wool, and tied labels to their tunics with the name of that new disease—"trench-foot." Those medical officers looked serious as the number of cases increased.

"This is getting beyond a joke," they said. "It is pulling down the battalion strength worse than wounds."

Brigadiers and divisional generals were gloomy, and cursed the new affliction of their men. Some of them said it was due to damned carelessness, others were inclined to think it due to deliberate malingering at a time when there were many cases of self-inflicted wounds by men who shot their fingers away, or their toes, to get out of the trenches.

There was no look of malingering on the faces of those boys who were being carried pick-a-back to the ambulance-trains at Remy siding, near Poperinghe, with both feet crippled and tied up in bundles of cotton-wool. The pain was martyrizing, like that of men tied to burning fagots for conscience' sake. In one battalion of the 49th (West Riding) Division there were over four hundred cases in that winter of '15. Other battalions in the Ypres salient suffered as much.

It was not until the end of the winter, when oil was taken up to the trenches and rubbing drill was ordered, two or three times a day, that the malady of trench-foot was reduced, and at last almost eliminated.

The spirit of the men fought against all that misery, resisted it, and would not be beaten by it.

A sergeant of the West Riding Division was badly wounded as he stood thigh-high in water. A bomb or a trench-mortar smashed one of his legs into a pulp of bloody flesh and splintered bone. Word was passed down to the field ambulance, and a surgeon came up, splashed to the neck in mud, with his instruments held high. The operation was done in the water, red with the blood of the wounded man, who was then brought down, less a leg, to the field hospital. He was put on one side as a man about to die... But that evening he chattered cheerfully, joked with the priest who came to anoint him, and wrote a letter to his wife.

"I hope this will find you in the pink, as it leaves me," he began. He mentioned that he had had an "accident" which had taken one of his legs away. "But the youngsters will like to play with my wooden peg," he wrote, and discussed the joke of it. The people round his bed marveled at him, though day after day they saw great courage; such courage as that of another man who was brought in mortally wounded and lay next to a comrade on the operating table.

"Stick it, lad!" he said, "stick it!" and turned his head a little to look at his friend.

Many of our camps were hardly better than the trenches. Only by duck-boards could one walk about the morass in which huts were built and tents were pitched. In the wagon lines gunners tried in vain to groom their horses, and floundered about in their gum boots, cursing the mud which clogged bits and chains and bridles, and could find no comfort anywhere between Dickebusch and Locre.

IV

The Hohenzollern redoubt, near Fosse 8, captured by the 9th Scottish Division in the battle of Loos, could not be held then under concentrated gun-fire from German batteries, and the Scots, and the Guards who followed them, after heavy losses, could only cling on to part of a communication trench (on the southeast side of the earthworks) nicknamed "Big Willie," near another trench called "Little Willie." Our enemies forced their way back into some of their old trenches in this outpost beyond their main lines, and in spite of the chaos produced by our shell-fire built up new parapets and sand-bag barricades, flung out barbed wire, and dug themselves into this graveyard where their dead and ours were strewn.

Perhaps there was some reason why our generals should covet possession of the Hohenzollern redoubt, some good military reason beyond the spell of a high-sounding name. I went up there one day when it was partly ours and stared at its rigid waves of mine-craters and trench parapets and upheaved chalk, dazzling white under a blue sky, and failed to see any beauty in the spot, or any value in it—so close to the German lines that one could not cough for fear of losing one's head. It seemed to me a place not to gain and not to hold. If I had been a general (appalling thought!) I should have said: "Let the enemy have that little hell of his. Let men live there among half-buried bodies and crawling lice, and the stench of rotting flesh. There is no good in it for us, and for him will be an abomination, dreaded by his men."

But our generals desired it. They hated to think that the enemy should have crawled back to it after our men had been there. They decided to "bite it off," that blunt nose which was thrust forward to our line. It was an operation that would be good to report in the official *communique.* Its capture would, no doubt, increase the morale of our men after their dead had been buried and their wounded patched up and their losses forgotten.

It was to the 46th Midland Division that the order of assault was given on October 13th, and into the trenches went the lace-makers of Nottingham, and the potters of the Five Towns, and the boot-makers of Leicester, North Staffordshires, and Robin Hoods and Sherwood Foresters, on the night of the 12th.

On the following morning our artillery concentrated a tremendous fire upon the redoubt, followed at 1 P.M. by volumes of smoke and gas. The chief features on this part of the German line were, on the right, a group of colliers' houses known as the Corons de Pekin, and a slag heap known as the Dump, to the northeast of that bigger dump called Fosse 8, and on the left another group of cottages, and another black hillock farther to the right of the Fosse. These positions were in advance of the Hohenzollern redoubt which our troops were to attack.

It was not an easy task. It was hellish. Intense as our artillery fire had been, it failed to destroy the enemy's barbed wire and front trenches sufficiently to clear the way, and the Germans were still working their machine-guns when the fuses were lengthened, the fire lifted, and the gas-clouds rolled away.

I saw that bombardment on the morning of Wednesday, October 13th, and the beginning of the attack from a slag heap close to some of our heavy guns. It was a fine, clear day, and some of the French miners living round the pit-heads on our side of the battle line climbed up iron ladders and coal heaps, roused to a new interest in the spectacle of war which had become a monotonous and familiar thing in their lives, because the intensity of our gun-fire and the volumes of smoke-clouds, and a certain strange, whitish vapor which was wafted from our lines toward the enemy stirred their imagination, dulled by the daily din of guns, to a sense of something beyond the usual flight of shells

"The English are attacking again!" was the message which brought out these men still living among ruined cottages on the edge of the slaughter-fields. They stared into the mist, where, beyond the brightness of the autumn sun, men were about to fight and die. It was the same scene that I had watched when I went up to the Loos redoubt in the September battle—a flat, bare, black plain, crisscrossed with the whitish earth of the trenches rising a little toward Loos and then falling again so that in the village there only the Tower Bridge was visible, with its steel girders glinting, high over the horizon line. To the left the ruins of Hulluch fretted the low-lying clouds of smoke, and beyond a huddle of broken houses far away was the town of Haisnes. Fosse 8 and the Hohenzollern redoubt were hummocks of earth faintly visible through drifting clouds of thick, sluggish vapor.

On the edge of this battleground the fields were tawny under the golden light of the autumn sun, and the broken towers of village churches, red roofs shattered by shell-fire, trees stripped bare of all leaves before the wind of autumn touched them, were painted in clear outlines against the gray-blue of the sky.

Our guns had been invisible. Not one of all those batteries which were massed over a wide stretch of country could be located before the battle by a searching glass. But when the bombardment began it seemed as though our shells came from every field and village for miles back, behind the lines.

The glitter of those bursting shells stabbed through the smoke of their explosion with little, twinkling flashes, like the sparkle of innumerable mirrors heliographing messages of death. There was one incessant roar rising and falling in waves of prodigious sound. The whole line of battle was in a grayish murk, which obscured all landmarks, so that even the Tower Bridge was but faintly visible.

Presently, when our artillery lifted, there were new clouds rising from the ground and spreading upward in a great dense curtain of a fleecy texture. They came from our smoke-shells, which were to mask our infantry attack. Through them and beyond them rolled another wave of cloud, a thinner, whiter vapor, which clung to the ground and then curled forward to the enemy's lines.

"That's our gas!" said a voice on one of the slag heaps, amid a group of observers—English and French officers.

"And the wind is dead right for it," said another voice. "The Germans will get a taste of it this time!"

Then there was silence, and some of those observers held their breath as though that gas had caught their own throats and choked them a little. They tried to pierce through that bar of cloud to see the drama behind its curtain—men caught in those fumes, the terror-stricken flight before its advance, the sudden cry of the enemy trapped in their dugouts. Imagination leaped out, through invisibility, to the realization of the things that were happening beyond.

From our place of observation there were brief glimpses of the human element in this scene of impersonal powers and secret forces. Across a stretch of flat ground beyond some of those zigzag lines of trenches little black things were scurrying forward. They were not bunched together in close groups, but scattered. Some of them seemed to hesitate, and then to fall and lie where they fell, others hurrying on until they disappeared in the drifting clouds.

It was the foremost line of our infantry attack, led by the bombers. The Germans were firing tempests of shells. Some of them were curiously colored, of a pinkish hue, or with orange-shaped puffs of vivid green. They were poison-shells giving out noxious gases. All the chemistry of death was poured out on both sides—and through it went the men of the Midland Division.

The attack on the right was delivered by a brigade of Staffordshire men, who advanced in four lines toward the Big Willie trench which formed the southeast side of the Hohenzollern redoubt. The leading companies, who were first over our own parapets, made a quick rush, half blinded by the smoke and the gaseous vapors which filled the air, and were at once received by a deadly fire from many machine-guns. It swept their ranks, and men fell on all sides. Others ran on in little parties flung out in extended order.

Young officers behaved with desperate gallantry, and as they fell cheered their men on, while others ran forward shouting, followed by numbers which dwindled at every yard, so that only a few reached the Big Willie trench in the first assault.

A bombing-party of North Staffordshire men cleared thirty yards of the trench by the rapidity with which they flung their hand-grenades at the German bombers who endeavored to keep them out, and again and again they kept at bay a tide of field-gray men, who swarmed up the communication trenches, by a series of explosions which blew many of them to bits as bomb after bomb was hurled into their mass. Other Germans followed, flinging their own stick-bombs.

The Staffordshires did not yield until nearly every man was wounded and many were killed. Even then they retreated yard by yard, still flinging grenades almost with the rhythm of a sower who scatters his seed, each motion of the hand and arm letting go one of those steel pomegranates which burst with the noise of a high-explosive shell.

The survivors fell back to the other side of a barricade made in the Big Willie trench by some of their men behind. Behind them again was another barrier, in case the first should be rushed.

It seemed as if they might be rushed now, for the Germans were swarming up Big Willie with strong bombing-parties, and would soon blast a way through unless they were thrust beyond the range of hand-grenades. It was a young lieutenant named Hawker, with some South Staffordshire men, who went forward to meet this attack and kept the enemy back until four o'clock in the afternoon, when only a few living men stood among the dead and they had to fall back to the second barrier.

Darkness now crept over the battlefield and filled the trenches, and in the darkness the wounded men were carried back to the rear, while those who had escaped worked hard to strengthen their defenses by sand-bags and earthworks, knowing that their only chance of life lay in fierce industry.

Early next morning an attempt was made by other battalions to come to the relief of those who held on behind those barriers in Big Willie trench. They were Nottingham men—Robin Hoods and other Sherwood lads—and they came across the open ground in two directions, attacking the west as well as the east ends of the German communication trenches which formed the face of the Hohenzollern redoubt.

They were supported by rifle grenade-fire, but their advance was met by intense fire from artillery and machine-guns, so that many were blown to bits or mangled or maimed, and none could reach their comrades in Big Willie trench.

While one brigade of the Midland men had been fighting like this on the right, another brigade had been engaged on the left. It contained Sherwood, Leicester, and Lincoln men, who, on the afternoon of October 13th, went forward to the assault with very desperate endeavor. Advancing in four lines, the leading companies were successful in reaching the Hohenzollern redoubt, smashed through the barbed wire, part of which was uncut, and reached the Fosse trench which forms the north base of the salient.

Machine-gun fire cut down the first two lines severely and the two remaining lines were heavily shelled by German artillery. It was an hour in which the courage of those men was agonized. They were exposed on naked ground swept by bullets, the atmosphere was heavy with gas and smoke; all the abomination of battle—he moaning of the wounded, the last cries of the dying, the death-crawl of stricken beings holding their broken limbs and their entrails—was around them, and in front a hidden enemy with unlimited supplies of ammunition and a better position.

The Robin Hoods and the men of Lincoln and Leicestershire were sustained in that shambles by the spirit that had come to them through the old yeoman stock in which their traditions were rooted, and those who had not fallen went forward, past their wounded comrades, past these poor, bloody, moaning men, to the German trenches behind the redoubt.

At 2.15 P.M. some Monmouth men came up in support, and while their bombers were at work some of the Lincolns pushed up with a machine-gun to a point within sixty yards from the Fosse trench, where they stayed till dark, and then were forced to fall back.

At this time parties of bombers were trying to force their way up the Little Willie trench on the extreme left of the redoubt, and here ghastly fighting took place. Some of the Leicesters made a dash three hundred yards up the trench, but were beaten back by overpowering numbers of German bombers and bayonet-men, and again and again other Midland lads went up that alleyway of death, flinging their grenades until they fell or until few comrades were left to support them as they stood among their dead and dying.

Single men held on, throwing and throwing, until there was no strength in their arms to hurl another bomb, or until death came to them. Yet the business went on through the darkness of the afternoon, and into the deeper darkness of the night, lit luridly at moments by the white illumination of German flares and by the flash of bursting shells.

Isolated machine-guns in uncaptured parts of the redoubt still beat a tattoo like the ruffle of war-drums, and from behind the barriers in the Big Willie trench came the sharp crack of English rifles, and dull explosions of other bombs flung by other Englishmen very hard pressed that night.

In the outer trenches, at the nose of the salient, fresh companies of Sherwood lads were feeling their way along, mixed up confusedly with comrades from other companies, wounded or spent with fighting, but determined to hold the ground they had won.

Some of the Robin Hoods up Little Willie trench were holding out desperately and almost at the last gasp, when they were relieved by other Sherwoods, and it was here that a young officer named Vickers was found in the way that won him his V.C.

Charles Geoffrey Vickers stood there for hours against a horde of men eager for his death, eager to get at the men behind him. But they could not approach. He and his fellow-bombers kept twenty yards or more clear before them, and any man who flung himself forward was the target of a hand-grenade.

From front and from flank German bombs came whizzing, falling short sometimes, with a blasting roar that tore down lumps of trench, and sometimes falling very close—close enough to kill.

Vickers saw some of his best men fall, but he kept the barrier still intact by bombing and bombing.

When many of his comrades were dead or wounded, he wondered how long the barrier would last, and gave orders for another to be built behind him, so that when the rush came it would be stopped behind him—and over him.

Men worked at that barricade, piling up sand-bags, and as it was built that young lieutenant knew that his own retreat was being cut off and that he was being coffined in that narrow space. Two other men were with him—I never learned their names—and they were hardly enough to hand up bombs as quickly as he wished to throw them.

Away there up the trench the Germans were waiting for a pounce. Though wounded so that he felt faint and giddy, he called out for more bombs. "More!" he said, "More!" and his hand was like a machine reaching out and throwing.

Rescue came at last, and the wounded officer was hauled over the barricade which he had ordered to be built behind him, closing up his way of escape.

All through October 14th the Midland men of the 46th Division held on to their ground, and some of the Sherwoods made a new attack, clearing the enemy out of the east portion of the redoubt.

It was lucky that it coincided with a counter-attack made by the enemy at a different point, because it relieved the pressure there. Bombing duels continued hour after hour, and human nature could hardly have endured so long a struggle without fatigue beyond the strength of men.

So it seems; yet when a brigade of Guards came up on the night of October 15th the enemy attacked along the whole line of redoubts, and the Midland men, who were just about to leave the trenches, found themselves engaged in a new action. They had to fight again before they could go, and they fought like demons or demigods for their right of way and home, and bombed the enemy back to his holes in the ground.

So ended the assault on the Hohenzollern by the Midland men of England, whose division, years later, helped to break the Hindenburg line along the great canal south of St.-Quentin.

What good came of it mortal men cannot say, unless the generals who planned it hold the secret. It cost a heavy price in life and agony. It demonstrated the fighting spirit of many English boys who did the best they could, with the rage, and fear, and madness of great courage, before they died or fell, and it left some living men, and others who relieved them in Big Willie and Little Willie trenches, so close to the enemy that one could hear them cough, or swear in guttural whispers.

And through the winter of '15, and the years that followed, the Hohenzollern redoubt became another Hooge, as horrible as Hooge, as deadly, as damnable in its filthy perils, where men of English blood, and Irish, and Scottish, took their turn, and hated it, and counted themselves lucky if they escaped from its prison-house, whose walls stank of new and ancient death.

* * * * *

Among those who took their turn in the hell of the Hohenzollern were the men of the 12th Division, New Army men, and all of the old stock and spirit of England, bred in the shires of Norfolk and Suffolk, Gloucester and Bedford, and in Surrey, Kent, Sussex, and Middlesex (which meant London), as the names of their battalions told. In September they relieved the Guards and cavalry at Loos; in December they moved on to Givenchy, and in February they began a long spell at the Hohenzollern. It was there the English battalions learned the worst things of war and showed the quality of English courage.

A man of Kent, named Corporal Cotter, of the Buffs, was marvelous in spirit, stronger than the flesh.

On the night of March 6th an attack was made by his company along an enemy trench, but his own bombing—party was cut off, owing to heavy casualties in the center of the attack. Things looked serious and Cotter went back under heavy fire to report and bring up more bombs.

On the return journey his right leg was blown off close below the knee and he was wounded in both arms. By a kind of miracle—the miracle of human courage—he did not drop down and die in the mud of the trench, mud so deep that unwounded men found it hard to walk—but made his way along fifty yards of trench toward the crater where his comrades were hard pressed. He came up to Lance-corporal Newman, who was bombing with his sector to the right of the position. Cotter called to him and directed him to bomb six feet toward where help was most needed, and worked his way forward to the crater where the Germans had developed a violent counter-attack.

Men fell rapidly under the enemy's bomb-fire, but Cotter, with only one leg, and bleeding from both arms, steadied his comrades, who were beginning to have the wind-up, as they say, issued orders, controlled the fire, and then altered dispositions to meet the attack. It was repulsed after two hours' fighting, and only then did Cotter allow his wounds to be bandaged. From the dug—out where he lay while the bombardment still continued he called out cheery words to the men, until he was carried down, fourteen hours later. He received the V. C., but died of his wounds.

Officers and men vied with one another, yet not for honor or reward, round these craters of the Hohenzollern, and in the mud, and the fumes of shells, and rain-swept darkness, and all the black horror of such a time and place, sometimes in groups and sometimes quite alone, did acts of supreme valor. When all the men in one of these infernal craters were dead or wounded Lieut. Lea Smith, of the Buffs, ran forward with a Lewis gun, helped by

Private Bradley, and served it during a fierce attack by German bombers until it jammed.

Then he left the gun and took to bombing, and that single figure of his, flinging grenades like an overarm bowler, kept the enemy at bay until reinforcements reached him.

Another officer of the Buff's—by name Smeltzer—withdrew his platoon under heavy fire, and, although he was wounded, fought his way back slowly to prevent the enemy from following up. The men were proud of his gallantry, but when he was asked what he had done he could think of nothing except that "when the Boches began shelling I got into a dugout, and when they stopped I came out again."

There were many men like that who did amazing things and, in the English way, said nothing of them. Of that modesty was Capt. Augrere Dawson, of the West Kents, who did not bother much about a bullet he met on his way to a crater, though it traveled through his chest to his shoulder-blade. He had it dressed, and then went back to lead his men, and remained with them until the German night attack was repulsed. He was again wounded, this time in the thigh, but did not trouble the stretcher-men (they had a lot to do on the night of March 18th and 19th), and trudged back alone.

It was valor that was paid for by flesh and blood. The honors gained by the 12th Division in a few months of trench warfare—one V. C., sixteen D. S. C.'s, forty-five Military Crosses, thirty-four Military Medals—were won by the loss in casualties of more than fourteen thousand men. That is to say, the losses of their division in that time, made up by new drafts, was 100 per cent.; and the Hohenzollern took the highest toll of life and limbs.

V

I heard no carols in the trenches on Christmas Eve in 1915, but afterward, when I sat with a pint of water in each of my top-boots, among a company of men who were wet to the knees and slathered with moist mud, a friend of mine raised his hand and said, "Listen!"

Through the open door came the music of a mouth—organ, and it was playing an old tune:

God rest ye, merry gentlemen.
Let nothing you dismay,
For Jesus Christ, our Saviour,
Was born on Christmas Day.

Outside the wind was howling across Flanders with a doleful whine, rising now and then into a savage violence which rattled the window-panes, and beyond the booming of its lower notes was the faint, dull rumble of distant guns.

"Christmas Eve!" said an officer. "Nineteen hundred and fifteen years ago... and now—this!"

He sighed heavily, and a few moments later told a funny story, which was followed by loud laughter. And so it was, I think, in every billet in Flanders and in every dugout that Christmas Eve, where men thought of the meaning of the day, with its message of peace and goodwill, and contrasted it with the great, grim horror of the war, and spoke a few words of perplexity; and then, after that quick sigh (how many comrades had gone since last Christmas Day!), caught at a jest, and had the courage of laughter. It was queer to find the spirit of Christmas, the little tendernesses of the old tradition, the toys and trinkets of its feast-day, in places where Death had been busy—and where the spirit of evil lay in ambush!

So it was when I went through Armentieres within easy range of the enemy's guns. Already six hundred civilians—mostly women and children—had been killed there. But, still, other women were chatting together through broken window-panes, and children were staring into little shops (only a few yards away from broken roofs and shell-broken walls) where Christmas toys were on sale.

A wizened boy, in a pair of soldier's boots—a French Hop o' My Thumb in the giant's boots—was gazing wistfully at some tin soldiers, and inside the shop a real soldier, not a bit like the tin one, was buying some Christmas cards worked by a French artist in colored wools for the benefit of English Tommies, with the aid of a dictionary. Other soldiers read their legends and laughed at them: "My heart is to you." "Good luck." "To the success!" "Remind France."

The man who was buying the cards fumbled with French money, and looked up sheepishly at me, as if shy of the sentiment upon which he was spending it.

"The people at home will be glad of 'em," he said. "I s'pose one can't forget Christmas altogether. Though it ain't the same thing out here."

Going in search of Christmas, I passed through a flooded countryside and found only scenes of war behind the lines, with gunners driving their batteries and limber down a road that had become a river-bed, fountains of spray rising about their mules and wheels, military motor-cars lurching in the mud beyond the pave, despatch-riders side-slipping in a wild way through boggy tracks, supply—columns churning up deep ruts.

And then into the trenches at Neuve Chapelle. If Santa Claus had come that way, remembering those grown-up boys of ours, the old man with his white beard must have lifted his red gown high—waist-high—when he waded up some of the communication trenches to the firing-lines, and he would have staggered and slithered, now with one top-boot deep in sludge, now with the other slipping off the trench boards into five feet of water, as I had to do, grasping with futile hands at slimy sandbags to save a headlong plunge into icy water.

And this old man of peace, who loved all boys and the laughter of youth, would have had to duck very low and make sudden bolts across open spaces, where parapets and earthworks had silted down, in order to avoid those sniping bullets which came snapping across the dead ground from a row of slashed trees and a few scarred ruins on the edge of the enemy's lines.

But sentiment of that sort was out of place in trenches less than a hundred yards away from men lying behind rifles and waiting to kill.

There was no spirit of Christmas in the tragic desolation of the scenery of which I had brief glimpses when I stood here and there nakedly (I felt) in those ugly places, when the officer who was with me said, "It's best to get a move on here," and, "This road is swept by machine—gun fire," and, "I don't like this corner; it's quite unhealthy."

But that absurd idea—of Santa Claus in the trenches—came into my head several times, and I wondered whether the Germans would fire a whizz-bang at him or give a burst of machine-gun fire if they caught the glint of his red cloak.

Some of the soldiers had the same idea. In the front-line trench a small group of Yorkshire lads were chaffing one another.

"Going to hang your boots up outside the dugout?" asked a lad, grinning down at an enormous pair of waders belonging to a comrade.

"Likely, ain't it?" said the other boy. "Father Christmas would be a bloody fool to come out here... They'd be full of water in the morning."

"You'll get some presents," I said. "They haven't forgotten you at home."

At that word "home" the boy flushed and something went soft in his eyes for a moment. In spite of his steel helmet and mud-stained uniform, he was a girlish-looking fellow—perhaps that was why his comrades were chaffing him—and I fancy the thought of Christmas made him yearn back to some village in Yorkshire.

Most of the other men with whom I spoke treated the idea of Christmas with contemptuous irony.

"A happy Christmas!" said one of them, with a laugh. "Plenty of crackers about this year! Tom Smith ain't in it."

"And I hope we're going to give the Boches some Christmas presents," said another. "They deserve it, I don't think!"

"No truce this year?" I asked.

"A truce?... We're not going to allow any monkey—tricks on the parapets. To hell with Christmas charity and all that tosh. We've got to get on with the war. That's my motto."

Other men said: "We wouldn't mind a holiday. We're fed up to the neck with all this muck."

The war did not stop, although it was Christmas Eve, and the only carol I heard in the trenches was the loud, deep chant of the guns on both sides, and the shrill soprano of whistling shells, and the rattle on the keyboards of machine-guns. The enemy was putting more shells into a bit of trench in revenge for a raid. To the left some shrapnel shells were bursting, and behind the lines our "heavies" were busily at work firing at long range.

"On earth peace, good-will toward men."

The message was spoken at many a little service on both sides of that long line where great armies were entrenched with their death-machines, and the riddle of life and faith was rung out by the Christmas bells which came clashing on the rain-swept wind, with the reverberation of great guns.

Through the night our men in the trenches stood in their waders, and the dawn of Christmas Day was greeted, not by angelic songs, but by the splutter of rifle-bullets all along the line.

VI

There was more than half a gale blowing on the eve of the new year, and the wind came howling with a savage violence across the rain-swept fields, so that the first day of a fateful year had a stormy birth, and there was no peace on earth.

Louder than the wind was the greeting of the guns to another year of war. I heard the New-Year's chorus when I went to see the last of the year across the battlefields. Our guns did not let it die in silence. It went into the tomb of the past, with all its tragic memories, to thunderous salvos, carrying death with them. The "heavies" were indulging in a special strafe this New—Year's eve. As I went down a road near the lines by Loos I saw, from concealed positions, the flash of gun upon gun. The air was swept by an incessant rush of shells, and the roar of all this artillery stupefied one's sense of sound. All about me in the village of Annequin, through which I walked, there was no other sound, no noise of human life. There were no New-Year's eve rejoicings among those rows of miners' cottages on the edge of the battlefield. Half those little red-brick houses were blown to pieces, and when here and there through a cracked window-pane I saw a woman's white face peering out upon me as I passed I felt as though I had seen a ghost-face in some black pit of hell.

For it was hellish, this place wrecked by high explosives and always under the fire of German guns. That any human being should be there passed all belief. From a shell-hole in a high wall I looked across the field of battle, where many of our best had died. The Tower Bridge of Loos stood grim and gaunt above the sterile fields. Through the rain and the mist loomed the long black ridge of Notre Dame de Lorette, where many poor bodies lay in the rotting leaves. The ruins of Haisnes and Hulluch were jagged against the sky-line. And here, on New—Year's eve, I saw no sign of human life and heard no sound of it, but stared at the broad desolation and listened to the enormous clangor of great guns.

* * * * *

Coming back that day through Bethune I met some very human life. It was a big party of bluejackets from the Grand Fleet, who had come to see what "Tommy" was doing in the war. They went into the trenches and saw a good deal, because the Germans made a bombing raid in that sector and the naval men did their little bit by the side of the lads in khaki, who liked this visit. They discovered the bomb store and opened such a Brock's benefit that the enemy must have been shocked with surprise. One young marine was bomb-slinging for four hours, and grinned at the prodigious memory as though he had had the time of his life. Another confessed to me that he preferred rifle-grenades, which he fired off all night until the dawn. There was no sleep in the dugouts, and every hour was a long thrill.

"I don't mind saying," said a petty officer who had fought in several naval actions during the war and is a man of mark, "that I had a fair fright when I was doing duty on the fire-step. 'I suppose I've got to look through a periscope,' I said. 'Not you,' said the sergeant. 'At night you puts your head over the parapet.' So over the parapet I put my head, and presently I saw something moving between the lines. My rifle began to shake. Germans! Moving, sure enough, over the open ground. I fixed bayonet and prepared for an attack... But I'm blessed if it wasn't a swarm of rats!"

The soldiers were glad to show Jack the way about the trenches, and some of them played up a little audaciously, as, for instance, when a young fellow sat on the top of the parapet at dawn.

"Come up and have a look, Jack," he said to one of the bluejackets.

"Not in these trousers, old mate!" said that young man.

"All as cool as cucumbers," said a petty officer, "and take the discomforts of trench life as cheerily as any men could. It's marvelous. Good luck to them in the new year!"

* * * * *

Behind the lines there was banqueting by men who were mostly doomed to die, and I joined a crowd of them in a hall at Lillers on that New-Year's day.

They were the heroes of Loos—or some of them—Camerons and Seaforths, Argyll and Sutherland Highlanders, Gordons and King's Own Scottish Borderers, who, with the London men, were first on Hill 70 and away to the Cite St.-Auguste. They left many comrades there, and their battalions have been filled up with new drafts—of the same type as themselves and of the same grit—but that day no ghost of grief, no dark shadow of gloom, was upon any of the faces upon which I looked round a festive board in a long, French hall, to which their wounded came in those days of the September battle.

There were young men there from the Scottish universities and from Highland farms, sitting shoulder to shoulder in a jolly comradeship which burst into song between every mouthful of the feast. On the platform above the banqueting-board a piper was playing, when I came in, and this hall in France was filled with the wild strains of it.

"And they're grand, the pipes," said one of the Camerons. "When I've been sae tired on the march I could have laid doon an' dee'd the touch o' the pipes has fair lifted me up agen."

The piper made way for a Kiltie at the piano, and for Highlanders, who sang old songs full of melancholy, which seemed to make the hearts of his comrades grow glad as when they helped him with "The Bonnie, Bonnie Banks of Loch Lomond." But the roof nearly flew off the hall to "The March of the Cameron Men," and the walls were greatly strained when the regimental marching song broke at every verse into wild Highland shouts and the war-cry which was heard at Loos of "Camerons, forward!" "Forward, Camerons!"

"An Englishman is good," said one of the Camerons, leaning over the table to me, "and an Irishman is good, but a Scot is the best of all." Then he struck the palm of one hand with the fist of another. "But the London men," he said, with a fine, joyous laugh at some good memory, "are as good as any fighting-men in France. My word, ye should have seen 'em on September 25th. And the London Irish were just lions!"

Out in the rain-slashed street I met the colonel of a battalion of Argylls and Sutherlands, with several of his officers; a tall, thin officer with a long stride, who was killed when another year had passed. He beckoned to me and said: "I'm going the rounds of the billets to wish the men good luck in the new year. It's a strain on the constitution, as I have to drink their health each time!"

He bore the strain gallantly, and there was something noble and chivalrous in the way he spoke to all his men, gathered together in various rooms in old Flemish houses, round plum-pudding from home or feasts provided by the army cooks. To each group of men he made the same kind of speech, thanking them from his heart for all their courage.

"You were thanked by three generals," he said, "after your attack at Loos, and you upheld the old reputation of the regiment. I'm proud of you. And afterward, in November, when you had the devil of a time in the trenches, you stuck it splendidly and came out with high spirits. I wish you all a happy new year, and whatever the future may bring I know I can count on you."

In every billet there were three cheers for the colonel, and another three for the staff captain, and though the colonel protested that he was afraid of spending a night in the guard-room (there were shouts of laughter at this), he drank his sip of neat whisky, according to the custom of the day.

"Toodle-oo, old bird!" said a kilted cockney, halfway up a ladder, on which he swayed perilously, being very drunk; but the colonel did not hear this familiar way of address.

In many billets and in many halls the feast of New Year's day was kept in good comradeship by men who had faced death together, and who in the year that was coming fought in many battles and fell on many fields.

VII

The Canadians who were in the Ypres salient in January, 1916, and for a long time afterward, had a grim way of fighting. The enemy never knew what they might do next. When they were most quiet they were most dangerous. They used cunning as well as courage, and went out on red-Indian adventures over No Man's Land for fierce and scientific slaughter.

I remember one of their early raids in the salient, when a big party of them—all volunteers—went out one night with intent to get through the barbed wire outside a strong German position, to do a lot of killing there. They had trained for the job and thought out every detail of this hunting expedition. They blacked their faces so that they would not show white in the enemy's flares. They fastened flash-lamps to their bayonets so that they might see their victims. They wore rubber gloves to save their hands from being torn on the barbs of the wire.

Stealthily they crawled over No Man's Land, crouching in shell-holes every time a rocket rose and made a glimmer of light. They took their time at the wire, muffling the snap of it by bits of cloth. Reliefs crawled up with more gloves, and even with tins of hot cocoa. Then through the gap into the German trenches, and there were screams of German soldiers, terror-shaken by the flash of light in their eyes, and black faces above them, and bayonets already red with blood. It was butcher's work, quick and skilful, like red-Indian scalping. Thirty Germans were killed before the Canadians went back, with only two casualties... The Germans were horrified by this sudden slaughter. They dared not come out on patrol work. Canadian scouts crawled down to them and insulted them, ingeniously, vilely, but could get no answer. Later they trained their machine—guns on German working-parties and swept crossroads on which supplies came up, and the Canadian sniper, in one shell-hole or another, lay for hours in sulky patience, and at last got his man... They had to pay for all this, at Maple Copse, in June of '15, as I shall tell. But it was a vendetta which did not end until the war ended, and the Canadians fought the Germans with a long, enduring, terrible, skilful patience which at last brought them to Mons on the day before armistice.

I saw a good deal of the Canadians from first to last, and on many days of battle saw the tough, hard fighting spirit of these men. Their generals believed in common sense applied to war, and not in high mysteries and secret rites which cannot be known outside the circle of initiation. I was impressed by General Currie, whom I met for the first time in that winter of 1915-16, and wrote at the time that I saw in him "a leader of men who in open warfare might win great victories by doing the common-sense thing rapidly and decisively, to the surprise of an enemy working by elaborate science. He would, I think, astound them by the simplicity of his smashing stroke." Those words of mine were fulfilled—on the day when the Canadians helped to break the Drocourt-Queant line, and when they captured Cambrai, with English troops on their right, who shared their success. General Currie, who became the Canadian Corps Commander, did not spare his men. He led them forward whatever the cost, but there was something great and terrible in his simplicity and sureness of judgment, and this real—estate agent (as he was before he took to soldiering) was undoubtedly a man of strong ability, free from those trammels of red tape and tradition which swathed round so many of our own leaders.

He cut clean to the heart of things, ruthlessly, like a surgeon, and as I watched that man, immense in bulk, with a heavy, thoughtful face and stern eyes that softened a little when he smiled, I thought of him as Oliver Cromwell. He was severe as a disciplinarian, and not beloved by many men. But his staff-officers, who stood in awe of him, knew that he demanded truth and honesty, and that his brain moved quickly to sure decisions and saw big problems broadly and with understanding. He had good men with him—mostly amateurs—but with hard business heads and the same hatred of red tape and niggling ways which belonged to their chief. So the Canadian Corps became a powerful engine on our side when it had learned many lessons in blood and tragedy. They organized their publicity side in the same masterful way, and were determined that what Canada did the world should know—and damn all censorship. They bought up English artists, photographers, and writing—men to record their exploits. With Lord Beaverbrook in England they engineered Canadian propaganda with immense energy, and Canada believed her men made up the British army and did all the fighting. I do not blame them, and only wish that the English soldier should have been given his share of the honors that belonged to him—the lion's share.

VIII

The Canadians were not the only men to go out raiding. It became part of the routine of war, that quick killing in the night, for English and Scottish and Irish and Welsh troops, and some had luck with it, and some men liked it, and to others it was a horror which they had to do, and always it was a fluky, nervy job, when any accident might lead to tragedy.

I remember one such raid by the 12th West Yorks in January of '15, which was typical of many others, before raids developed into minor battles, with all the guns at work.

There were four lieutenants who drew up the plan and called for volunteers, and it was one of these who went out first and alone to reconnoiter the ground and to find the best way through the German barbed wire. He just slipped out over the parapet and disappeared into the darkness. When he came back he had a wound in the wrist—it was just the bad luck of a chance bullet—but brought in valuable knowledge. He had found a gap in the enemy's wire which would give an open door to the party of visitors. He had also tested the wire farther along, and thought it could be cut without much bother.

"Good enough!" was the verdict, and a detachment started out for No Man's Land, divided into two parties.

The enemy trenches were about one hundred yards away, which seems a mile in the darkness and the loneliness of the dead ground. At regular intervals the German rockets flared up so that the hedges and wire and parapets along their line were cut out ink-black against the white illumination, and the two patrols of Yorkshiremen who had been crawling forward stopped and crouched lower and felt themselves revealed, and then when darkness hid them again went on.

The party on the left were now close to the German wire and under the shelter of a hedge. They felt their way along until the two subalterns who were leading came to the gap which had been reported by the first explorer. They listened intently and heard the German sentry stamping his feet and pacing up and down. Presently he began to whistle softly, utterly unconscious of the men so close to him—so close now that any stumble, any clatter of arms, any word spoken, would betray them.

The two lieutenants had their revolvers ready and crept forward to the parapet. The men had to act according to instinct now, for no order could be given, and one of them found his instinct led him to clamber right into the German trench a few yards away from the sentry, but on the other side of the traverse. He had not been there long, holding his breath and crouching like a wolf, before footsteps came toward him and he saw the glint of a cigarette.

It was a German officer going his round. The Yorkshire boy sprang on to the parapet again, and lay across it with his head toward our lines and his legs dangling in the German trench. The German officer's cloak brushed his heels, but the boy twisted round a little and stared at him as he passed. But he passed, and presently the sentry began to whistle again, some old German tune which cheered him in his loneliness. He knew nothing of the eyes watching him through the darkness nor of his nearness to death.

It was the first lieutenant who tried to shoot him. But the revolver was muddy and would not fire. Perhaps a click disturbed the sentry. Anyhow, the moment had come for quick work. It was the sergeant who sprang upon him, down from the parapet with one pounce. A frightful shriek, with the shrill agony of a boy's voice, wailed through the silence. The sergeant had his hand about the German boy's throat and tried to strangle him and to stop another dreadful cry.

The second officer made haste. He thrust his revolver close to the struggling sentry and shot him dead, through the neck, just as he was falling limp from a blow on the head given by the butt-end of the weapon which had failed to fire. The bullet did its work, though it passed through the sergeant's hand, which had still held the man by the throat. The alarm had been raised and German soldiers were running to the rescue.

"Quick!" said one of the officers.

There was a wild scramble over the parapet, a drop into the wet ditch, and a race for home over No Man's Land, which was white under the German flares and noisy with the waspish note of bullets.

The other party were longer away and had greater trouble to find a way through, but they, too, got home, with one officer badly wounded, and wonderful luck to escape so lightly. The enemy suffered from "the jumps" for several nights afterward, and threw bombs into their own barbed wire, as though the English were out there again. And at the sound of those bombs the West Yorks laughed all along their trenches.

IX

It was always astonishing, though afterward familiar in those battlefields of Flanders, to find oneself in the midst of so many nationalities and races and breeds of men belonging to that British family of ours which sent its sons to sacrifice. In those trenches there were all the ways of speech, all the sentiment of place and history, all the creeds and local customs and songs of old tradition which belong to the mixture of our blood wherever it is found about the world.

The skirl of the Scottish bagpipes was heard through all the years of war over the Flemish marshlands, and there were Highlanders and Lowlanders with every dialect over the border. In one line of trenches the German soldiers listened to part-songs sung in such trained harmony that it was as if a battalion of opera-singers had come into the firing-line. The Welshmen spoke their own language. For a time no officer received his command unless he spoke it as fluently as running water by Aberystwyth, and even orders were given in this tongue until a few Saxons, discovered in the ranks, failed to form fours and know their left hand from their right in Welsh.

The French-Canadians did not need to learn the language of the peasants in these market towns. Soldiers from Somerset used many old Saxon words which puzzled their cockney friends, and the Lancashire men brought the northern bur with them and the grit of the northern spirit. And Ireland, though she would not have conscription, sent some of the bravest of her boys out there, and in all the bloodiest battles since that day at Mons the old fighting qualities of the Irish race shone brightly again, and the blood of her race has been poured out upon these tragic fields.

One of the villages behind the lines of Arras was so crowded with Irish boys at the beginning of '16 that I found it hard not to believe that a part of old Ireland itself had found its way to Flanders. In one old outhouse the cattle had not been evicted. Twelve Flemish cows lay cuddled up together on the ground floor in damp straw, which gave out a sweet, sickly stench, while the Irish soldiers lived upstairs in the loft, to which they climbed up a tall ladder with broken rungs.

I went up the ladder after them—it was very shaky in the middle—and, putting my head through the loft, gave a greeting to a number of dark figures lying in the same kind of straw that I had smelled downstairs. One boy was sitting with his back to the beams, playing a penny whistle very softly to himself, or perhaps to the rats under the straws.

"The craytures are that bold," said a boy from County Cork, "that when we first came in they sat up smilin' and sang 'God Save Ireland.' Bedad, and it's the truth I'm after tellin' ye."

The billets were wet and dirty. But it was good to be away from the shells, even if the rain came through the beams of a broken roof and soaked through the plaster of wattle walls. The Irish boys were good at making wood fires in these old barns and pigsties, if there were a few bricks about to make a hearth, and, sure, a baked potato was no Protestant with a grudge against the Pope.

There were no such luxuries in the trenches when the Dublins and the Munsters were up in the firing-line at the Hohenzollern. The shelling was so violent that it was difficult to get up the supplies, and some of the boys had to fall back on their iron rations. It was the only complaint which one of them made when I asked him what he thought of his first experience under fire.

"It was all right, sorr, and not so bad as I'd been after thinking, if only my appetite had not been bigger than my belt, at all."

The spirit of these Irishmen was shown by some who had just come out from the old country to join their comrades in the firing-line. When the Germans put over a number of shells, smashing the trenches and wounding men, the temper of the lads broke out, and they wanted to get over the parapet and make a dash for the enemy. "'Twould taych him a lesson," they told their officers, who had some trouble in restraining them.

These newcomers had to take part in the digging which goes on behind the lines at night—out in the open, without the shelter of a trench. It was nervous work, especially when the German flares went up, silhouetting their figures on the sky-line, and when one of the enemy's machine-guns began to chatter. But the Irish boys found the heart for a jest, and one of them, resting on his spade a moment, stared over to the enemy's lines and said, "May the old devil take the spalpeen who works that typewriter!"

It was a scaring, nerve-racking time for those who had come fresh to the trenches, some of those boys who had not guessed the realities of war until then. But they came out proudly—"with their tails up," said one of their officers—after their baptism of fire.

The drum-and-fife band of the Munsters was practising in an old barn on the wayside, and presently, in honor of visitors—who were myself and another—the pipers were sent for. They were five tall lads, who came striding down the street of Flemish cottages, with the windbags under their arms, and then, with the fife men sitting on the straw around them and the drummers standing with their sticks ready, they took their breath for "the good old Irish tune" demanded by the captain.

It was a tune which men could not sing very safely in Irish yesterdays, and it held the passion of many rebellious hearts and the yearning of them.

Oh, Paddy dear, and did you hear the news that's going round? The shamrock is forbid by law to grow on Irish ground.

She's the most distressful country that ever yet was seen; They're hanging men and women there for wearing of the green.

Then the pipers played the "March of O'Neill," a wild old air as shrill and fierce as the spirit of the men who came with their Irish battle-cries against Elizabeth's pikemen and Cromwell's Ironsides.

I thought then that the lads who still stayed back in Ireland, and the old people there, would have been glad to stand with me outside that Flemish barn and to hear the old tunes of their race played by the boys who were out there fighting.

I think they would have wept a little, as I saw tears in the eyes of an Irish soldier by my side, for it was the spirit of Ireland herself, with all her poetry, and her valor, and her faith in liberty, which came crying from those pipes, and I wished that the sound of them could carry across the sea.

That was a year before I saw the Irish battalions come out of Guichy, a poor remnant of the strength that had gone in, all tattered and torn, and caked with the filth of battle, and hardly able to stagger along. But they pulled themselves up a little, and turned eyes left when they passed their brigadier, who called out words of praise to them.

It was more than a year later than that when I saw the last of them, after a battle in Flanders, when they were massacred, and lay in heaps round German redoubts, up there in the swamps.

X

Early in the morning of February 23d there was a clear sky with a glint of sun in it, and airplanes were aloft as though it would be a good flying-day. But before midday the sky darkened and snow began to fall, and then it snowed steadily for hours, so that all the fields of Flanders were white.

There was a strange, new beauty in the war zone which had changed all the pictures of war by a white enchantment. The villages where our soldiers were billeted looked as though they were expecting a visit from Santa Claus. The snow lay thick on the thatch and in soft, downy ridges on the red-tiled roofs. It covered, with its purity, the rubbish heaps in Flemish farmyards and the old oak beams of barns and sheds where British soldiers made their beds of straw. Away over the lonely country which led to the trenches, every furrow in the fields was a thin white ridge, and the trees, which were just showing a shimmer of green, stood ink-black against the drifting snow-clouds, with a long white streak down each tall trunk on the side nearest to the wind. The old windmills of Flanders which looked down upon the battlefields had been touched by the softly falling flakes, so that each rib of their sails and each rung of their ladders and each plank of their ancient timbers was outlined like a frosty cobweb.

Along the roads of war our soldiers tramped through the blizzard with ermine mantles over their mackintosh capes, and mounted men with their heads bent to the storm were like white knights riding through a white wilderness. The long columns of motor-lorries, the gun—limbers drawn up by their batteries, the field ambulances by the clearing hospitals, were all cloaked in snow, and the tramp and traffic of an army were hushed in the great quietude.

In the trenches the snow fell thickly and made white pillows of the piled sand-bags and snow-men of sentries standing in the shelter of the traverses.

The tarpaulin roofs and timbered doorways of dugouts were so changed by the snowflakes that they seemed the dwelling-places of fairy folks or, at least, of Pierrot and Columbine in a Christmas hiding-place, and not of soldiers stamping their feet and blowing on their fingers and keeping their rifles dry.

In its first glamour of white the snow gave a beauty even to No Man's Land, making a lace-work pattern of barbed wire, and lying very softly over the tumbled ground of mine-fields, so that all the ugliness of destruction and death was hidden under this canopy. The snowflakes fluttered upon stark bodies there, and shrouded them tenderly. It was as though all the doves of peace were flying down to fold their wings above the obscene things of war.

For a little while the snow brought something like peace. The guns were quieter, for artillery observation was impossible. There could be no sniping, for the scurrying flakes put a veil between the trenches. The airplanes which went up in the morning came down quickly to the powdered fields and took shelter in their sheds. A great hush was over the war zone, but there was something grim, suggestive of tragic drama, in this silent countryside, so white even in the darkness, where millions of men were waiting to kill one another.

Behind the lines the joke of the snow was seen by soldiers, who were quick to see a chance of fun. Men who had been hurling bombs in the Ypres salient bombarded one another with hand-grenades, which burst noiselessly except for the shouts of laughter that signaled a good hit.

French soldiers were at the same game in one village I passed, where the snow-fight was fast and furious, and some of our officers led an attack upon old comrades with the craft of trappers and an expert knowledge of enfilade fire. The white peace did not last long. The ermine mantle on the battlefield was stained by scarlet patches as soon as men could see to fight again.

XI

For some days in that February of 1916 the war correspondents in the Chateau of Tilques, from which they made their expeditions to the line, were snowed up like the army round them. Not even the motor-cars could move through that snow which drifted across the roads. We sat indoors talking—high treason sometimes—pondering over the problem of a war from which there seemed no way out, becoming irritable with one another's company, becoming passionate in argument about the ethics of war, the purpose of man, the gospel of Christ, the guilt of Germany, and the dishonesty of British politicians. Futile, foolish arguments, while men were being killed in great numbers, as daily routine, without result!

Officers of a division billeted nearby came in to dine with us, some of them generals with elaborate theories on war and a passionate hatred of

Germany, seeing no other evil in the world; some of them brigadiers with tales of appalling brutality (which caused great laughter), some of them battalion officers with the point of view of those who said, *"Morituri te saluant!"*

There was one whose conversation I remember (having taken notes of it before I turned in that night). It was a remarkable conversation, summing up many things of the same kind which I had heard in stray sentences by other officers, and month by month, years afterward, heard again, spoken with passion. This officer who had come out to France in 1914 and had been fighting ever since by a luck which had spared his life when so many of his comrades had fallen round him, did not speak with passion. He spoke with a bitter, mocking irony. He said that G.H.Q. was a close corporation in the hands of the military clique who had muddled through the South African War, and were now going to muddle through a worse one. They were, he said, intrenched behind impregnable barricades of old, moss-eaten traditions, red tape, and caste privilege. They were, of course, patriots who believed that the Empire depended upon their system. They had no doubt of their inherent right to conduct the war, which was "their war," without interference or criticism or publicity. They spent many hours of the days and nights in writing letters to one another, and those who wrote most letters received most decorations, and felt, with a patriotic fire within their breasts, that they were getting on with the war.

Within their close corporation there were rivalries, intrigues, perjuries, and treacheries like those of a medieval court. Each general and staff-officer had his followers and his sycophants, who jostled for one another's jobs, fawned on the great man, flattered his vanity, and made him believe in his omniscience. Among the General Staff there were various grades—G.S.O. I, G.S.O. II, G.S.O. III, and those in the lower grades fought for a higher grade with every kind of artfulness, and diplomacy and back-stair influence. They worked late into the night. That is to say, they went back to their offices after dining at mess—"so frightfully busy, you know, old man!"—and kept their lights burning, and smoked more cigarettes, and rang one another up on the telephone with futile questions, and invented new ways of preventing something from being down somewhere. The war to them was a far-off thing essential to their way of life, as miners in the coal-fields are essential to statesmen in Downing Street, especially in cold weather. But it did not touch their souls or their bodies. They did not see its agony, or imagine it, or worry about it. They were always cheerful, breezy, bright with optimism. They made a little work go a long way. They were haughty and arrogant with subordinate officers, or at the best affable and condescending, and to superior officers they said, "Yes, sir," "No, sir," "Quite so, sir," to any statement, however absurd in its ignorance and dogmatism. If a major-general said, "Wagner was a mountebank in music," G.S.O. III, who had once studied at Munich, said, "Yes, sir," or, "You think so, sir? Of course you're right."

If a lieutenant-colonel said, "Browning was not a poet," a staff captain, who had read Browning at Cambridge with passionate admiration, said: "I quite agree with you, sir. And who do you think was a poet, sir?"

It was the army system. The opinion of a superior officer was correct, always. It did not admit of contradiction. It was not to be criticized. Its ignorance was wisdom.

G. H. Q. lived, said our guest, in a world of its own, rose-colored, remote from the ugly things of war. They had heard of the trenches, yes, but as the West End hears of the East End—a nasty place where common people lived. Occasionally they visited the trenches as society folk go slumming, and came back proud of having seen a shell burst, having braved the lice and the dirt.

"The trenches are the slums," said our guest. "We are the Great Unwashed. We are the Mud-larks."

There was a trench in the salient called J. 3. It was away out in advance of our lines. It was not connected with our own trench system. It had been left derelict by both sides and was a ditch in No Man's Land. But our men were ordered to hold it—"to save sniping." A battalion commander protested to the Headquarters Staff. There was no object in holding J. 3. It was a target for German guns and a temptation to German miners.

"J. 3," came the staff command, "must be held until further orders."

We lost five hundred men in holding it. The trench and all in it were thrown up by mines. Among those killed was the Hon. Lyndhurst Bruce, the husband of Camille Clifford, with other husbands of women unknown.

Our guest told the story of the massacre in Neuve Chapelle. "This is a death sentence," said the officers who were ordered to attack. But they attacked, and died, with great gallantry, as usual.

"In the slums," said our guest, "we are expected to die if G. H. Q. tells us so, or if the corps arranges our funeral. And generally we do."

That night, when the snow lay on the ground, I listened to the rumbling of the gunning away in the salient, and seemed to hear the groans of men at Hooge, at St.-Eloi, in other awful places. The irony of that guest of ours was frightful. It was bitter beyond justice, though with truth in the mockery, the truth of a soul shocked by the waste of life and heroism;... when I met him later in the war he was on the staff.

XII

The world—our side of it—held its breath and felt its own heart-beat when, in February of that year '15, the armies of the German Crown Prince launched their offensive against the French at Verdun. It was the biggest offensive since their first drive down to the Marne; and as the days passed and they hurled fresh masses of men against the French and brought up new guns to replace their losses, there was no doubt that in this battle the Germans were trying by all their weight to smash their way to victory through the walls which the French had built against them by living flesh and spirit.

"Will they hold?" was the question which every man among us asked of his neighbor and of his soul.

On our front there was nothing of war beyond the daily routine of the trenches and the daily list of deaths and wounds. Winter had closed down upon us in Flanders, and through its fogs and snows came the news of that conflict round Verdun to the waiting army, which was ours. The news was bad, yet not the worst. Poring over maps of the French front, we in our winter quarters saw with secret terror, some of us with a bluster of false optimism, some of us with unjustified despair, that the French were giving ground, giving ground slowly, after heroic resistance, after dreadful massacre, and steadily. They were falling back to the inner line of forts, hard pressed. The Germans, in spite of monstrous losses under the flail of the *soixante-quinzes,* were forcing their way from slope to slope, capturing positions which all but dominated the whole of the Verdun heights.

"If the French break we shall lose the war," said the pessimist.

"The French will never lose Verdun," said the optimist.

"Why not? What are your reasons beyond that cursed optimism which has been our ruin? Why announce things like that as though divinely inspired? For God's sake let us stare straight at the facts."

"The Germans are losing the war by this attack on Verdun. They are just pouring their best soldiers into the furnace—burning the flower of their army. It is our gain. It will lead in the end to our victory."

"But, my dear good fool, what about the French losses? Don't they get killed, too? The German artillery is flogging them with shell-fire from seventeen-inch guns, twelve-inch, nine-inch, every bloody and monstrous engine. The French are weak in heavy artillery. For that error, which has haunted them from the beginning, they are now paying with their life's blood—the life blood of France."

"You are arguing on emotion and fear. Haven't you learned yet that the attacking side always loses more than the defense?"

"That is a sweeping statement. It depends on relative man-power and gun-power. Given a superiority of guns and men, and attack is cheap. Defense is blown off the earth. Otherwise how could we ever hope to win?"

"I agree. But the forces at Verdun are about equal, and the French have the advantage of position. The Germans are committing suicide."

"Humbug! They know what they are doing. They are the greatest soldiers in Europe."

"Led by men with bone heads."

"By great scientists."

"By the traditional rules of medievalism. By bald—headed vultures in spectacles with brains like penny-in—the-slot machines. Put in a penny and out comes a rule of war. Mad egoists! Colossal blunderers! Efficient in all things but knowledge of life."

"Then God help our British G.H.Q.!"

A long silence. The silence of men who see monstrous forces at work, in which human lives are tossed like straws in flame. A silence reaching back to old ghosts of history, reaching out to supernatural aid. Then from one speaker or another a kind of curse and a kind of prayer.

"Hell!... God help us all!"

So it was in our mess where war correspondents and censors sat down together after futile journeys to dirty places to see a bit of shell-fire, a few dead bodies, a line of German trenches through a periscope, a queue of wounded men outside a dressing station, the survivors of a trench raid, a bombardment before a "minor operation," a trench-mortar "stunt," a new part of the line... Verdun was the only thing that mattered in March and April until France had saved herself and all of us.

XIII

The British army took no part in that battle of Verdun, but rendered great service to France at that time. By February of 1915 we had taken over a new line of front, extending from our positions round Loos southward to the country round Lens and Arras. It was to this movement in February that Marshal Joffre made allusion when, in a message to our Commander-in-Chief on March 2d, he said that "the French army remembered that its recent call on the comradeship of the British army met with an immediate and complete response."

By liberating an immense number of French troops of the Tenth Army and a mass of artillery from this part of the front, we had the good fortune to be of great service to France at a time when she needed many men and guns to repel the assault upon Verdun.

Some of her finest troops—men who had fought in many battles and had held the trenches with most dogged courage—were here in this sector of the western front, and many batteries of heavy and light artillery had been in these positions since the early months of the war. It was, therefore, giving a new and formidable strength to the defense of Verdun when British troops replaced them at the time the enemy made his great attack.

The French went away from this part of their battlefront with regret and emotion. To them it was sacred ground, this line from the long ridge of Notre Dame de Lorette, past Arras, the old capital of Artois, to Hebuterne, where it linked up with the British army already on the Somme. Every field here was a graveyard of their heroic dead.

I went over all the ground which we now held, and saw the visible reminders of all that fighting which lay strewn there, and told the story of all the struggle there by the upheaval of earth, the wreckage of old trenches, the mine—craters and shell-holes, and the litter of battle in every part of that countryside.

I went there first—to the hill of Notre Dame de Lorette looking northward to Lens, and facing the Vimy Ridge, which the enemy held as a strong barrier against us above the village of Souchez and Ablain St.-Nazaire and Neuville St.-Vaast, which the French had captured—when they were still there; and I am glad of that, for I saw in their places the men who had lived there and fought there as one may read in the terrible and tragic narrative of war by Henri Barbusse in *Le Feu.*

I went on such a day as Barbusse describes. (Never once did he admit any fine weather to alleviate the suffering of his comrades, thereby exaggerating their misery somewhat.) It was raining, and there was a white, dank mist through the trees of the Bois de Bouvigny on the way to the spur of Notre Dame. It clung to the undergrowth, which was torn by shell-fire, and to every blade of grass growing rankly round the lips of shell-craters in which were bits of red rag or old bones, the red pantaloons of the first French armies who had fought through those woods in the beginning of the war.

I roamed about a graveyard there, where shells had smashed down some of the crosses, but had not damaged the memorial to the men who had stormed up the slope of Notre Dame de Lorette and had fallen when their comrades chased the Germans to the village below.

A few shells came over the hill as I pushed through the undergrowth with a French captain, and they burst among the trees with shattering boughs. I remember that little officer in a steel helmet, and I could see a Norman knight as his ancestor with a falcon as his crest. He stood so often on the sky-line, in full view of the enemy (I was thankful for the mist), that I admired but deplored his audacity. Without any screen to hide us we walked down the hillside, gathering clots of greasy mud in our boots, stumbling, and once sprawling. Another French captain joined us and became the guide.

"This road is often 'Marmite,'" he said, "but I have escaped so often I have a kind of fatalism."

I envied his faith, remembering two eight-inch shells which a few minutes before had burst in our immediate neighborhood, cutting off twigs of trees and one branch with a scatter of steel as sharp as knives and as heavy as sledge-hammers.

Then for the first time I went into Ablain St.-Nazaire, which afterward I passed through scores of times on the way to Vimy when that ridge was ours. The ragged ruin of its church was white and ghostly in the mist. On the right of the winding road which led through it was Souchez Wood, all blasted and riven, and beyond a huddle of bricks which once was Souchez village.

"Our men have fallen on every yard of this ground," said the French officer. "Their bodies lie thick below the soil. Poor France! Poor France!"

He spoke with tragedy in his eyes and voice, seeing the vision of all that youth of France which even then, in March of '16, had been offered up in vast sacrifice to the greedy devils of war. Rain was slashing down now, beating a tattoo on the steel helmets of a body of French soldiers who stood shivering by the ruined walls while trench-mortars were making a tumult in the neighborhood. They were the men of Henri Barbusse—his comrades. There were middle-aged men and boys mixed together in a confraternity of misery. They were plastered with wet clay, and their boots were enlarged grotesquely by the clots of mud on them. Their blue coats were soddened, and the water dripped out of them and made pools round their feet. They were unshaven, and their wet faces were smeared with the soil of the trenches.

"How goes it?" said the French captain with me.

"It does not go," said the French sergeant. "'Cre nom de Dieu!—my men are not gay to-day. They have been wet for three weeks and their bones are aching. This place is not a Bal Tabourin. If we light even a little fire we ask for trouble. At the sight of smoke the dirty Boche starts shelling again. So we do not get dry, and we have no warmth, and we cannot make even a cup of good hot coffee. That dirty Boche up there on Vimy looks out of his deep tunnels and laughs up his sleeve and says those poor devils of Frenchmen are not gay to-day! That is true, mon Capitaine. Mais, que voulez-vous? C'est pour la France."

"Oui. C'est pour la France."

The French captain turned away and I could see that he pitied those comrades of his as we went over cratered earth to the village of Neuville St.-Vaast.

"Poor fellows," he said, presently. "Not even a cup of hot coffee!... That is war! Blood and misery. Glory, yes—afterward! But at what a price!"

So we came to Neuville St.-Vaast, a large village once with a fine church, old in history, a schoolhouse, a town hall, many little streets of comfortable houses under the shelter of the friendly old hill of Vimy, and within easy walk of Arras; then a frightful rubbish heap mingled with unexploded shells, the twisted iron of babies' perambulators, bits of dead bodies, and shattered farm-carts.

Two French soldiers carried a stretcher on which a heavy burden lay under a blood-soaked blanket.

"It is a bad wound?" asked the captain.

The men laid the stretcher down, breathing hard, and uncovered a face, waxen, the color of death. It was the face of a handsome man with a pointed beard, breathing snuffily through his nose.

"He may live as far as the dressing station," said one of the Frenchmen. "It was a trench-mortar which blew a hole in his body just now, over there."

The man jerked his head toward a barricade of sand—bags at the end of a street of ruin.

Two other men walked slowly toward us with a queer, hobbling gait. Both of them were wounded in the legs, and had tied rags round their wounds tightly. They looked grave, almost sullen, staring at us as they passed, with brooding eyes.

"The German trench-mortars are very evil," said the captain.

We poked about the ruins, raising our heads cautiously above sand-bags to look at the German lines cut into the lower slopes of Vimy, and thrust out by communication trenches to the edge of the village in which we walked. A boy officer came up out of a hole and saluted the captain, who stepped back and said, in an emotional way:

"Tiens! C'est toi, Edouard?"

"Oui, mon Capitaine."

The boy had a fine, delicate, Latin face, with dark eyes and long, black eyelashes.

"You are a lieutenant, then? How does it go, Edouard?"

"It does not go," answered the boy like that French sergeant in Ablain St.-Nazaire. "This is a bad place. I lose my men every day. There were three killed yesterday, and six wounded. To-day already there are two killed and ten wounded."

Something broke in his voice.

"Ce n'est pas bon du tout, du tout!" ("It is not good at all, at all!")

The captain clapped him on the shoulders, tried to cheer him.

"Courage, mon vieux!"

The rain shot down on us. Our feet slithered in deep, greasy mud. Sharp stabs of flame vomited out of the slopes of Vimy. There was the high, long-drawn scream of shells in flight to Notre Dame de Lorette. Batteries of *soixante-quinzes* were firing rapidly, and their shells cut through the air above us like scythes. The caldron in this pit of war was being stirred up. Another wounded poilu was carried past us, covered by a bloody blanket like the other one. From slimy sand-bags and wet ruins came the sickening stench of human corruption. A boot with some pulp inside protruded from a mud—bank where I stood, and there was a human head, without eyes or nose, black, and rotting in the puddle of a shell—hole. Those were relics of a battle on May 9th, a year before, when swarms of boys, of the '16 class, boys of eighteen, the flower of French youth, rushed forward from the crossroads at La Targette, a few hundred yards away, to capture these ruins of Neuville St.-Vaast. They captured them, and it cost them seven thousand in killed and wounded—at least three thousand dead. They fought like young demons through the flaming streets. They fell in heaps under the German barrage-fire. Machine—guns cut them down as though they were ripe corn under the sickle. But these French boys broke the Prussian Guard that day.

Round about, over all this ground below Notre Dame de Lorette and the fields round Souchez, the French had fought ferociously, burrowing below earth at the Labyrinth—sapping, mining, gaining a network of trenches, an isolated house, a huddle of ruins, a German sap-head, by frequent rushes and the frenzy of those who fight vith their teeth and hands, flinging themselves on the bodies of their enemy, below ground in the darkness, or above ground between ditches and sand-bags. So for something like fifteen months they fought, by Souchez and the Labyrinth, until in February of '16 they went away after greeting our khaki men who came into their old places and found the bones and bodies of Frenchmen there, as I found, white, rat-gnawed bones, in disused trenches below Notre Dame when the rain washed the earth down and uncovered them.

XIV

It was then, in that February of '15, that the city of Arras passed for defense into British hands and became from that time on one of our strongholds on the edge of the battlefields so that it will be haunted forever by the ghosts of those men of ours whom I saw there on many days of grim fighting, month after month, in snow and sun and rain, in steel helmets and stink-coats, in muddy khaki and kilts, in queues of wounded (three thousand at a time outside the citadel), in billets where their laughter and music were scornful of high velocities, in the surging tide of traffic that poured through to victory that cost as much sometimes as defeat.

When I first went into Arras during its occupation by the French I remembered a day, fifteen months before, near the town of St.-Pol in Artois, where I was caught up in one of those tides of fugitives which in those early days of war used to roll back in a state of terror before the German invasion. "Where do they come from?" I asked, watching this long procession of gigs and farmers' carts and tramping women and children. The answer told me everything. "They are bombarding Arras, m'sieur."

Since then "They" had never ceased to bombard Arras. From many points of view, as I had come through the countryside at night, I had seen the flashes of shells over that city and had thought of the agony inside. Four days before I went in first it was bombarded with one hundred and fifty seventeen-inch shells, each one of which would destroy a cathedral. It was with a sense of being near to death—not a pleasant feeling, you understand—that I went into Arras for the first time and saw what had happened to it.

I was very near to the Germans. No more than ten yards away, when I stood peering through a hole in the wall of the Maison Rouge in the suburb of Blangy—it was a red-brick villa, torn by shells, with a piano in the parlor which no man dared to play, behind a shelter of sand-bags—and no more than two hundred yards away from the enemy's lines when I paced up and down the great railway station of Arras, where no trains ever traveled. For more than a year the enemy had been encamped outside the city, and for all that time had tried to batter a way into and through it. An endless battle had surged up against its walls, but in spite of all their desperate attacks no German soldier had set foot inside the city except as a prisoner of war. Many thousands of young Frenchmen had given their blood to save it.

The enemy had not been able to prevail over flesh and blood and the spirit of heroic men, but he had destroyed the city bit by bit. It was pitiful beyond all expression. It was worse than looking upon a woman whose beauty had been scarred by bloody usage.

For Arras was a city of beauty—a living expression in stone of all the idealism in eight hundred years of history, a most sweet and gracious place. Even then, after a year's bombardment, some spiritual exhalation of human love and art came to one out of all this ruin. When I entered the city and wandered a little in its public gardens before going into its dead heart—the Grande Place—I felt the strange survival. The trees here were slashed by shrapnel. Enormous shell-craters had plowed up those pleasure-grounds. The shrubberies were beaten down.

Almost every house had been hit, every building was scarred and slashed, but for the most part the city still stood, so that I went through many long streets and passed long lines of houses, all deserted, all dreadful in their silence and desolation and ruin.

Then I came to the cathedral of St.-Vaast. It was an enormous building of the Renaissance, not beautiful, but impressive in its spaciousness and dignity. Next to it was the bishop's palace, with long corridors and halls, and a private chapel. Upon these walls and domes the fury of great shells had spent itself. Pillars as wide in girth as giant trees had been snapped off to the base. The dome of the cathedral opened with a yawning chasm. High explosives burst through the walls. The keystones of arches were blown out, and masses of masonry were piled into the nave and aisles.

As I stood there, rooks had perched in the broken vaulting and flew with noisy wings above the ruined altars. Another sound came like a great beating of wings, with a swifter rush. It was a shell, and the vibration of it stirred the crumbling masonry, and bits of it fell with a clatter to the littered floor. On the way to the ruin of the bishop's chapel I passed a group of stone figures. They were the famous "Angels of Arras" removed from some other part of the building to what might have been a safer place.

Now they were fallen angels, mangled as they lay. But in the chapel beyond, where the light streamed through the broken panes of stained-glass windows, one figure stood untouched in all this ruin. It was a tall statue of Christ standing in an attitude of meekness and sorrow, as though in the presence of those who crucified Him.

Yet something more wonderful than this scene of tragedy lived in the midst of it. Yet there were still people living in Arras.

They lived an underground life, for the most part, coming up from the underworld to blink in the sunlight, to mutter a prayer or a curse or two, to gaze for a moment at any change made by a new day's bombardment, and then to burrow down again at the shock of a gun.

Through low archways just above the pavement, I looked down into some of the deep-vaulted cellars where the merchants used to stock their wine, and saw old women, and sometimes young women there, cooking over little stoves, pottering about iron bedsteads, busy with domestic work. Some of them looked up as I passed, and my eyes and theirs stared into each other. The women's faces were lined and their eyes sunken. They had the look of people who have lived through many agonies and have more to suffer.

Not all these citizens of Arras were below ground. There was a greengrocer's shop still carrying on a little trade. I went into another shop and bought some picture post-cards of the ruins within a few yards of it. The woman behind the counter was a comely soul, and laughed because she had no change. Only two days before a seventeen-inch shell had burst fifty yards or so away from her shop, which was close enough for death. I marveled at the risk she took with cheerful smiles. Was it courage or stupidity?

One of the old women in the street grasped my arm in a friendly way and called me cher petit ami, and described how she had been nearly killed a hundred times. When I asked her why she stayed she gave an old woman's cackling laugh and said, *"Que voulez-vous, jeune homme?"* which did not seem a satisfactory answer. As dusk crept into the streets of Arras I saw small groups of boys and girls. They seemed to come out of holes in the ground to stare at this Englishman in khaki. "Are you afraid of the shells?" I asked. They grimaced up at the sky and giggled. They had got used to the hell of it all, and dodged death as they would a man with a whip, shouting with laughter beyond the length of his lash. In one of the vaulted cellars underground, when English soldiers first went in, there lived a group of girls who gave them wine to drink, and kisses for a franc or two, and the Circe cup of pleasure, if they had time to stay. Overhead shells were howling. Their city was stricken with death. These women lived like witches in a cave—a strange and dreadful life.

I walked to the suburb of Blangy by way of St.-Nicolas and came to a sinister place. Along the highroad from Arras to Douai was a great factory of some kind—probably for beet sugar—and then a street of small houses with back yards and gardens much like those in our own suburbs. Holes had been knocked through the walls of the factory and houses, the gardens had been barricaded with barbed wire and sand-bags, and the passage from house to house and between the overturned boilers of the factory formed a communication trench to the advanced outpost in the last house held by the French, on the other side of which is the enemy. As we made our way through these ruined houses we had to walk very quietly and to speak in whispers. In the last house of all, which was a combination of fort and dugout, absolute silence was necessary, for there were German soldiers only ten yards away, with trench-mortars and bombs and rifles always ready to snipe across the walls. Through a chink no wider than my finger I could see the red-brick ruins of the houses inhabited by the enemy and the road to Douai... The road to Douai as seen through this chink was a tangle of broken bricks.

The enemy was so close to Arras when the French held it that there were many places where one had to step quietly and duck one's head, or get behind the shelter of a broken wall, to avoid a sniper's bullet or the rattle of bullets from a machine-gun.

As I left Arras in that November evening, darkness closed in its ruined streets and shells were crashing over the city from French guns, answered now and then by enemy batteries. But in a moment of rare silence I heard the chime of a church clock. It seemed like the sweet voice of that old-time peace in Arras before the days of its agony, and I thought of that solitary bell sounding above the ruins in a ghostly way.

XV

While we hung on the news from Verdun—it seemed as though the fate of the world were in Fort Douaumont—our own lists of death grew longer.

In the casualty clearing station by Poperinghe more mangled men lay on their stretchers, hobbled to the ambulance-trains, groped blindly with one hand clutching at a comrade's arm. More, and more, and more, with head wounds, and body wounds, with trench-feet, and gas.

"O Christ!" said one of them whom I knew. He had been laid on a swing-bed in the ambulance-train.

"Now you will be comfortable and happy," said the R.A.M.C. orderly.

The boy groaned again. He was suffering intolerable agony, and, grasping a strap, hauled himself up a little with a wet sweat breaking out on his forehead.

Another boy came along alone, with one hand in a big bandage. He told me that it was smashed to bits, and began to cry. Then he smudged the tears away and said:

"I'm lucky enough. I saw many fellows killed."

So it happened, day by day, but the courage of our men endured.

It seemed impossible to newcomers that life could exist at all under the shell-fire which the Germans flung over our trenches and which we flung over theirs. So it seemed to the Irish battalions when they held the lines round Loos, by that Hohenzollern redoubt which was one of our little hells.

"Things happened," said one of them, "which in other times would have been called miracles. We all had hairbreadth escapes from death." For days they were under heavy fire, with 9.2's flinging up volumes of sand and earth and stones about them. Then waves of poison-gas. Then trench-mortars and bombs.

"It seemed like years!" said one of the Irish crowd. "None of us expected to come out alive."

Yet most of them had the luck to come out alive that time, and over a midday mess in a Flemish farmhouse they had hearty appetites for bully beef and fried potatoes, washed down by thin red wine and strong black coffee.

Round Ypres, and up by Boesinghe and Hooge—you remember Hooge?—the 14th, 20th, and 6th Divisions took turns in wet ditches and in shell-holes, with heavy crumps falling fast and roaring before they burst like devils of hell. On one day there were three hundred casualties in one battalion The German gun-fire lengthened, and men were killed on their way out to "rest"—camps to the left of the road between Poperinghe and Vlamertinghe.

* * * * *

On March 28th the Royal Fusiliers and the Northumberland Fusiliers—the old Fighting Fifth—captured six hundred yards of German trenches near St.-Eloi and asked for trouble, which, sure enough, came to them who followed them. Their attack was against a German stronghold built of earth and sand-bags nine feet high, above a nest of trenches in the fork of two roads from St.-Eloi to Messines. They mined beneath this place and it blew up with a roaring blast which flung up tons of soil in a black mass. Then the Fusiliers dashed forward, flinging bombs through barbed wire and over sand-bags which had escaped the radius of the mine-burst—in one jumbled mass of human bodies in a hurry to get on, to kill, and to come back. One German machine-gun got to work on them. It was knocked out by a bomb flung by an officer who saved his company. The machine—gunners were bayoneted. Elsewhere there was chaos out of which living men came, shaking and moaning.

I saw the Royal Fusiliers and Northumberland Fusiliers come back from this exploit, exhausted, caked from head to foot in wet clay. Their steel helmets were covered with sand-bagging, their trench-waders, their rifles, and smoke helmets were all plastered by wet, white earth, and they looked a ragged regiment of scarecrows gathered from the fields of France. Some of them had shawls tied about their helmets, and some of them wore the shiny black helmets of the Jaeger Regiment and the gray coats of German soldiers. They had had luck. They had not left many comrades behind, and they had come out with life to the good world. Tired as they were, they came along as though to carnival. They had proved their courage through an ugly job. They had done "damn well," as one of them remarked; and they were out of the shell-fire which ravaged the ground they had taken, where other men lay.

XVI

At the beginning of March there was a little affair—costing a lot of lives—in the neighborhood of St.-Eloi, up in the Ypres salient. It was a struggle for a dirty hillock called the Bluff, which had been held for a long time by the 3d Division under General Haldane, whose men were at last relieved, after weary months in the salient, by the 17th Division commanded by General Pilcher. The Germans took advantage of the change in defense by a sudden attack after the explosion of a mine, and the men of the 17th Division, new to this ground, abandoned a position of some local importance.

General Haldane was annoyed. It was ground of which he knew every inch. It was ground which men of his had died to hold. It was very annoying—using a feeble word—to battalion officers and men of the 3d Division—Suffolks and King's Own Liverpools, Gordons and Royal Scots—who had first come out of the salient, out of its mud and snow and slush and shell-fire, to a pretty village far behind the lines, on the road to Calais, where they were getting back to a sense of normal life again. Sleeping in snug billets, warming their feet at wood fires, listening with enchantment to the silence about them, free from the noise of artillery. They were hugging themselves with the thought of a month of this... Then because they had been in the salient so long and had held this line so stubbornly, they were ordered back again to recapture the position lost by new men.

After a day of field sports they were having a boxing—match in an old barn, very merry and bright, before that news came to them. General Haldane had given me a quiet word about it, and I watched the boxing, and the faces of all those men, crowded round the ring, with pity for the frightful disappointment that was about to fall on them, like a sledge-hammer. I knew some of their officers—Colonel Dyson of the Royal Scots, and Captain Heathcote, who hated the war and all its ways with a deadly hatred, having seen much slaughter of men and of their own officers. Colonel Dyson was the seventeenth commanding officer of his battalion, which had been commanded by every officer down to second lieutenant, and had only thirty men left of the original crowd. They had been slain in large numbers in that "holding attack" by Hooge on September 25th, during the battle of Loos, as I have told. Now they were "going in" again, and were very sorry for themselves, but hid their feelings from their men. The men were tough and stalwart lads, tanned by the wind and rain of a foul winter, thinned down by the ordeal of those months in the line under daily bouts of fire. In a wooden gallery of the barn a mass of them lay in deep straw, exchanging caps, whistling, shouting, in high spirits. Not yet did they know the call-back to the salient. Then word was passed to them after the boxing finals. That night they had to march seven miles to entrain for the railroad nearest to Ypres. I saw them march away, silently, grimly, bravely, without many curses.

They were to recapture the Bluff, and early on the morning of March 2d, before dawn had risen, I went out to the salient and watched the bombardment which preceded the attack. There was an incessant tumult of guns, and the noise rolled in waves across the flat country of the salient and echoed back from Kemmel Hill and the Wytschaete Ridge. There was a white frost over the fields, and all the battle-front was veiled by a mist which clung round the villages and farmsteads behind the lines and made a dense bank of gray fog below the rising ground.

This curtain was rent with flashes of light and little glinting stars burst continually over one spot, where the Bluff was hidden beyond Zillebeke Lake. When daybreak came, with the rim of a red sun over a clump of trees in the east, the noise of guns increased in spasms of intensity like a rising storm. Many batteries of heavy artillery were firing salvos. Field-guns, widely scattered, concentrated their fire upon one area, where their shells were bursting with a twinkle of light. Somewhere a machine-gun was at work with sharp, staccato strokes, like an urgent knocking at the door. High overhead was the song of an airplane coming nearer, with a high, vibrant humming. It was an enemy searching through the mist down below him for any movement of troops or trains.

It was the 76th Brigade of the 3d Division which attacked at four thirty-two that morning, and they were the Suffolks, Gordons, and King's Own Liverpools who led the assault, commanded by General Pratt. They flung themselves into the German lines in the wake of a heavy barrage fire, smashing through broken belts of wire and stumbling in and out of shell-craters. The Germans, in their front-lines, had gone to cover in deep dugouts which they had built with feverish haste on the Bluff and its neighborhood during the previous ten days and nights. At first only a few men, not more than a hundred or so, could be discovered alive. The dead were thick in the maze of trenches, and our men stumbled across them.

The living were in a worse state than the dead, dazed by the shell-fire, and cold with terror when our men sprang upon them in the darkness before dawn. Small parties were collected and passed back as prisoners—marvelously lucky men if they kept their sanity as well as their lives after all that hell about them. Hours later, when our battalions had stormed their way up other trenches into a salient jutting out of the German line and beyond the boundary of the objective that had been given to them, other living men were found to be still hiding in the depths of other dugouts and could not be induced to come out. Terror kept them in those holes, and they were like wild beasts at bay, still dangerous because they had their bombs and rifles. An ultimatum was shouted down to them by men too busy for persuasive talk. "If you don't come out you'll be blown in." Some of them came out and others were blown to bits. After that the usual thing happened, the thing that inevitably happened in all these little murderous attacks and counter-attacks. The enemy concentrated all its power of artillery on that position captured by our men, and day after day hurled over storms of shrapnel and high explosives, under which our men cowered until many were killed and more wounded. The first attack on the Bluff and its recapture cost us three thousand casualties, and that was only the beginning of a daily toll of life and limbs in that neighborhood of hell. Through driving snowstorms shells went rushing across that battleground, ceaselessly in those first weeks of March, but the 3d Division repulsed the enemy's repeated attacks in bombing fights which were very fierce on both sides.

I went to General Pilcher's headquarters at Reninghelst on March 4th, and found the staff of the 17th Division frosty in their greeting, while General Pratt, the brigadier of the 3d Division, was conducting the attack in their new territory. General Pilcher himself was much shaken. The old gentleman had been at St.-Eloi when the bombardment had begun on his men. With Captain

Rattnag his A. D. C. he lay for an hour in a ditch with shells screaming overhead and bursting close. More than once when I talked with him he raised his head and listened nervously and said: "Do you hear the guns?... They are terrible."

I was sorry for him, this general who had many theories on war and experimented in light-signals, as when one night I stood by his side in a dark field, and had a courteous old-fashioned dignity and gentleness of manner. He was a fine old English gentleman and a gallant soldier, but modern warfare was too brutal for him. Too brutal for all those who hated its slaughter.

Those men of the 3d Division—the "Iron Division," as it was called later in the war—remained in a hideous turmoil of wet earth up by the Bluff until other men came to relieve them and take over this corner of hell.

What remained of the trenches was deep in water and filthy mud, where the bodies of many dead Germans lay under a litter of broken sand-bags and in the holes of half-destroyed dugouts. Nothing could be done to make it less horrible. Then the weather changed and became icily cold, with snow and rain.

One dugout which had been taken for battalion headquarters was six feet long by four wide, and here in this waterlogged hole lived three officers of the Royal Scots to whom a day or two before I had wished "good luck."

The servants lived in the shaft alongside which was a place measuring four feet by four feet. There were no other dugouts where men could get any shelter from shells or storms, and the enemy's guns were never silent.

But the men held on, as most of our men held on, with a resignation to fate and a stoic endurance beyond that ordinary human courage which we seemed to know before the war.

The chaplain of this battalion had spent all the long night behind the lines, stoking fires and going round the cook-houses and looking at his wrist-watch to see how the minutes were crawling past. He had tea, rum, socks, oil, and food all ready for those who were coming back, and the lighted braziers were glowing red.

At the appointed time the *padre* went out to meet his friends, pressing forward through the snow and listening for any sound of footsteps through the great hush.

But there was no sound except the soft flutter of snowflakes. He strained his eyes for any moving shadows of men. But there was only darkness and the falling snow.

Two hours passed, and they seemed endless to that young chaplain whose brain was full of frightful apprehensions, so that they were hours of anguish to him.

Then at last the first men appeared. "I've never seen anything so splendid and so pitiful," said the man who had been waiting for them.

They came along at about a mile an hour, sometimes in groups, sometimes by twos or threes, holding on to each other, often one by one. In this order they crept through the ruined villages in the falling snow, which lay thick upon the masses of fallen masonry. There was a profound silence about them, and these snow-covered men were like ghosts walking through cities of death.

No man spoke, for the sound of a human voice would have seemed a danger in this great white quietude. They were walking like old men, weak-kneed, and bent under the weight of their packs and rifles.

Yet when the young padre greeted them with a cheery voice that hid the water in his heart every one had a word and a smile in reply, and made little jests about their drunken footsteps, for they were like drunken men with utter weariness.

"What price Charlie Chaplin now, sir?" was one man's joke.

The last of those who came back—and there were many who never came back—were some hours later than the first company, having found it hard to crawl along that Via Dolorosa which led to the good place where the braziers were glowing.

It was a heroic episode, for each one of these men was a hero, though his name will never be known in the history of that silent and hidden war. And yet it was an ordinary episode, no degree worse in its hardship than what happened all along the line when there was an attack or counter-attack in foul weather.

The marvel of it was that our men, who were very simple men, should have "stuck it out" with that grandeur of courage which endured all things without self-interest and without emotion. They were unconscious of the virtue that was in them.

XVII

Going up to the line by Ypres, or Armentieres, or Loos, I noticed in those early months of 1916 an increasing power of artillery on our side of the lines and a growing intensity of gun-fire on both sides.

Time was, a year before, when our batteries were scattered thinly behind the lines and when our gunners had to be thrifty of shells, saving them up anxiously for hours of great need, when the S O S rocket shot up a green light from some battered trench upon which the enemy was concentrating "hate."

Those were ghastly days for gunner officers, who had to answer telephone messages calling for help from battalions whose billets were being shelled to pieces by long—range howitzers, or from engineers whose working-parties were being sniped to death by German field-guns, or from a brigadier who wanted to know, plaintively, whether the artillery could not deal with a certain gun which was enfilading a certain trench and piling up the casualties. It was hard to say: "Sorry!... We've got to go slow with ammunition."

That, now, was ancient history. For some time the fields had grown a new crop of British batteries. Month after month our weight of metal increased, and while the field-guns had been multiplying at a great rate the "heavies" had been coming out, too, and giving a deeper and more sonorous tone to that swelling chorus which rolled over the battlefields by day and night.

There was a larger supply of shells for all those pieces, and no longer the same need for thrift when there was urgent need for artillery support. Retaliation was the order of the day, and if the enemy asked for trouble by any special show of "hate" he got it quickly and with a double dose.

Compared with the infantry, the gunners had a chance of life, except in places where, as in the salient, the German observers stared down at them from high ground and saw every gun flash and registered every battery. Going round the salient one day with General Burstall—and a very good name, too!—who was then the Canadian gunner-general, I was horrified at the way in which the enemy had the accurate range of our guns and gun-pits and knocked them out with deadly shooting.

Here and there our amateur gunners—quick to learn their job—found a good place, and were able to camouflage their position for a time, and give praise to the little god of Luck, until one day sooner or later they were discovered and a quick move was necessary if they were not caught too soon.

So it was with a battery in the open fields beyond Kemmel village, where I went to see a boy who had once been a rising hope of Fleet Street.

He was new to his work and liked the adventure of it—that was before his men were blown to bits around him and he was sent down as a tragic case of shell-shock—and as we walked through the village of Kemmel he chatted cheerfully about his work and life and found it topping. His bright, luminous eyes were undimmed by the scene around him. He walked in a jaunty, boyish way through that ruined place. It was not a pleasant place. Kemmel village, even in those days, had been blown to bits, except where, on the outskirts, the chateau with its racing-stables remained untouched—"German spies!" said the boy—and where a little grotto to Our Lady of Lourdes was also unscathed. The church was battered and broken, and there were enormous shell-pits in the churchyard and open vaults where old dead had been tumbled out of their tombs. We walked along a sunken road and then to a barn in open fields. The roof was pierced by shrapnel bullets, which let in the rain on wet days and nights, but it was cozy otherwise in the room above the ladder where the officers had their mess. There were some home-made chairs up there, and

Kirchner prints of naked little ladies were tacked up to the beams, among the trench maps, and round the fireplace where logs were burning was a canvas screen to let down at night. A gramophone played merry music and gave a homelike touch to this parlor in war.

"A good spot!" I said. "Is it well hidden?"

"As safe as houses," said the captain of the battery. "Touching wood, I mean."

There were six of us sitting at a wooden plank on trestles, and at those words five young men rose with a look of fright on their faces and embraced the beam supporting the roof of the barn.

"What's happened?" I asked, not having heard the howl of a shell.

"Nothing," said the boy, "except touching wood. The captain spoke too loudly."

We went out to the guns which were to do a little shooting, and found them camouflaged from aerial eyes in the grim desolation of the battlefield, all white after a morning's snowstorm, except where the broken walls of distant farmhouses and the windmills on Kemmel Hill showed black as ink.

The gunners could not see their target, which had been given to them through the telephone, but they knew it by the figures giving the angle of fire.

"It's a pumping-party in a waterlogged trench," said a bright-eyed boy by my side (he was one of the rising hopes of Fleet Street before he became a gunner officer in Flanders). "With any luck we shall get 'em in the neck, and I like to hear the Germans squeal... And my gun's ready first, as usual."

The officer commanding shouted through a tin megaphone, and the battery fired, each gun following its brother at a second interval, with the staccato shock of a field-piece, which is more painful than the dull roar of a "heavy."

A word came along the wire from the officer in the observation post a mile away.

Another order was called through the tin mouthpiece.

"Repeat!"

"We've got'em," said the young gentleman by my side, in a cheerful way.

The officer with the megaphone looked across and smiled.

"We may as well give them a salvo. They won't like it a bit."

A second or two later there was a tremendous crash as the four guns fired together. "Repeat!" came the high voice through the megaphone.

The still air was rent again... In a waterlogged trench, which we could not see, a German pumping-party had been blown to bits.

The artillery officers took turns in the observation posts, sleeping for the night in one of the dugouts behind the front trench instead of in the billet below.

The way to the observation post was sometimes a little vague, especially in frost-and-thaw weather, when parts of the communication trenches slithered down under the weight of sand-bags.

The young officer who walked with luminous eyes and eager step found it necessary to crawl on his stomach before he reached his lookout station from which he looked straight across the enemy's trenches. But, once there, it was pretty comfortable and safe, barring a direct hit from above or a little mining operation underneath.

He made a seat of a well-filled sand-bag (it was rather a shock when he turned it over one day to get dry side up and found a dead Frenchman there), and smoked Belgian cigars for the sake of their aroma, and sat there very solitary and watchful.

The rats worried him a little—they were bold enough to bare their teeth when they met him down a trench, and there was one big fellow called Cuthbert, who romped round his dugout and actually bit his ear one night. But these inconveniences did not seem to give any real distress to the soul of youth, out there alone and searching for human targets to kill... until one day, as I have said, everything snapped in him and the boy was broken.

It was on the way back from Kemmel village one day that I met a queer apparition through a heavy snowstorm. It was a French civilian in evening dress—boiled shirt, white tie, and all—with a bowler hat bent to the storm.

Tomlinson, the great Tomlinson, was with me, and shook his head.

"It isn't true," he said. "I don't believe it... We're mad, that's all!... The whole world is mad, so why should we be sane?"

We stared after the man who went into the ruin of Kemmel, to the noise of gun-fire, in evening dress, without an overcoat, through a blizzard of snow.

A little farther down the road we passed a signboard on the edge of a cratered field. New words had been painted on it in good Roman letters.

Cimetiere reserve

Tomlinson, the only Tomlinson, regarded it gravely and turned to me with a world of meaning in his eyes. Then he tapped his forehead and laughed.

"Mad!" he said. "We're all mad!"

XVIII

In that winter of discontent there was one great body of splendid men whose spirits had sunk to zero, seeing no hope ahead of them in that warfare of trenches and barbed wire. The cavalry believed they were "bunkered" forever, and that all their training and tradition were made futile by the digging in of armies. Now and again, when the infantry was hard pressed, as in the second battle of Ypres and the battle of Loos, they were called on to leave their horses behind and take a turn in the trenches, and then they came back again, less some of their comrades, into dirty billets remote from the fighting-lines, to exercise their horses and curse the war.

Before they went into the line in February of '16 I went to see some of those cavalry officers to wish them good luck, and saw them in the trenches and afterward when they came out. In the headquarters of a squadron of "Royals"—the way in was by a ladder through the window—billeted in a village, which on a day of frost looked as quaint and pretty as a Christmas card, was a party of officers typical of the British cavalry as a whole.

A few pictures cut out of *La Vie Parisienne* were tacked on to the walls to remind them of the arts and graces of an older mode of life, and to keep them human by the sight of a pretty face (oh, to see a pretty girl again!).

Now they were going to change this cottage for the trenches, this quiet village with a church-bell chiming every hour, for the tumult in the battle-front—this absolute safety for the immediate menace of death. They knew already the beastliness of life in trenches. They had no illusions about "glory." But they were glad to go, because activity was better than inactivity, and because the risk would give them back their pride, and because the cavalry should fight anyhow and somehow, even if a charge or a pursuit were denied them.

They had a hot time in the trenches. The enemy's artillery was active, and the list of casualties began to tot up. A good officer and a fine fellow was killed almost at the outset, and men were horribly wounded. But all those troopers showed a cool courage.

Things looked bad for a few minutes when a section of trenches was blown in, isolating one platoon from another. A sergeant-major made his way back from the damaged section, and a young officer who was going forward to find out the extent of damage met him on the way.

"Can I get through?" asked the officer.

"I've got through," was the answer, "but it's chancing one's luck."

The officer "chanced his luck," but did not expect to come back alive. Afterward he tried to analyze his feelings for my benefit.

"I had no sense of fear," he said, "but a sort of subconscious knowledge that the odds were against me if I went on, and yet a conscious determination to go on at all costs and find out what had happened."

He came back, covered with blood, but unwounded. In spite of all the unpleasant sights in a crumpled trench, he had the heart to smile when in the middle of the night one of the sergeants approached him with an amiable suggestion.

"Don't you think it would be a good time, sir, to make a slight attack upon the enemy?"

There was something in those words, "a slight attack," which is irresistibly comic to any of us who know the conditions of modern trench war. But they were not spoken in jest.

So the cavalry did its "bit" again, though not as cavalry, and I saw some of them when they came back, and they were glad to have gone through that bloody business so that no man might fling a scornful word as they passed with their horses.

"It is queer," said my friend, "how we go from this place of peace to the battlefield, and then come back for a spell before going up again. It is like passing from one life to another."

In that cavalry mess I heard queer conversations. Those officers belonged to the old families of England, the old caste of aristocracy, but the foul outrage of the war—the outrage against all ideals of civilization—had made them think, some of them for the first time, about the structure of social life and of the human family.

They hated Germany as the direct cause of war, but they looked deeper than that and saw how the leaders of all great nations in Europe had maintained the philosophy of forms and had built up hatreds and fears and alliances over the heads of the peoples whom they inflamed with passion or duped with lies.

"The politicians are the guilty ones," said one cavalry officer. "I am all for revolution after this bloody massacre. I would hang all politicians, diplomats, and so-called statesmen with strict impartiality."

"I'm for the people," said another. "The poor, bloody people, who are kept in ignorance and then driven into the shambles when their rulers desire to grab some new part of the earth's surface or to get their armies going because they are bored with peace."

"What price Christianity?" asked another, inevitably. "What have the churches done to stop war or preach the gospel of Christ? The Bishop of London, the Archbishop of Canterbury, all those conventional, patriotic, cannon—blessing, banner-baptizing humbugs. God! They make me tired!"

Strange words to hear in a cavalry mess! Strange turmoil in the souls of men! They were the same words I had heard from London boys in Ypres, spoken just as crudely. But many young gentlemen who spoke those words have already forgotten them or would deny them.

XIX

The winter of 1915-16 passed with its misery, and spring came again to France and Flanders with its promise of life, fulfilled in the beauty of wild flowers and the green of leaves where the earth was not made barren by the fire of war and all trees killed.

For men there was no promise of life, but only new preparations for death, and continued killing.

The battle of Verdun was still going on, and France had saved herself from a mortal blow at the heart by a desperate, heroic resistance which cost her five hundred and fifty thousand in dead and wounded. On the British front there were still no great battles, but those trench raids, artillery duels, mine fighting, and small massacres which filled the casualty clearing stations with the average amount of human wreckage. The British armies were being held in leash for a great offensive in the summer. New divisions were learning the lessons of the old divisions, and here and there generals were doing a little fancy work to keep things merry and bright.

So it was when some mines were exploded under the German earthworks on the lower slopes of the Vimy Ridge, where the enemy had already blown several mines and taken possession of their craters. It was to gain those craters, and new ones to be made by our mine charges, that the 74th Brigade of the 25th Division, a body of Lancashire men, the 9th Loyal North Lancashires and the 11th Royal Fusiliers, with a company of Royal Engineers and some Welsh pioneers, were detailed for the perilous adventure of driving in the mine shafts, putting tremendous charges of high explosives in the sapheads, and rushing the German positions.

It was on the evening of May 15th, after two days of wet and cloudy weather preventing the enemy's observation, that our heavy artillery fired a short number of rounds to send the Germans into their dugouts. A few minutes later the right group of mines exploded with a terrific roar and blew in two of the five old German craters. After the long rumble of heaving earth had been stilled there was just time enough to hear the staccato of a German machine-gun. Then there was a second roar and a wild upheaval of soil when the left group of mines destroyed two more of the German craters and knocked out the machine-gun.

The moment for the infantry attack had come, and the men were ready. The first to get away were two lieutenants of the 9th Loyal North Lancashires, who rushed forward with their assaulting-parties to the remaining crater on the extreme left, which had not been blown up.

With little opposition from dazed and terror-stricken Germans, bayoneted as they scrambled out of the chaotic earth, our men flung themselves into those smoking pits and were followed immediately by working-parties, who built up bombing posts with earth and sand-bags on the crater lip and began to dig out communication trenches leading to them. The assaulting-parties of the Lancashire Fusiliers were away at the first signal, and were attacking the other groups of craters under heavy fire.

The Germans were shaken with terror because the explosion of the mines had killed and wounded a large number of them, and through the darkness there rang out the cheers of masses of men who were out for blood. Through the darkness there now glowed a scarlet light, flooding all that turmoil of earth and men with a vivid, red illumination, as flare after flare rose high into the sky from several points of the German line. Later the red lights died down, and then other rockets were fired, giving a green light to this scene of war.

The German gunners were now at work in answer to those beacons of distress, and with every caliber of gun from howitzers to minenwerfers they shelled our front-lines for two hours and killed for vengeance. They were too late to stop the advance of the assaulting troops, who were fighting in the craters against groups of German bombers who tried to force their way up to the rescue of a position already lost. One of our officers leading the assault on one of the craters on the right was killed very quickly, but his men were not checked, and with individual resolution and initiative, and the grit of the Lancashire man in a tight place, fought on grimly, and won their purpose.

A young lieutenant fell dead from a bullet wound after he had directed his men to their posts from the lip of a new mine-crater, as coolly as though he were a master of ceremonies in a Lancashire ballroom. Another, a champion bomb-thrower, with a range of forty yards, flung his hand-grenades at the enemy with untiring skill and with a fierce contempt of death, until he was killed by an answering shot. The N.C.O.'s took up the command and the men "carried on" until they held all the chain of craters, crouching and panting above mangled men.

They were hours of anguish for many Germans, who lay wounded and half buried, or quite buried, in the chaos, of earth made by those mine-craters now doubly upheaved. Their screams and moans sounding above the guns, the frantic cries of men maddened under tons of earth, which kept them prisoners in deep pits below the crater lips, and awful inarticulate noises of human pain coming out of that lower darkness beyond the light of the rockets, made up a chorus of agony more than our men could endure, even in the heat of battle. They shouted across to the German grenadiers:

"We will cease fire if you will, and let you get in your wounded... Cease fire for the wounded!"

The shout was repeated, and our bombers held their hands, still waiting for an answer. But the answer was a new storm of bombs, and the fighting went on, and the moaning of the men who were helpless and unhelped.

Working-parties followed up the assault to "consolidate" the position. They did amazing things, toiling in the darkness under abominable shell-fire, and by daylight had built communication trenches with head-cover from the crater lips to our front-line trenches.

But now it was the enemy's turn—the turn of his guns, which poured explosive fire into those pits, churning up the earth again, mixing it with new flesh and blood, and carving up his own dead; and it was the turn of his bombers, who followed this fire in strong assaults upon the Lancashire lads, who, lying among their killed and wounded, had to repel those fierce attacks.

On May 17th I went to see General Doran of the 25th Division, an optimistic old gentleman who took a bright view of things, and Colonel Crosby, who was acting—brigadier of the 74th Brigade, which had made the attack. He, too, was enthusiastic about the situation, though his brigade had suffered eight hundred casualties in a month of routine warfare.

In my simple way I asked him a direct question:

"Do you think your men can hold on to the craters, sir?"

Colonel Crosby stared at me sternly.

"Certainly. The position cannot be retaken overground. We hold it strongly."

As he spoke an orderly came into his billet (a small farmhouse), saluted, and handed him a pink slip, which was a telephone message. I watched him read it, and saw the sudden pallor of his face, and noticed how the room shook with the constant reverberation of distant gun-fire. A big bombardment was in progress over Vimy way.

"Excuse me," said the colonel; "things seem to be happening. I must go at once."

He went through the window, leaping the sill, and a look of bad tidings went with him.

His men had been blown out of the craters.

A staff officer sat in the brigade office, and when the acting-brigadier had gone raised his head and looked across to me.

"I am a critic of these affairs," he said. "They seem to me too expensive. But I'm here to do what I am told."

We did not regain the Vimy craters until a year afterward, when the Canadians and Scottish captured all the Vimy Ridge in a great assault.

XX

The winter of discontent had passed. Summer had come with a wealth of beauty in the fields of France this side the belt of blasted earth. The grass was a tapestry of flowers, and tits and warblers and the golden oriole were making music in the woods. At dusk the nightingale sang as though no war were near its love, and at broad noonday a million larks rose above the tall wheat with a great high chorus of glad notes.

Among the British armies there was hope again, immense faith that believed once more in an ending to the war. Verdun had been saved. The enemy had been slaughtered. His reserves were thin and hard to get (so said Intelligence) and the British, stronger than they had ever been, in men, and guns, and shells, and aircraft, and all material of war, were going to be launched in a great offensive. No more trench warfare. No more dying in ditches. Out into the open, with an Army of Pursuit (Rawlinson's) and a quick break-through. It was to be "The Great Push." The last battles were to be fought before the year died again, though many men would die before that time.

Up in the salient something happened to make men question the weakness of the enemy, but the news did not spread very far and there was a lot to do elsewhere, on the Somme, where the salient seemed a long way off. It was the Canadians to whom it happened, and it was an ugly thing.

On June 2d a flame of fire from many batteries opened upon their lines in Sanctuary Wood and Maple Copse, beyond the lines of Ypres, and tragedy befell them. I went to see those who lived through it and stood in the presence of men who had escaped from the very pits of that hell which had been invented by human beings out of the earth's chemistry, and yet had kept their reason.

The enemy's bombardment began suddenly, with one great crash of guns, at half past eight on Friday morning. Generals Mercer and Williams had gone up to inspect the trenches at six o'clock in the morning.

It had been almost silent along the lines when the enemy's batteries opened fire with one enormous thunderstroke, which was followed by continuous salvos. The shells came from nearly every point of the compass—north, east, and south. The evil spell of the salient was over our men again.

In the trenches just south of Hooge were the Princess Patricia's Light Infantry, with some battalions of the Royal Canadian Regiment south of them, and some of the Canadian Mounted Rifles (who had long been dismounted), and units from another Canadian division at the extreme end of their line of front. It was those men who had to suffer the tempest of the enemy's shells.

Earth below them opened up into great craters as high-explosive shells burst continually, flinging up masses of soil, flattening out breastworks and scattering sand-bags into dust.

Canadians in the front trenches held on in the midst of this uproar. "They took it all," said one of the officers, and in that phrase, spoken simply by a man who was there, too, lies the spirit of pride and sacrifice. "They took it all" and did not budge, though the sky seemed to be opening above them and the earth below them.

The bombardment continued without a pause for five hours, by which time most of our front trenches had been annihilated. At about a quarter past one the enemy's guns lifted a little, and through the dense smoke-clouds which made a solid bar across No Man's Land appeared a mass of German infantry. They wore their packs and full field-kit, as though they had come to stay.

Perhaps they expected that no one lived in the British trenches, and it was a reasonable idea, but wrong. There were brave men remaining there, alive and determined to fight. Although the order for retirement had been given, single figures here and there were seen to get over the broken parapets and go forward to meet the enemy halfway. They died to a man, fighting. It seemed to me one of the most pitiful and heroic things of this war, that little crowd of men, many of them wounded, some of them dazed and deaf, stumbling forward to their certain death to oppose the enemy's advance.

From the network of trenches behind, not altogether smashed, there was time for men to retire to a second line of defense, if they were still unwounded and had strength to go. An officer—Captain Crossman—in command of one of these support companies, brought several men out of a trench, but did not follow on. He turned again, facing the enemy, and was last seen—"a big, husky man," says one of his comrades—as he fired his revolver and then flung it into a German's face.

Colonel Shaw of the 1st Battalion, C.M.R., rallied eighty men out of the Cumberland dugouts, and died fighting. The Germans were kept at bay for some time, but they flung their bombs into the square of men, so that very few remained alive. When only eight were still fighting among the bodies of their comrades these tattered and blood-splashed men, standing there fiercely contemptuous of the enemy and death, were ordered to retire by Major Palmer, the last officer among them.

Meanwhile the battalions in support were holding firm in spite of the shell-fire, which raged above them also, and it was against this second line of Canadians that the German infantry came up—and broke.

In the center the German thrust was hard toward Zillebeke Lake. Here some of the Canadian Rifles were in support, and as soon as the infantry attack began they were ordered forward to meet and check the enemy. An officer in command of one of their battalions afterward told me that he led his men across country to Maple Copse under such a fire as he had never seen. Because of the comrades in front, in dire need of help, no notice was taken as the wounded fell, but the others pressed on as fast as they could go.

Maple Copse was reached, and here the men halted and awaited the enemy with another battalion who were already holding this wood of six or seven acres. When the German troops arrived they may have expected to meet no great resistance. They met a withering fire, which caused them bloody losses. The Canadians had assembled at various points, which became strongholds of defense with machine-guns and bomb stores, and the men held their fire until the enemy was within close range, so that they worked havoc among them. But the German guns never ceased and many Canadians fell. Col. E. H. Baker, a member of the Canadian Parliament, fell with a piece of shell in his lung.

Hour after hour our gunners fed their breeches and poured out shells. The edge of the salient was swept with fire, and, though the Canadian losses were frightful, the Germans suffered also, so that the battlefield was one great shambles. Our own wounded, who were brought back, owe their lives to the stretcher-bearers, who were supreme in devotion. They worked in and out across that shell-swept ground hour after hour through the day and night, rescuing many stricken men at a great cost in life to themselves. Out of one party of twenty only five remained alive. "No one can say," said one of their officers, "that the Canadians do not know how to die."

No one would deny that.

Out of three thousand men in the Canadian 8th Brigade their casualties were twenty-two hundred.

There were 151 survivors from the 1st Battalion Canadian Mounted Rifles, 130 from the 4th Battalion, 350 from the 5th, 520 from the 2nd. Those are the figures of massacre.

Eleven days later the Canadians took their revenge. Their own guns were but a small part of the huge orchestra of "heavies" and field batteries which played the devil's tattoo upon the German positions in our old trenches. It was annihilating, and the German soldiers had to endure the same experience as their guns had given to Canadian troops on the same ground. Trenches already battered were smashed again. The earth, which was plowed with shells in their own attack, was flung up again by our shells. It was hell again for poor human wretches.

The Canadian troops charged at two o'clock in the morning. Their attack was directed to the part of the line from the southern end of Sanctuary Wood to Mount Gorst, about a mile, which included Armagh Wood, Observatory Hill, and Mount Gorst itself.

The attack went quickly and the men expected greater trouble. The enemy's shell-fire was heavy, but the Canadians got through under cover of their own guns, which had lengthened their fuses a little and continued an intense bombardment behind the enemy's first line. The men advanced in open order and worked downward and southward into their old positions.

In one place of attack about forty Germans, who fought desperately, were killed almost to a man, just as Colonel Shaw had died on June 2d with his party of eighty men who had rallied round him. It was one shambles for another, and the Germans were not less brave, it seems.

One officer and one hundred and thirteen men surrendered. The officer was glad to escape from the death to which he had resigned himself when our bombardment began.

"I knew how it would be," he said. "We had orders to take this ground, and took it; but we knew you would come back again. You had to do so. So here I am."

Parts of the line were deserted, except by the dead. In one place the stores which had been buried by the Canadians before they left were still there, untouched by the enemy. Our bombardment had made it impossible for his troops to consolidate their position and to hold the line steady.

They had just taken cover in the old bits of trench, in shell-holes and craters, and behind scattered sand-bags, and had been pounded there. The Canadians were back again.

PART FIVE

THE HEART OF A CITY AMIENS IN TIME OF WAR

I

During the battles of the Somme in 1916, and afterward in periods of progress and retreat over the abominable fields, the city of Amiens was the capital of the British army. When the battles began in July of that year it was only a short distance away from the fighting-lines; near enough to hear the incessant roar of gun-fire on the French front and ours, and near enough to get, by motor-car or lorry, in less than thirty minutes, to places where men were being killed or maimed or blinded in the routine of the day's work. One went out past Amiens station and across a little stone bridge which afterward, in the enemy's advance of 1918, became the mark for German high velocities along the road to Querrieux, where Rawlinson had his headquarters of the Fourth Army in an old chateau with pleasant meadows round it and a stream meandering through fields of buttercups in summer-time. Beyond the dusty village of Querrieux with its white cottages, from which the plaster fell off in blotches as the war went on, we went along the straight highroad to Albert, through the long and straggling village of Lahoussoye, where Scottish soldiers in reserve lounged about among frowsy peasant women and played solemn games with "the bairns"; and so, past camps and hutments on each side of the road, to the ugly red-brick town where the Golden Virgin hung head downward from the broken tower of the church with her Babe outstretched above the fields of death as though as a peace-offering to this world at war.

One could be killed any day in Albert. I saw men blown to bits there the clay after the battles of the Somme began. It was in the road that turned to the right, past the square to go to Meaulte and on to Fricourt. There was a tide of gun transport swirling down the road, bringing up new ammunition for the guns that were firing without a pause over Fricourt and Mametz. The high scream of a shell came through a blue sky and ended on its downward note with a sharp crash. For a few minutes the transport column was held up while a mass of raw flesh which a second before had been two living men and their horses was cleared out of the way. Then the gun wagons went at a harder pace down the road, raising a cloud of white dust out of which I heard the curses of the drivers, swearing in a foul way to disguise their fear.

I went through Albert many scores of times to the battlefields beyond, and watched its process of disintegration through those years, until it was nothing but a wild scrap heap of read brick and twisted iron, and, in the last phase, even the Golden Virgin and her Babe, which had seemed to escape all shell-fire by miraculous powers, lay buried beneath a mass of masonry. Beyond were the battlefields of the Somme where every yard of ground is part of the great graveyard of our youth.

So Amiens, as I have said, was not far away from the red heart of war, and was clear enough to the lines to be crowded always with officers and men who came out between one battle and another, and by "lorry-jumping" could reach this city for a few hours of civilized life, according to their views of civilization. To these men—boys, mostly—who had been living in lousy ditches under hell fire, Amiens was Paradise, with little hells for those who liked them. There were hotels in which they could go get a bath, if they waited long enough or had the luck to be early on the list. There were streets of shops with plate-glass windows unbroken, shining, beautiful. There were well-dressed women walking about, with kind eyes, and children as dainty, some of them, as in High Street, Kensington, or Prince's Street, Edinburgh. Young officers, who had plenty of money to spend—because there was no chance of spending money between a row of blasted trees and a ditch in which bits of dead men were plastered into the parapet—invaded the shops and bought fancy soaps, razors, hair-oil, stationery, pocketbooks, knives, flash-lamps, top-boots (at a fabulous price), khaki shirts and collars, gramophone records, and the latest set of Kirchner prints. It was the delight of spending, rather than the joy of possessing, which made them go from one shop to another in search of things they could carry hack to the line—that and the lure of girls behind the counters, laughing, bright-eyed girls who understood their execrable French, even English spoken with a Glasgow accent, and were pleased to flirt for five minutes with any group of young fighting-men—who broke into roars of laughter at the gallantry of some Don Juan among them with the gift of audacity, and paid outrageous prices for the privilege of stammering out some foolish sentiment in broken French, blushing to the roots of their hair (though captains and heroes) at their own temerity with a girl who, in another five minutes, would play the same part in the same scene with a different group of boys.

I used to marvel at the patience of these girls. How bored they must have been with all this flirtation, which led to nothing except, perhaps, the purchase of a bit of soap at twice its proper price! They knew that these boys would leave to go back to the trenches in a few hours and that some of them would certainly be dead in a few days. There could be no romantic episode, save of a transient kind, between them and these good-looking lads in whose eyes there were desire and hunger, because to them the plainest girl was Womanhood, the sweet, gentle, and feminine side of life, as opposed to the cruelty, brutality, and ugliness of war and death. The shopgirls of Amiens had no illusions. They had lived too long in war not to know the realities. They knew the risks of transient love and they were not taking them—unless conditions were very favorable. They attended strictly to business and hoped to make a lot of money in the shop, and were, I think, mostly good girls—as virtuous as life in wartime may let girls be—wise beyond their years, and with pity behind their laughter for these soldiers who tried to touch their hands over the counters, knowing that many of them were doomed to die for France and England. They had their own lovers—boys in blue somewhere between Vaux-sur-Somme and Hartmanns—weilerkopf—and apart from occasional intimacies with English officers quartered in Amiens for long spells, left the traffic of passion to other women who walked the streets.

II

The Street of the Three Pebbles—la rue des Trois Cailloux—which goes up from the station through the heart of Amiens, was the crowded highway. Here were the best shops—the hairdresser, at the left-hand side, where all day long officers down from the line came in to have elaborate luxury in the way of close crops with *friction d'eau de quinine,* shampooing, singeing, oiling, not because of vanity, but because of the joyous sense of cleanliness and perfume after the filth and stench of life in the desolate fields; then the booksellers' (Madame Carpentier et *fille*) on the right-hand side, which was not only the rendezvous of the miscellaneous crowd buying stationery and *La Vie Parisienne,* but of the intellectuals who spoke good French and bought good books and liked ten minutes' chat with the mother and daughter. (Madame was an Alsatian lady with vivid memories of 1870, when, as a child, she had first learned to hate Germans.) She hated them now with a fresh, vital hatred, and would have seen her own son dead a hundred times—he was a soldier in Saloniki—rather than that France should make a compromise peace with the enemy. She had been in Amiens, as I was, on a dreadful night of August of 1914, when the French army passed through in retreat from Bapaume, and she and the people of her city knew for the first time that the Germans were close upon them. She stood in the crowd as I did—in the darkness, watching that French column pass with their transport, and their wounded lying on the baggage wagons, men of many regiments mixed up, the light of the street lamps shining on the casques of cuirassiers with their long horsehair tails, leading their stumbling horses, and foot soldiers, hunched under their packs, marching silently with dragging steps. Once in a while one of the soldiers left the ranks and came on to the sidewalk, whispering to a group of dark shadows. The crowds watched silently, in a curious, dreadful silence, as though stunned. A woman near me spoke in a low voice, and said, *"Nous sommes perdus!"* Those were the only words I heard or remembered.

That night in the station of Amiens the boys of a new class were being hurried away in truck trains, and while their army was in retreat sang "La Marseillaise," as though victory were in their hearts. Next day the German army under von Kluck entered Amiens, and ten days afterward passed through it on the way to Paris. Madame Carpentier told me of the first terror of the people when the field-gray men came down the Street of the Three Pebbles and entered their shops. A boy selling oranges fainted when a German stretched out his hand to buy some. Women hid behind their counters when German boots stamped into their shops. But Madame Carpentier was not afraid. She knew the Germans and their language. She spoke frank words to German officers, who saluted her respectfully enough. "You will never get to Paris... France and England will be too strong for you... Germany will be destroyed before this war ends." They laughed at her and said: "We shall be in Paris in a week from now. Have you a little diary, Madame?" Madame Carpentier was haughty with them. Some women of Amiens—poor drabs—did not show any haughtiness, nor any pride, with the enemy who crowded into the city on their way toward Paris. A girl told me that she was looking through the window of a house that faced the Place de la Gare, and saw a number of German soldiers dancing round a piano-organ which was playing to them. They were dancing with women of the town, who were laughing and screeching in the embrace of big, blond Germans. The girl who was watching was only a schoolgirl then. She knew very little of the evil of life, but enough to know that there was something in this scene degrading to womanhood and to France. She turned from the window and flung herself on her bed and wept bitterly...

I used to call in at the bookshop for a chat now and then with Madame and Mademoiselle Carpentier, while a crowd of officers came in and out. Madame was always merry and bright in spite of her denunciations of the *"Sale Boches—les brigands, les bandits!"* and Mademoiselle put my knowledge of French to a severe but pleasant test. She spoke with alarming rapidity, her words tumbling over one another in a cascade of volubility delightful to hear but difficult to follow. She had a strong mind—masterly in her methods of business—so that she could serve six customers at once and make each one think that her attention was entirely devoted to his needs—and a very shrewd and critical idea of military strategy and organization. She had but a poor opinion of British generals and generalship, although a wholehearted admiration for the gallantry of British officers and men; and she had an intimate knowledge of our preparations, plans, failures, and losses. French liaison-officers confided to her the secrets of the British army; and English officers trusted her with many revelations of things "in the wind." But Mademoiselle Carpentier had discretion and loyalty and did not repeat these things to people who had no right to know. She would have been far more efficient as a staff officer than many of the young gentlemen with red tabs on their tunics who came into the shop, flipping beautiful top-boots with riding-crops, sitting on the counter, and turning over the pages of *La Vie* for the latest convention in ladies' legs.

Mademoiselle was a serious musician, so her mother told me, but her musical studies were seriously interrupted by business and air raids, which one day ceased in Amiens altogether after a night of horror, when hundreds of houses were smashed to dust and many people killed, and the Germans brought their guns close to the city—close enough to scatter high velocities about its streets—and the population came up out of their cellars, shaken by the terror of the night, and fled. I passed the bookshop where Mademoiselle was locking up the door of this house which had escaped by greater luck than its neighbors. She turned as I passed and raised her hand with a grave gesture of resignation and courage. *"Ils ne passeront pas!"* she said. It was the spirit of the courage of French womanhood which spoke in those words.

III

That was in the last phase of the war, but the Street of the Three Pebbles had been tramped up and down for two years before then by the British armies on the Somme, with the French on their right. I was never tired of watching those crowds and getting into the midst of them, and studying their types. All the types of young English manhood came down this street, and some of their faces showed the strain and agony of war, especially toward the end of the Somme battles, after four months or more of slaughter. I saw boys with a kind of hunted look in their eyes; and Death was the hunter. They stared into the shop windows in a dazed way, or strode along with packs on their backs, looking neither to the right nor to the left, and white, haggard faces, as expressionless as masks. Tomorrow or the next day, perhaps, the Hunter would track them down. Other English officers showed no sign at all of apprehension or lack of nerve-control, although the psychologist would have detected disorder of soul in the rather deliberate note of hilarity with which they greeted their friends, in gusts of laughter, for no apparent cause, at "Charlie's bar," where they would drink three cocktails apiece on an empty stomach, and in their tendency to tell tales of horror as things that were very funny. They dined and wined in Amiens at the "Rhin," the "Godebert," or the "Cathedrale," with a kind of spiritual exaltation in good food and drink, as though subconsciously they believed that this might be their last dinner in life, with good pals about them. They wanted to make the best of it—and damn the price. In that spirit many of them went after other pleasures—down the byways of the city, and damned the price again, which was a hellish one. Who blames them? It was war that was to blame, and those who made war possible.

Down the rue des Trois Cailloux, up and down, up and down, went English, and Scottish, and Irish, and Welsh, and Canadian, and Australian, and New Zealand fighting—men. In the winter they wore their trench-coats all splashed and caked up to the shoulders with the white, chalky mud of the Somme battlefields, and their top—boots and puttees were plastered with this mud, and their faces were smeared with it after a lorry drive or a tramp down from the line. The rain beat with a metallic tattoo on their steel hats. Their packs were all sodden.

French poilus, detrained at Amiens station for a night on their way to some other part of the front, jostled among British soldiers, and their packs were a wonder to see. They were like traveling tinkers, with pots and pans and boots slung about their faded blue coats, and packs bulging with all the primitive needs of life in the desert of the battlefields beyond civilization. They were unshaven, and wore their steel casques low over their foreheads, without gaiety, without the means of buying a little false hilarity, but grim and sullen—looking and resentful of English soldiers walking or talking with French *cocottes.*

IV

I saw a scene with a French poilu one day in the Street of the Three Pebbles, during those battles of the Somme, when the French troops were fighting on our right from Maricourt southward toward Roye. It was like a scene from "Gaspard." The poilu was a middle-aged man, and very drunk on some foul spirit which he had bought in a low cafe down by the river. In the High Street he was noisy, and cursed God for having allowed the war to happen, and the French government for having sentenced him and all poor *sacre poilus* to rot to death in the trenches, away from their wives and children, without a thought for them; and nothing but treachery in Paris:

"Nous sommes trahis!" said the man, raising his arms. "For the hundredth time France is betrayed."

A crowd gathered round him, listening to his drunken denunciations. No one laughed. They stared at him with a kind of pitying wonderment. An *agent de police* pushed his way between the people and caught hold of the soldier by the wrist and tried to drag him away. The crowd murmured a protest, and then suddenly the poilu, finding himself in the hands of the police, on this one day out of the trenches—after five months—flung himself on the pavement in a passion of tears and supplication.

"*Je suis pere de famille!... Je suis un soldat de France!... Dans les tranchees pour cinq mois!... Qu'est-ce que mes camarades vont dire, 'cre nom de Dieu? et mon capitaine? C'est emmordant apres toute ma service comme brave soldat. Mais, quoi donc, mon vieux!"*

"Viens donc, saligaud," growled the agent de police.

The crowd was against the policeman. Their murmurs rose to violent protest on behalf of the poilu.

"C'est un heros, tout de meme. Cinq mois dans les tranches! C'est affreux! Mais oui, il est soul, mais pour—quoi pas! Apres cinq mois sur le front qu'est-ce que cela signifie? Ca n'a aucune importance!"

A dandy French officer of Chasseurs Alpins stepped into the center of the scene and tapped the policeman on the shoulder.

"Leave him alone. Don't you see he is a soldier? Sacred name of God, don't you know that a man like this has helped to save France, while you pigs stand at street corners watching petticoats?"

He stooped to the fallen man and helped him to stand straight.

"Be off with you, mon brave, or there will be trouble for you."

He beckoned to two of his own Chasseurs and said:

"Look after that poor comrade yonder. He is un peu etoile."

The crowd applauded. Their sympathy was all for the drunken soldier of France.

V

Into a small *estaminet* at the end of the rue des Trois Cailloux, beyond the Hotel de Ville, came one day during the battles of the Somme two poilus, grizzled, heavy men, deeply bronzed, with white dust in their wrinkles, and the earth of the battlefields ingrained in the skin of their big, coarse hands. They ordered two "little glasses" and drank them at one gulp. Then two more.

"See what I have got, my little cabbage," said one of them, stooping to the heavy pack which he had shifted from his shoulders to the other seat beside him. "It is something to make you laugh."

"And what is that, my old one?" said a woman sitting on the other side of the marble-topped table, with another woman of her own class, from the market nearby.

The man did not answer the question, but fumbled into his pack, laughing a little in a self-satisfied way.

"I killed a German to get it," he said. "He was a pig of an officer, a dirty Boche. Very chic, too, and young like a schoolboy."

One of the women patted him on the shoulder. Her eyes glistened.

"Did you slit his throat, the dirty dog? Eh, I'd like to get my fingers round the neck of a dirty Boche!"

"I finished him with a grenade," said the poilu. "It was good enough. It knocked a hole in him as large as a cemetery. See then, my cabbage. It will make you smile. It is a funny kind of mascot, eh?"

He put on the table a small leather pouch stained with a blotch of reddish brown. His big, clumsy fingers could hardly undo the little clasp.

"He wore this next his heart," said the man. "Perhaps he thought it would bring him luck. But I killed him all the same! 'Cre nom de Dieu!"

He undid the clasp, and his big fingers poked inside the flap of the pouch.

"It was from his woman, his German grue. Perhaps even now she doesn't know he's dead. She thinks of him wearing this next to his heart. 'Cre nom de Dieu! It was I that killed him a week ago!"

He held up something in his hand, and the light through the *estaminet* window gleamed on it. It was a woman's lock of hair, like fine-spun gold.

The two women gave a shrill cry of surprise, and then screamed with laughter. One of them tried to grab the hair, but the poilu held it high, beyond her reach, with a gruff command of, "Hands off!" Other soldiers and women in the *estaminet* gathered round staring at the yellow tress, laughing, making ribald conjectures as to the character of the woman from whose head it had come. They agreed that she was fat and ugly, like all German women, and a foul slut.

"She'll never kiss that fellow again," said one man. "Our old one has cut the throat of that pig of a Boche!"

"I'd like to cut off all her hair and tear the clothes off her back," said one of the women. "The dirty drab with yellow hair! They ought to be killed, every one of them, so that the human race should by rid of them!"

"Her lover is a bit of clay, anyhow," said the other woman. "A bit of dirt, as our poilus will do for all of them."

The soldier with the woman's hair in his hand stroked it across his forefinger.

"All the same it is pretty. Like gold, eh? I think of the woman, sometimes. With blue eyes, like a German girl I kissed in Paris-a dancing-girl!"

There was a howl of laughter from the two women.

"The old one is drunk. He is amorous with the German cow!"

"I will keep it as a mascot," said the poilu, scrunching it up and thrusting it into his pouch. "It'll keep me in mind of that saligaud of a German officer I killed. He was a chic fellow, tout de meme. A boy."

VI

Australians slouched up the Street of the Three Pebbles with a grim look under their wide-brimmed hats, having come down from Pozieres, where it was always hell in the days of the Somme fighting. I liked the look of them, dusty up to the eyes in summer, muddy up to their eyes in winter—these gipsy fellows, scornful of discipline for discipline's sake, but desperate fighters, as simple as children in their ways of thought and speech (except for frightful oaths), and looking at life, this life of war and this life in Amiens, with frank, curious eyes, and a kind of humorous contempt for death, and disease, and English Tommies, and French girls, and "the whole damned show," as they called it. They were lawless except for the laws to which their souls gave allegiance. They behaved as the equals of all men, giving no respect to generals or staff-officers or the devils of hell. There was a primitive spirit of manhood in them, and they took what they wanted, and were ready to pay for it in coin or in disease or in wounds. They had no conceit of themselves in a little, vain way, but they reckoned themselves the only fighting-men, simply, and without boasting. They were hard as steel, and finely tempered. Some of them were ruffians, but most of them were, I imagine, like those English yeomen who came into France with the Black Prince, men who lived "rough," close to nature, of sturdy independence, good-humored, though fierce in a fight, and ruthless. That is how they seemed to me, in a general way, though among them were boys of a more delicate fiber, and sensitive, if one might judge by their clear-cut features and wistful eyes. They had money to spend beyond the dreams of our poor Tommy. Six shillings and sixpence a day and remittances from home. So they pushed open the doors of any restaurant in Amiens and sat down to table next to English officers, not abashed, and ordered anything that pleased their taste, and wine in plenty.

In that High Street of Amiens one day I saw a crowd gathered round an Australian, so tall that he towered over all other heads. It was at the corner of the rue de Corps Nu sans Teste, the Street of the Naked Body without a Head, and I suspected trouble. As I pressed on the edge of the crowd I heard the Australian ask, in a loud, slow drawl, whether there was any officer about who could speak French. He asked the question gravely, but without anxiety. I pushed through the crowd and said: "I speak French. What's the trouble?"

I saw then that, like the French poilu I have described, this tall Australian was in the grasp of a French agent de police, a small man of whom he took no more notice than if a fly had settled on his wrist. The Australian was not drunk. I could see that he had just drunk enough to make his brain very clear and solemn. He explained the matter deliberately, with a slow choice of words, as though giving evidence of high matters before a court. It appeared that he had gone into the *estaminet* opposite with four friends. They had ordered five glasses of porto, for which they had paid twenty centimes each, and drank them. They then ordered five more glasses of *porto* and paid the same price, and drank them. After this they took a stroll up and down the street, and were bored, and went into the *estaminet* again, and ordered five more glasses of porto. It was then the trouble began. But it was not the Australian who began it. It was the woman behind the bar. She served five glasses more of *porto* and asked for thirty centimes each.

"Twenty centimes," said the Australian. "Vingt, Madame."

"Mais non! Trente centimes, chaque verre! Thirty, my old one. Six sous, comprenez?"

"No comprennye," said the Australian. "Vingt centimes, or go to hell."

The woman demanded the thirty centimes; kept on demanding with a voice more shrill.

"It was her voice that vexed me," said the Australian. "That and the bloody injustice."

The five Australians drank the five glasses of porto, and the tall Australian paid the thirty centimes each without further argument. Life is too short for argument. Then, without words, he took each of the five glasses, broke it at the stem, and dropped it over the counter.

"You will see, sir," he said, gravely, "the justice of the matter on my side."

But when they left the *estaminet* the woman came shrieking into the street after them. Hence the *agent de police* and the grasp on the Australian's wrist.

"I should be glad if you would explain the case to this little Frenchman," said the soldier. "If he does not take his hand off my wrist I shall have to kill him."

"Perhaps a little explanation might serve," I said.

I spoke to the *agent de police* at some length, describing the incident in the cafe. I took the view that the lady was wrong in increasing the price so rapidly. The *agent* agreed gravely. I then pointed out that the Australian was a very large-sized man, and that in spite of his quietude he was a man in the habit of killing Germans. He also had a curious dislike of policemen.

"It appears to me," I said, politely, "that for the sake of your health the other end of the street is better than this."

The a*gent de police* released his grip from the Australian's wrist and saluted me.

"Vous avez raison, monsieur. Je vous remercie. Ces Australiens sont vraiment formidables, n'est-ce pas?"

He disappeared through the crowd, who were smiling with a keen sense of understanding. Only the lady of the *estaminet* was unappeased.

"They are bandits, these Australians!" she said to the world about her.

The tall Australian shook hands with me in a comradely way.

"Thanks for your trouble," he said. "It was the injustice I couldn't stick. I always pay the right price. I come from Australia."

I watched him go slouching down the rue des Trois Cailloux, head above all the passers-by. He would be at Pozieres again next day.

VII

I was billeted for a time with other war correspondents in an old house in the rue Amiral Courbet, on the way to the river Somme from the Street of the Three Pebbles, and with a view of the spire of the cathedral, a wonderful thing of delicate lines and tracery, graven with love in every line, by Muirhead Bone, and from my dormer window. It was the house of Mme. de la Rochefoucauld, who lived farther out of the town, but drove in now and then to look at this little mansion of hers at the end of a courtyard behind wrought-iron gates. It was built in the days before the Revolution, when it was dangerous to be a fine lady with the name of Rochefoucauld. The furniture was rather scanty, and was of the Louis Quinze and Empire periods. Some portraits of old gentlemen and ladies of France, with one young fellow in a scarlet coat, who might have been in the King's Company of the Guard about the time when Wolfe scaled the Heights of Abraham, summoned up the ghosts of the house, and I liked to think of them in these rooms and going in their sedan-chairs across the little courtyard to high mass at the cathedral or to a game of bezique in some other mansion, still standing in the quiet streets of Amiens, unless in a day in March of 1918 they were destroyed with many hundreds of houses by bombs and gun-fire. My little room was on the floor below the garret, and here at night, after a long day in the fields up by Pozieres or Martinpuich or beyond, by Ligny-Tilloy, on the way to Bapaume, in the long struggle and slaughter over every inch of ground, I used to write my day's despatch, to be taken next day (it was before we were allowed to use the military wires) by King's Messenger to England.

Those articles, written at high speed, with an impressionism born out of many new memories of tragic and heroic scenes, were interrupted sometimes by air-bombardments. Hostile airmen came often to Amiens during the Somme fighting, to unload their bombs as near to the station as they could guess, which was not often very near. Generally they killed a few women and children and knocked a few poor houses and a shop or two into a wild rubbish heap of bricks and timber. While I wrote, listening to the crashing of glass and the anti-aircraft fire of French guns from the citadel, I used to wonder subconsciously whether I should suddenly be hurled into chaos at the end of an unfinished sentence, and now and again in spite of my desperate conflict with time to get my message done (the censors were waiting for it downstairs) I had to get up and walk into the passage to listen to the infernal noise in the dark city of Amiens. But I went back again and bent over my paper, concentrating on the picture of war which I was trying to set down so that the world might see and understand, until once again, ten minutes later or so, my will-power would weaken and the little devil of fear would creep up to my heart and I would go uneasily to the door again to listen. Then once more to my writing... Nothing touched the house in the rue Amiral Courbet while we were there. But it was into my bedroom that a shell went crashing after that night in March when Amiens was badly wrecked, and we listened to the noise of destruction all around us from a room in the Hotel du Rhin on the other side of the way. I should have been sleeping still if I had slept that night in my little old bedroom when the shell paid a visit.

There were no lights allowed at night in Amiens, and when I think of darkness I think of that city in time of war, when all the streets were black tunnels and one fumbled one's way timidly, if one had no flash-lamp, between the old houses with their pointed gables, coming into sharp collision sometimes with other wayfarers. But up to midnight there were little lights flashing for a second and then going out, along the Street of the Three Pebbles and in the dark corners of side-streets. They were carried by girls seeking to entice English officers on their way to their billets, and they clustered like glowworms about the side door of the Hotel du Rhin after nine o'clock, and outside the railings of the public gardens. As one passed, the bright bull's-eye from a pocket torch flashed in one's eyes, and in the radiance of it one saw a girl's face, laughing, coming very close, while her fingers felt for one's badge.

"How dark it is to-night, little captain! Are you not afraid of darkness? I am full of fear. It is so sad, this war, so dismal! It is comradeship that helps one now!... A little love... a little laughter, and then—who knows?"

A little love... a little laughter—alluring words to boys out of one battle, expecting another, hating it all, lonely in their souls because of the thought of death, in exile from their own folk, in exile from all womanhood and tender, feminine things, up there in the ditches and shellcraters of the desert fields, or in the huts of headquarters staffs, or in reserve camps behind the fighting-line. A little love, a little laughter, and then—who knows? The sirens had whispered their own thoughts. They had translated into pretty French the temptation of all the little devils in their souls.

"Un peu d'amour-"

One flash-lamp was enough for two down a narrow street toward the riverside, and then up a little dark stairway to a lamp-lit room... Presently this poor boy would be stricken with disease and wish himself dead.

VIII

In the Street of the Three Pebbles there was a small estaminet into which I went one morning for a cup of coffee, while I read an Amiens news-sheet made up mostly of extracts translated from the leading articles of English papers. (There was never any news of French fighting beyond the official communique and imaginary articles of a romantic kind written by French journalists in Paris about episodes of war.) In one corner of the estaminet was a group of bourgeois gentlemen talking business for a time, and then listening to a monologue from the woman behind the counter. I could not catch many words of the conversation, owing to the general chatter, but when the man went out the woman and I were left alone together, and she came over to me and put a photograph down on the table before me, and, as though carrying on her previous train of thought, said, in French, of course:

"Yes, that is what the war has done to me."

I could not guess her meaning. Looking at the photograph, I saw it was of a young girl in evening dress with her hair coiled in an artistic way and a little curl on each cheek. Madame's daughter, I thought, looking up at the woman standing in front of me in a grubby bodice and tousled hair. She looked a woman of about forty, with a wan face and beaten eyes.

"A charming young lady," I said, glancing again at the portrait.

The woman repeated her last sentence, word for word.

"Yes... that is what the war has done to me."

I looked up at her again and saw that she had the face of the young girl in the photograph, but coarsened, aged, raddled, by the passing years and perhaps by tragedy.

"It is you?" I asked.

"Yes, in 1913, before the war. I have changed since then—n'est-ce pas, Monsieur?"

"There is a change," I said. I tried not to express my thought of how much change.

"You have suffered in the war—more than most people?"

"Ah, I have suffered!"

She told me her story, and word for word, if I could have written it down then, it would have read like a little novel by Guy de Maupassant. She was the daughter of people in Lille, well-to-do merchants, and before the war married a young man of the same town, the son of other manufacturers. They had two children and were very happy. Then the war came. The enemy drove down through Belgium, and one day drew near and threatened Lille. The parents of the young couple said: "We will stay. We are too old to leave our home, and it is better to keep watch over the factory. You must go, with the little ones, and there is no time to lose."

There was no time to lose. The trains were crowded with fugitives and soldiers—mostly soldiers. It was necessary to walk. Weeping, the young husband and wife said farewell to their parents and set out on the long trail, with the two babies in a perambulator, under a load of bread and wine, and a little maid carrying some clothes in a bundle. For days they tramped the roads until they were all dusty and bedraggled and footsore, but glad to be getting farther away from that tide of field-gray men which had now swamped over Lille. The young husband comforted his wife. "Courage!" he said. "I have money enough to carry us through the war. We will set up a little shop somewhere." The maid wept bitterly now and then, but the young husband said: "We will take care of you, Margot. There is nothing to fear. We are lucky in our escape." He was a delicate fellow, rejected for military service, but brave. They came to Amiens, and hired the *estaminet* and set up business. There was a heavy debt to work off for capital and expenses before they would make money, but they were doing well. The mother was happy with her children, and the little maid had dried her tears. Then one day the young husband went away with the little maid and all the money, leaving his wife in the *estaminet* with a big debt to pay and a broken heart.

"That is what the war has done to me," she said again, picking up the photograph of the girl in the evening frock with a little curl on each cheek.

"C'est triste, Madame!"

"Oui, c'est triste, Monsieur!"

But it was not war that had caused her tragedy, except that it had unloosened the roots of her family life. Guy de Maupassant would have given just such an ending to his story.

IX

Some of our officers stationed in Amiens, and billeted in private houses, became very friendly with the families who received them. Young girls of good middle class, the daughters of shopkeepers and schoolmasters, and merchants in a good way of business, found it delightful to wait on handsome young Englishmen, to teach them French, to take walks with them, and to arrange musical evenings with other girl friends who brought their young officers and sang little old French songs with them or English songs in the prettiest French accent. These young officers of ours found the home life very charming. It broke the monotony of exile and made them forget the evil side of war. They paid little gallantries to the girls, bought them boxes of chocolate until fancy chocolate was forbidden in France, and presented flowers to decorate the table, and wrote amusing verses in their autograph albums or drew sketches for them. As this went on they gained to the privilege of brotherhood, and there were kisses before saying "good night" outside bedroom doors, while the parents downstairs were not too watchful, knowing the ways of young people, and lenient because of their happiness. Then a day came in each one of these households when the officer billeted there was ordered away to some other place. What tears! What lamentations! And what promises never to forget little Jeanne with her dark tresses, or Suzanne with the merry eyes! Were they not engaged? Not formally, perhaps, but in honor and in love. For a time letters arrived, eagerly waited for by girls with aching hearts. Then picture post-cards with a line or two of affectionate greeting. Then nothing. Nothing at all, month after month, in spite of all the letters addressed with all the queer initials for military units. So it happened again and again, until bitterness crept into girls' hearts, and hardness and contempt.

"In my own little circle of friends," said a lady of Amiens, "I know eighteen girls who were engaged to English officers and have been forsaken. It is not fair. It is not good. Your English young men seem so serious, far more serious than our French boys. They have a look of shyness which we find delightful. They are timid, at first, and blush when one pays a pretty compliment. They are a long time before they take liberties. So we trust them, and take them seriously, and allow intimacies which we should refuse to French boys unless formally engaged. But it is all camouflage. At heart your English young men are just flirts. They play with us, make fools of us, steal our hearts, and then go away, and often do not send so much as a post-card. Not even one little post-card to the girls who weep their hearts out for them! You English are all hypocrites. You boast that you 'play the game.' I know your phrase. It is untrue.

"You play with good girls as though they were grues, and that no Frenchman would dare to do. He knows the difference between good girls and bad girls, and behaves, with reverence to those who are good. When the English army goes away from France it will leave many bitter memories because of that."

X

It was my habit to go out at night for a walk through Amiens before going to bed, and generally turned river-ward, for even on moonless nights there was always a luminance over the water and one could see to walk along the quayside. Northward and eastward the sky was quivering with flashes of white light, like summer lightning, and now and then there was a long, vivid glare of red touching the high clouds with rosy feathers; one of our dumps, or one of the enemy's, had been blown up by that gun-fire, sullen and menacing, which never ceased for years. In that quiet half-hour, alone, or with some comrade, like Frederic Palmer or Beach Thomas, as tired and as thoughtful as oneself after a long day's journeying in the swirl of war, one's brain roved over the scenes of battle, visualizing anew, and in imagination, the agony up there, the death which was being done by those guns, and the stupendous sum of all this conflict. We saw, after all, only one patch of the battlefields of the world, and yet were staggered by the immensity of its massacre, by the endless streams of wounded, and by the growth of those little forests of white crosses behind the fighting-lines. We knew, and could see at any moment in the mind's eye—even in the darkness of an Amiens night—the vastness of the human energy which was in motion along all the roads to Paris and from Boulogne and Dieppe and Havre to the fighting-lines, and in every village on the way the long columns of motor-lorries bringing up food and ammunition, the trains on their way to the army rail-heads with material of war and more food and more shells, the Red Cross trains crowded with maimed and injured boys, the ambulances clearing the casualty stations, the troops marching forward from back roads to the front, from which many would never come marching back, the guns and limbers and military transports and spare horses, along hundreds of miles of roads—all the machinery of slaughter on the move. It was staggering in its enormity, in its detail, and in its activity. Yet beyond our sphere in the British section of the western front there was the French front, larger than ours, stretching right through France, and all their roads were crowded with the same traffic, and all their towns and villages were stirred by the same activity and for the same purpose of death, and all their hospitals were crammed with the wreckage of youth. On the other side of the lines the Germans were busy in the same way, as busy as soldier ants, and the roads behind their front were cumbered by endless columns of transport and marching men, and guns and ambulances laden with bashed, blinded, and bleeding boys. So it was in Italy, in Austria, in Saloniki, and Bulgaria, Serbia, Mesopotamia, Egypt... In the silence of Amiens by night, under the stars, with a cool breath of the night air on our foreheads, with a glamour of light over the waters of the Somme, our spirit was stricken by the thought of this world-tragedy, and cried out in anguish against this bloody crime in which all humanity was involved. The senselessness of it! The futility! The waste! The mockery of men's faith in God!...

Often Palmer and I—dear, grave old Palmer, with sphinx-like face and honest soul—used to trudge along silently, with just a sigh now and then, or a groan, or a sudden cry of "O God!... O Christ!" It was I, generally, who spoke those words, and Palmer would say: "Yes... and it's going to last a long time yet. A long time... It's a question who will hold out twenty-four hours longer than the other side. France is tired, more tired than any of us. Will she break first? Somehow I think not. They are wonderful! Their women have a gallant spirit... How good it is, the smell of the trees to-night!"

Sometimes we would cross the river and look back at the cathedral, high and beautiful above the huddle of old, old houses on the quayside, with a faint light on its pinnacle and buttresses and immense blackness beyond them.

"Those builders of France loved their work," said Palmer. "There was always war about the walls of this cathedral, but they went on with it, stone by stone, without hurry."

We stood there in a long silence, not on one night only, but many times, and out of those little dark streets below the cathedral of Amiens came the spirit of history to teach our spirit with wonderment at the nobility and the brutality of men, and their incurable folly, and their patience with tyranny.

"When is it all going to end, Palmer, old man?"

"The war, or the folly of men?"

"The war. This cursed war. This bloody war."

"Something will break one day, on our side or the other. Those who hold out longest and have the best reserves of man-power."

We were starting early next day—before dawn—to see the beginning of another battle. We walked slowly over the little iron bridge again, through the vegetable market, where old men and women were unloading cabbages from a big wagon, then into the dark tunnel of the rue des Augustins, and so to the little old mansion of Mme. de la Rochefoucauld in the rue Amiral Courbet. There was a light burning in the window of the censor's room. In there the colonel was reading *The Times* in the Louis Quinze with a grave pucker on his high, thin forehead. He could not get any grasp of the world's events. There was an attack on the censor by Northcliffe. Now what did he mean by that? It was really very unkind of him, after so much civility to him. Charteris would be furious. He would bang the telephone—but—dear, dear, why should people be so violent? War correspondents were violent on the slightest provocation. The world itself was very violent. And it was all so dangerous. Don't you think so, Russell?

The cars were ordered for five o'clock. Time for bed.

XI

The night in Amiens was dark and sinister when rain fell heavily out of a moonless sky. Hardly a torch-lamp flashed out except where a solitary woman scurried down the wet streets to lonely rooms. There were no British officers strolling about. They had turned in early, to hot baths and unaccustomed beds, except for one or two, with their burberries buttoned tight at the throat, and sopping field-caps pulled down about the ears, and top—boots which went splash, splash through deep puddles as they staggered a little uncertainly and peered up at dark corners to find their whereabouts, by a dim sense of locality and the shapes of the houses. The rain pattered sharply on the pavements and beat a tattoo on leaden gutters and slate roofs. Every window was shuttered and no light gleamed through.

On such a night I went out with Beach Thomas, as often before, wet or fine, after hard writing.

"A foul night," said Thomas, setting off in his quick, jerky step. "I like to feel the rain on my face."

We turned down as usual to the river. It was very dark—the rain was heavy on the quayside, where there was a group of people bareheaded in the rain and chattering in French, with gusts of laughter.

"Une bouteille de champagne!" The words were spoken in a clear boy's voice, with an elaborate caricature of French accent, in musical cadence, but unmistakably English.

"A drunken officer," said Thomas.

"Poor devil!"

We drew near among the people and saw a young officer arm in arm with a French peasant—one of the market porters—telling a tale in broken French to the audience about him, with comic gesticulations and extraor dinary volubility.

A woman put her hand on my shoulder and spoke in French.

"He has drunk too much bad wine. His legs walk away from him. He will be in trouble, Monsieur. And a child—no older than my own boy who is fighting in the Argonne."

"Apportez-moi une bouteille de champagne, vite!..." said the young officer. Then he waved his arm and said: "J'ai perdu mon cheval" ("A kingdom for a bloody horse!"), "as Shakespeare said. *Y a-t'il quelqu'un qui a vu mon sacre cheval?* In other words, if I don't find that four-legged beast which led to my damnation I shall be shot at dawn. Fusille, comprenez? On va me fusiller par un mur blanc—or is it une mure blanche? quand l'aurore se leve avec les couleurs d'une rose et l'odeur d'une jeune fille lavee et parfumee. Pretty good that, eh, what? But the fact remains that unless I find my steed, my charger, my war-horse, which in reality does not belong to me at all, because I pinched it from the colonel, I shall be shot as sure as fate, and, alas! I do not want to die. I am too young to die, and meanwhile I desire encore une bouteille de champagne!"

The little crowd of citizens found a grim humor in this speech, one-third of which they understood. They laughed coarsely, and a man said:

"Quel drole de type! Quel numero!"

But the woman who had touched me on the sleeve spoke to me again.

"He says he has lost his horse and will be shot as a deserter. Those things happen. My boy in the Argonne tells me that a comrade of his was shot for hiding five days with his young woman. It would be sad if this poor child should be condemned to death."

I pushed my way through the crowd and went up to the officer.

"Can I help at all?"

He greeted me warmly, as though he had known me for years.

"My dear old pal, you can indeed! First of all I want a bottle of champagne-une bouteille de champagne-" it was wonderful how much music he put into those words—"and after that I want my runaway horse, as I have explained to these good people who do not understand a bloody word, in spite of my excellent French accent. I stole the colonel's horse to come for a joy-ride to Amiens. The colonel is one of the best of men, but very touchy, very touchy indeed. You would be surprised. He also has the worst horse in the world, or did, until it ran away half an hour ago into the blackness of this hell which men call Amiens. It is quite certain that if I go back without that horse most unpleasant things will happen to a gallant young British officer, meaning myself, who with most innocent intentions of cleansing his soul from the filth of battle, from the horror of battle, from the disgusting fear of battle—oh yes, I've been afraid all right, and so have you unless you're a damned hero or a damned liar—desired to get as far as this beautiful city (so fair without, so foul within!) in order to drink a bottle, or even two or three, of rich, sparkling wine, to see the loveliness of women as they trip about these pestilential streets, to say a little prayer in la cathedrale, and then to ride back, refreshed, virtuous, knightly, all through the quiet night, to deliver up the horse whence I had pinched it, and nobody any the wiser in the dewy morn. You see, it was a good scheme."

"What happened?" I asked.

"It happened thuswise," he answered, breaking out into fresh eloquence, with fantastic similes and expressions of which I can give only the spirit. "Leaving a Pozieres, which, as you doubtless know, unless you are a bloody staff-officer, is a place where the devil goes about like a roaring lion seeking whom he may devour, where he leaves his victims' entrails hanging on to barbed wire, and where the bodies of your friends and mine lie decomposing in muddy holes—you know the place?—I put my legs across the colonel's horse, which was in the wagonlines, and set forth for Amiens. That horse knew that I had pinched him—forgive my slang. I should have said it in the French language, vole—and resented me. Thrice was I nearly thrown from his back. Twice did he entangle himself in barbed wire deliberately. Once did I have to coerce him with many stripes to pass a tank. Then the heavens opened upon us and it rained. It rained until I was wet to the skin, in spite of sheltering beneath a tree, one branch of which, owing to the stubborn temper of my steed, struck me a stinging blow across the face. So in no joyful spirit I came at last to Amiens, this whited sepulcher, this Circe's capital, this den of thieves, this home of vampires. There I dined, not wisely, but too well. I drank of the flowing cup—une bouteille de champagne—and I met a maiden as ugly as sin, but beautiful in my eyes after Pozieres—you understand—and accompanied her to her poor lodging—in a most verminous place, sir—where we discoursed upon the problems of life and love. O youth! O war! O hell!... My horse, that brute who resented me, was in charge of an 'ostler, whom I believe verily is a limb of Satan, in the yard without. It was late when I left that lair of Circe, where young British officers, even as myself, are turned into swine. It was late and dark, and I was drunk. Even now I am very drunk. I may say that I am becoming drunker and drunker."

It was true. The fumes of bad champagne were working in the boy's brain, and he leaned heavily against me.

"It was then that that happened which will undoubtedly lead to my undoing, and blast my career as I have blasted my soul. The horse was there in the yard, but without saddle or bridle.

"'Where is my saddle and where is my bridle, oh, naughty 'ostler?' I shouted, in dismay.

"The 'ostler, who, as I informed you, is one of Satan's imps, answered in incomprehensible French, led the horse forth from the yard, and, giving it a mighty blow on the rump, sent it clattering forth into the outer darkness. In my fear of losing it—for I must be at Pozieres at dawn—I ran after it, but it ran too fast in the darkness, and I stopped and tried to grope my way back to the stableyard to kill that 'ostler, thereby serving God, and other British officers, for he was the devil's agent. But I could not find the yard again. It had disappeared! It was swallowed up in Cimmerian gloom. So I was without revenge and without horse, and, as you will perceive, sir—unless you are a bloody staff-officer who doesn't perceive anything—I am utterly undone. I am also horribly drunk, and I must apologize for leaning so heavily on your arm. It's awfully good of you, anyway, old man."

The crowd was mostly moving, driven indoors by the rain. The woman who had spoken to me said, "I heard a horse's hoofs upon the bridge, la-bas."

Then she went away with her apron over her head.

Thomas and I walked each side of the officer, giving him an arm. He could not walk straight, and his legs played freakish tricks with him. All the while he talked in a strain of high comedy interlarded with grim little phrases, revealing an underlying sense of tragedy and despair, until his speech thickened and he became less fluent. We spent a fantastic hour searching for his horse. It was like a nightmare in the darkness and rain. Every now and then we heard, distinctly, the klip-klop of a horse's hoofs, and went off in that direction, only to be baffled by dead silence, with no sign of the animal. Then again, as we stood listening, we heard the beat of hoofs on hard pavements, in the opposite direction, and walked that way, dragging the boy, who was getting more and more incapable of walking upright. At last we gave up hope of finding the horse, though the young officer kept assuring us that he must find it at all costs. "It's a point of honor," he said, thickly. "Not my horse, you know Doctor's horse. Devil to pay to-morrow."

He laughed foolishly and said:

"Always devil to pay in morning."

We were soaked to the skin.

"Come home with me," I said. "We can give you a shake-down."

"Frightfully good, old man. Awfully sorry, you know, and all that. Are you a blooming general, or something? But I must find horse."

By some means we succeeded in persuading him that the chase was useless and that it would be better for him to get into our billet and start out next morning, early. We dragged him up the rue des Augustins, to the rue Amiral Courbet. Outside the iron gates I spoke to him warningly:

"You've got to be quiet. There are staff-officers inside..."

"What?... Staff officers?... Oh, my God!"

The boy was dismayed. The thought of facing staff-officers almost sobered him; did, indeed, sober his brain for a moment, though not his legs.

"It's all right," I said. "Go quietly, and I will get you upstairs safely."

It was astonishing how quietly he went, hanging on to me. The little colonel was reading The Times in the salon. We passed the open door, and saw over the paper his high forehead puckered with perplexity as to the ways of the world. But he did not raise his head or drop The Times at the sound of our entry. I took the boy upstairs to my room and guided him inside. He said, "Thanks awfully," and then lay down on the floor and fell into so deep a sleep that I was scared and thought for a moment he might be dead. I went downstairs to chat with the little colonel and form an alibi in case of trouble. An hour later, when I went into my room, I found the boy still lying as I had left him, without having stirred a limb. He was a handsome fellow, with his head hanging limply across his right arm and a lock of damp hair falling across his forehead. I thought of a son of mine, who in a few years would be as old as he, and I prayed God mine might be spared this boy's tragedy... Through the night he slept in a drugged way, but just at dawn he woke up and stretched himself, with a queer little moan. Then he sat up and said:

"Where am I?"

"In a billet at Amiens. You lost your horse last night and I brought you here."

Remembrance came into his eyes and his face was swept with a sudden flush of shame and agony.

"Yes... I made a fool of myself. The worst possible. How can I get back to Pozieres?"

"You could jump a lorry with luck."

"I must. It's serious if I don't get back in time. In any case, the loss of that horse—"

He thought deeply for a moment, and I could see that his head was aching to the beat of sledge-hammers.

"Can I wash anywhere?"

I pointed to a jug and basin, and he said, "Thanks, enormously."

He washed hurriedly, and then stared down with a shamed look at his muddy uniform, all creased and bedraggled. After that he asked if he could get out downstairs, and I told him the door was unlocked.

He hesitated for a moment before leaving my room.

"I am sorry to have given you all this trouble. It was very decent of you. Many thanks."

The boy was a gentleman when sober. I wonder if he died at Pozieres, or farther on by the Butte de Warlencourt... A week later I saw an advertisement in an Amiens paper: "Horse found. Brown, with white sock on right foreleg. Apply—"

I have a fancy it was the horse for which we had searched in the rain.

XII

The quickest way to the cathedral is down a turning on the right-hand side of the Street of the Three Pebbles. Charlie's bar was on the left-hand side of the street, always crowded after six o'clock by officers of every regiment, drinking egg-nogs, Martinis, Bronxes, sherry cobblers, and other liquids, which helped men marvelously to forget the beastliness of war, and gave them the gift of laughter, and made them careless of the battles which would have to be fought. Young staff-officers were there, explaining carefully how hard worked they were and how often they went under shell-fire. The fighting officers, English, Scottish, Irish, Welsh, jeered at them, laughed hugely at the latest story of mirthful horror, arranged rendezvous at the Godebert restaurant, where they would see the beautiful Marguerite (until she transferred to la cathedrale in the same street) and our checks which Charlie cashed at a discount, with a noble faith in British honesty, not often, as he told me, being hurt by a "stumor." Charlie's bar was wrecked by shell-fire afterward, and he went to Abbeville and set up a more important establishment, which was wrecked, too, in a fierce air raid, before the paint was dry on the walls.

The cathedral was a shrine to which many men and women went all through the war, called into its white halls by the spirit of beauty which dwelt there, and by its silence and peace. The great west door was screened from bomb-splinters by sand-bags piled high, and inside there were other walls of sand-bags closing in the sanctuary and some of the windows. But these signs of war did not spoil the majesty of the tall columns and high roof, nor the loveliness of the sculptured flowers below the clerestory arches, nor the spiritual mystery of those great, dim aisles, where light flickered and shadows lurked, and the ghosts of history came out of their tombs to pace these stones again where five, six, seven centuries before they had walked to worship God, in joy or in despair, or to show their beauty of young womanhood—peasant girl or princess—to lovers gazing by the pillars, or to plight their troth as royal brides, or get a crown for their heads, or mercy for their dead bodies in velvet-draped coffins.

Our soldiers went in there, as many centuries before other English soldiers, who came out with Edward the Black Prince, by way of Crecy, or with Harry the King, through Agincourt. Five hundred years hence, if Amiens cathedral still stands, undamaged by some new and monstrous conflict in a world of incurable folly, the generation of that time will think now and then, perhaps, of the English lads in khaki who tramped up the highway of this nave with their field-caps under their arms, each footstep leaving the imprint of a wet boot on the old flagstones, awed by the silence and the spaciousness, with a sudden heartache for a closer knowledge, or some knowledge, of the God worshiped there—the God of Love—while, not far away, men were killing one another by high explosives, shells, hand-grenades, mines, machine-guns, bayonets, poison-gas, trench-mortars, tanks, and, in close fighting, with short daggers like butchers' knives, or clubs with steel knobs. I watched the faces of the men who entered here. Some of them, like the Australians and New-Zealanders, unfamiliar with cathedrals, and not religious by instinct or training, wandered round in a wondering way, with a touch of scorn, even of hostility, now and then, for these mysteries—the chanting of the Office, the tinkling of the bells at the high mass—which were beyond their understanding, and which they could not link up with any logic of life, as they knew it now, away up by Bapaume or Bullecourt, where God had nothing to do, seemingly, with a night raid into Boche lines, when they blew a party of Germans to bits by dropping Stoke bombs down their dugout, or with the shrieks of German boys, mad with fear, when the Australians jumped on them in the darkness and made haste with their killing. All the same, this great church was wonderful, and the Australians, scrunching their slouch-hats, stared up at the tall columns to the clerestory arches, and peered through the screen to the golden sun upon the high-altar, and touched old tombs with their muddy hands, reading the dates on them—1250, 1155, 1415—with astonishment at their antiquity. Their clean-cut hatchet faces, sun—baked, tanned by rain and wind, their simple blue-gray eyes, the fine, strong grace of their bodies, as they stood at ease in this place of history, struck me as being wonderfully like all that one imagines of those English knights and squires—Norman-English—who rode through

France with the Black Prince. It is as though Australia had bred back to the old strain. Our own English soldiers were less arresting to the eye, more dapper and neat, not such evident children of nature. Gravely they walked up the aisles, standing in groups where a service was in progress, watching the movements of the priests, listening to the choir and organ with reverent, dreamy eyes. Some of them—country lads—thought back, I fancy, to some village church in England where they had sung hymns with mother and sisters in the days before the war. England and that little church were a long way off now, perhaps all eternity away. I saw one boy standing quite motionless, with wet eyes, without self-consciousness. This music, this place of thoughtfulness, had made something break in his heart... Some of our young officers, but not many, knelt on the cane chairs and prayed, face in hands. French officers crossed themselves and their medals tinkled as they walked up the aisles. Always there were women in black weeds kneeling before the side—altars, praying to the Virgin for husbands and sons, dead or alive, lighting candles below holy pictures and statues. Our men tiptoed past them, holding steel hats or field—caps, and putting their packs against the pillars. On the steps of the cathedral I heard two officers talking one day.

"How can one reconcile all this with the war?"

"Why not?... I suppose we're fighting for justice and all that. That's what *The Daily Mail tells us."*

"Seriously, old man. Where does Christ come in?"

"He wasn't against righteous force. He chased the money-changers out of the Temple."

"Yes, but His whole teaching was love and forgiveness. 'Thou shalt not kill.' 'Little children, love one another!' 'Turn the other cheek.'. .. Is it all sheer tosh? If so, why go on pretending?... Take chaplains in khaki—these lieutenant-colonels with black crosses. They make me sick. It's either one thing or the other. Brute force or Christianity. I am harking back to the brute—force theory. But I'm not going to say 'God is love' one day and then prod a man in the stomach the next. Let's be consistent."

"The other fellows asked for it. They attacked first."

"Yes, but we are all involved. Our diplomacy, our secret treaties, our philosophical dope over the masses, our imperial egotism, our trade rivalries—all that was a direct challenge of Might against Right. The Germans are more efficient and more logical—that's all. They prepared for the inevitable and struck first. We knew the inevitable was coming, but didn't prepare, being too damned inefficient... I have a leaning toward religion. Instinctively I'm for Christ. But it doesn't work in with efficiency and machine-guns."

"It belongs to another department, that's all. We're spiritual and animal at the same time. In one part of my brain I'm a gentleman. In another, a beast.

It's conflict. We can't eliminate the beast, but we can control it now and then when it gets too obstreperous, and that's where religion helps. It's the high ideal—otherworldliness."

"The Germans pray to the same God. Praise Christ and ask for victory."

"Let them. It may do them a bit of good. It seems to me God is above all the squabbles of humanity—doesn't care a damn about them!—but the human soul can get into touch with the infinite and the ideal, even while he is doing butcher's work, and beastliness. That doesn't matter very much. It's part of the routine of life."

"But it does matter. It makes agony and damnation in the world. It creates cruelty and tyranny, and all bloody things. Surely if we believe in God—anyhow in Christian ethics—this war is a monstrous crime in which all humanity is involved."

"The Hun started it... Let's go and give the glad eye to Marguerite."

At night, in moonlight, Amiens cathedral was touched with a new spirituality, a white magic beyond all words of beauty. On many nights of war I walked round the cathedral square, looking up at that grand mass of masonry with all its pinnacles and buttresses gleaming like silver and its sculptured tracery like lacework, and a flood of milky light glamorous on walls in which every stone was clear-cut beyond a vast shadow-world. How old it was! How many human eyes through many centuries had come in the white light of the moon to look at this dream in stone enshrining the faith of men! The Revolution had surged round these walls, and the screams of wild women, and their shrill laughter, and their cries for the blood of aristocrats, had risen from this square. Pageants of kingship and royal death had passed across these pavements through the great doors there. Peasant women, in the darkness, had wept against these walls, praying for God's pity for their hearts. Now the English officers were lighting cigarettes in the shelter of a wall, the outline of their features—knightly faces—touched by the moonlight. There were flashes of gun-fire in the sky beyond the river.

"A good night for a German air raid," said one of the officers.

"Yes, a lovely night for killing women in their sleep," said the other man.

The people of Amiens were sleeping, and no light gleamed through their shutters.

XIII

Coming away from the cathedral through a side-street going into the rue des Trois Cailloux, I used to pass the Palais de Justice—a big, grim building, with a long flight of steps leading up to its doorways, and above the portico the figure of Justice, blind, holding her scales. There was no justice there during the war, but rooms full of French soldiers with smashed faces, blind, many of them, like that woman in stone. They used to sit, on fine days, on the flight of steps, a tragic exhibition of war for passers-by to see. Many of them revealed no faces, but were white masks of cotton-wool, bandaged round their heads. Others showed only the upper parts of their faces, and the places where their jaws had been were tied up with white rags. There were men without noses, and men with half their scalps torn away. French children used to stare through the railings at them, gravely, with childish curiosity, without pity. English soldiers gave them a passing glance, and went on to places where they might be made like this, without faces, or jaws, or noses, or eyes. By their uniforms I saw that there were Chasseurs Alpins, and Chasseurs d'Afrique, and young infantrymen of the line, and gunners. They sat, without restlessness, watching the passers-by if they had eyes to see, or, if blind, feeling the breeze about them, and listening to the sound of passing feet.

XIV

The prettiest view of Amiens was from the banks of the Somme outside the city, on the east side, and there was a charming walk along the tow-path, past market-gardens going down to the river on the opposite bank, and past the gardens of little chalets built for love-in-idleness in days of peace. They were of fantastic architecture—these Cottages where well-to-do citizens of Amiens used to come for week-ends of boating and fishing—and their garden gates at the end of wooden bridges over back-waters were of iron twisted into the shapes of swans or flowers, and there were snails of terra-cotta on the chimney-pots, and painted woodwork on the walls, in the worst taste, yet amusing and pleasing to the eye in their green bowers. I remember one called Mon Idee, and wondered that any man should be proud of such a freakish conception of a country house. They were abandoned during the war, except one or two used for casual rendezvous between French officers and their light o' loves, and the tow-path was used only by stray couples who came out for loneliness, and British soldiers walking out with French girls. The market-gardeners punted down the river in long, shallow boats, like gondolas, laden high with cabbages, cauliflowers, and asparagus, and farther up-stream there was a boat-house where orderlies from the New Zealand hospital in Amiens used to get skiffs for an hour's rowing, leaning on their oars to look at the picture of the cathedral rising like a mirage beyond the willows and the encircling water, with fleecy clouds above its glittering roof, or lurid storm-clouds with the red glow of sunset beneath their wings. In the dusk or the darkness there was silence along the banks but for a ceaseless throbbing of distant gun-fire, rising sometimes to a fury of drumming when the French *soixante-quinze* was at work, outside Roye and the lines beyond Suzanne. It was what the French *call la rafale des tambours de la mort*—the ruffle of the drums of death. The winding waters of the Somme flowed in higher reaches through the hell of war by Biaches and St.-Christ, this side of Peronne, where dead bodies floated in slime and blood, and there was a litter of broken bridges and barges, and dead trees, and ammunition-boxes. The river itself was a highway into hell, and there came back upon its tide in slow-moving barges the wreckage of human life, fresh from the torturers. These barges used to unload their cargoes of maimed men at a carpenter's yard just below the bridge, outside the city, and often as I passed I saw human bodies being lifted out and carried on stretchers into the wooden sheds. They were the bad cases—French boys wounded in the abdomen or lungs, or with their limbs torn off, or hopelessly shattered. It was an agony for them to be moved, even on the stretchers. Some of them cried out in fearful anguish, or moaned like wounded animals, again and again. Those sounds spoiled the music of the lapping water and the whispering of the willows and the song of birds. The sight of these tortured boys, made useless in life, took the color out of the flowers and the beauty out of that vision of the great cathedral, splendid above the river. Women watched them from the bridge, straining their eyes as the bodies were carried to the bank. I think some of them looked for their own men. One of them spoke to me one day.

"That is what the Germans do to our sons. Bandits! Assassins!"

"Yes. That is war, Madame."

She put a skinny hand on my arm.

"Will it go on forever, this war? Until all the men are killed?"

"Not so long as that, Madame. Some men will be left alive. The very old and the very young, and the lucky ones, and those behind the lines."

"The Germans are losing many men, Monsieur?"

"Heaps, Madame. I have seen their bodies strewn about the fields."

"Ah, that is good! I hope all German women will lose their sons, as I have lost mine."

"Where was that, Madame?"

"Over there."

She pointed up the Somme.

"He was a good son. A fine boy. It seems only yesterday he lay at my breast. My man weeps for him. They were good comrades."

"It is sad, Madame."

"Ah, but yes. It is sad! Au revoir, Monsieur."

"Au revoir, Madame."

XV

There was a big hospital in Amiens, close to the railway station, organized by New Zealand doctors and nurses. I went there one day in the autumn of 1914, when the army of von Kluck had passed through the city and gone beyond. The German doctors had left behind the instruments abandoned by an English unit sharing the retreat. The French doctor who took me round told me the enemy had behaved well in Amiens. At least he had refrained from atrocities. As I went through the long wards I did not guess that one day I should be a patient there. That was two years later, at the end of the Somme battles. I was worn out and bloodless after five months of hard strain and nervous wear and tear. Some bug had bitten me up in the fields where lay the unburied dead.

"Trench fever," said the doctor.

"You look in need of a rest," said the matron. "My word, how white you are! Had a hard time, eh, like the rest of them?"

I lay in bed at the end of the officers' ward, with only one other bed between me and the wall. That was occupied by the gunner-general of the New Zealand Division. Opposite was another row of beds in which officers lay sleeping, or reading, or lying still with wistful eyes.

"That's all right. You're going to die!" said a rosy—cheeked young orderly, after taking my temperature and feeling my pulse. It was his way of cheering a patient up. He told me how he had been torpedoed in the Dardanelles while he was ill with dysentery. He indulged in reminiscences with the New Zealand general who had a grim gift of silence, but glinting eyes. In the bed on my left was a handsome boy with a fine, delicate face, a subaltern in the Coldstream Guards, with a pile of books at his elbow—all by Anatole France. It was the first time I had ever laid in hospital, and I felt amazingly weak and helpless, but interested in my surroundings. The day nurse, a tall, buxom New Zealand girl whom the general chaffed with sarcastic humor, and who gave back more than she got, went off duty with a cheery, "Good night, all!" and the night nurse took her place, and made a first visit to each bed. She was a dainty little woman with the complexion of a delicate rose and large, luminous eyes. She had a nunlike look, utterly pure, but with a spiritual fire in those shining eyes of hers for all these men, who were like children in her hands. They seemed glad at her coming.

"Good evening, sister!" said one man after another, even one who had laid with his eyes closed for an hour or more, with a look of death on his face.

She knelt down beside each one, saying, "How are you to-night?" and chatting in a low voice, inaudible to the bed beyond. From one bed I heard a boy's voice say: "Oh, don't go yet, sister! You have only given me two minutes, and I want ten, at least. I am passionately in love with you, you know, and I have been waiting all day for your beauty!"

There was a gust of laughter in the ward.

"The child is at it again!" said one of the officers.

"When are you going to write me another sonnet?" asked the nurse. "The last one was much admired."

"The last one was rotten," said the boy. "I have written a real corker this time. Read it to yourself, and don't drop its pearls before these swine."

"Well, you must be good, or I won't read it at all."

An officer of the British army, who was also a poet, hurled the bedclothes off and sat on the edge of his bed in his pajamas.

"I'm fed up with everything! I hate war! I don't want to be a hero! I don't want to die! I want to be loved!... I'm a glutton for love!"

In his pajamas the boy looked a child, no older than a schoolboy who was mine and who still liked to be tucked up in bed by his mother. With his tousled hair and his petulant grimace, this lieutenant might have been Peter Pan, from Kensington. The night nurse pretended to chide him. It was a very gentle chiding, but as abruptly as he had thrown off his clothes he snuggled under them again and said: "All right, I'll be good. Only I want a kiss before I go to sleep."

I became good friends with that boy, who was a promising young poet, and a joyous creature no more fit for war than a child of ten, hating the muck and horror of it, not ashamed to confess his fear, with a boyish wistfulness of hope that he might not be killed, because he loved life. But he was killed... I had a letter from his stricken mother months afterward. The child was "Missing" then, and her heart cried out for him.

Opposite my bed was a middle-aged man from Lancashire—I suppose he had been in a cotton-mill or a factory—a hard-headed, simple-hearted fellow, as good as gold, and always speaking of "the wife." But his nerves had gone to pieces and he was afraid to sleep because of the dreams that came to him.

"Sister," he said, "don't let me go to sleep. Wake me up if you see me dozing. I see terrible things in my dreams. Frightful things. I can't bear it."

"You will sleep better to-night," she said. "I am putting something in your milk. Something to stop the dreaming."

But he dreamed. I lay awake, feverish and restless, and heard the man opposite muttering and moaning, in his sleep. Sometimes he would give a long, quivering sigh, and sometimes start violently, and then wake up in a dazed way, saying:

"Oh, my God! Oh, my God!" trembling with fear, so that the bed was shaken. The night nurse was always by his side in a moment when he called out, hushing him down, whispering to him.

"I see pools of blood and bits of dead bodies in my sleep," he told me. "It's what I saw up at Bazentin. There was a fellow with his face blown off, walking about. I see him every night. Queer, isn't it? Nerves, you know. I didn't think I had a nerve in my body before this war."

The little night nurse came to my bedside.

"Can't you sleep?"

"I'm afraid not. My heart is thumping in a queer way. May I smoke?"

She put a cigarette between my lips and lighted a match.

"Take a few whiffs and then try to sleep. You need lots of sleep."

In the ward there was only the glimmer of night lights in red glasses, and now and then all through the night matches were lighted, illuminating the room for a second, followed by the glowing end of a cigarette shining like a star in the darkness.

The sleeping men breathed heavily, tossed about violently, gave strange jerks and starts. Sometimes they spoke aloud in their sleep.

"That isn't a dud, you fool! It will blow us to hell."

"Now then, get on with it, can't you?"

"Look out! They're coming! Can't you see them moving by the wire?"

The spirit of war was in that ward and hunted them even in their sleep; lurking terrors surged up again in their subconsciousness. Sights which they had tried to forget stared at them through their closed eyelids. The daylight came and the night nurse slipped away, and the day nurse shook one's shoulders and said: "Time to wash and shave. No malingering!"

It was the discipline of the hospital. Men as weak as rats had to sit up in bed, or crawl out of it, and shave themselves.

"You're merciless!" I said, laughing painfully when the day nurse dabbed my back with cold iodine at six o'clock on a winter morning, with the windows wide open.

"Oh, there's no mercy in this place!" said the strong-minded girl. "It's kill or cure here, and no time to worry."

"You're all devils," said the New Zealand general. "You don't care a damn about the patients so long as you have all the beds tidy by the time the doctor comes around. I'm a general, I am, and you can't order ME about, and if you think I'm going to shave at this time in the morning you are jolly well mistaken. I am down with dysentery, and don't you forget it. I didn't get through the Dardanelles to be murdered at Amiens."

"That's where you may be mistaken, general," said the imperturbable girl. "I have to carry out orders, and if they lead to your death it's not my responsibility. I'm paid a poor wage for this job, but I do my duty, rough or smooth, kill or cure."

"You're a vampire. That's what you are."

"I'm a nurse."

"If ever I hear you're going to marry a New Zealand boy I'll warn him against you."

"He'll be too much of a fool to listen to you."

"I've a good mind to marry you myself and beat you every morning."

"Modern wives have strong muscles. Look at my arm!"

*　　　*　　　*　　　*　　　*

Three nights in one week there were air raids, and as the German mark was the railway station we were in the center of the danger-zone. There was a frightful noise of splintering glass and smashing timber between each crash of high explosives. The whine of shrapnel from the anti—aircraft guns had a sinister note, abominable in the ears of those officers who had come down from the fighting—lines nerve-racked and fever-stricken. They lay very quiet. The night nurse moved about from bed to bed, with her flash-lamp. Her face was pale, but she showed no other sign of fear and was braver than her patients at that time, though they had done the hero's job all right.

It was in another hospital a year later, when I lay sick again, that an officer, a very gallant gentleman, said, "If there is another air raid I shall go mad." He had been stationed near the blast-furnace of Les Izelquins, near Bethune, and had been in many air raids, when over sixty-three shells had blown his hut to bits and killed his men, until he could bear it no more. In the Amiens hospital some of the patients had their heads under the bedclothes like little children.

XVI

The life of Amiens ended for a while, and the city was deserted by all its people, after the night of March 30, 1918, which will be remembered forever to the age-long history of Amiens as its night of greatest tragedy. For a week the enemy had been advancing across the old battlefields after the first onslaught in the morning of March 21st, when our lines were stormed and broken by his men's odds against our defending troops. We war correspondents had suffered mental agonies like all who knew what had happened better than the troops themselves. Every day after the first break-through we pushed out in different directions—Hamilton Fyfe and I went together sometimes until we came up with the backwash of the great retreat, ebbing back and back, day after day, with increasing speed, until it drew very close to Amiens. It was a kind of ordered chaos, terrible to see. It was a chaos like that of upturned ant-heaps, but with each ant trying to rescue its eggs and sticks in a persistent, orderly way, directed by some controlling or communal intelligence, only instead of eggs and sticks these soldier-ants of ours, in the whole world behind our front-lines, were trying to rescue heavy guns, motor-lorries, tanks, ambulances, hospital stores, ordnance stores, steam-rollers, agricultural implements, transport wagons, railway engines, Y.M.C.A. tents, gun-horse and mule columns, while rear-guard actions were being fought within gunfire of them and walking wounded were hobbling back along the roads in this uproar of traffic, and word came that a further retreat was happening and that the enemy had broken through again...

Amiens seemed threatened on the morning when, to the north, Albert was held by a mixed crowd of Scottish and English troops, too thin, as I could see when I passed through them, to fight any big action, with an enemy advancing rapidly from Courcellette and outflanking our line by Montauban and Fricourt. I saw our men marching hastily in retreat to escape that tightening net, and while the southern side of Amiens was held by a crowd of stragglers with cyclist battalions, clerks from headquarters staffs, and dismounted cavalry, commanded by Brigadier-General Carey, sent down hurriedly to link them together and stop a widening gap until the French could get to our relief on the right and until the Australians had come down from Flanders. There was nothing on that day to prevent the Germans breaking through to Amiens except the courage of exhausted boys thinly strung out, and the lagging footsteps of the Germans themselves, who had suffered heavy losses all the way and were spent for a while by their progress over the wild ground of the old fighting-fields. Their heavy guns were far behind, unable to keep pace with the storm troops, and the enemy was relying entirely on machine-guns and a few field-guns, but most of our guns were also out of action, captured or falling back to new lines, and upon the speed with which the enemy could mass his men for a new assault depended the safety of Amiens and the road to Abbeville and the coast. If he could hurl fresh divisions of men against our line on that last night of March, or bring up strong forces of cavalry, or armored cars, our line would break and Amiens would be lost, and all our work would be in jeopardy. That was certain. It was visible. It could not be concealed by any camouflage of hope or courage.

It was after a day on the Somme battlefields, passing through our retiring troops, that I sat down, with other war correspondents and several officers, to a dinner in the old Hotel du Rhin in Amiens. It was a dismal meal, in a room where there had been much laughter and, throughout the battles of the Somme, in 1916, a coming and going of generals and staffs and officers of all grades, cheery and high-spirited at these little tables where there were good wine and not bad food, and putting away from their minds for the time being the thought of tragic losses or forlorn battles in which they might fall. In the quietude of the hotel garden, a little square plot of grass bordered by flower-beds, I had had strange conversations with boys who had revealed their souls a little, after dinner in the darkness, their faces bared now and then by the light of cigarettes or the flare of a match.

"Death is nothing," said one young officer just down from the Somme fields for a week's rest-cure for jangled nerves. "I don't care a damn for death; but it's the waiting for it, the devilishness of its uncertainty, the sight of one's pals blown to bits about one, and the animal fear under shell-fire, that break one's pluck... My nerves are like fiddle-strings."

In that garden, other men, with a queer laugh now and then between their stories, had told me their experiences in shell-craters and ditches under frightful fire which had "wiped out" their platoons or companies. A bedraggled stork, the inseparable companion of a waddling gull, used to listen to the conferences, with one leg tucked under his wing, and its head on one side, with one watchful, beady eye fixed on the figures in khaki—until suddenly it would clap its long bill rapidly in a wonderful imitation of machine-gun fire—"Curse the bloody bird!" said officers startled by this evil and reminiscent noise—and caper with ridiculous postures round the imperturbable gull... Beyond the lines, from the dining-room, would come the babble of many tongues and the laughter of officers telling stories against one another over their bottles of wine, served by Gaston the head-waiter, between our discussions on strategy—he was a strategist by virtue of service in the trenches and several wounds—or by "Von Tirpitz," an older, whiskered man, or by Joseph, who had a high, cackling laugh and strong views against the fair sex, and the inevitable cry, "C'est la guerre!" when officers complained of the service... There had been merry parties in this room, crowded with the ghosts of many heroic fellows, but it was a gloomy gathering on that evening at the end of March when we sat there for the last time. There were there officers who had lost their towns, and "Dadoses" (Deputy Assistant Director of Ordnance Supplies) whose stores had gone up in smoke and flame, and a few cavalry officers back from special leave and appalled by what had happened in their absence, and a group of Y.M.C.A. officials who had escaped by the skin of their teeth from huts now far behind the German lines, and censors who knew that no blue pencil could hide the truth of the retreat, and war correspondents who had to write the truth and hated it.

Gaston whispered gloomily behind my chair: *"Mon petit caporal"*—he called me that because of a fancied likeness to the young Napoleon—*"dites donc. Vous croyex quils vont passer par Amiens? Non, ce n'est pas possible, ca! Pour la deuxieme fois? Non. Je refuse a le croire. Mais c'est mauvais, c'est affreux, apres tant de sacrifice!"*

Madame, of the cash-desk, sat in the dining-room, for company's sake, fixing up accounts as though the last day of reckoning had come...as it had. Her hair, with its little curls, was still in perfect order. She had two dabs of color on her cheeks, as usual, but underneath a waxen pallor. She was working out accounts with a young officer, who smoked innumerable cigarettes to steady his nerves. "Von Tirpitz" was going round in an absent-minded way, pulling at his long whiskers.

The war correspondents talked together. We spoke gloomily, in low voices, so that the waiters should not hear.

"If they break through to Abbeville we shall lose the coast."

"Will that be a win for the Germans, even then?"

"It will make it hell in the Channel."

"We shall transfer our base to St.-Nazaire."

"France won't give in now, whatever happens. And England never gives in."

"We're exhausted, all the same. It's a question of man-power."

"They're bound to take Albert to-night or to-morrow."

"I don't see that at all. There's still a line..."

"A line! A handful of tired men."

"It will be the devil if they get into Villers-Bretonneux to-night. It commands Amiens. They could blow the place off the map."

"They won't."

"We keep on saying, 'They won't.' We said, 'They won't get the Somme crossings!' but they did. Let's face it squarely, without any damned false optimism. That has been our curse all through."

"Better than your damned pessimism."

"It's quite possible that they will be in this city tonight. What is to keep them back? There's nothing up the road."

"It would look silly if we were all captured to-night. How they would laugh!"

"We shouldn't laugh, though. I think we ought to keep an eye on things."

"How are we to know? We are utterly without means of communication. Anything may happen in the night."

Something happened then. It was half past seven in the evening. There were two enormous crashes outside the windows of the Hotel du Rhin. All the windows shook and the whole house seemed to rock. There was a noise of rending wood, many falls of bricks, and a cascade of falling glass. Instinctively and instantly a number of officers threw themselves on the floor to escape flying bits of steel and glass splinters blown sideways. Then some one laughed.

"Not this time!"

The officers rose from the floor and took their places at the table, and lit cigarettes again. But they were listening. We listened to the loud hum of airplanes, the well known "zooz-zooz" of the Gothas' double fuselage. More bombs were dropped farther into the town, with the same sound of explosives and falling masonry. The anti—aircraft guns got to work and there was the shrill chorus of shrapnel shells winging over the roofs.

"Bang!... Crash!"

That was nearer again.

Some of the officers strolled out of the dining room.

"They're making a mess outside. Perhaps we'd better get away before it gets too hot."

Madame from the cash-desk turned to her accounts again. I noticed the increasing pallor of her skin beneath the two dabs of red. But she controlled her nerves pluckily; even smiled, too, at the young officer who was settling up for a group of others.

The moon had risen over the houses of Amiens. It was astoundingly bright and beautiful in a clear sky and still air, and the streets were flooded with white light, and the roofs glittered like silver above intense black shadows under the gables, where the rays were barred by projecting walls.

"Curse the moon!" said one officer. "How I hate its damned light"

But the moon, cold and smiling, looked down upon the world at war and into this old city of Amiens, in which bombs were bursting. Women were running close to the walls. Groups of soldiers made a dash from one doorway to another. Horses galloped with heavy wagons up the Street of the Three Pebbles, while shrapnel flickered in the sky above them and paving-stones were hurled up in bursts of red fire and explosions. Many horses were killed by flying chunks of steel. They lay bleeding monstrously so that there were large pools of blood around them.

An officer came into the side door of the Hotel du Rhin. He was white under his steel hat, which he pushed back while he wiped his forehead.

"A fellow was killed just by my side." he said. "We were standing in a doorway together and something caught him in the face. He fell like a log, without a sound, as dead as a door-nail."

There was a flight of midges in the sky, droning with that double note which vibrated like 'cello strings, very loudly, and with that sinister noise I could see them quite clearly now and then as they passed across the face of the moon, black, flitting things, with a glitter of shrapnel below them. From time to time they went away until they were specks of silver and black; but always they came back again, or others came, with new stores of bombs which they unloaded over Amiens. So it went on all through the night.

I went up to a bedroom and lay on a bed, trying to sleep. But it was impossible. My will-power was not strong enough to disregard those crashes in the streets outside, when houses collapsed with frightful falling noises after bomb explosions. My inner vision foresaw the ceiling above me pierced by one of those bombs, and the room in which I lay engulfed in the chaos of this wing of the Hotel du Rhin. Many times I said, "To hell with it all... I'm going to sleep," and then sat up in the darkness at the renewal of that tumult and switched on the electric light. No, impossible to sleep! Outside in the corridor there was a stampede of heavy boots. Officers were running to get into the cellars before the next crash, which might fling them into the dismal gulfs. The thought of that cellar pulled me down like the law of gravity. I walked along the corridor, now deserted, and saw a stairway littered with broken glass, which my feet scrunched. There were no lights in the basement of the hotel, but I had a flash-lamp, going dim, and by its pale eye fumbled my way to a stone passage leading to the cellar. That flight of stone steps was littered also with broken glass. In the cellar itself was a mixed company of men who had been dining earlier in the evening, joined by others who had come in from the streets for shelter. Some of them had dragged down mattresses from the bedrooms and were lying there in their trench-coats, with their steel hats beside them. Others were sitting on wooden cases, wearing their steel hats, while there were others on their knees, and their faces in their hands, trying to sleep. There were some of the town majors who had lost their towns, and some Canadian cavalry officers, and two or three private soldiers, and some motor-drivers and orderlies, and two young cooks of the hotel lying together on dirty straw. By one of the stone pillars of the vaulted room two American war correspondents—Sims and Mackenzie—were sitting on a packing-case playing cards on a board between them. They had stuck candles in empty wine-bottles, and the flickering light played on their faces and cast deep shadows under their eyes. I stood watching these men in that cellar and thought what a good subject it would be for the pencil of Muirhead Bone. I wanted to get a comfortable place. There was only one place on the bare stones, and when I lay down there my bones ached abominably, and it was very cold. Through an aperture in the window came a keen draft and I could see in a square of moonlit sky a glinting star. It was not much of a cellar. A direct hit on the Hotel du Rhin would make a nasty mess in this vaulted room and end a game of cards. After fifteen minutes I became restless, and decided that the room upstairs, after all, was infinitely preferable to this damp cellar and these hard stones. I returned to it and lay down on the bed again and switched off the light. But the noises outside, the loneliness of the room, the sense of sudden death fluking overhead, made me sit up again and listen intently. The Gothas were droning over Amiens again. Many houses round about were being torn and shattered. What a wreckage was being made of the dear old city! I paced up and down the room, smoking cigarettes, one after another, until a mighty explosion, very close, made all my nerves quiver. No, decidedly, that cellar was the best place. If one had to die it was better to be in the company of friends. Down I went again, meeting an officer whom I knew well. He, too, was a wanderer between the cellar and the abandoned bedrooms.

"I am getting bored with this," he said. "It's absurd to think that this filthy cellar is any safer than upstairs. But the dugout sense calls one down. Anyhow, I can't sleep."

We stood looking into the cellar. There was something comical as well as sinister in the sight of the company there sprawled on the mattresses, vainly trying to extract comfort out of packing-cases for pillows, or gas-bags on steel hats. One friend of ours, a cavalry officer of the old school, looked a cross between Charlie Chaplin and Ol' Bill, with a fierce frown above his black mustache. Sims and Mackenzie still played their game of cards, silently, between the guttering candles.

I think I went from the cellar to the bedroom, and from the bedroom to the cellar, six times that night. There was never ten minutes' relief from the drone of Gothas, who were making a complete job of Amiens. It was at four in the morning that I met the same officer who saw me wandering before.

"Let us go for a walk," he said. "The birds will be away by dawn."

It was nothing like dawn when we went out of the side door of the Hotel du Rhin and strolled into the Street of the Three Pebbles. There was still the same white moonlight, intense and glittering, but with a paler sky. It shone down upon dark pools of blood and the carcasses of horses and fragments of flesh, from which a sickly smell rose. The roadway was littered with bits of timber and heaps of masonry. Many houses had collapsed into wild chaos, and others, though still standing, had been stripped of their wooden frontages and their walls were scarred by bomb-splinters. Every part of the old city, as we explored it later, had been badly mauled, and hundreds of houses were utterly destroyed. The air raid ceased at 4.30 A.M., when the first light of dawn came into the sky....

That day Amiens was evacuated, by command of the French military authorities, and the inhabitants trailed out of the city, leaving everything behind them. I saw the women locking up their shops—where there were any doors to shut or their shop still standing. Many people must have been killed and buried in the night beneath their own houses—I never knew how many. The fugitives escaped the next phase of the tragedy in Amiens when, within a few hours, the enemy sent over the first high velocities, and for many weeks afterward scattered them about the city, destroying many other houses. A fire started by these shells formed a great gap between the rue des Jacobins and the rue des Trois Cailloux, where there had been an arcade and many good shops and houses. I saw the fires smoldering about charred beams and twisted ironwork when I went through the city after the day of exodus.

XVII

It was a pitiful adventure to go through Amiens in the days of its desolation, and we who had known its people so well hated its loneliness. All abandoned towns have a tragic aspect—I often think of Douai, which was left with all its people under compulsion of the enemy—but Amiens was strangely sinister with heaps of ruins in its narrow streets, and the abominable noise of high-velocity shells in flight above its roofs, and crashing now in one direction and now in another.

One of our sentries came out of a little house near the Place and said:

"Keep as much as possible to the west side of the town, sir. They've been falling pretty thick on the east side. Made no end of a mess!"

On the way back from Villers-Bretonneux and the Australian headquarters, on the left bank of the Somme, we ate sandwiches in the public gardens outside the Hotel du Rhin. There were big shell-holes in the flower-beds, and trees had been torn down and flung across the pathway, and there was a broken statue lying on the grass. Some French and English soldiers tramped past. Then there was no living soul about in the place which had been so crowded with life, with pretty women and children, and young officers doing their shopping, and the business of a city at work.

"It makes one understand what Rome was like after the barbarians had sacked and left it," said a friend of mine.

"There is something ghastly about it," said another.

We stood round the Hotel du Rhin, shut up and abandoned. The house next door had been wrecked, and it was scarred and wounded, but still stood after that night of terror.

One day during its desolation I went to a banquet in Amiens, in the cellars of the Hotel de Ville. It was to celebrate the Fourth of July, and an invitation had been sent to me by the French commandant de place and the English A. P. M.

It was a *beau geste,* gallant and romantic in those days of trouble, when Amiens was still closely beleaguered, but safer now that Australians and British troops were holding the lines strongly outside, with French on their right southward from Boves and Hangest Wood. The French commandant had procured a collection of flags and his men had decorated the battered city with the Tricolor. It even fluttered above some of the ruins, as though for the passing of a pageant. But only a few cars entered the city and drew up to the Town Hall, and then took cover behind the walls.

Down below, in the cellars, the damp walls were garlanded with flowers from the market-gardens of the Somme, now deserted by their gardeners, and roses were heaped on the banqueting-table. General Monash, commanding the Australian corps, was there, with the general of the French division on his right. A young American officer sat very grave and silent, not, perhaps, understanding much of the conversation about him, because most of the guests were French officers, with Senators and Deputies of Amiens and its Department. There was good wine to drink from the cold vaults of the Hotel de Ville, and with the scent of rose and hope for victory in spite of all disasters—the German offensive had been checked and the Americans were now coming over in a tide—it was a cheerful luncheon-party. The old general, black-visaged, bullet-headed, with a bristly mustache like a French bull—terrier, sat utterly silent, eating steadily and fiercely. But the French *commandant de place*, as handsome as Athos, as gay as D'Artagnan, raised his glass to England and France, to the gallant Allies, and to all fair women. He became reminiscent of his days as a sous-lieutenant. He remembered a girl called Marguerite—she was exquisite; and another called Yvonne—he had adored her. O life! O youth!... He had been a careless young devil, with laughter in his heart....

XVIII

I suppose it was three months later when I saw the first crowds coming back to their homes in Amiens. The tide had turned and the enemy was in hard retreat. Amiens was safe again! They had never had any doubt of this homecoming after that day nearly three months before, when, in spite of the enemy's being so close, Foch said, in his calm way, "I guarantee Amiens." They believed what Marshal Foch said. He always knew. So now they were coming back again with their little bundles and their babies and small children holding their hands or skirts, according as they had received permits from the French authorities. They were the lucky ones whose houses still existed. They were conscious of their own good fortune and came chattering very cheerfully from the station up the Street of the Three Pebbles, on their way to their streets. But every now and then they gave a cry of surprise and dismay at the damage done to other people's houses.

"O la la! Regardez ca! c'est affreux!"

There was the butcher's shop, destroyed; and the house of poor little Madeleine; and old Christopher's workshop; and the milliner's place, where they used to buy their Sunday hats; and that frightful gap where the Arcade had been. Truly, poor Amiens had suffered martyrdom; though, thank God, the cathedral still stood in glory, hardly touched, with only one little shellhole through the roof.

Terrible was the damage up the rue de Beauvais and the streets that went out of it. To one rubbish heap which had been a corner house two girls came back. Perhaps the French authorities had not had that one on their list. The girls came tripping home, with light in their eyes, staring about them, ejaculating pity for neighbors whose houses had been destroyed. Then suddenly they stood outside their own house and saw that the direct hit of a shell had knocked it to bits. The light went out of their eyes. They stood there staring, with their mouths open... Some Australian soldiers stood about and watched the girls, understanding the drama.

"Bit of a mess, missy!" said one of them. "Not much left of the old home, eh?"

The girls were amazingly brave. They did not weep. They climbed up a hillock of bricks and pulled out bits of old, familiar things. They recovered the whole of a child's perambulator, with its wheels crushed. With an air of triumph and shrill laughter they turned round to the Australians.

"Pour les bebes!" they cried.

"While there's life there's hope," said one of the Australians, with sardonic humor.

So the martyrdom of Amiens was at an end, and life came back to the city that had been dead, and the soul of the city had survived. I have not seen it since then, but one day I hope I shall go back and shake hands with Gaston the waiter and say, *"Comment ca va, mon vieux?"* ("How goes it, my old one?") and stroll into the bookshop and say, "Bon jour, mademoiselle!" and walk round the cathedral and see its beauty in moonlight again when no one will look up and say, "Curse the moon!"

There will be many ghosts in the city at night—the ghosts of British officers and men who thronged those streets in the great war and have now passed on.

PART SIX.

PSYCHOLOGY ON THE SOMME

I

All that had gone before was but a preparation for what now was to come. Until July 1 of 1916 the British armies were only getting ready for the big battles which were being planned for them by something greater than generalship—by the fate which decides the doom of men.

The first battles by the Old Contemptibles, down from Mons and up by Ypres, were defensive actions of rear—guards holding the enemy back by a thin wall of living flesh, while behind the New Armies of our race were being raised.

The battles of Festubert, Neuve Chapelle, Loos, and all minor attacks which led to little salients, were but experimental adventures in the science of slaughter, badly bungled in our laboratories. They had no meaning apart from providing those mistakes by which men learn; ghastly mistakes, burning more than the fingers of life's children. They were only diversions of impatience in the monotonous routine of trench warfare by which our men strengthened the mud walls of their School of Courage, so that the new boys already coming out might learn their lessons without more grievous interruption than came from the daily visits of that Intruder to whom the fees were paid. In those two years it was France which fought the greatest battles, flinging her sons against the enemy's ramparts in desperate, vain attempts to breach them. At Verdun, in the months that followed the first month of '16, it was France which sustained the full weight of the German offensive on the western front and broke its human waves, until they were spent in a sea of blood, above which the French poilus, the "hairy ones," stood panting and haggard, on their death-strewn rocks. The Germans had failed to deal a fatal blow at the heart of France. France held her head up still, bleeding from many wounds, but defiant still; and the German High Command, aghast at their own losses—six hundred thousand casualties—already conscious, icily, of a dwindling man-power which one day would be cut off at its source, rearranged their order of battle and shifted the balance of their weight eastward, to smash Russia. Somehow or other they must smash a way out by sledge-hammer blows, left and right, west and east, from that ring of nations which girdled them. On the west they would stand now on the defensive, fairly sure of their strength, but well aware that it would be tried to the utmost by that enemy which, at the back of their brains (at the back of the narrow brains of those bald-headed vultures on the German General Staff), they most feared as their future peril—England. They had been fools to let the British armies grow up and wax so strong. It was the folly of the madness by which they had flung the gauntlet down to the souls of proud peoples arrayed against them.

Our armies were now strong and trained and ready. We had about six hundred thousand bayonet-men in France and Flanders and in England, immense reserves to fill up the gaps that would be made in their ranks before the summer foliage turned to russet tints.

Our power in artillery had grown amazingly since the beginning of the year. Every month I had seen many new batteries arrive, with clean harness and yellow straps, and young gunners who were quick to get their targets. We were strong in "heavies," twelve-inchers, 9.2's, eight-inchers, 4.2's, mostly howitzers, with the long-muzzled sixty-pounders terrible in their long range and destructiveness. Our aircraft had grown fast, squadron upon squadron, and our aviators had been trained in the school of General Trenchard, who sent them out over the German lines to learn how to fight, and how to scout, and how to die like little gentlemen.

For a time our flying-men had gone out on old-fashioned "buses"—primitive machines which were an easy prey to the fast-flying Fokkers who waited for them behind a screen of cloud and then "stooped" on them like hawks sure of their prey. But to the airdrome near St.-Omer came later models, out of date a few weeks after their delivery, replaced by still more powerful types more perfectly equipped for fighting. Our knights-errant of the air were challenging the German champions on equal terms, and beating them back from the lines unless they flew in clusters. There were times when our flying-men gained an absolute supremacy by greater daring—there was nothing they did not dare—and by equal skill. As a caution, not wasting their strength in unequal contests. It was a sound policy, and enabled them to come back again in force and hold the field for a time by powerful concentrations. But in the battles of the Somme our airmen, at a heavy cost of life, kept the enemy down a while and blinded his eyes.

The planting of new airdromes between Albert and Amiens, the long trail down the roads of lorries packed with wings and the furniture of aircraft factories, gave the hint, to those who had eyes to see, that in this direction a merry hell was being prepared.

There were plain signs of massacre at hand all the way from the coast to the lines. At Etaples and other places near Boulogne hospital huts and tents were growing like mushrooms in the night. From casualty clearing stations near the front the wounded—the human wreckage of routine warfare—were being evacuated "in a hurry" to the base, and from the base to England. They were to be cleared out of the way so that all the wards might be empty for a new population of broken men, in enormous numbers. I went down to see this clearance, this tidying up. There was a sinister suggestion in the solitude that was being made for a multitude that was coming.

"We shall be very busy," said the doctors.

"We must get all the rest we can now," said the nurses.

"In a little while every bed will be filled," said the matrons.

Outside one hut, with the sun on their faces, were four wounded Germans, Wurtemburgers and Bavarians, too ill to move just then. Each of them had lost a leg under the surgeon's knife. They were eating strawberries, and seemed at peace. I spoke to one of them.

"Wie befinden sie sich?"

"Ganz wohl; wir sind zufrieden mit unsere behandlung."

I passed through the shell-shock wards and a yard where the "shell-shocks" sat about, dumb, or making queer, foolish noises, or staring with a look of animal fear in their eyes. From a padded room came a sound of singing. Some idiot of war was singing between bursts of laughter. It all seemed so funny to him, that war, so mad!

"We are clearing them out," said the medical officer. "There will be many more soon."

How soon? That was a question nobody could answer. It was the only secret, and even that was known in London, where little ladies in society were naming the date, "in confidence," to men who were directly concerned with it—having, as they knew, only a few more weeks, or days, of certain life. But I believe there were not many officers who would have surrendered deliberately all share in "The Great Push." In spite of all the horror which these young officers knew it would involve, they had to be "in it" and could not endure the thought that all their friends and all their men should be there while they were "out of it." A decent excuse for the safer side of it—yes. A staff job, the Intelligence branch, any post behind the actual shambles—and thank God for the luck. But not an absolute shirk.

Tents were being pitched in many camps of the Somme, rows and rows of bell tents and pavilions stained to a reddish brown. Small cities of them were growing up on the right of the road between Amiens and Albert—at Dernancourt and Daours and Vaux-sous-Corbie. I thought they might be for troops in reserve until I saw large flags hoisted to tall staffs and men of the R.A.M.C. busy painting signs on large sheets stretched out on the grass. It was always the same sign—the Sign of the Cross that was Red.

There was a vast traffic of lorries on the roads, and trains were traveling on light railways day and night to railroads just beyond shell-range. What was all the weight they carried? No need to ask. The "dumps" were being filled, piled up, with row upon row of shells, covered by tarpaulin or brushwood when they were all stacked. Enormous shells, some of them, like gigantic pigs without legs. Those were for the fifteen-inchers, or the 9.2's. There was enough high-explosive force littered along those roads above the Somme to blow cities off the map.

"It does one good to see," said a cheery fellow. "The people at home have been putting their backs into it. Thousands of girls have been packing those things. Well done, Munitions!"

I could take no joy in the sight, only a grim kind of satisfaction that at least when our men attacked they would have a power of artillery behind them. It might help them to smash through to a finish, if that were the only way to end this long-drawn suicide of nations.

My friend was shocked when I said:

"Curse all munitions!"

II

The British armies as a whole were not gloomy at the approach of that new phase of war which they called "The Great Push," as though it were to be a glorified football-match. It is difficult, perhaps impossible, to know the thoughts of vast masses of men moved by some sensational adventure. But a man would be a liar if he pretended that British troops went forward to the great attack with hangdog looks or any visible sign of fear in their souls. I think most of them were uplifted by the belief that the old days of trench warfare were over forever and that they would break the enemy's lines by means of that enormous gun-power behind them, and get him "on the run." There would be movement, excitement, triumphant victories—and then the end of the war. In spite of all risks it would be enormously better than the routine of the trenches. They would be getting on with the job instead of standing still and being shot at by invisible earth-men.

"If we once get the Germans in the open we shall go straight through them."

That was the opinion of many young officers at that time, and for once they agreed with their generals.

It seemed to be a question of getting them in the open, and I confess that when I studied the trench maps and saw the enemy's defensive earthworks thirty miles deep in one vast maze of trenches and redoubts and barbed wire and tunnels I was appalled at the task which lay before our men. They did not know what they were being asked to do.

They had not seen, then, those awful maps.

We were at the height and glory of our strength. Out of England had come the flower of our youth, and out of Scotland and Wales and Canada and Australia and New Zealand. Even out of Ireland, with the 16th Division of the south and west, and the 36th of Ulster. The New Armies were made up of all the volunteers who had answered the call to the colors, not waiting for the conscription by class, which followed later. They were the ardent ones, the young men from office, factory, shop, and field, university and public school. The best of our intelligence were there, the noblest of our manhood, the strength of our heart, the beauty of our soul, in those battalions which soon were to be flung into explosive fires.

III

In the month of May a new type of manhood was filling the old roads behind the front.

I saw them first in the little old town of St.-Pol, where always there was a coming and going of French and English soldiers. It was market-day and the Grande Place (not very grand) was crowded with booths and old ladies in black, and young girls with checkered aprons over their black frocks, and pigs and clucking fowls. Suddenly the people scattered, and there was a rumble and rattle of wheels as a long line of transport wagons came through the square.

"By Jove!... Australians!"

There was no mistaking them. Their slouch-hats told one at a glance, but without them I should have known. They had a distinctive type of their own, which marked them out from all other soldiers of ours along those roads of war.

They were hatchet-faced fellows who came riding through the little old market town; British unmistakably, yet not English, not Irish, nor Scottish, nor Canadian. They looked hard, with the hardness of a boyhood and a breeding away from cities or, at least, away from the softer training of our way of life. They had merry eyes (especially for the girls round the stalls), but resolute, clean-cut mouths, and they rode their horses with an easy grace in the saddle, as though born to riding, and drove their wagons with a recklessness among the little booths that was justified by half an inch between an iron axle and an old woman's table of colored ribbons.

Those clean-shaven, sun-tanned, dust-covered men, who had come out of the hell of the Dardanelles and the burning drought of Egyptian sands, looked wonderfully fresh in France. Youth, keen as steel, with a flash in the eyes, with an utter carelessness of any peril ahead, came riding down the street.

They were glad to be there. Everything was new and good to them (though so old and stale to many of us), and after their adventures in the East they found it splendid to be in a civilized country, with water in the sky and in the fields, with green trees about them, and flowers in the grass, and white people who were friendly.

When they came up in the train from Marseilles they were all at the windows, drinking in the look of the French landscape, and one of their officers told me that again and again he heard the same words spoken by those lads of his.

"It's a good country to fight for... It's like being home again."

At first they felt chilly in France, for the weather had been bad for them during the first weeks in April, when the wind had blown cold and rain-clouds had broken into sharp squalls.

Talking to the men, I saw them shiver a little and heard their teeth chatter, but they said they liked a moist climate with a bite in the wind, after all the blaze and glare of the Egyptian sun.

One of their pleasures in being there was the opportunity of buying sweets! "They can't have too much of them," said one of the officers, and the idea that those hard fellows, whose Homeric fighting qualities had been proved, should be enthusiastic for lollipops seemed to me an amusing touch of character. For tough as they were, and keen as they were, those Australian soldiers were but grown-up children with a wonderful simplicity of youth and the gift of laughter.

I saw them laughing when, for the first time, they tried on the gas-masks which none of us ever left behind when we went near the fighting-line. That horror of war on the western front was new to them.

Poison-gas was not one of the weapons used by the Turks, and the gas-masks seemed a joke to the groups of Australians trying on the headgear in the fields, and changing themselves into obscene specters ... But one man watching them gave a shudder and said, "It's a pity such splendid boys should have to risk this foul way of death." They did not hear his words, and we heard their laughter again.

On that first day of their arrival I stood in a courtyard with a young officer whose gray eyes had a fine, clear light, which showed the spirit of the man, and as we talked he pointed out some of the boys who passed in and out of an old barn. One of them had done fine work on the Peninsula, contemptuous of all risks. Another had gone out under heavy fire to bring in a wounded friend... "Oh, they are great lads!" said the captain of the company. "But now they want to get at the Germans and finish the job quickly. Give them a fair chance and they'll go far."

They went far, from that time to the end, and fought with a simple, terrible courage.

They had none of the discipline imposed upon our men by Regular traditions. They were gipsy fellows, with none but the gipsy law in their hearts, intolerant of restraint, with no respect for rank or caste unless it carried strength with it, difficult to handle behind the lines, quick-tempered, foul-mouthed, primitive men, but lovable, human, generous souls when their bayonets were not red with blood. Their discipline in battle was the best. They wanted to get to a place ahead. They would fight the devils of hell to get there.

The New-Zealanders followed them, with rosy cheeks like English boys of Kent, and more gentle manners than the other "Anzacs," and the same courage. They went far, too, and set the pace awhile in the last lap. But that, in the summer of '16, was far away.

In those last days of June, before the big battles began, the countryside of the Somme valley was filled with splendor. The mustard seed had spread a yellow carpet in many meadows so that they were Fields of the Cloth of Gold, and clumps of red clover grew like flowers of blood. The hedges about the villages of Picardy were white with elderflower and drenched with scent. It was haymaking time and French women and children were tossing the hay on wooden pitchforks during hot days which came between heavy rains. Our men were marching through that beauty, and were conscious of it, I think, and glad of life.

IV

Boulogne was a port through which all our youth passed between England and the long, straight road which led to No Man's Land. The seven-day-leave men were coming back by every tide, and all other leave was canceled.

New "drafts" were pouring through the port by tens of thousands—all manner of men of all our breed marching in long columns from the quayside, where they had orders yelled at them through megaphones by A.P.M.'s, R.T.O.'s, A.M.L.O.'s, and other blue tabbed officers who dealt with them as cattle for the slaughterhouses. I watched them landing from the transports which came in so densely crowded with the human freight that the men were wedged together on the decks like herrings in barrels. They crossed from one boat to another to reach the gangways, and one by one, interminably as it seemed, with rifle gripped and pack hunched, and steel hat clattering like a tinker's kettle, came down the inclined plank and lurched ashore. They were English lads from every country; Scots, Irish, Welsh, of every regiment; Australians, New-Zealanders, South Africans, Canadians, West Indian negroes of the Garrison Artillery; Sikhs, Pathans, and Dogras of the Indian Cavalry. Some of them had been sick and there was a greenish pallor on their faces.

Most of them were deeply tanned. Many of them stepped on the quayside of France for the first time after months of training, and I could tell those, sometimes, by the furtive look they gave at the crowded scene about them, and by a sudden glint in their eyes, a faint reflection of the emotion that was in them, because this was another stage on their adventure of war, and the drawbridge was down at last between them and the enemy. That was all, just that look, and lips tightened now grimly, and the pack hunched higher. Then they fell in by number and marched away, with Redcaps to guard them, across the bridge, into the town of Boulogne and beyond to the great camp near Etaples (and near the hospital, so that German aircraft had a good argument for smashing Red Cross huts), where some of them would wait until somebody said, "You're wanted." They were wanted in droves as soon as the fighting began on the first day of July.

The bun shops in Boulogne were filled with nurses, V.A.D.'s, all kinds of girls in uniforms which glinted with shoulder-straps and buttons. They ate large quantities of buns at odd hours of mornings and afternoons. Flying-men and officers of all kinds waiting for trains crowded the Folkestone Hotel and restaurants, where they spent two hours over luncheon and three hours over dinner, drinking red wine, talking "shop"—the shop of trench-mortar units, machine-gun sections, cavalry squadrons, air-fighting, gas schools, and anti-gas schools. Regular inhabitants of Boulogne, officers at the base, passed to inner rooms with French ladies of dangerous appearance, and the transients envied them and said: "Those fellows have all the luck! What's their secret? How do they arrange these cushie jobs?" From open windows came the music of gramophones. Through half-drawn curtains there were glimpses of khaki tunics and Sam Brown belts in juxtaposition with silk blouses and coiled hair and white arms. Opposite the Folkestone there was a park of ambulances driven by "Scottish women," who were always on the move from one part of the town to the other. Motor-cars came hooting with staff-officers, all aglow in red tabs and armbands, thirsty for little cocktails after a dusty drive. Everywhere in the streets and on the esplanade there was incessant saluting. The arms of men were never still. It was like the St. Vitus disease. Tommies and Jocks saluted every subaltern with an automatic gesture of convulsive energy. Every subaltern acknowledged these movements and in turn saluted a multitude of majors, colonels, and generals. The thing became farcical, a monstrous absurdity of human relationship, yet pleasing to the vanity of men lifted up above the lowest caste. It seemed to me an intensification of the snob instinct in the soul of man. Only the Australians stood out against it, and went by all officers except their own with a careless slouch and a look of "To hell with all that handwagging."

Seated on high stools in the Folkestone, our young officers clinked their cocktails, and then whispered together.

"When's it coming?"

"In a few days... I'm for the Gommecourt sector."

"Do you think we shall get through?"

"Not a doubt of it. The cavalry are massing for a great drive. As soon as we make the gap they'll ride into the blue."

"By God!... There'll be some slaughter"

"I think the old Boche will crack this time."

"Well, cheerio!"

There was a sense of enormous drama at hand, and the excitement of it in boys' hearts drugged all doubt and fears. It was only the older men, and the introspective, who suffered from the torture of apprehension. Even timid fellows in the ranks were, I imagine, strengthened and exalted by the communal courage of their company or battalion, for courage as well as fear is infectious, and the psychology of the crowd uplifts the individual to immense heights of daring when alone he would be terror—stricken. The public-school spirit of pride in name and tradition was in each battalion of the New Army, extended later to the division, which became the unit of esprit de corps. They must not "let the battalion down." They would do their damnedest to get farther than any other crowd, to bag more prisoners, to gain more "kudos." There was rivalry even among the platoons and the companies. "A" Company would show "B" Company the way to go! Their sergeant-major was a great fellow! Their platoon commanders were fine kids! With anything like a chance—

In that spirit, as far as I, an outsider could see and hear, did our battalions of boys march forward to "The Great Push," whistling, singing, jesting, until their lips were dry and their throats parched in the dust, and even the merriest jesters of all were silent under the weight of their packs and rifles. So they moved up day by day, through the beauty of that June in France, thousands of men, hundreds of thousands to the edge of the battlefields of the Somme, where the enemy was intrenched in fortress positions and where already, before the last days of June, gunfire was flaming over a vast sweep of country.

V

On the 1st of July, 1916, began those prodigious battles which only lulled down at times during two and a half years more, when our British armies fought with desperate sacrificial valor beyond all previous reckoning; when the flower of our youth was cast into that furnace month after month, recklessly, with prodigal, spendthrift haste; when those boys were mown down in swaths by machine-guns, blown to bits by shell-fire, gassed in thousands, until all that country became a graveyard; when they went forward to new assaults or fell back in rearguard actions with a certain knowledge that they had in their first attack no more than one chance in five of escape, next time one chance in four, then one chance in three, one chance in two, and after that no chance at all, on the line of averages, as worked out by their experience of luck. More boys came out to take their places, and more, and more, conscripts following volunteers, younger brothers following elder brothers. Never did they revolt from the orders that came to them. Never a battalion broke into mutiny against inevitable martyrdom. They were obedient to the command above them. Their discipline did not break. However profound was the despair of the individual, and it was, I know, deep as the wells of human tragedy in many hearts, the mass moved as it was directed, backward or forward, this way and that, from one shambles to another, in mud and in blood, with the same massed valor as that which uplifted them before that first day of July with an intensified pride in the fame of their divisions, with a more eager desire for public knowledge of their deeds, with a loathing of war's misery, with a sense of its supreme folly, yet with a refusal in their souls to acknowledge defeat or to stop this side of victory. In each battle there were officers and men who risked death deliberately, and in a kind of ecstasy did acts of superhuman courage; and because of the number of these feats the record of them is monotonous, dull, familiar. The mass followed their lead, and even poor coward-hearts, of whom there were many, as in all armies, had courage enough, as a rule, to get as far as the center of the fury before their knees gave way or they dropped dead.

Each wave of boyhood that came out from England brought a new mass of physical and spiritual valor as great as that which was spent, and in the end it was an irresistible tide which broke down the last barriers and swept through in a rush to victory, which we gained at the cost of nearly a million dead, and a high sum of living agony, and all our wealth, and a spiritual bankruptcy worse than material loss, so that now England is for a time sick to death and drained of her old pride and power.

VI

I remember, as though it were yesterday in vividness and a hundred years ago in time, the bombardment which preceded the battles of the Somme. With a group of officers I stood on the high ground above Albert, looking over to Gommecourt and Thiepval and La Boisselle, on the left side of the German salient, and then, by crossing the road, to Fricourt, Mametz, and Montauban on the southern side. From Albert westward past Thiepval Wood ran the little river of the Ancre, and on the German side the ground rose steeply to Usna Hill by La Boisselle, and to Thiepval Chateau above the wood. It was a formidable defensive position, one fortress girdled by line after line of trenches, and earthwork redoubts, and deep tunnels, and dugouts in which the German troops could live below ground until the moment of attack. The length of our front of assault was about twenty miles round the side of the salient to the village of Bray, on the Somme, where the French joined us and continued the battle.

From where we stood we could see a wide panorama of the German positions, and beyond, now and then, when the smoke of shellfire drifted, I caught glimpses of green fields and flower patches beyond the trench lines, and church spires beyond the range of guns rising above clumps of trees in summer foliage. Immediately below, in the foreground, was the village of Albert, not much ruined then, with its red-brick church and tower from which there hung, head downward, the Golden Virgin with her Babe outstretched as though as a peace-offering over all this strife. That leaning statue, which I had often passed on the way to the trenches, was now revealed brightly with a golden glamour, as sheets of flame burst through a heavy veil of smoke over the valley. In a field close by some troops were being ticketed with yellow labels fastened to their backs. It was to distinguish them so that artillery observers might know them from the enemy when their turn came to go into the battleground. Something in the sight of those yellow tickets made me feel sick. Away behind, a French farmer was cutting his grass with a long scythe, in steady, sweeping strokes. Only now and then did he stand to look over at the most frightful picture of battle ever seen until then by human eyes. I wondered, and wonder still, what thoughts were passing through that old brain to keep him at his work, quietly, steadily, on the edge of hell. For there, quite close and clear, was hell, of man's making, produced by chemists and scientists, after centuries in search of knowledge. There were the fires of hate, produced out of the passion of humanity after a thousand years of Christendom and of progress in the arts of beauty. There was the devil-worship of our poor, damned human race, where the most civilized nations of the world were on each side of the bonfires. It was worth watching by a human ant.

I remember the noise of our guns as all our batteries took their parts in a vast orchestra of drumfire. The tumult of the fieldguns merged into thunderous waves. Behind me a fifteen-inch "Grandmother" fired single strokes, and each one was an enormous shock. Shells were rushing through the air like droves of giant birds with beating wings and with strange wailings. The German lines were in eruption. Their earthworks were being tossed up, and fountains of earth sprang up between columns of smoke, black columns and white, which stood rigid for a few seconds and then sank into the banks of fog. Flames gushed up red and angry, rending those banks of mist with strokes of lightning. In their light I saw trees falling, branches tossed like twigs, black things hurtling through space. In the night before the battle, when that bombardment had lasted several days and nights, the fury was intensified. Red flames darted hither and thither like little red devils as our trench mortars got to work. Above the slogging of the guns there were louder, earth-shaking noises, and volcanoes of earth and fire spouted as high as the clouds. One convulsion of this kind happened above Usna Hill, with a long, terrifying roar and a monstrous gush of flame.

"What is that?" asked some one.

"It must be the mine we charged at La Boisselle. The biggest that has xever been."

It was a good guess. When, later in the battle, I stood by the crater of that mine and looked into its gulf I wondered how many Germans had been hurled into eternity when the earth had opened. The grave was big enough for a battalion of men with horses and wagons, below the chalk of the crater's lips. Often on the way to Bapaume I stepped off the road to look into that white gulf, remembering the moment when I saw the gust of flame that rent the earth about it.

VII

There was the illusion of victory on that first day of the Somme battles, on the right of the line by Fricourt, and it was not until a day or two later that certain awful rumors I had heard from wounded men and officers who had attacked on the left up by Gommecourt, Thiepval, and Serre were confirmed by certain knowledge of tragic disaster on that side of the battle-line.

The illusion of victory, with all the price and pain of it, came to me when I saw the German rockets rising beyond the villages of Mametz and Montauban and our barrage fire lifting to a range beyond the first lines of German trenches, and our support troops moving forward in masses to captured ground. We had broken through! By the heroic assault of our English and Scottish troops. West Yorks, Yorks and Lancs, Lincolns, Durhams, Northumberland Fusiliers, Norfolks and Berkshires, Liverpools, Manchesters, Gordons, and Royal Scots, all those splendid men I had seen marching to their lines. We had smashed through the ramparts of the German fortress, through that maze of earthworks and tunnels which had appalled me when I saw them on the maps, and over which I had gazed from time to time from our front-line trenches when those places seemed impregnable. I saw crowds of prisoners coming back under escort, fifteen hundred had been counted in the first day, and they had the look of a defeated army. Our lightly wounded men, thousands of them, were shouting and laughing as they came down behind the lines, wearing German caps and helmets. From Amiens civilians straggled out along the roads as far as they were allowed by military police, and waved hands and cheered those boys of ours. "Vive l'Angleterre!" cried old men, raising their hats. Old women wept at the sight of those gay wounded, the lightly touched, glad of escape, rejoicing in their luck and in the glory of life which was theirs still and cried out to them with shrill words of praise and exultation.

"Nous les aurons les sales Boches! Ah, ils sont foutus, ces bandits! C'est la victoire, grace a vous, petits soldats anglais!"

Victory! The spirit of victory in the hearts of fighting men, and of women excited by the sight of those bandaged heads, those bare, brawny arms splashed with blood, those laughing heroes.

It looked like victory, in those days, as war correspondents, we were not so expert in balancing the profit and loss as afterward we became. When I went into Fricourt on the third day of battle, after the last Germans, who had clung on to its ruins, had been cleared out by the Yorkshires and Lincolns of the 21st Division, that division which had been so humiliated at Loos and now was wonderful in courage, and when the Manchesters and Gordons of the 30th Division had captured Montauban and repulsed fierce counter-attacks.

It looked like victory, because of the German dead that lay there in their battered trenches and the filth and stench of death over all that mangled ground, and the enormous destruction wrought by our guns, and the fury of fire which we were still pouring over the enemy's lines from batteries which had moved forward.

I went down flights of steps into German dugouts, astonished by their depth and strength. Our men did not build like this. This German industry was a rebuke to us, yet we had captured their work and the dead bodies of their laborers lay in those dark caverns, killed by our bombers, who had flung down handgrenades. I drew back from those fat corpses. They looked monstrous, lying there crumpled up, amid a foul litter of clothes, stickbombs, old boots, and bottles. Groups of dead lay in ditches which had once been trenches, flung into chaos by that bombardment I had seen. They had been bayoneted. I remember one man, an elderly fellow sitting up with his back to a bit of earth with his hands half raised. He was smiling a little, though he had been stabbed through the belly and was stone dead. Victory! some of the German dead were young boys, too young to be killed for old men's crimes, and others might have been old or young. One could not tell, because they had no faces, and were just masses of raw flesh in rags and uniforms. Legs and arms lay separate, without any bodies thereabouts.

Outside Montauban there was a heap of our own dead. Young Gordons and Manchesters of the 30th Division, they had been caught by blasts of machinegun fire, but our dead seemed scarce in the places where I walked.

Victory? Well, we had gained some ground, and many prisoners, and here and there some guns. But as I stood by Montauban I saw that our line was a sharp salient looped round Mametz village and then dipping sharply southward to Fricourt. O God! had we only made another salient after all that monstrous effort? To the left there was fury at La Boisselle, where a few broken trees stood black on the skyline on a chalky ridge. Storms of German shrapnel were bursting there, and machineguns were firing in spasms. In Contalmaison, round a chateau which stood high above ruined houses, shells were bursting with thunderclaps, our shells. German gunners in invisible batteries were sweeping our lines with barrage fire, it roamed up and down this side of Montauban Wood, just ahead of me, and now and then shells smashed among the houses and barns of Fricourt, and over Mametz there was suddenly a hurricane of "hate." Our men were working like ants in those muck heaps, a battalion moved up toward Boisselle. From a ridge above Fricourt, where once I had seen a tall crucifix between two trees, which our men called the "Poodles," a body of men came down and shrapnel burst among them and they fell and disappeared in tall grass. Stretcher bearers came slowly through Fricourt village with living burdens. Some of them were German soldiers carrying our wounded and their own. Walking wounded hobbled slowly with their arms round each other's shoulders, Germans and English together. A boy in a steel hat stopped me and held up a bloody hand. "A bit of luck!" he said. "I'm off, after eighteen months of it."

German prisoners came down with a few English soldiers as their escort. I saw distant groups of them, and a shell smashed into one group and scattered it. The living ran, leaving their dead. Ambulances driven by daring fellows drove to the far edge of Fricourt, not a healthy place, and loaded up with wounded from a dressing station in a tunnel there.

It was a wonderful picture of war in all its filth and shambles. But was it Victory? I knew then that it was only a breach in the German bastion, and that on the left, Gommecourt way, there had been black tragedy.

VIII

On the left, where the 8th and 10th Corps were directing operations, the assault had been delivered by the 4th, 29th, 36th, 49th, 32nd, 8th, and 56th Divisions.

The positions in front of them were Gommecourt and Beaumont Hamel on the left side of the River Ancre, and Thiepval Wood on the right side of the Ancre leading up to Thiepval Chateau on the crest of the cliff. These were the hardest positions to attack, because of the rising ground and the immense strength of the enemy's earthworks and tunneled defenses. But our generals were confident that the gun power at their disposal was sufficient to smash down that defensive system and make an easy way through for the infantry. They were wrong. In spite of that tornado of shell-fire which I had seen tearing up the earth, many tunnels were still unbroken, and out of them came masses of German machine-gunners and riflemen, when our infantry rose from their own trenches on that morning of July 1st.

Our guns had shifted their barrage forward at that moment, farther ahead of the infantry than was afterward allowed, the men being trained to follow close to the lines of bursting shells, trained to expect a number of casualties from their own guns—it needs some training—in order to secure the general safety gained by keeping the enemy below ground until our bayonets were round his dugouts.

The Germans had been trained, too, to an act of amazing courage. Their discipline, that immense power of discipline which dominates men in the mass, was strong enough to make them obey the order to rush through that barrage of ours, that advancing wall of explosion and, if they lived through it, to face our men in the open with massed machine-gun fire. So they did; and as English, Irish, Scottish, and Welsh battalions of our assaulting divisions trudged forward over what had been No Man's Land, machine-gun bullets sprayed upon them, and they fell like grass to the scythe. Line after line of men followed them, and each line crumpled, and only small groups and single figures, seeking comradeship, hurried forward. German machine-gunners were bayoneted as their thumbs were still pressed to their triggers. In German front-line trenches at the bottom of Thiepval Wood, outside Beaumont Hamel and on the edge of Gommecourt Park, the field-gray men who came out of their dugouts fought fiercely with stick-bombs and rifles, and our officers and men, in places where they had strength enough, clubbed them to death, stuck them with bayonets, and blew their brains out with revolvers at short range. Then those English and Irish and Scottish troops, grievously weak because of all the dead and wounded behind them, struggled through to the second German line, from which there came a still fiercer rattle of machine-gun and rifle-fire. Some of them broke through that line, too, and went ahead in isolated parties across the wild crater land, over chasms and ditches and fallen trees, toward the highest ground, which had been their goal. Nothing was seen of them. They disappeared into clouds of smoke and flame. Gunner observers saw rockets go up in far places—our rockets—showing that outposts had penetrated into the German lines. Runners came back—survivors of many predecessors who had fallen on the way—with scribbled messages from company officers. One came from the Essex and King's Own of the 4th Division, at a place called Pendant Copse, southeast of Serre. "For God's sake send us bombs." It was impossible to send them bombs. No men could get to them through the deep barrage of shell-fire which was between them and our supporting troops. Many tried and died.

The Ulster men went forward toward Beaumont Hamel with a grim valor which was reckless of their losses. Beaumont Hamel was a German fortress. Machine-gun fire raked every yard of the Ulster way. Hundreds of the Irish fell. I met hundreds of them wounded—tall, strong, powerful men, from Queen's Island and Belfast factories, and Tyneside Irish and Tyneside Scots.

"They gave us no chance," said one of them—a sergeant-major. "They just murdered us."

But bunches of them went right into the heart of the German positions, and then found behind them crowds of Germans who had come up out of their tunnels and flung bombs at them. Only a few came back alive in the darkness.

Into Thiepval Wood men of ours smashed their way through the German trenches, not counting those who fell, and killing any German who stood in their way. Inside that wood of dead trees and charred branches they reformed, astonished at the fewness of their numbers. Germans coming up from holes in the earth attacked them, and they held firm and took two hundred prisoners. Other Germans came closing in like wolves, in packs, and to a German officer who said, "Surrender!" our men shouted, "No surrender!" and fought in Thiepval Wood until most were dead and only a few wounded crawled out to tell that tale.

The Londoners of the 56th Division had no luck at all. Theirs was the worst luck because, by a desperate courage in assault, they did break through the German lines at Gommecourt. Their left was held by the London Rifle Brigade. The Rangers and the Queen Victoria Rifles—the old "Vics "—formed their center. Their right was made up by the London Scottish, and behind came the Queen's Westminsters and the Kensingtons, who were to advance through their comrades to a farther objective. Across a wide No Man's Land they suffered from the bursting of heavy crumps, and many fell. But they escaped annihilation by machine-gun fire and stormed through the upheaved earth into Gommecourt Park, killing many Germans and sending back batches of prisoners. They had done what they had been asked to do, and started building up barricades of earth and sand-bags, and then found they were in a death-trap. There were no troops on their right or left. They had thrust out into a salient, which presently the enemy saw. The German gunners, with deadly skill, boxed it round with shell-fire, so that the Londoners were inclosed by explosive walls, and then very slowly and carefully drew a line of bursting shells up and down, up and down that captured ground, ravaging its earth anew and smashing the life that crouched there—London life.

I have written elsewhere (in The Battles of the Somme) how young officers and small bodies of these London men held the barricades against German attacks while others tried to break a way back through that murderous shell-fire, and how groups of lads who set out on that adventure to their old lines were shattered so that only a few from each group crawled back alive, wounded or unwounded.

At the end of the day the Germans acted with chivalry, which I was not allowed to tell at the time. The general of the London Division (Philip Howell) told me that the enemy sent over a message by a low-flying airplane, proposing a truce while the stretcher-bearers worked, and offering the service of their own men in that work of mercy. This offer was accepted without reference to G.H.Q., and German stretcher-bearers helped to carry our wounded to a point where they could be reached.

Many, in spite of that, remained lying out in No Man's Land, some for three or four days and nights. I met one man who lay out there wounded, with a group of comrades more badly hurt than he was, until July 6th. At night he crawled over to the bodies of the dead and took their water-bottles and "iron" rations, and so brought drink and food to his stricken friends. Then at last he made his way through roving shells to our lines and even then asked to lead the stretcher-bearers who volunteered on a search-party for his "pals."

"Physical courage was very common in the war," said a friend of mine who saw nothing of war. "It is proved that physical courage is the commonest quality of mankind, as moral courage is the rarest." But that soldier's courage was spiritual, and there were many like him in the battles of the Somme and in other later battles as tragic as those.

IX

I have told how, before "The Big Push," as we called the beginning of these battles, little towns of tents were built under the sign of the Red Cross. For a time they were inhabited only by medical officers, nurses, and orderlies, busily getting ready for a sudden invasion, and spending their surplus energy, which seemed inexhaustible, on the decoration of their camps by chalk-lined paths, red crosses painted on canvas or built up in red and white chalk on leveled earth, and flowers planted outside the tents—all very pretty and picturesque in the sunshine and the breezes over the valley of the Somme.

On the morning of battle the doctors, nurses, and orderlies waited for their patients and said, "Now we shan't be long!" They were merry and bright with that wonderful cheerfulness which enabled them to face the tragedy of mangled manhood without horror, and almost, it seemed, without pity, because it was their work, and they were there to heal what might be healed. It was with a rush that their first cases came, and the M.O.'s whistled and said, "Ye gods! how many more?" Many more. The tide did not slacken. It became a spate brought down by waves of ambulances. Three thousand wounded came to Daours on the Somme, three thousand to Corbie, thousands to Dernancourt, Heilly, Puchevillers, Toutencourt, and many other "clearing stations."

At Daours the tents were filled to overflowing, until there was no more room. The wounded were laid down on the grass to wait their turn for the surgeon's knife. Some of them crawled over to haycocks and covered themselves with hay and went to sleep, as I saw them sleeping there, like dead men. Here and there shell-shocked boys sat weeping or moaning, and shaking with an ague. Most of the wounded were quiet and did not give any groan or moan. The lightly wounded sat in groups, telling their adventures, cursing the German machine-gunners. Young officers spoke in a different way, and with that sporting spirit which they had learned in public schools praised their enemy.

"The machine-gunners are wonderful fellows—topping. Fight until they're killed. They gave us hell."

Each man among those thousands of wounded had escaped death a dozen times or more by the merest flukes of luck. It was this luck of theirs which they hugged with a kind of laughing excitement.

"It's a marvel I'm here! That shell burst all round me. Killed six of my pals. I've got through with a blighty wound. No bones broken... God! What luck!"

The death of other men did not grieve them. They could not waste this sense of luck in pity. The escape of their own individuality, this possession of life, was a glorious thought. They were alive! What luck! What luck!

We called the hospital at Corbie the "Butcher's Shop." It was in a pretty spot in that little town with a big church whose tall white towers looked down a broad sweep of the Somme, so that for miles they were a landmark behind the battlefields. Behind the lines during those first battles, but later, in 1918, when the enemy came nearly to the gates of Amiens, a stronghold of the Australians, who garrisoned it and sniped pigeons for their pots off the top of the towers, and took no great notice of "whizz-bangs" which broke through the roofs of cottages and barns. It was a safe, snug place in July of '16, but that Butcher's Shop at a corner of the square was not a pretty spot. After a visit there I had to wipe cold sweat from my forehead, and found myself trembling in a queer way. It was the medical officer—a colonel—who called it that name. "This is our Butcher's Shop," he said, cheerily. "Come and have a look at my cases. They're the worst possible; stomach wounds, compound fractures, and all that. We lop off limbs here all day long, and all night. You've no idea!"

I had no idea, but I did not wish to see its reality. The M.O. could not understand my reluctance to see his show. He put it down to my desire to save his time—and explained that he was going the rounds and would take it as a favor if I would walk with him. I yielded weakly, and cursed myself for not taking to flight. Yet, I argued, what men are brave enough to suffer I ought to have the courage to see... I saw and sickened.

These were the victims of "Victory" and the red fruit of war's harvest-fields. A new batch of "cases" had just arrived. More were being brought in on stretchers. They were laid down in rows on the floor-boards. The colonel bent down to some of them and drew their blankets back, and now and then felt a man's pulse. Most of them were unconscious, breathing with the hard snuffle of dying men. Their skin was already darkening to the death-tint, which is not white. They were all plastered with a gray clay and this mud on their faces was, in some cases, mixed with thick clots of blood, making a hard incrustation from scalp to chin.

"That fellow won't last long," said the M. O., rising from a stretcher. "Hardly a heart-beat left in him. Sure to die on the operating-table if he gets as far as that... Step back against the wall a minute, will you?"

We flattened ourselves against the passage wall while ambulance-men brought in a line of stretchers. No sound came from most of those bundles under the blankets, but from one came a long, agonizing wail, the cry of an animal in torture.

"Come through the wards," said the colonel. "They're pretty bright, though we could do with more space and light."

In one long, narrow room there were about thirty beds, and in each bed lay a young British soldier, or part of a young British soldier. There was not much left of one of them. Both his legs had been amputated to the thigh, and both his arms to the shoulder-blades.

"Remarkable man, that," said the colonel. "Simply refuses to die. His vitality is so tremendous that it is putting up a terrific fight against mortality... There's another case of the same kind; one leg gone and the other going, and one arm. Deliberate refusal to give in. 'You're not going to kill me, doctor,' he said. 'I'm going to stick it through.' What spirit, eh?"

I spoke to that man. He was quite conscious, with bright eyes. His right leg was uncovered, and supported on a board hung from the ceiling. Its flesh was like that of a chicken badly carved-white, flabby, and in tatters. He thought I was a surgeon, and spoke to me pleadingly:

"I guess you can save that leg, sir. It's doing fine. I should hate to lose it."

I murmured something about a chance for it, and the M. O. broke in cheerfully.

"You won't lose it if I can help it. How's your pulse? Oh, not bad. Keep cheerful and we'll pull you through." The man smiled gallantly.

"Bound to come off," said the doctor as we passed to another bed. "Gas gangrene. That's the thing that does us down."

In bed after bed I saw men of ours, very young men, who had been lopped of limbs a few hours ago or a few minutes, some of them unconscious, some of them strangely and terribly conscious, with a look in their eyes as though staring at the death which sat near to them, and edged nearer.

"Yes," said the M. O., "they look bad, some of 'em, but youth is on their side. I dare say seventy-five per cent. will get through. If it wasn't for gas gangrene—"

He jerked his head to a boy sitting up in bed, smiling at the nurse who felt his pulse.

"Looks fairly fit after the knife, doesn't he? But we shall have to cut higher up. The gas again. I'm afraid he'll be dead before to-morrow. Come into the operating-theater. It's very well equipped."

I refused that invitation. I walked stiffly out of the Butcher's Shop of Corbie past the man who had lost both arms and both legs, that vital trunk, past rows of men lying under blankets, past a stench of mud and blood and anesthetics, to the fresh air of the gateway, where a column of ambulances had just arrived with a new harvest from the fields of the Somme.

"Come in again, any time!" shouted out the cheery colonel, waving his hand.

I never went again, though I saw many other Butcher's Shops in the years that followed, where there was a great carving of human flesh which was of our boyhood, while the old men directed their sacrifice, and the profiteers grew rich, and the fires of hate were stoked up at patriotic banquets and in editorial chairs.

X

The failure on the left hardly balanced by the partial success on the right caused a sudden pause in the operations, camouflaged by small attacks on minor positions around and above Fricourt and Mametz. The Lincolns and others went over to Fricourt Wood and routed out German machine-gunners. The West Yorks attacked the sunken road at Fricourt. The Dorsets, Manchesters, Highland Light Infantry, Lancashire Fusiliers, and Borderers of the 32d Division were in possession of La Boisselle and clearing out communication trenches to which the Germans were hanging on with desperate valor. The 21st Division—Northumberland Fusiliers, Durhams, Yorkshires-were making a flanking attack on Contalmaison, but weakened after their heavy losses on the first day of battle. The fighting for a time was local, in small copses—Lozenge Wood, Peak Wood, Caterpillar Wood, Acid Drop Copse—where English and German troops fought ferociously for yards of ground, hummocks of earth, ditches.

G. H. Q. had been shocked by the disaster on the left and the failure of all the big hopes they had held for a break-through on both sides of the German positions. Rumors came to us that the Commander-in-Chief had decided to restrict future operations to minor actions for strengthening the line and to abandon the great offensive. It was believed by officers I met that Sir Henry Rawlinson was arguing, persuading, in favor of continued assaults on the grand scale.

Whatever division of opinion existed in the High Command I do not know; it was visible to all of us that for some days there were uncertainty of direction, hesitation, conflicting orders. On July 7th the 17th Division, under General Pilcher, attacked Contalmaison, and a whole battalion of the Prussian Guard hurried up from Valenciennes and, thrown on to the battlefield without maps or guidance, walked into the barrage which covered the advance of our men and were almost annihilated. But although some bodies of our men entered Contalmaison, in an attack which I was able to see, they were smashed out of it again by storms of fire followed by masses of men who poured out from Mametz Wood. The Welsh were attacking Mametz Wood.

They were handled, as Marbot said of his men in a Napoleonic battle, "like turnips." Battalion commanders received orders in direct conflict with one another. Bodies of Welshmen were advanced, and then retired, and left to lie nakedly without cover, under dreadful fire. The 17th Division, under General Pilcher, did not attack at the expected time. There was no co-ordination of divisions; no knowledge among battalion officers of the strategy or tactics of a battle in which their men were involved.

"Goodness knows what's happening," said an officer I met near Mametz. He had been waiting all night and half a day with a body of troops who had expected to go forward, and were still hanging about under harassing fire.

On July 9th Contalmaison was taken. I saw that attack very clearly, so clearly that I could almost count the bricks in the old chateau set in a little wood, and saw the left-hand tower knocked off by the direct hit of a fifteen-inch shell. At four o'clock in the afternoon our guns concentrated on the village, and under the cover of that fire our men advanced on three sides of it, hemmed it in, and captured it with the garrison of the 122d Bavarian Regiment, who had suffered the agonies of hell inside its ruins. Now our men stayed in the ruins, and this time German shells smashed into the chateau and the cottages and left nothing but rubbish heaps of brick through which a few days later I went walking with the smell of death in my nostrils. Our men were now being shelled in that place.

Beyond La Boisselle, on the left of the Albert-Bapaume road, there had been a village called Ovillers. It was no longer there. Our guns has removed every trace of it, except as it lay in heaps of pounded brick. The Germans had a network of trenches about it, and in their ditches and their dugouts they fought like wolves. Our 12th Division was ordered to drive them out—a division of English county troops, including the Sussex, Essex, Bedfords, and Middlesex—and those country boys of ours fought their way among communication trenches, burrowed into tunnels, crouched below hummocks of earth and brick, and with bombs and bayonets and broken rifles, and boulders of stone, and German stick-bombs, and any weapon that would kill, gained yard by yard over the dead bodies of the enemy, or by the capture of small batches of cornered men, until after seventeen days of this one hundred and forty men of the 3rd Prussian Guard, the last of their garrison, without food or water, raised a signal of surrender, and came out with their hands up. Ovillers was a shambles, in a fight of primitive earth-men like human beasts. Yet our men were not beast-like. They came out from those places—if they had the luck to come out—apparently unchanged, without any mark of the beast on them, and when they cleansed themselves of mud and filth, boiled the lice out of their shirts, and assembled in a village street behind the lines, they whistled, laughed, gossiped, as though nothing had happened to their souls—though something had really happened, as now we know.

It was not until July 14th that our High Command ordered another general attack after the local fighting which had been in progress since the first day of battle. Our field-batteries, and some of our "heavies," had moved forward to places like Montauban and Contalmaison—where German shells came searching for them all day long—and new divisions had been brought up to relieve some of the men who had been fighting so hard and so long. It was to be an attack on the second German line of defense on the ridges by the village of Bazentin le Grand and Bazentin le Petit to Longueval on the right and Delville Wood. I went up in the night to see the bombardment and the beginning of the battle and the swirl of its backwash, and I remember now the darkness of villages behind the lines through which our cars crawled, until we reached the edge of the battlefields and saw the sky rent by incessant flames of gun-fire, while red tongues of flames leaped up from burning villages. Longueval was on fire, and the two Bazentins, and another belt of land in France, so beautiful to see, even as I had seen it first between the sand-bags of our parapets, was being delivered to the charcoal-burners.

I have described that night scene elsewhere, in all its deviltry, but one picture which I passed on the way to the battlefield could not then be told. Yet it was significant of the mentality of our High Command, as was afterward pointed out derisively by Sixte von Arnim. It proved the strange unreasoning optimism which still lingered in the breasts of old-fashioned generals in spite of what had happened on the left on the first day of July, and their study of trench maps, and their knowledge of German machine-guns. By an old mill-house called the Moulin Vivier, outside the village of Meaulte, were masses of cavalry—Indian cavalry and Dragoons—drawn up densely to leave a narrow passageway for field-guns and horse-transport moving through the village, which was in utter darkness. The Indians sat like statues on their horses, motionless, dead silent. Now and again there was a jangle of bits. Here and there a British soldier lit a cigarette and for a second the little flame of his match revealed a bronzed face or glinted on steel helmets.

Cavalry!... So even now there was a serious purpose behind the joke of English soldiers who had gone forward on the first day, shouting, "This way to the gap!" and in the conversation of some of those who actually did ride through Bazentin that day.

A troop or two made their way over the cratered ground and skirted Delville Wood; the Dragoon Guards charged a machine-gun in a cornfield, and killed the gunners. Germans rounded up by them clung to their stirrup leathers crying: "Pity! Pity!" The Indians lowered their lances, but took prisoners to show their chivalry. But it was nothing more than a beau geste. It was as futile and absurd as Don Quixote's charge of the windmill. They were brought to a dead halt by the nature of the ground and machine-gun fire which killed their horses, and lay out that night with German shells searching for their bodies.

One of the most disappointed men in the army was on General Haldane's staff. He was an old cavalry officer, and this major of the old, old school (belonging in spirit to the time of Charles Lever) was excited by the thought that there was to be a cavalry adventure. He was one of those who swore that if he had his chance he would "ride into the blue." It was the chance he wanted and he nursed his way to it by delicate attentions to General Haldane. The general's bed was not so comfortable as his. He changed places. He even went so far as to put a bunch of flowers on the general's table in his dugout.

"You seem very attentive to me, major," said the general, smelling a rat.

Then the major blurted out his desire. Could he lead a squadron round Delville Wood? Could he take that ride into the blue? He would give his soul to do it.

"Get on with your job," said General Haldane.

That ride into the blue did not encourage the cavalry to the belief that they would be of real value in a warfare of trench lines and barbed wire, but for a long time later they were kept moving backward and forward between the edge of the battlefields and the back areas, to the great incumbrance of the roads, until they were "guyed" by the infantry, and irritable, so their officers told me, to the verge of mutiny. Their irritability was cured by dismounting them for a turn in the trenches, and I came across the Household Cavalry digging by the Coniston Steps, this side of Thiepval, and cursing their spade-work.

In this book I will not tell again the narrative of that, fighting in the summer and autumn of 1916, which I have written with many details of each day's scene in my collected despatches called The Battles of the Somme. There is little that I can add to those word-pictures which I wrote day by day, after haunting experiences amid the ruin of those fields, except a summing-up of their effect upon the mentality of our men, and upon the Germans who were in the same "blood-bath," as they called it, and a closer analysis of the direction and mechanism of our military machine.

Looking back upon those battles in the light of knowledge gained in the years that followed, it seems clear that our High Command was too prodigal in its expenditure of life in small sectional battles, and that the army corps and divisional staffs had not established an efficient system of communication with the fighting units under their control. It seemed to an outsider like myself that a number of separate battles were being fought without reference to one another in different parts of the field. It seemed as though our generals, after conferring with one another over telephones, said, "All right, tell So-and-so to have a go at Thiepval," or, "To-day we will send such-and-such a division to capture Delville Wood," or, "We must get that line of trenches outside Bazentin." Orders were drawn up on the basis of that decision and passed down to brigades, who read them as their sentence of death, and obeyed with or without protest, and sent three or four battalions to assault a place which was covered by German batteries round an arc of twenty miles, ready to open out a tempest of fire directly a rocket rose from their infantry, and to tear up the woods and earth in that neighborhood if our men gained ground. If the whole battle-line moved forward the German fire would have been dispersed, but in these separate attacks on places like Trones Wood and Delville Wood, and later on High Wood, it was a vast concentration of explosives which plowed up our men.

So it was that Delville Wood was captured and lost several times and became "Devil's" Wood to men who lay there under the crash and fury of massed gun-fire until a wretched remnant of what had been a glorious brigade of youth crawled out stricken and bleeding when relieved by another brigade ordered to take their turn in that devil's caldron, or to recapture it when German bombing-parties and machine-gunners had followed in the wake of fire, and had crouched again among the fallen trees, and in the shell-craters and ditches, with our dead and their dead to keep them company. In Delville Wood the South African Brigade of the 9th Division was cut to pieces, and I saw the survivors come out with few officers to lead them.

In Trones Wood, in Bernafay Wood, in Mametz Wood, there had been great slaughter of English troops and Welsh. The 18th Division and the 38th suffered horribly. In Delville Wood many battalions were slashed to pieces before these South Africans. And after that came High Wood.. . All that was left of High Wood in the autumn of 1916 was a thin row of branchless trees, but in July and August there were still glades under heavy foliage, until the branches were lopped off and the leaves scattered by our incessant fire. It was an important position, vital for the enemy's defense, and our attack on the right flank of the Pozieres Ridge, above Bazentin and Delville Wood, giving on the reverse slope a fine observation of the enemy's lines above Martinpuich and Courcellette away to Bapaume. For that reason the Germans were ordered to hold it at all costs, and many German batteries had registered on it to blast our men out if they gained a foothold on our side of the slope or theirs.

So High Wood became another hell, on a day of great battle—September 14, 1916—when for the first time tanks were used, demoralizing the enemy in certain places, though they were too few in number to strike a paralyzing blow. The Londoners gained part of High Wood at frightful cost and then were blown out of it. Other divisions followed them and found the wood stuffed with machine-guns which they had to capture through hurricanes of bullets before they crouched in craters amid dead Germans and dead English, and then were blown out like the Londoners, under shell-fire, in which no human life could stay for long.

The 7th Division was cut up there. The 33d Division lost six thousand men in an advance against uncut wire in the wood, which they were told was already captured.

Hundreds of men were vomiting from the effect of gas-shells, choking and blinded. Behind, the transport wagons and horses were smashed to bits.

The divisional staffs were often ignorant of what was happening to the fighting-men when the attack was launched. Light signals, rockets, heliographing, were of small avail through the dust—and smoke-clouds. Forward observing officers crouching behind parapets, as I often saw them, and sometimes stood with them, watched fires burning, red rockets and green, gusts of flame, and bursting shells, and were doubtful what to make of it all. Telephone wires trailed across the ground for miles, were cut into short lengths by shrapnel and high explosive. Accidents happened as part of the inevitable blunders of war. It was all a vast tangle and complexity of strife.

On July 17th I stood in a tent by a staff-officer who was directing a group of heavy guns supporting the 3d Division. He was tired, as I could see by the black lines under his eyes and tightly drawn lips. On a camp-table in front of him, upon which he leaned his elbows, there was a telephone apparatus, and the little bell kept ringing as we talked. Now and then a shell burst in the field outside the tent, and he raised his head and said: "They keep crumping about here. Hope they won't tear this tent to ribbons....That sounds like a gas-shell."

Then he turned to the telephone again and listened to some voice speaking.

"Yes, I can hear you. Yes, go on. 'Our men seen leaving High Wood.' Yes. 'Shelled by our artillery.' Are you sure of that? I say, are you sure they were our men? Another message. Well, carry on. 'Men digging on road from High Wood southeast to Longueval.' Yes, I've got that. 'They are our men and not Boches.' Oh, hell!... Get off the line. Get off the line, can't you?... 'Our men and not Boches.' Yes, I have that. 'Heavily shelled by our guns.'"

The staff-officer tapped on the table with a lead-pencil a tattoo, while his forehead puckered. Then he spoke into the telephone again.

"Are you there, 'Heavies'?... Well, don't disturb those fellows for half an hour. After that I will give you new orders. Try and confirm if they are our men."

He rang off and turned to me.

"That's the trouble. Looks as if we had been pounding our own men like hell. Some damn fool reports 'Boches.' Gives the reference number. Asks for the 'Heavies'. Then some other fellow says: 'Not Boches. For God's sake cease fire!' How is one to tell?"

I could not answer that question, but I hated the idea of our men sent forward to capture a road or a trench or a wood and then "pounded" by our guns. They had enough pounding from the enemy's guns. There seemed a missing link in the system somewhere. Probably it was quite inevitable.

Over and over again the wounded swore to God that they had been shelled by our own guns. The Londoners said so from High Wood. The Australians said so from Mouquet Farm. The Scots said so from Longueval! They said: "Why the hell do we get murdered by British gunners? What's the good of fighting if we're slaughtered by our own side?"

In some cases they were mistaken. It was enfilade fire from German batteries. But often it happened according to the way of that telephone conversation in the tent by Bronfay Farm.

The difference between British soldiers and German soldiers crawling over shell-craters or crouching below the banks of a sunken road was no more than the difference between two tribes of ants. Our flying scouts, however low they flew, risking the Archies and machine-gun bullets, often mistook khaki for field gray, and came back with false reports which led to tragedy.

XI

People who read my war despatches will remember my first descriptions of the tanks and those of other correspondents. They caused a sensation, a sense of excitement, laughter which shook the nation because of the comicality, the grotesque surprise, the possibility of quicker victory, which caught hold of the imagination of people who heard for the first time of those new engines of war, so beast-like in appearance and performance. The vagueness of our descriptions was due to the censorship, which forbade, wisely enough, any technical and exact definition, so that we had to compare them to giant toads, mammoths, and prehistoric animals of all kinds. Our accounts did, however, reproduce the psychological effect of the tanks upon the British troops when these engines appeared for the first time to their astonished gaze on September 13th. Our soldiers roared with laughter, as I did, when they saw them lolloping up the roads. On the morning of the great battle of September 15th the presence of the tanks going into action excited all the troops along the front with a sense of comical relief in the midst of the grim and deadly business of attack. Men followed them, laughing and cheering. There was a wonderful thrill in the airman's message, "Tank walking up the High Street of Flers with the British army cheering behind." Wounded boys whom I met that morning grinned in spite of their wounds at our first word about the tanks. "Crikey!" said a cockney lad of the 47th Division. "I can't help laughing every time I think of them tanks. I saw them stamping down German machine-guns as though they were wasps' nests." The adventures of Creme de Menthe, Cordon Rouge, and the Byng Boys, on both sides of the Bapaume road, when they smashed down barbed wire, climbed over trenches, sat on German redoubts, and received the surrender of German prisoners who held their hands up to these monsters and cried, "Kamerad!" were like fairy-tales of war by H. G. Wells.

Yet their romance had a sharp edge of reality as I saw in those battles of the Somme, and afterward, more grievously, in the Cambrai salient and Flanders, when the tanks were put out of action by direct hits of field-guns and nothing of humankind remained in them but the charred bones of their gallant crews.

Before the battle in September of '16 I talked with the pilots of the first tanks, and although they were convinced of the value of these new engines of war and were out to prove it, they did not disguise from me nor from their own souls that they were going forth upon a perilous adventure with the odds of luck against them. I remember one young pilot—a tiny fellow like a jockey, who took me on one side and said, "I want you to do me a favor," and then scribbled down his mother's address and asked me to write to her if "anything" happened to him.

He and other tank officers were anxious. They had not complete confidence in the steering and control of their engines. It was a difficult and clumsy kind of gear, which was apt to break down at a critical moment, as I saw when I rode in one on their field of maneuver. These first tanks were only experimental, and the tail arrangement was very weak. Worse than all mechanical troubles was the short-sighted policy of some authority at G.H.Q., who had insisted upon A.S.C. drivers being put to this job a few days before the battle, without proper training.

"It is mad and murderous," said one of the officers, "These fellows may have pluck, all right—I don't doubt it—but they don't know their engines, nor the double steering trick, and they have never been under shell-fire. It is asking for trouble."

As it turned out, the A.S.C. drivers proved their pluck, for the most part, splendidly, but many tanks broke down before they reached the enemy's lines, and in that action and later battles there were times when they bitterly disappointed the infantry commanders and the troops.

Individual tanks, commanded by gallant young officers and served by brave crews, did astounding feats, and some of these men came back dazed and deaf and dumb, after forty hours or more of fighting and maneuvering within steel walls, intensely hot, filled with the fumes of their engines, jolted and banged about over rough ground, and steering an uncertain course, after the loss of their "tails," which had snapped at the spine. But there had not been anything like enough tanks to secure an annihilating surprise over the enemy as afterward was attained in the first battle of Cambrai; and the troops who had been buoyed up with the hope that at last the machine—gun evil was going to be scotched were disillusioned and dejected when they saw tanks ditched behind the lines or nowhere in sight when once again they had to trudge forward under the flail of machine-gun bullets from earthwork redoubts. It was a failure in generalship to give away our secret before it could be made effective.

I remember sitting in a mess of the Gordons in the village of Franvillers along the Albert road, and listening to a long monologue by a Gordon officer on the future of the tanks. He was a dreamer and visionary, and his fellow-officers laughed at him.

"A few tanks are no good," he said. "Forty or fifty tanks are no good on a modern battle-front. We want hundreds of tanks, brought up secretly, fed with ammunition by tank carriers, bringing up field-guns and going into action without any preliminary barrage. They can smash through the enemy's wire and get over his trenches before he is aware that an attack has been organized. Up to now all our offensives have been futile because of our preliminary advertisement by prolonged bombardment. The tanks can bring back surprise to modern warfare, but we must have hundreds of them."

Prolonged laughter greeted this speech. But the Celtic dreamer did not smile. He was staring into the future... And what he saw was true, though he did not live to see it, for in the Cambrai battle of November 11th the tanks did advance in hundreds, and gained an enormous surprise over the enemy, and led the way to a striking victory, which turned to tragedy because of risks too lightly taken.

XII

One branch of our military machine developed with astonishing rapidity and skill during those Somme battles. The young gentlemen of the Air Force went "all out" for victory, and were reckless in audacity. How far they acted under orders and against their own judgment of what was sensible and sound in fighting-risks I do not know. General Trenchard, their supreme chief, believed in an aggressive policy at all costs, and was a Napoleon in this war of the skies, intolerant of timidity, not squeamish of heavy losses if the balance were tipped against the enemy. Some young flying-men complained to me bitterly that they were expected to fly or die over the German lines, whatever the weather or whatever the risks. Many of them, after repeated escapes from anti-aircraft shells and hostile craft, lost their nerve, shirked another journey, found themselves crying in their tents, and were sent back home for a spell by squadron commanders, with quick observation for the breaking-point; or made a few more flights and fell to earth like broken birds.

Sooner or later, apart from rare cases, every man was found to lose his nerve, unless he lost his life first. That was a physical and mental law. But until that time these flying-men were the knights-errant of the war, and most of them did not need any driving to the risks they took with boyish recklessness.

They were mostly boys—babes, as they seemed to me, when I saw them in their tents or dismounting from their machines. On "dud" days, when there was no visibility at all, they spent their leisure hours joy-riding to Amiens or some other town where they could have a "binge." They drank many cocktails and roared with laughter over, bottles of cheap champagne, and flirted with any girl who happened to come within their orbit. If not allowed beyond their tents, they sulked like baby Achilles, reading novelettes, with their knees hunched up, playing the gramophone, and ragging each other.

There was one child so young that his squadron leader would not let him go out across the battle-lines to challenge any German scout in the clouds or do any of the fancy "stunts" that were part of the next day's program. He went to bed sulkily, and then came back again, in his pajamas, with rumpled hair.

"Look here, sir," he said. "Can't I go? I've got my wings. It's perfectly rotten being left behind."

The squadron commander, who told me of the tale, yielded.

"All right. Only don't do any fool tricks."

Next morning the boy flew off, played a lone hand, chased a German scout, dropped low over the enemy's lines, machine-gunned infantry on the march, scattered them, bombed a train, chased a German motor-car, and after many adventures came back alive and said, "I've had a rare old time!"

On a stormy day, which loosened the tent poles and slapped the wet canvas, I sat in a mess with a group of flying-officers, drinking tea out of a tin mug. One boy, the youngest of them, had just brought down his first "Hun." He told me the tale of it with many details, his eyes alight as he described the fight. They had maneuvered round each other for a long time. Then he shot his man en passant. The machine crashed on our side of the lines. He had taken off the iron crosses on the wings, and a bit of the propeller, as mementoes. He showed me these things (while the squadron commander, who had brought down twenty-four Germans, winked at me) and told me he was going to send them home to hang beside his college trophies... I guessed he was less than nineteen years old. Such a kid!... A few days later, when I went to the tent again, I asked about him. "How's that boy who brought down his first 'Hun'?" The squadron commander said:

"Didn't you hear? He's gone west. Brought down in a dog-fight. He had a chance of escape, but went back to rescue a pal... a nice boy."

They became fatalists after a few fights, and believed in their luck, or their mascots—teddy-bears, a bullet that had missed them, china dolls, a girl's lock of hair, a silver ring. Yet at the back of their brains, most Of them, I fancy, knew that it was only a question of time before they "went west," and with that subconscious thought they crowded in all life intensely in the hours that were given to them, seized all chance of laughter, of wine, of every kind of pleasure within reach, and said their prayers (some of them) with great fervor, between one escape and another, like young Paul Bensher, who has revealed his soul in verse, his secret terror, his tears, his hatred of death, his love of life, when he went bombing over Bruges.

On the mornings of the battles of the Somme I saw them as the heralds of a new day of strife flying toward the lines in the first light of dawn. When the sun rose its rays touched their wings, made them white like cabbage butterflies, or changed them to silver, all a sparkle. I saw them fly over the German positions, not changing their course. Then all about them burst black puffs of German shrapnel, so that many times I held my breath because they seemed in the center of the burst. But generally when the cloud cleared they were flying again, until they disappeared in the mists over the enemy's country. There they did deadly work, in single fights with German airmen, or against great odds, until they had an air space to themselves and skimmed the earth like albatrosses in low flight, attacking machine-gun nests, killing or scattering the gunners by a burst of bullets from their Lewis guns, dropping bombs on German wagon transports, infantry, railway trains (one man cut a train in half and saw men and horses falling out), and ammunition—dumps, directing the fire of our guns upon living targets, photographing new trenches and works, bombing villages crowded with German troops. That they struck terror into these German troops was proved afterward when we went into Bapaume and Peronne and many villages from which the enemy retreated after the battles of the Somme. Everywhere there were signboards on which was written *"Flieger Schutz!"* (aircraft shelter) or German warnings of: "Keep to the sidewalks. This road is constantly bombed by British airmen."

They were a new plague of war, and did for a time gain a complete mastery of the air. But later the Germans learned the lesson of low flying and night bombing, and in 1917 and 1918 came back in greater strength and made the nights horrible in camps behind the lines and in villages, where they killed many soldiers and more civilians.

The infantry did not believe much in our air supremacy at any time, not knowing what work was done beyond their range of vision, and seeing our machines crashed in No Man's Land, and hearing the rattle of machine-guns from hostile aircraft above their own trenches.

"Those aviators of ours," a general said to me, "are the biggest liars in the world. Cocky fellows claiming impossible achievements. What proof can they give of their preposterous tales? They only go into the air service because they haven't the pluck to serve in the infantry."

That was prejudice. The German losses were proof enough of our men's fighting skill and strength, and German prisoners and German letters confirmed all their claims. But we were dishonest in our reckoning from first to last, and the British public was hoodwinked about our losses. "Three of our machines are missing." "Six of our machines are missing." Yes, but what about the machines which crashed in No Man's Land and behind our lines? They were not missing, but destroyed, and the boys who had flown in them were dead or broken.

To the end of the war those aviators of ours searched the air for their adventures, fought often against overwhelming numbers, killed the German champions in single combat or in tourneys in the sky, and let down tons of high explosives which caused great death and widespread destruction; and in this work they died like flies, and one boy's life—one of those laughing, fatalistic, intensely living boys—was of no more account in the general sum of slaughter than a summer midge, except as one little unit in the Armies of the Air.

XIII

I am not strong enough in the science of psychology to understand the origin of laughter and to get into touch with the mainsprings of gaiety. The sharp contrast between normal ethics and an abnormality of action provides a grotesque point of view arousing ironical mirth. It is probable also that surroundings of enormous tragedy stimulate the sense of humor of the individual, so that any small, ridiculous thing assumes the proportion of monstrous absurdity. It is also likely—certain, I think—that laughter is an escape from terror, a liberation of the soul by mental explosion, from the prison walls of despair and brooding. In the Decameron of Boccaccio a group of men and women encompassed by plague retired into seclusion to tell one another mirthful immoralities which stirred their laughter. They laughed while the plague destroyed society around them and when they knew that its foul germs were on the prowl for their own bodies... So it was in this war, where in many strange places and in many dreadful days there was great laughter. I think sometimes of a night I spent with the medical officers of a tent hospital in the fields of the Somme during those battles. With me as a guest went a modern Falstaff, a "ton of flesh," who "sweats to death and lards the lean earth as he walks along."

He was a man of many anecdotes, drawn from the sinks and stews of life, yet with a sense of beauty lurking under his coarseness, and a voice of fine, sonorous tone, which he managed with art and a melting grace.

On the way to the field hospital he had taken more than one nip of whisky. His voice was well oiled when he sang a greeting to a medical major in a florid burst of melody from Italian opera. The major was a little Irish medico who had been through the South African War and in tropical places, where he had drunk fire-water to kill all manner of microbes. He suffered abominably from asthma and had had a heart-seizure the day before our dinner at his mess, and told us that he would drop down dead as sure as fate between one operation and another on "the poor, bloody wounded" who never ceased to flow into his tent. But he was in a laughing mood, and thirsty for laughter-making liquid. He had two whiskies before the dinner began to wet his whistle. His fellow-officers were out for an evening's joy, but nervous of the colonel, an austere soul who sat at the head of the mess with the look of a man afraid that merriment might reach outrageous heights beyond his control. A courteous man he was, and rather sad. His presence for a time acted as a restraint upon the company, until all restraint was broken by the Falstaff with me, who told soul-crashing stories to the little Irish major across the table and sang love lyrics to the orderly who brought round the cottage pie and pickles. There was a tall, thin young surgeon who had been carving up living bodies all day and many days, and now listened to that fat rogue with an intensity of delight that lit up his melancholy eyes, watching him gravely between gusts of deep laughter, which seemed to come from his boots. There was another young surgeon, once of Barts', who made himself the cup-server of the fat knight and kept his wine at the brim, and encouraged him to fresh audacities of anecdotry, with a humorous glance at the colonel's troubled face... The colonel was forgotten after dinner. The little Irish major took the lid off the boiling pot of mirth. He was entirely mad, as he assured us, between dances of a wild and primitive type, stories of adventure in far lands, and spasms of asthmatic coughing, when he beat his breast and said, "A pox in my bleeding heart!"

Falstaff was playing Juliet to the Romeo of the tall young surgeon, singing falsetto like a fat German angel dressed in loose-fitting khaki, with his belt undone. There were charades in the tent. The boy from Barts' did remarkable imitations of a gamecock challenging a rival bird, of a cow coming through a gate, of a general addressing his troops (most comical of all). Several glasses were broken. The corkscrew was disregarded as a useless implement, and whisky-bottles were decapitated against the tent poles. I remember vaguely the crowning episode of the evening when the little major was dancing the Irish jig with a kitchen chair; when Falstaff was singing the Prologue of Pagliacci to the stupefied colonel; when the boy, once of Barts', was roaring like a lion under the mess table, and when the tall, melancholy surgeon was at the top of the tent pole, scratching himself like a gorilla in his native haunts... Outside, the field hospital was quiet, under a fleecy sky with a crescent moon. Through the painted canvas of the tent city candle-light glowed with a faint rose-colored light, and the Red Cross hung limp above the camp where many wounded lay, waking or sleeping, tossing in agony, dying in unconsciousness. Far away over the fields, rockets were rising above the battle-lines. The sky was flickering with the flush of gun-fire. A red glare rose and spread below the clouds where some ammunition-dump had been exploded... Old Falstaff fell asleep in the car on the way back to our quarters, and I smiled at the memory of great laughter in the midst of tragedy.

XIV

The struggle of men from one low ridge to another low ridge in a territory forty miles wide by more than twenty miles deep, during five months of fighting, was enormous in its intensity and prolongation of slaughter, wounding, and endurance of all hardships and terrors of war. As an eye-witness I saw the full scope of the bloody drama. I saw day by day the tidal waves of wounded limping back, until two hundred and fifty thousand men had passed through our casualty clearing stations, and then were not finished. I went among these men when the blood was wet on them, and talked with hundreds of them, and heard their individual narratives of escapes from death until my imagination was saturated with the spirit of their conflict of body and soul. I saw a green, downy countryside, beautiful in its summer life, ravaged by gun-fire so that the white chalk of its subsoil was flung above the earth and grass in a wide, sterile stretch of desolation pitted with shell-craters, ditched by deep trenches, whose walls were hideously upheaved by explosive fire, and littered yard after yard, mile after mile, with broken wire, rifles, bombs, unexploded shells, rags of uniform, dead bodies, or bits of bodies, and all the filth of battle. I saw many villages flung into ruin or blown clean off the map. I walked into such villages as Contalmaison, Martinpuich, Le Sars, Thilloy, and at last Bapaume, when a smell of burning and the fumes of explosives and the stench of dead flesh rose up to one's nostrils and one's very soul, when our dead and German dead lay about, and newly wounded came walking through the ruins or were carried shoulder high on stretchers, and consciously and subconsciously the living, unwounded men who went through these places knew that death lurked about them and around them and above them, and at any second might make its pounce upon their own flesh. I saw our men going into battle with strong battalions and coming out of it with weak battalions. I saw them in the midst of battle at Thiepval, at Contalmaison, at Guillemont, by Loupart Wood, when they trudged toward lines of German trenches, bunching a little in groups, dodging shell-bursts, falling in single figures or in batches, and fighting over the enemy's parapets. I sat with them in their dugouts before battle and after battle, saw their bodies gathered up for burial, heard their snuffle of death in hospital, sat by their bedside when they were sorely wounded. So the full tragic drama of that long conflict on the Somme was burned into my brain and I was, as it were, a part of it, and I am still seared with its remembrance, and shall always be.

But however deep the knowledge of tragedy, a man would be a liar if he refused to admit the heroism, the gallantry of youth, even the gaiety of men in these infernal months. Psychology on the Somme was not simple and straightforward. Men were afraid, but fear was not their dominating emotion, except in the worst hours. Men hated this fighting, but found excitement in it, often exultation, sometimes an intense stimulus of all their senses and passions before reaction and exhaustion. Men became jibbering idiots with shell-shock, as I saw some of them, but others rejoiced when they saw our shells plowing into the enemy's earthworks, laughed at their own narrow escapes and at grotesque comicalities of this monstrous deviltry. The officers were proud of their men, eager for their honor and achievement. The men themselves were in rivalry with other bodies of troops, and proud of their own prowess. They were scornful of all that the enemy might do to them, yet acknowledged his courage and power. They were quick to kill him, yet quick also to give him a chance of life by surrender, and after that were—nine times out of ten—chivalrous and kindly, but incredibly brutal on the rare occasions when passion overcame them at some tale of treachery. They had the pride of the skilled laborer in his own craft, as machine-gunners, bombers, raiders, trench-mortar—men, and were keen to show their skill, whatever the risks. They were healthy animals, with animal courage as well as animal fear, and they had, some of them, a spiritual and moral fervor which bade them risk death to save a comrade, or to save a position, or to kill the fear that tried to fetter them, or to lead men with greater fear than theirs. They lived from hour to hour and forgot the peril or the misery that had passed, and did not forestall the future by apprehension unless they were of sensitive mind, with the worst quality men might have in modern warfare—imagination.

They trained themselves to an intense egotism within narrow boundaries. Fifty yards to the left, or five hundred, men were being pounded to death by shell-fire. Fifty yards to the right, or five hundred, men were being mowed down by machine-gun fire. For the time being their particular patch was quiet. It was their luck. Why worry about the other fellow? The length of a traverse in a ditch called a trench might make all the difference between heaven and hell. Dead bodies were being piled up on one side of the traverse. A shell had smashed into the platoon next door. There was a nasty mess. Men sat under their own mud-bank and scooped out a tin of bully beef and hoped nothing would scoop them out of their bit of earth. This protective egotism seemed to me the instinctive soul-armor of men in dangerous places when I saw them in the line. In a little way, not as a soldier, but as a correspondent, taking only a thousandth part of the risks of fighting-men, I found myself using this self-complacency. They were strafing on the left. Shells were pitching on the right. Very nasty for the men in either of those places. Poor devils! But meanwhile I was on a safe patch, it seemed. Thank Heaven for that!

"Here," said an elderly officer—one of those rare exalted souls who thought that death was a little thing to give for one's country's sake—"here we may be killed at any moment!"

He spoke the words in Contalmaison with a glow in his voice, as though announcing glad tidings to a friend who was a war artist camouflaged as a lieutenant and new to the scene of battle.

"But," said the soldier-artist, adjusting his steel hat nervously, "I don't want to be killed! I hate the idea of it!"

He was the normal man. The elderly officer was abnormal. The normal man, soldier without camouflage, had no use for death at all, unless it was in connection with the fellow on the opposite side of the way. He hated the notion of it applied to himself. He fought ferociously, desperately, heroically, to escape it. Yet there were times, many times, when he paid not the slightest attention to the near neighborhood of that grisly specter, because in immediate, temporary tranquillity he thrust the thought from his mind, and smoked a cigarette, and exchanged a joke with the fellow at his elbow. There were other times when, in a state of mental exaltation, or spiritual self-sacrifice, or physical excitement, he acted regardless of all risks and did mad, marvelous, almost miraculous things, hardly conscious of his own acts, but impelled to do as he did by the passion within him—passion of love, passion of hate, passion of fear, or passion of pride. Those men, moved like that, were the leaders, the heroes, and groups followed them sometimes because of their intensity of purpose and the infection of their emotion, and the comfort that came from their real or apparent self-confidence in frightful situations. Those who got through were astonished at their own courage. Many of them became convinced consciously or subconsciously that they were immune from shells and bullets. They walked through harassing fire with a queer sense of carelessness. They had escaped so often that some of them had a kind of disdain of shell-bursts, until, perhaps, one day something snapped in their nervous system, as often it did, and the bang of a door in a billet behind the lines, or a wreath of smoke from some domestic chimney, gave them a sudden shock of fear. Men differed wonderfully in their nerve-resistance, and it was no question of difference in courage.

In the mass all our soldiers seemed equally brave. In the mass they seemed astoundingly cheerful. In spite of all the abomination of that Somme fighting our troops before battle and after battle—a few days after—looked bright-eyed, free from haunting anxieties, and were easy in their way of laughter. It was optimism in the mass, heroism in the mass. It was only when one spoke to the individual, some friend who bared his soul a second, or some soldier-ant in the multitude, with whom one talked with truth, that one saw the hatred of a man for his job, the sense of doom upon him, the weakness that was in his strength, the bitterness of his grudge against a fate that forced him to go on in this way of life, the remembrance of a life more beautiful which he had abandoned—all mingled with those other qualities of pride and comradeship, and that illogical sense of humor which made up the strange complexity of his psychology.

XV

It was a colonel of the North Staffordshires who revealed to me the astounding belief that he was "immune" from shell-fire, and I met other men afterward with the same conviction. He had just come out of desperate fighting in the neighborhood of Thiepval, where his battalion had suffered heavily, and at first he was rude and sullen in the hut. I gaged him as a hard Northerner, without a shred of sentiment or the flicker of any imaginative light; a stern, ruthless man. He was bitter in his speech to me because the North Staffords were never mentioned in my despatches. He believed that this was due to some personal spite—not knowing the injustice of our military censorship under the orders of G.H.Q.

"Why the hell don't we get a word?" he asked. "Haven't we done as well as anybody, died as much?"

I promised to do what I could—which was nothing—to put the matter right, and presently he softened, and, later was amazingly candid in self-revelation.

"I have a mystical power," he said. "Nothing will ever hit me as long as I keep that power which comes from faith. It is a question of absolute belief in the domination of mind over matter. I go through any barrage unscathed because my will is strong enough to turn aside explosive shells and machine-gun bullets. As matter they must obey my intelligence. They are powerless to resist the mind of a man in touch with the Universal Spirit, as I am."

He spoke quietly and soberly, in a matter-of-fact way. I decided that he was mad. That was not surprising. We were all mad, in one way or another or at one time or another. It was the unusual form of madness that astonished me. I envied him his particular "kink." I wished I could cultivate it, as an aid to courage. He claimed another peculiar form of knowledge. He knew before each action, he told me, what officers and men of his would be killed in battle. He looked at a man's eyes and knew, and he claimed that he never made a mistake... He was sorry to possess that second sight, and it worried him.

There were many men who had a conviction that they would not be killed, although they did not state it in the terms expressed by the colonel of the North Staffordshires, and it is curious that in some cases I know they were not mistaken and are still alive. It was indeed a general belief that if a man funked being hit he was sure to fall, that being the reverse side of the argument.

I saw the serene cheerfulness of men in the places of death at many times and in many places, and I remember one group of friends on the Somme who revealed that quality to a high degree. It was when our front-line ran just outside the village of Martinpuich to Courcelette, on the other side of the Bapaume road, and when the 8th-10th Gordons were there, after their fight through Longueval and over the ridge. It was the little crowd I have mentioned before in the battle of Loos, and it was Lieut. John Wood who took me to the battalion headquarters located under some sand-bags in a German dug—out. All the way up to Contalmaison and beyond there were the signs of recent bloodshed and of present peril. Dead horses lay about, disemboweled by shell-fire. Legs and arms protruded from shell-craters where bodies lay half buried. Heavy crumps came howling through the sky and bursting with enormous noise here, there, and everywhere over that vast, desolate battlefield, with its clumps of ruin and rows of dead trees. It was the devil's hunting-ground and I hated every yard of it. But John Wood, who lived in it, was astoundingly cheerful, and a fine, sturdy, gallant figure, in his kilted dress, as he climbed over sand-bags, walked on the top of communication trenches (not bothering to take cover) and skirting round hedges of barbed wire, apparently unconscious of the "crumps" that were bursting around. I found laughter and friendly greeting in a hole in the earth where the battalion staff was crowded. The colonel was courteous, but busy. He rather deprecated the notion that I should go up farther, to the ultimate limit of our line. It was no use putting one's head into trouble without reasonable purpose, and the German guns had been blowing in sections of his new-made trenches. But John Wood was insistent that I should meet "old Thom," afterward in command of the battalion. He had just been buried and dug out again. He would like to see me. So we left the cover of the dugout and took to the open again. Long lines of Jocks were digging a support trench—digging with a kind of rhythmic movement as they threw up the earth with their shovels. Behind them was another line of Jocks, not working. They lay as though asleep, out in the open. They were the dead of the last advance. Captain Thom was leaning up against the wall of the front-line trench, smoking a cigarette, with his steel hat on the back of his head—a handsome, laughing figure. He did not look like a man who had just been buried and dug out again.

"It was a narrow shave," he said. "A beastly shell covered me with a ton of earth... Have a cigarette, won't you?"

We gossiped as though in St. James's Street. Other young Scottish officers came up and shook hands, and said: "Jolly weather, isn't it? What do you think of our little show?" Not one of them gave a glance at the line of dead men over there, behind their parados. They told me some of the funny things that had happened lately in the battalion, some grim jokes by tough Jocks. They had a fine crowd of men. You couldn't beat them. "Well, good morning! Must get on with the job." There was no anguish there, no sense of despair, no sullen hatred of this life, so near to death. They seemed to like it... They did not really like it. They only made the best of it, without gloom. I saw they did not like this job of battle, one evening in their mess behind the line. The colonel who commanded them at the time, Celt of the Celts, was in a queer mood. He was a queer man, aloof in his manner, a little "fey." He was annoyed with three of his officers who had come back late from three days' Paris leave. They were giants, but stood like schoolboys before their master while he spoke ironical, bitter words. Later in the evening he mentioned casually that they must prepare to go into the line again under special orders. What about the store of bombs, small-arms ammunition, machine-guns?

The officers were stricken into silence. They stared at one another as though to say: "What does the old man mean? Is this true?" One of them became rather pale, and there was a look of tragic resignation in his eyes. Another said, "Hell!" in a whisper. The adjutant answered the colonel's questions in a formal way, but thinking hard and studying the colonel's face anxiously.

"Do you mean to say we are going into the line again, sir? At once?"

The colonel laughed.

"Don't look so scared, all of you! It's only a field-day for training."

The officers of the Gordons breathed more freely. Poof! They had been fairly taken in by the "old man's" leg-pulling... No, it was clear they did not find any real joy in the line. They would not choose a front-line trench as the most desirable place of residence.

XVI

In queer psychology there was a strange mingling of the pitiful and comic—among a division (the 35th) known as the Bantams. They were all volunteers, having been rejected by the ordinary recruiting-officer on account of their diminutive stature, which was on an average five feet high, descending to four feet six. Most of them came from Lancashire, Cheshire, Durham, and Glasgow, being the dwarfed children of industrial England and its mid-Victorian cruelties. Others were from London, banded together in a battalion of the Middlesex Regiment. They gave a shock to our French friends when they arrived as a division at the port of Boulogne.

"Name of a dog!" said the quayside loungers. "England is truly in a bad way. She is sending out her last reserves!"

"But they are the soldiers of Lilliput!" exclaimed others.

"It is terrible that they should send these little ones," said kind-hearted fishwives.

Under the training of General Pi, who commanded them, they became smart and brisk in the ranks. They saluted like miniature Guardsmen, marched with quick little steps like clockwork soldiers. It was comical to see them strutting up and down as sentries outside divisional headquarters, with their bayonets high above their wee bodies. In trench warfare they did well—though the fire-step had to be raised to let them see over the top—and in one raid captured a German machine-gun which I saw in their hands, and hauled it back (a heavier weight than ours) like ants struggling with a stick of straw. In actual battle they were hardly strong enough and could not carry all that burden of fighting-kit—steel helmet, rifle, hand-grenades, shovels, empty sand-bags—with which other troops went into action. So they were used as support troops mostly, behind the Black Watch and other battalions near Bazentin and Longueval, and there these poor little men dug and dug like beavers and crouched in the cover they made under damnable fire, until many of them were blown to bits. There was no "glory" in their job, only filth and blood, but they held the ground and suffered it all, not gladly. They had a chance of taking prisoners at Longueval, where they rummaged in German dugouts after the line had been taken by the 15th Scottish Division and the 3d, and they brought back a number of enormous Bavarians who were like the Brobdingnagians to these little men of Lilliput and disgusted with that humiliation. I met the whole crowd of them after that adventure, as they sat, half naked, picking the lice out of their shirts, and the conversation I had with them remains in my memory because of its grotesque humor and tragic comicality. They were excited and emotional, these stunted men. They cursed the war with the foulest curses of Scottish and Northern dialects. There was one fellow—the jester of them all—whose language would have made the poppies blush. With ironical laughter, outrageous blasphemy, grotesque imagery, he described the suffering of himself and his mates under barrage fire, which smashed many of them into bleeding pulp. He had no use for this war. He cursed the name of "glory." He advocated a trade—unionism among soldiers to down tools whenever there was a threat of war. He was a Bolshevist before Bolshevism. Yet he had no liking for Germans and desired to cut them into small bits, to slit their throats, to disembowel them. He looked homeward to a Yorkshire town and wondered what his missus would say if she saw him scratching himself like an ape, or lying with his head in the earth with shells bursting around him, or prodding Germans with a bayonet. "Oh," said that five-foot hero, "there will be a lot of murder after this bloody war. What's human life? What's the value of one man's throat? We're trained up as murderers—I don't dislike it, mind you—and after the war we sha'n't get out of the habit of it. It'll come nat'ral like!"

He was talking for my benefit, egged on to further audacities by a group of comrades who roared with laughter and said: "Go it, Bill! That's the stuff!" Among these Lilliputians were fellows who sat aloof and sullen, or spoke of their adventure with its recent horror in their eyes. Some of them had big heads on small bodies, as though they suffered from water on the brain... Many of them were sent home afterward. General Haldane, as commander of the 6th Corps, paraded them, and poked his stick at the more wizened ones, the obviously unfit, the degenerates, and said at each prod, "You can go... You. ..You...." The Bantam Division ceased to exist.

They afforded many jokes to the army. One anecdote went the round. A Bantam died—of disease ("and he would," said General Haldane)—and a comrade came to see his corpse.

"Shut ze door ven you come out," said the old woman of his billet. "Fermez la porte, mon vieux."

The living Bantam went to see the dead one, and came downstairs much moved by grief.

"I've seed poor Bill," he said.

"As-tu ferme la porte?" said the old woman, anxiously.

The Bantam wondered at the anxious inquiry; asked the reason of it.

"C'est a cause du chat!" said the old woman. "Ze cat, Monsieur, 'e 'ave 'ad your friend in ze passage tree time already to-day. Trois fois!"

Poor little men born of diseased civilization! They were volunteers to a man, and some of them with as much courage as soldiers twice their size.

They were the Bantams who told me of the Anglican padre at Longueval. It was Father Hall of Mirfield, attached to the South African Brigade. He came out to a dressing station established in the one bit of ruin which could be used for shelter, and devoted himself to the wounded with a spiritual fervor. They were suffering horribly from thirst, which made their tongues swell and set their throats on fire.

"Water!" they cried. "Water! For Christ's sake, water!"

There was no water, except at a well in Longueval, under the fire of German snipers, who picked off our men when they crawled down like wild dogs with their tongues lolling out. There was one German officer there in a shell-hole not far from the well, who sat with his revolver handy, and he was a dead shot.

But he did not shoot the padre. Something in the face and figure of that chaplain, his disregard of the bullets snapping about him, the upright, fearless way in which he crossed that way of death, held back the trigger-finger of the German officer and he let him pass. He passed many times, untouched by bullets or machine-gun fire, and he went into bad places, pits of horror, carrying hot tea, which he made from the well water for men in agony.

XVII

During these battles I saw thousands of German prisoners, and studied their types and physiognomy, and, by permission of Intelligence officers, spoke with many of them in their barbed-wire cages or on the field of battle when they came along under escort. Some of them looked degraded, bestial men. One could imagine them guilty of the foulest atrocities. But in the mass they seemed to me decent, simple men, remarkably like our own lads from the Saxon counties of England, though not quite so bright and brisk, as was only natural in their position as prisoners, with all the misery of war in their souls. Afterward they worked with patient industry in the prison-camps and established their own discipline, and gave very little trouble if well handled. In each crowd of them there were fellows who spoke perfect English, having lived in England as waiters and hairdressers, or clerks or mechanics. It was with them I spoke most because it was easiest, but I know enough German to talk with the others, and I found among them all the same loathing of war, the same bewilderment as to its causes, the same sense of being driven by evil powers above them. The officers were different. They lost a good deal of their arrogance, but to the last had excuses ready for all that Germany had done, and almost to the last professed to believe that Germany would win. Their sense of caste was in their nature. They refused to travel in the same carriages with their men, to stay even for an hour in the same inclosures with them. They regarded them, for the most part, as inferior beings. And there were castes even among the officers. I remember that in the last phase, when we captured a number of cavalry officers, these elegant sky-blue fellows held aloof from the infantry officers and would not mix with them. One of them paced up and down all night alone, and all next day, stiff in the corsets below that sky-blue uniform, not speaking to a soul, though within a few yards of him were many officers of infantry regiments.

Our men treated their prisoners, nearly always, after the blood of battle was out of their eyes, with a good—natured kindness that astonished the Germans themselves. I have seen them filling German water-bottles at considerable trouble, and the escorts, two or three to a big batch of men, were utterly trustful of them. "Here, hold my rifle, Fritz," said one of our men, getting down from a truck-train to greet a friend.

An officer standing by took notice of this.

"Take your rifle back at once! Is that the way to guard your prisoners?"

Our man was astonished.

"Lor' bless you, sir, they don't want no guarding. They're glad to be took. They guard themselves."

"Your men are extraordinary," a German officer told me. "They asked me whether I would care to go down at once or wait till the barrage had passed."

He seemed amazed at that thoughtfulness for his comfort. It was in the early days of the Somme fighting, and crowds of our men stood on the banks above a sunken road, watching the prisoners coming down. This officer who spoke to me had an Iron Cross, and the men wanted to see it and handle it.

"Will they give it back again?" he asked, nervously, fumbling at the ribbon.

"Certainly," I assured him.

He handed it to me, and I gave it to the men, who passed it from one to the other and then back to the owner.

"Your men are extraordinary," he said. "They are wonderful."

One of the most interesting prisoners I met on the field of battle was a tall, black-bearded man whom I saw walking away from La Boisselle when that place was smoking with shell-bursts. An English soldier was on each side of him, and each man carried a hand-bag, while this black-bearded giant chatted with them.

It was a strange group, and I edged nearer to them and spoke to one of the men.

"Who's this? Why do you carry his bags?"

"Oh, we're giving him special privileges," said the man. "He stayed behind to look after our wounded. Said his job was to look after wounded, whoever they were. So there he's been, in a dugout bandaging our lads; and no joke, either. It's hell up there. We're glad to get out of it."

I spoke to the German doctor and walked with him. He discussed the philosophy of the war simply and with what seemed like sincerity.

"This war!" he said, with a sad, ironical laugh. "We go on killing one another-to no purpose. Europe is being bled to death and will be impoverished for long years. We Germans thought it was a war for Kultur—our civilization. Now we know it is a war against Kultur, against religion, against all civilization."

"How will it end?" I asked him.

"I see no end to it," he answered. "It is the suicide of nations. Germany is strong, and England is strong, and France is strong. It is impossible for one side to crush the other, so when is the end to come?"

I met many other prisoners then and a year afterward who could see no end of the massacre. They believed the war would go on until living humanity on all sides revolted from the unceasing sacrifice. In the autumn of 1918, when at last the end came in sight, by German defeat, unexpected a few months before even by the greatest optimist in the British armies, the German soldiers were glad. They did not care how the war ended so long as it ended. Defeat? What did that matter? Was it worse to be defeated than for the race to perish by bleeding to death?

XVIII

The struggle for the Pozieres ridge and High Wood lasted from the beginning of August until the middle of September—six weeks of fighting as desperate as any in the history of the world until that time. The Australians dealt with Pozieres itself, working round Moquet Farm, where the Germans refused to be routed from their tunnels, and up to the Windmill on the high ground of Pozieres, for which there was unceasing slaughter on both sides because the Germans counter-attacked again and again, and waves of men surged up and fell around that mound of forsaken brick, which I saw as a reddish cone through flame and smoke.

Those Australians whom I had seen arrive in France had proved their quality. They had come believing that nothing could be worse than their ordeal in the Dardanelles. Now they knew that Pozieres was the last word in frightfulness. The intensity of the shell-fire under which they lay shook them, if it did not kill them. Many of their wounded told me that it had broken their nerve. They would never fight again without a sense of horror.

"Our men are more highly strung than the English," said one Australian officer, and I was astonished to hear these words, because those Australians seemed to me without nerves, and as tough as gristle in their fiber.

They fought stubbornly, grimly, in ground so ravaged with fire that the earth was finely powdered. They stormed the Pozieres ridge yard by yard, and held its crest under sweeping barrages which tore up their trenches as soon as they were dug and buried and mangled their living flesh. In six weeks they suffered twenty thousand casualties, and Pozieres now is an Australian graveyard, and the memorial that stands there is to the ghosts of that splendid youth which fell in heaps about that plateau and the slopes below. Many English boys of the Sussex, West Kents, Surrey, and Warwick regiments, in the 18th Division, died at their side, not less patient in sacrifice, not liking it better. Many Scots of the 15th and 9th Divisions, many New-Zealanders, many London men of the 47th and 56th Divisions, fell, killed or wounded, to the right of them, on the way to Martinpuich, and Eaucourt l'Abbaye and Flers, from High Wood and Longueval, and Bazentin. The 3d Division of Yorkshires and Northumberland Fusiliers, Royal Scots and Gordons, were earning that name of the Iron Division, and not by any easy heroism. Every division in the British army took its turn in the blood-bath of the Somme and was duly blooded, at a cost of 25 per cent. and sometimes 50 per cent. of their fighting strength. The Canadians took up the struggle at Courcelette and captured it in a fierce and bloody battle. The Australians worked up on the right of the Albert-Bapaume road to Thilloy and Ligny Thilloy. On the far left the fortress of Thiepval had fallen at last after repeated and frightful assaults, which I watched from ditches close enough to see our infantry—Wiltshires and Worcesters of the 25th Division—trudging through infernal fire. And then at last, after five months of superhuman effort, enormous sacrifice, mass-heroism, desperate will-power, and the tenacity of each individual human ant in this wild ant-heap, the German lines were smashed, the Australians surged into Bapaume, and the enemy, stricken by the prolonged fury of our attack, fell back in a far and wide retreat across a country which he laid waste, to the shelter of his Hindenburg line, from Bullecourt to St.-Quentin.

XIX

The goal of our desire seemed attained when at last we reached Bapaume after these terrific battles in which all our divisions, numbering nearly a million men, took part, with not much difference in courage, not much difference in average of loss. By the end of that year's fighting our casualties had mounted up to the frightful total of four hundred thousand men. Those fields were strewn with our dead. Our graveyards were growing forests of little white crosses. The German dead lay in heaps. There were twelve hundred corpses littered over the earth below Loupart Wood, in one mass, and eight hundred of them were German. I could not walk without treading on them there. When I fell in the slime I clutched arms and legs. The stench of death was strong and awful.

But our men who had escaped death and shell-shock kept their sanity through all this wilderness of slaughter, kept—oh, marvelous!—their spirit of humor, their faith in some kind of victory. I was with the Australians on that day when they swarmed into Bapaume, and they brought out trophies like men at a country fair... I remember an Australian colonel who came riding with a German beer-mug at his saddle... Next day, though shells were still bursting in the ruins, some Australian boys set up some painted scenery which they had found among the rubbish, and chalked up the name of the "Coo-ee Theater."

The enemy was in retreat to his Hindenburg line, over a wide stretch of country which he laid waste behind him, making a desert of French villages and orchards and parks, so that even the fruit-trees were cut down, and the churches blown up, and the graves ransacked for their lead. It was the enemy's first retreat on the western front, and that ferocious fighting of the British troops had smashed the strongest defenses ever built in war, and our raw recruits had broken the most famous regiments of the German army, so in spite of all tragedy and all agony our men were not downcast, but followed up their enemy with a sense of excitement because it seemed so much like victory and the end of war.

When the Germans retreated from Gommecourt, where so many boys of the 56th (London) Division had fallen on the 1st of July, I went through that evil place by way of Fonquevillers (which we called "Funky Villas"), and, stumbling over the shell-craters and broken trenches and dead bodies between the dead masts of slashed and branchless trees, came into the open country to our outpost line. I met there a friendly sergeant who surprised me by referring in a casual way to a little old book of mine.

"This place," he said, glancing at me, "is a strange Street of Adventure."

It reminded me of another reference to that tale of mine when I was among a crowd of London lads who had just been engaged in a bloody fight at a place called The Hairpin.

A young officer sent for me and I found him in the loft of a stinking barn, sitting in a tub as naked as he was born.

"I just wanted to ask you," he said, "whether Katharine married Frank?"

The sergeant at Gommecourt was anxious to show me his own Street of Adventure.

"I belong to Toc-emmas," he said (meaning trench—mortars), "and my officers would be very pleased if you would have a look at their latest stunt. We've got a 9.2 mortar in Pigeon Wood, away beyond the infantry. It's never been done before and we're going to blow old Fritz out of Kite Copse."

I followed him into the blue, as it seemed to me, and we fell in with a young officer also on his way to Pigeon Wood. He was in a merry mood, in spite of harassing fire round about and the occasional howl of a 5.9. He kept stopping to look at enormous holes in the ground and laughing at something that seemed to tickle his sense of humor.

"See that?" he said. "That's old Charlie Lowndes's work."

At another pit in upheaved earth he said: "That's Charlie Lowndes again... Old Charlie gave 'em hell. He's a topping chap. You must meet him... My God! look at that!"

He roared with laughter again, on the edge of an unusually large crater.

"Who is Charlie?" I asked. "Where can I find him?"

"Oh, we shall meet him in Pigeon Wood. He's as pleased as Punch at having got beyond the infantry. First time it has ever been done. Took a bit of doing, too, with the largest size of Toc-emma."

We entered Pigeon Wood after a long walk over wild chaos, and, guided by the officer and sergeant, I dived down into a deep dugout just captured from the Germans, who were two hundred yards away in Kite Copse.

"What cheer, Charlie!" shouted the young officer.

"Hullo, fellow-my-lad!... Come in. We're getting gloriously binged on a rare find of German brandy."

"Topping and I've brought a visitor."

Capt. Charles Lowndes—"dear old Charlie"—received us most politely in one of the best dugouts I ever saw, with smoothly paneled walls fitted up with shelves, and good deal furniture made to match.

"This is a nice little home in hell," said Charles. "At any moment, of course, we may be blown to bits, but meanwhile it is very comfy down here, and what makes everything good is a bottle of rare old brandy and an unlimited supply of German soda-water. Also to add to the gaiety of indecent minds there is a complete outfit of ladies' clothing in a neighboring dugout. Funny fellows those German officers. Take a pew, won't you? and have a drink. Orderly!"

He shouted for his man and ordered a further supply of German soda-water.

We drank to the confusion of the enemy, in his own brandy and soda-water, out of his own mugs, sitting on his own chairs at his own table, and "dear old Charlie," who was a little etoile, as afterward I became, with a sense of deep satisfaction (the noise of shells seemed more remote), discoursed on war, which he hated, German psychology, trench-mortar barrages (they had simply blown the Boche out of Gommecourt), and his particular fancy stunt of stealing a march on the infantry, who, said Captain Lowndes, are "laps behind." Other officers crowded into the dugout. One of them said: "You must come round to mine. It's a blasted palace," and I went round later and he told me on the way that he had escaped so often from shell-bursts that he thought the average of luck was up and he was bound to get "done in" before long.

Charlie Lowndes dispensed drinks with noble generosity. There was much laughter among us, and afterward we went upstairs and to the edge of the wood, to which a heavy, wet mist was clinging, and I saw the trench-mortar section play the devil with Kite Copse, over the way. Late in the afternoon I took my leave of a merry company in that far-flung outpost of our line, and wished them luck. A few shells crashed through the wood as I left, but I was disdainful of them after that admirable brandy. It was a long walk back to "Funky Villas," not without the interest of arithmetical calculations about the odds of luck in harassing fire, but a thousand yards or so from Pigeon Wood I looked back and saw that the enemy had begun to "take notice." Heavy shells were smashing through the trees there ferociously. I hoped my friends were safe in their dugouts again....

And I thought of the laughter and gallant spirit of the young men, after five months of the greatest battles in the history of the world. It seemed to me wonderful.

XX

I have described what happened on our side of the lines, our fearful losses, the stream of wounded that came back day by day, the "Butchers' Shops," the agony in men's souls, the shell-shock cases, the welter and bewilderment of battle, the shelling of our own troops, the lack of communication between fighting units and the command, the filth and stench of the hideous shambles which were our battlefields. But to complete the picture of that human conflict in the Somme I must now tell what happened on the German side of the lines, as I was able to piece the tale together from German prisoners with whom I talked, German letters which I found in their abandoned dugouts, and documents which fell into the hands of our staff—officers.

Our men were at least inspirited by the knowledge that they were beating their enemy back, in spite of their own bloody losses. The Germans had not even that source of comfort, for whatever it might be worth under barrage fire. The mistakes of our generalship, the inefficiency of our staff-work, were not greater than the blunderings of the German High Command, and their problem was more difficult than ours because of the weakness of their reserves, owing to enormous preoccupation on the Russian front. The agony of their men was greater than ours.

To understand the German situation it must be remembered that from January to May, 1916, the German command on the western front was concentrating all its energy and available strength in man-power and gun—power upon the attack of Verdun. The Crown Prince had staked his reputation upon that adventure, which he believed would end in the capture of the strongest French fortress and the destruction of the French armies. He demanded men and more men, until every unit that could be spared from other fronts of the line had been thrown into that furnace. Divisions were called in from other theaters of war, and increased the strength on the western front to a total of about one hundred and thirty divisions.

But the months passed and Verdun still held out above piles of German corpses on its slopes, and in June Germany looked east and saw a great menace.

The Russian offensive was becoming violent. German generals on the Russian fronts sent desperate messages for help. "Send us more men," they said, and from the western front four divisions containing thirty-nine battalions were sent to them.

They must have been sent grudgingly, for now another menace threatened the enemy, and it was ours. The British armies were getting ready to strike. In spite of Verdun, France still had men enough—-withdrawn from that part of the line in which they had been relieved by the British—-to co-operate in a new attack.

It was our offensive that the German command feared most, for they had no exact knowledge of our strength or of the quality of our new troops. They knew that our army had grown prodigiously since the assault on Loos, nearly a year before.

They had heard of the Canadian reinforcements, and the coming of the Australians, and the steady increase of recruiting in England, and month by month they had heard the louder roar of our guns along the line, and had seen their destructive effect spreading and becoming more terrible. They knew of the steady, quiet concentration of batteries and divisions on the west and south of the Ancre.

The German command expected a heavy blow and, prepared for it, but as yet had no knowledge of the driving force behind it. What confidence they had of being able to resist the British attack was based upon the wonderful strength of the lines which they had been digging and fortifying since the autumn of the first year of war—"impregnable positions," they had called them—the inexperience of our troops, their own immense quantity of machine-guns, the courage and skill of their gunners, and their profound belief in the superiority of German generalship.

In order to prevent espionage during the coming struggle, and to conceal the movement of troops and guns, they ordered the civil populations to be removed from villages close behind their positions, drew cordons of military police across the country, picketed crossroads, and established a network of counter espionage to prevent any leakage of information.

To inspire the German troops with a spirit of martial fervor (not easily aroused to fever pitch after the bloody losses before Verdun) Orders of the Day were issued to the battalions counseling them to hold fast against the hated English, who stood foremost in the way of peace (that was the gist of a manifesto by Prince Rupprecht of Bavaria, which I found in a dugout at Montauban), and promising them a speedy ending to the war.

Great stores of material and munitions were concentrated at rail-heads and dumps ready to be sent up to the firing-lines, and the perfection of German organization may well have seemed flawless—before the attack began.

When they began they found that in "heavies" and in expenditure of high explosives they were outclassed.

They were startled, too, by the skill and accuracy of the British gunners, whom they had scorned as "amateurs," and by the daring of our airmen, who flew over their lines with the utmost audacity, "spotting" for the guns, and registering on batteries, communication trenches, crossroads, rail-heads, and every vital point of organization in the German war-machine working opposite the British lines north and south of the Ancre.

Even before the British infantry had left their trenches at dawn on July 1st, German officers behind the firing—lines saw with anxiety that all the organization which had worked so smoothly in times of ordinary trench—warfare was now working only in a hazardous way under a deadly storm of shells.

Food and supplies of all kinds could not be sent up to front-line trenches without many casualties, and sometimes could not be sent up at all. Telephone wires were cut, and communications broken between the front and headquarters staffs. Staff-officers sent up to report were killed on the way to the lines. Troops moving forward from reserve areas came under heavy fire and lost many men before arriving in the support trenches.

Prince Rupprecht of Bavaria, sitting aloof from all this in personal safety, must have known before July 1st that his resources in men and material would be strained to the uttermost by the British attack, but he could take a broader view than men closer to the scene of battle, and taking into account the courage of his troops (he had no need to doubt that), the immense strength of their positions, dug and tunneled beyond the power of high explosives, the number of his machine-guns, the concentration of his artillery, and the rawness of the British troops, he could count up the possible cost and believe that in spite of a heavy price to pay there would be no break in his lines.

At 7.30 A.M. on July 1st the British infantry, as I have told, left their trenches and attacked on the right angle down from Gommecourt, Beaumont Hamel, Thiepval, Ovillers, and La Boisselle, and eastward from Fricourt, below Mametz and Montauban. For a week the German troops—Bavarians and Prussians—had been crouching in their dugouts, listening to the ceaseless crashing of the British "drum-fire." In places like Beaumont Hamel, the men down in the deep tunnels—some of them large enough to hold a battalion and a half—were safe as long as they stayed there. But to get in or out was death. Trenches disappeared into a sea of shell-craters, and the men holding them—for some men had to stay on duty there—were blown to fragments.

Many of the shallower dugouts were smashed in by heavy shells, and officers and men lay dead there as I saw them lying on the first days of July, in Fricourt and Mametz and Montauban. The living men kept their courage, but below ground, under that tumult of bursting shells, and wrote pitiful letters to their people at home describing the horror of those hours.

"We are quite shut off from the rest of the world," wrote one of them. "Nothing comes to us. No letters. The English keep such a barrage on our approaches it is terrible. To-morrow evening it will be seven days since this bombardment began. We cannot hold out much longer. Everything is shot to pieces."

Thirst was one of their tortures. In many of the tunneled shelters there was food enough, but the water could not be sent up. The German soldiers were maddened by thirst. When rain fell many of them crawled out and drank filthy water mixed with yellow shell-sulphur, and then were killed by high explosives. Other men crept out, careless of death, but compelled to drink. They crouched over the bodies of the men who lay above, or in, the shell-holes, and lapped up the puddles and then crawled down again if they were not hit.

When our infantry attacked at Gommecourt and Beaumont Hamel and Thiepval they were received by waves of machine-gun bullets fired by men who, in spite of the ordeal of our seven days' bombardment, came out into the open now, at the moment of attack which they knew through their periscopes was coming. They brought their guns above the shell-craters of their destroyed trenches under our barrage and served them. They ran forward even into No Man's Land, and planted their machine-guns there, and swept down our men as they charged. Over their heads the German gunners flung a frightful barrage, plowing gaps in the ranks of our men.

On the left, by Gommecourt and Beaumont Hamel, the British attack failed, as I have told, but southward the "impregnable" lines were smashed by a tide of British soldiers as sand castles are overwhelmed by the waves. Our men swept up to Fricourt, struck straight up to Montauban on the right, captured it, and flung a loop round Mametz village.

For the German generals, receiving their reports with great difficulty because runners were killed and telephones broken, the question was: "How will these British troops fight in the open after their first assault? How will our men stand between the first line and the second?"

As far as the German troops were concerned, there were no signs of cowardice, or "low morale" as we called it more kindly, in those early days of the struggle. They fought with a desperate courage, holding on to positions in rearguard actions when our guns were slashing them and when our men were getting near to them, making us pay a heavy price for every little copse or gully or section of trench, and above all serving their machine-guns at La Boisselle, Ovillers, above Fricourt, round Contalmaison, and at all points of their gradual retreat, with a wonderful obstinacy, until they were killed or captured. But fresh waves of British soldiers followed those who were checked or broken.

After the first week of battle the German General Staff had learned the truth about the qualities of those British "New Armies" which had been mocked and caricatured in German comic papers. They learned that these "amateur soldiers" had the qualities of the finest troops in the world—not only extreme valor, but skill and cunning, not only a great power of endurance under the heaviest fire, but a spirit of attack which was terrible in its effect. They were fierce bayonet fighters. Once having gained a bit of earth or a ruined village, nothing would budge them unless they could be blasted out by gun-fire. General Sixt von Arnim put down some candid notes in his report to Prince Rupprecht.

"The English infantry shows great dash in attack, a factor to which immense confidence in its overwhelming artillery greatly contributes. .. It has shown great tenacity in defense. This was especially noticeable in the case of small parties, which, when once established with machine-guns in the corner of a wood or a group of houses, were very difficult to drive out."

The German losses were piling up. The agony of the German troops under our shell-fire was reaching unnatural limits of torture. The early prisoners I saw—Prussians and Bavarians of the 14th Reserve Corps—were nerve-broken, and told frightful stories of the way in which their regiments had been cut to pieces. The German generals had to fill up the gaps, to put new barriers of men against the waves of British infantry. They flung new troops into the line, called up hurriedly from reserve depots.

Now, for the first time, their staff-work showed signs of disorder and demoralization. When the Prussian Guards Reserves were brought up from Valenciennes to counter—attack at Contalmaison they were sent on to the battlefield without maps or local guides, and walked straight into our barrage. A whole battalion was cut to pieces and many others suffered frightful things. Some of the prisoners told me that they had lost three-quarters of their number in casualties, and our troops advanced over heaps of killed and wounded.

The 122d Bavarian Regiment in Contalmaison was among those which suffered horribly. Owing to our ceaseless gun-fire, they could get no food-supplies and no water. The dugouts were crowded, so that they had to take turns to get into these shelters, and outside our shells were bursting over every yard of ground.

"Those who went outside," a prisoner told me, "were killed or wounded. Some of them had their heads blown off, and some of them their arms. But we went on taking turns in the hole, although those who went outside knew that it was their turn to die, most likely. At last most of those who came into the hole were wounded, some of them badly, so that we lay in blood." That is one little picture in a great panorama of bloodshed.

The German command was not thinking much about the human suffering of its troops. It was thinking of the next defensive line upon which they would have to fall back if the pressure of the British offensive could be maintained—the Longueval-Bazentin-Pozires line. It was getting nervous. Owing to the enormous efforts made in the Verdun offensive, the supplies of ammunition were not adequate to the enormous demand.

The German gunners were trying to compete with the British in continuity of bombardments and the shells were running short. Guns were wearing out under this incessant strain, and it was difficult to replace them. General von Gallwitz received reports of "an alarmingly large number of bursts in the bore, particularly in field-guns."

General von Arnim complained that "reserve supplies of ammunition were only available in very small quantities." The German telephone system proved "totally inadequate in consequence of the development which the fighting took." The German air service was surprisingly weak, and the British airmen had established temporary mastery.

"The numerical superiority of the enemy's airmen," noted General von Arnim, "and the fact that their machines were better made, became disagreeably apparent to us, particularly in their direction of the enemy's artillery fire and in bomb-dropping."

On July 15th the British troops broke the German second line at Longueval and the Bazentins, and inflicted great losses upon the enemy, who fought with their usual courage until the British bayonets were among them.

A day or two later the fortress of Ovillers fell, and the remnants of the garrison—one hundred and fifty strong—after a desperate and gallant resistance in ditches and tunnels, where they had fought to the last, surrendered with honor.

Then began the long battle of the woods—Devil's Wood, High Wood, Trones Wood—continued through August with most fierce and bloody fighting, which ended in our favor and forced the enemy back, gradually but steadily, in spite of the terrific bombardments which filled those woods with shell-fire and the constant counter-attacks delivered by the Germans.

"Counter-attack!" came the order from the German staff, and battalions of men marched out obediently to certain death, sometimes with incredible folly on the part of their commanding officers, who ordered these attacks to be made without the slightest chance of success.

I saw an example of that at close range during a battle at Falfemont Farm, near Guillemont. Our men had advanced from Wedge Wood, and I watched them from a trench just south of this, to which I had gone at a great pace over shell-craters and broken wire, with a young observing officer who had been detailed to report back to the guns. (Old "Falstaff," whose songs and stories had filled the tent under the Red Cross with laughter, toiled after us gallantly, but grunting and sweating under the sun like his prototype, until we lost him in our hurry.) Presently a body of Germans came out of a copse called Leuze Wood, on rising ground, faced round among the thin, slashed trees of Falfemont, and advanced toward our men, shoulder to shoulder, like a solid bar. It was sheer suicide. I saw our men get their machineguns into action, and the right side of the living bar frittered away, and then the whole line fell into the scorched grass. Another line followed. They were tall men, and did not falter as they came forward, but it seemed to me they walked like men conscious of going to death. They died. The simile is outworn, but it was exactly as though some invisible scythe had mown them down.

In all the letters written during those weeks of fighting and captured by us from dead or living men there was one cry of agony and horror.

"I stood on the brink of the most terrible days of my life," wrote one of them. "They were those of the battle of the Somme. It began with a night attack on August 13th and 14th. The attack lasted till the evening of the 18th, when the English wrote on our bodies in letters of blood, 'It is all over with you.' A handful of half-mad, wretched creatures, worn out in body and mind, were all that was left of a whole battalion. We were that handful."

The losses of many of the German battalions were staggering (yet not greater than our own), and by the middle of August the morale of the troops was severely shaken. The 117th Division by Pozires suffered very heavily. The 11th Reserve and 157th Regiments each lost nearly three-quarters of their effectives. The 9th Reserve Corps had also lost heavily. The 9th Reserve Jager Battalion lost about three-quarters, the 84th Reserve and 86th Reserve over half. On August 10th the 16th Division had six battalions in reserve.

By August 19th, owing to the large number of casualties, the greater part of those reserves had been absorbed into the front and support trenches, leaving as available reserves two exhausted battalions.

The weakness of the division and the absolute necessity of reinforcing it led to the 15th Reserve Infantry Regiment (2d Guards Division) being brought up to strengthen the right flank in the Leipzig salient. This regiment had suffered casualties to the extent of over 50 percent west of Pozires during the middle of July, and showed no eagerness to return to the fight. These are but a few examples of what was happening along the whole of the German front on the Somme.

It became apparent by the end of August that the enemy was in trouble to find fresh troops to relieve his exhausted divisions, and that the wastage was faster than the arrival of new men. It was noticeable that he left divisions in the line until incapable of further effort rather than relieving them earlier so that after resting they might again be brought on to the battlefield. The only conclusion to be drawn from this was that the enemy had not sufficient formations available to make the necessary reliefs.

In July three of these exhausted divisions were sent to the east, their place being taken by two new divisions, and in August three more exhausted divisions were sent to Russia, eight new divisions coming to the Somme front. The British and French offensive was drawing in all the German reserves and draining them of their life's blood.

"We entrained at Savigny," wrote a man of one of these regiments, "and at once knew our destination. It was our old blood-bath—the Somme."

In many letters this phrase was used. The Somme was called the "Bath of Blood" by the German troops who waded across its shell-craters and in the ditches which were heaped with their dead. But what I have described is only the beginning of the battle, and the bath was to be filled deeper in the months that followed.

XXI

The name (that "blood-bath") and the news of battle could not be hidden from the people of Germany, who had already been chilled with horror by the losses at Verdun, nor from the soldiers of reserve regiments quartered in French and Belgian towns like Valenciennes, St. Quentin, Cambrai, Lille, Bruges, and as far back as Brussels, waiting to go to the front, nor from the civil population of those towns, held for two years by their enemy—these blond young men who lived in their houses, marched down their streets, and made love to their women.

The news was brought down from the Somme front by Red Cross trains, arriving in endless succession, and packed with maimed and mangled men. German military policemen formed cordons round the railway stations, pushed back civilians who came to stare with somber eyes at these blanketed bundles of living flesh, but when the ambulances rumbled through the streets toward the hospitals—long processions of them, with the soles of men's boots turned up over the stretchers on which they lay quiet and stiff—the tale was told, though no word was spoken.

The tale of defeat, of great losses, of grave and increasing anxiety, was told clearly enough—as I read in captured letters—by the faces of German officers who went about in these towns behind the lines with gloomy looks, and whose tempers, never of the sweetest, became irritable and unbearable, so that the soldiers hated them for all this cursing and bullying. A certain battalion commander had a nervous breakdown because he had to meet his colonel in the morning.

"He is dying with fear and anxiety," wrote one of his comrades.

Other men, not battalion commanders, were even more afraid of their superior officers, upon whom this bad news from the Somme had an evil effect.

The bad news was spread by divisions taken out of the line and sent back to rest. The men reported that their battalions had been cut to pieces. Some of their regiments had lost three-quarters of their strength. They described the frightful effect of the British artillery—the smashed trenches, the shell-crater, the horror.

It was not good for the morale of men who were just going up there to take their turn.

The man who was afraid of his colonel "sits all day long writing home, with the picture of his wife and children before his eyes." He was afraid of other things.

Bavarian soldiers quarreled with Prussians, accused them (unjustly) of shirking the Somme battlefields and leaving the Bavarians to go to the blood-bath.

"All the Bavarian troops are being sent to the Somme (this much is certain, you can see no Prussians there), and this in spite of the losses the 1st Bavarian Corps suffered recently at Verdun! And how we did suffer!... It appears that we are in for another turn—at least the 5th Bavarian Division. Everybody has been talking about it for a long time. To the devil with it! Every Bavarian regiment is being sent into it, and it's a swindle."

It was in no cheerful mood that men went away to the Somme battlefields. Those battalions of gray-clad men entrained without any of the old enthusiasm with which they had gone to earlier battles. Their gloom was noticed by the officers.

"Sing, you sheeps' heads, sing!" they shouted.

They were compelled to sing, by order.

"In the afternoon," wrote a man of the 18th Reserve Division, "we had to go out again; we were to learn to sing. The greater part did not join in, and the song went feebly. Then we had to march round in a circle and sing, and that went no better. After that we had an hour off, and on the way back to billets we were to sing 'Deutschland uber Alles,' but this broke down completely. One never hears songs of the Fatherland any more."

They were silent, grave-eyed men who marched through the streets of French and Belgian towns to be entrained for the Somme front, for they had forebodings of the fate before them. Yet none of their forebodings were equal in intensity of fear to the frightful reality into which they were flung.

The journey to the Somme front, on the German side, was a way of terror, ugliness, and death. Not all the imagination of morbid minds searching obscenely for foulness and blood in the great, deep pits of human agony could surpass these scenes along the way to the German lines round Courcelette and Flers, Gueudecourt, Morval, and Lesboeufs.

Many times, long before a German battalion had arrived near the trenches, it was but a collection of nerve—broken men bemoaning losses already suffered far behind the lines and filled with hideous apprehension. For British long-range guns were hurling high explosives into distant villages, barraging crossroads, reaching out to rail-heads and ammunition-dumps, while British airmen were on bombing flights over railway stations and rest-billets and highroads down which the German troops came marching at Cambrai, Bapaume, in the valley between Irles and Warlencourt, at Ligny-Thilloy, Busigny, and many other places on the lines of route.

German soldiers arriving one morning at Cambrai by train found themselves under the fire of a single airplane which flew very low and dropped bombs. They exploded with heavy crashes, and one bomb hit the first carriage behind the engine, killing and wounding several men. A second bomb hit the station buildings, and there was a clatter of broken glass, the rending of wood, and the fall of bricks. All lights went out, and the German soldiers groped about in the darkness amid the splinters of glass and the fallen bricks, searching for the wounded by the sound of their groans. It was but one scene along the way to that blood-bath through which they had to wade to the trenches of the Somme.

Flights of British airplanes circled over the villages on the way. At Grevilliers, in August, eleven 112-16 bombs fell in the market square, so that the center of the village collapsed in a state of ruin, burying soldiers billeted there. Every day the British airmen paid these visits, meeting the Germans far up the roads on their way to the Somme, and swooping over them like a flying death. Even on the march in open country the German soldiers tramping silently along—not singing in spite of orders—were bombed and shot at by these British aviators, who flew down very low, pouring out streams of machine-gun bullets. The Germans lost their nerve at such times, and scattered into the ditches, falling over one another, struck and cursed by their *Unteroffizieren*, and leaving their dead and wounded in the roadway.

As the roads went nearer to the battlefields they were choked with the traffic of war, with artillery and transport wagons and horse ambulances, and always thousands of gray men marching up to the lines, or back from them, exhausted and broken after many days in the fires of hell up there. Officers sat on their horses by the roadside, directing all the traffic with the usual swearing and cursing, and rode alongside the transport wagons and the troops, urging them forward at a quicker pace because of stern orders received from headquarters demanding quicker movement. The reserves, it seemed, were desperately wanted up in the lines. The English were attacking again. .. God alone knew what was happening. Regiments had lost their way. Wounded were pouring back. Officers had gone mad. Into the midst of all this turmoil shells fell—shells from long-range guns. Transport wagons were blown to bits. The bodies and fragments of artillery horses lay all over the roads. Men lay dead or bleeding under the debris of gun-wheels and broken bricks. Above all the noise of this confusion and death in the night the hard, stern voices of German officers rang out, and German discipline prevailed, and men marched on to greater perils.

They were in the shell-zone now, and sometimes a regiment on the march was tracked all along the way by British gun-fire directed from airplanes and captive balloons. It was the fate of a captured officer I met who had detrained at Bapaume for the trenches at Contalmaison.

At Bapaume his battalion was hit by fragments of twelve-inch shells. Nearer to the line they came under the fire of eight-inch and six-inch shells. Four-point-sevens (4.7's) found them somewhere by Bazentin. At Contalmaison they marched into a barrage, and here the officer was taken prisoner. Of his battalion there were few men left.

It was so with the 3d Jager Battalion, ordered up hurriedly to make a counter-attack near Flers. They suffered so heavily on the way to the trenches that no attack could be made. The stretcher-bearers had all the work to do.

The way up to the trenches became more tragic as every kilometer was passed, until the stench of corruption was wafted on the wind, so that men were sickened, and tried not to breathe, and marched hurriedly to get on the lee side of its foulness. They walked now through places which had once been villages, but were sinister ruins where death lay in wait for German soldiers.

"It seems queer to me," wrote one of them, "that whole villages close to the front look as flattened as a child's toy run over by a steam-roller. Not one stone remains on another. The streets are one line of shell—holes. Add to that the thunder of the guns, and you will see with what feelings we come into the line—into trenches where for months shells of all caliber have rained... Flers is a scrap heap."

Again and again men lost their way up to the lines. The reliefs could only be made at night lest they should be discovered by British airmen and British gunners, and even if these German soldiers had trench maps the guidance was but little good when many trenches had been smashed in and only shell-craters could be found.

"In the front line of Flers," wrote one of these Germans, "the men were only occupying shell-holes. Behind there was the intense smell of putrefaction which filled the trench—almost unbearably. The corpses lie either quite insufficiently covered with earth on the edge of the trench or quite close under the bottom of the trench, so that the earth lets the stench through. In some places bodies lie quite uncovered in a trench recess, and no one seems to trouble about them. One sees horrible pictures—here an arm, here a foot, here a head, sticking out of the earth. And these are all German soldiers-heroes!

"Not far from us, at the entrance to a dugout, nine men were buried, of whom three were dead. All along the trench men kept on getting buried. What had been a perfect trench a few hours before was in parts completely blown in... The men are getting weaker. It is impossible to hold out any longer. Losses can no longer be reckoned accurately. Without a doubt many of our people are killed."

That is only one out of thousands of such gruesome pictures, true as the death they described, true to the pictures on our side of the line as on their side, which went back to German homes during the battles of the Somme. Those German soldiers were great letter-writers, and men sitting in wet ditches, in "fox-holes," as they called their dugouts, "up to my waist in mud," as one of them described, scribbled pitiful things which they hoped might reach their people at home, as a voice from the dead. For they had had little hope of escape from the blood—bath. "When you get this I shall be a corpse," wrote one of them, and one finds the same foreboding in many of these documents.

Even the lucky ones who could get some cover from the incessant bombardment by English guns began to lose their nerves after a day or two. They were always in fear of British infantry sweeping upon them suddenly behind the Trommelfeuer, rushing their dugouts with bombs and bayonets. Sentries became "jumpy," and signaled attacks when there were no attacks. The gas—alarm was sounded constantly by the clang of a bell in the trench, and men put on their heavy gas-masks and sat in them until they were nearly stifled.

Here is a little picture of life in a German dugout near the British lines, written by a man now dead:

"The telephone bell rings. 'Are you there? Yes, here's Nau's battalion.' 'Good. That is all.' Then that ceases, and now the wire is in again perhaps for the twenty-fifth or thirtieth time. Thus the night is interrupted, and now they come, alarm messages, one after the other, each more terrifying than the other, of enormous losses through the bombs and shells of the enemy, of huge masses of troops advancing upon us, of all possible possibilities, such as a train broken down, and we are tortured by all the terrors that the mind can invent. Our nerves quiver. We clench our teeth. None of us can forget the horrors of the night."

Heavy rain fell and the dugouts became wet and filthy.

"Our sleeping-places were full of water. We had to try and bail out the trenches with cooking-dishes. I lay down in the water with G-. We were to have worked on dugouts, but not a soul could do any more. Only a few sections got coffee. Mine got nothing at all. I was frozen in every limb, poured the water out of my boots, and lay down again."

Our men suffered exactly the same things, but did not write about them.

The German generals and their staffs could not be quite indifferent to all this welter of human suffering among their troops, in spite of the cold, scientific spirit with which they regarded the problem of war. The agony of the individual soldier would not trouble them. There is no war without agony. But the psychology of masses of men had to be considered, because it affects the efficiency of the machine.

The German General Staff on the western front was becoming seriously alarmed by the declining morale of its infantry under the increasing strain of the British attacks, and adopted stern measures to cure it. But it could not hope to cure the heaps of German dead who were lying on the battlefields, nor the maimed men who were being carried back to the dressing stations, nor to bring back the prisoners taken in droves by the French and British troops.

Before the attack on the Flers line, the capture of Thiepval, and the German debacle at Beaumont Hamel, in November, the enemy's command was already filled with a grave anxiety at the enormous losses of its fighting strength; was compelled to adopt new expedients for increasing the number of its divisions. It was forced to withdraw troops badly needed on other fronts, and the successive shocks of the British offensive reached as far as Germany itself, so that the whole of its recruiting system had to be revised to fill up the gaps torn out of the German ranks.

XXII

All through July and August the enemy's troops fought with wonderful and stubborn courage, defending every bit of broken woodland, every heap of bricks that was once a village, every line of trenches smashed by heavy shell-fire, with obstinacy.

It is indeed fair and just to say that throughout those battles of the Somme our men fought against an enemy hard to beat, grim and resolute, and inspired sometimes with the courage of despair, which was hardly less dangerous than the courage of hope.

The Australians who struggled to get the high ground at Pozieres did not have an easy task. The enemy made many counter-attacks against them. All the ground thereabouts was, as I have said, so smashed that the earth became finely powdered, and it was the arena of bloody fighting at close quarters which did not last a day or two, but many weeks. Mouquet Farm was like the phoenix which rose again out of its ashes. In its tunneled ways German soldiers hid and came out to fight our men in the rear long after the site of the farm was in our hands.

But the German troops were fighting what they knew to be a losing battle. They were fighting rear-guard actions, trying to gain time for the hasty digging of ditches behind them, trying to sell their lives at the highest price.

They lived not only under incessant gun-fire, gradually weakening their nerve-power, working a physical as well as a moral change in them, but in constant terror of British attacks.

They could never be sure of safety at any hour of the day or night, even in their deepest dugouts. The British varied their times of attack. At dawn, at noon, when the sun was reddening in the west, just before the dusk, in pitch darkness, even, the steady, regular bombardment that had never ceased all through the days and nights would concentrate into the great tumult of sudden drum-fire, and presently waves of men—English or Scottish or Irish, Australians or Canadians—would be sweeping on to them and over them, rummaging down into the dugouts with bombs and bayonets, gathering up prisoners, quick to kill if men were not quick to surrender.

In this way Thiepval was encircled so that the garrison there—the 180th Regiment, who had held it for two years—knew that they were doomed. In this way Guillemont and Ginchy fell, so that in the first place hardly a man out of two thousand men escaped to tell the tale of horror in German lines, and in the second place there was no long fight against the Irish, who stormed it in a wild, fierce rush which even machine-guns could not check. The German General Staff was getting flurried, grabbing at battalions from other parts of the line, disorganizing its divisions under the urgent need of flinging in men to stop this rot in the lines, ordering counter-attacks which were without any chance of success, so that thin waves of men came out into the open, as I saw them several times, to be swept down by scythes of bullets which cut them clean to the earth. Before September 15th they hoped that the British offensive was wearing itself out. It seemed to them at least doubtful that after the struggle of two and a half months the British troops could still have spirit and strength enough to fling themselves against new lines.

But the machinery of their defense was crumbling. Many of their guns had worn out, and could not be replaced quickly enough. Many batteries had been knocked out in their emplacements along the line of Bazentin and Longueval before the artillery was drawn back to Grand-court and a new line of safety. Battalion commanders clamored for greater supplies of hand-grenades, intrenching-tools, trench-mortars, signal rockets, and all kinds of fighting material enormously in excess of all previous requirements.

The difficulties of dealing with the wounded, who littered the battlefields and choked the roads with the traffic of ambulances, became increasingly severe, owing to the dearth of horses for transport and the longer range of British guns which had been brought far forward.

The German General Staff studied its next lines of defense away through Courcelette, Martinpuich, Lesboeufs, Morval, and Combles, and they did not look too good, but with luck and the courage of German soldiers, and the exhaustion—surely those fellows were exhausted!—of British troops—good enough.

On September 15th the German command had another shock when the whole line of the British troops on the Somme front south of the Ancre rose out of their trenches and swept over the German defenses in a tide.

Those defenses broke hopelessly, and the waves dashed through. Here and there, as on the German left at Morval and Lesboeufs, the bulwarks stood for a time, but the British pressed against them and round them. On the German right, below the little river of the Ancre, Courcelette fell, and Martinpuich, and at last, as I have written, High Wood, which the Germans desired to hold at all costs, and had held against incessant attacks by great concentration of artillery, was captured and left behind by the London men. A new engine of war had come as a demoralizing influence among German troops, spreading terror among them on the first day out of the tanks. For the first time the Germans were outwitted in inventions of destruction; they who had been foremost in all engines of death. It was the moment of real panic in the German lines—a panic reaching back from the troops to the High Command.

Ten days later, on September 25th, when the British made a new advance—all this time the French were pressing forward, too, on our right by Roye—Combles was evacuated without a fight and with a litter of dead in its streets; Gueudecourt, Lesboeufs, and Morval were lost by the Germans; and a day later Thiepval, the greatest fortress position next to Beaumont Hamel, fell, with all its garrison taken prisoners.

They were black days in the German headquarters, where staff-officers heard the news over their telephones and sent stern orders to artillery commanders and divisional generals, and after dictating new instructions that certain trench systems must be held at whatever price, heard that already they were lost.

It was at this time that the morale of the German troops on the Somme front showed most signs of breaking. In spite of all their courage, the ordeal had been too hideous for them, and in spite of all their discipline, the iron discipline of the German soldier, they were on the edge of revolt. The intimate and undoubted facts of this break in the morale of the enemy's troops during this period reveal a pitiful picture of human agony.

"We are now fighting on the Somme with the English," wrote a man of the 17th Bavarian Regiment. "You can no longer call it war. It is mere murder. We are at the focal-point of the present battle in Foureaux Wood (near Guillemont). All my previous experiences in this war—the slaughter at Ypres and the battle in the gravel-pit at Hulluch—are the purest child's play compared with this massacre, and that is much too mild a description. I hardly think they will bring us into the fight again, for we are in a very bad way."

"From September 12th to 27th we were on the Somme," wrote a man of the 10th Bavarians, "and my regiment had fifteen hundred casualties."

A detailed picture of the German losses under our bombardment was given in the diary of an officer captured in a trench near Flers, and dated September 22d.

"The four days ending September 4th, spent in the trenches, were characterized by a continual enemy bombardment that did not abate for a single instant. The enemy had registered on our trenches with light, as well as medium and heavy, batteries, notwithstanding that he had no direct observation from his trenches, which lie on the other side of the summit. His registering was done by his excellent air service, which renders perfect reports of everything observed.

"During the first day, for instance, whenever the slightest movement was visible in our trenches during the presence, as is usually the case, of enemy aircraft flying as low as three and four hundred yards, a heavy bombardment of the particular section took place. The very heavy losses during the first day brought about the resolution to evacuate the trenches during the daytime. Only a small garrison was left, the remainder withdrawing to a part of the line on the left of the Martinpuich-Pozieres road.

"The signal for a bombardment by 'heavies' was given by the English airplanes. On the first day we tried to fire by platoons on the airplanes, but a second airplane retaliated by dropping bombs and firing his machine-gun at our troops. Our own airmen appeared only once for a short time behind our lines.

"While many airplanes are observing from early morning till late at night, our own hardly ever venture near. The opinion is that our trenches cannot protect troops during a barrage of the shortest duration, owing to lack of dugouts.

"The enemy understands how to prevent, with his terrible barrage, the bringing up of building material, and even how to hinder the work itself. The consequence is that our trenches are always ready for an assault on his part. Our artillery, which does occasionally put a heavy barrage on the enemy trenches at a great expense of ammunition, cannot cause similar destruction to him. He can bring his building material up, can repair his trenches as well as build new ones, can bring up rations and ammunition, and remove the wounded.

"The continual barrage on our lines of communication makes it very difficult for us to ration and relieve our troops, to supply water, ammunition, and building material, to evacuate wounded, and causes heavy losses. This and the lack of protection from artillery fire and the weather, the lack of hot meals, the continual necessity of lying still in the same place, the danger of being buried, the long time the wounded have to remain in the trenches, and chiefly the terrible effect of the machine—and heavy-artillery fire, controlled by an excellent air service, has a most demoralizing effect on the troops.

"Only with the greatest difficulty could the men be persuaded to stay in the trenches under those conditions."

There were some who could not be persuaded to stay if they could see any chance of deserting or malingering. For the first time on our front the German officers could not trust the courage of their men, nor their loyalty, nor their sense of discipline. All this horror of men blown to bits over living men, of trenches heaped with dead and dying, was stronger than courage, stronger than loyalty, stronger than discipline. A moral rot was threatening to bring the German troops on the Somme front to disaster.

Large numbers of men reported sick and tried by every kind of trick to be sent back to base hospitals.

In the 4th Bavarian Division desertions were frequent, and several times whole bodies of men refused to go forward into the front line. The morale of men in the 393d Regiment, taken at Courcelette, seemed to be very weak. One of the prisoners declared that they gave themselves up without firing a shot, because they could trust the English not to kill them.

The platoon commander had gone away, and the prisoner was ordered to alarm the platoon in case of attack, but did not do so on purpose. They did not shoot with rifles or machine-guns and did not throw bombs.

Many of the German officers were as demoralized as the men, shirking their posts in the trenches, shamming sickness, and even leading the way to surrender. Prisoners of the 351st Regiment, which lost thirteen hundred men in fifteen days, told of officers who had refused to take their men up to the front-line, and of whole companies who had declined to move when ordered to do so. An officer of the 74th Landwehr Regiment is said by prisoners to have told his men during our preliminary bombardment to surrender as soon as we attacked.

A German regimental order says: "I must state with the greatest regret that the regiment, during this change of position, had to take notice of the sad fact that men of four of the companies, inspired by shameful cowardice, left their companies on their own initiative and did not move into line."

Another order contains the same fact, and a warning of what punishment may be meted out:

"Proofs are multiplying of men leaving the position without permission and hiding at the rear. It is our duty... each at his post—to deal with this fact with energy and success."

Many Bavarians complained that their officers did not accompany them into the trenches, but went down to the hospitals with imaginary diseases. In any case there was a great deal of real sickness, mental and physical. The ranks were depleted by men suffering from fever, pleurisy, jaundice, and stomach complaints of all kinds, twisted up with rheumatism after lying in waterlogged holes, lamed for life by bad cases of trench-foot, and nerve-broken so that they could do nothing but weep.

The nervous cases were the worst and in greatest number. Many men went raving mad. The shell-shock victims clawed at their mouths unceasingly, or lay motionless like corpses with staring eyes, or trembled in every limb, moaning miserably and afflicted with a great terror.

To the Germans (barely less to British troops) the Somme battlefields were not only shambles, but a territory which the devil claimed as his own for the torture of men's brains and souls before they died in the furnace fires. A spirit of revolt against all this crept into the minds of men who retained their sanity—a revolt against the people who had ordained this vast outrage against God and humanity.

Into German letters there crept bitter, burning words against "the millionaires—who grow rich out of the war," against the high people who live in comfort behind the lines. Letters from home inflamed these thoughts.

It was not good reading for men under shell-fire.

"It seems that you soldiers fight so that official stay-at-homes can treat us as female criminals. Tell me, dear husband, are you a criminal when you fight in the trenches, or why do people treat women and children here as such?...

"For the poor here it is terrible, and yet the rich, the gilded ones, the bloated aristocrats, gobble up everything in front of our very eyes... All soldiers—friend and foe—ought to throw down their weapons and go on strike, so that this war which enslaves the people more than ever may cease."

Thousands of letters, all in this strain, were reaching the German soldiers on the Somme, and they did not strengthen the morale of men already victims of terror and despair.

Behind the lines deserters were shot in batches. To those in front came Orders of the Day warning them, exhorting them, commanding them to hold fast.

"To the hesitating and faint-hearted in the regiment," says one of these Orders, "I would say the following:

"What the Englishman can do the German can do also. Or if, on the other hand, the Englishman really is a better and superior being, he would be quite justified in his aim as regards this war, viz., the extermination of the German. There is a further point to be noted: this is the first time we have been in the line on the Somme, and what is more, we are there at a time when things are more calm. The English regiments opposing us have been in the firing-line for the second, and in some cases even the third, time. Heads up and play the man!"

It was easy to write such documents. It was more difficult to bring up reserves of men and ammunition. The German command was harder pressed by the end of September.

From July 1st to September 8th, according to trustworthy information, fifty-three German divisions in all were engaged against the Allies on the Somme battlefront. Out of these fourteen were still in the line on September 8th.

Twenty-eight had been withdrawn, broken and exhausted, to quieter areas. Eleven more had been withdrawn to rest-billets. Under the Allies' artillery fire and infantry attacks the average life of a German division as a unit fit for service on the Somme was nineteen days. More than two new German divisions had to be brought into the front-line every week since the end of June, to replace those smashed in the process of resisting the Allied attack. In November it was reckoned by competent observers in the field that well over one hundred and twenty German divisions had been passed through the ordeal of the Somme, this number including those which have appeared there more than once.

XXIII

By September 25th, when the British troops made another attack, the morale of the German troops was reaching its lowest ebb. Except on their right, at Beaumont Hamel and Beaucourt, they were far beyond the great system of protective dugouts which had given them a sense of safety before July 1st. Their second and third lines of defense had been carried, and they were existing in shell-craters and trenches hastily scraped up under ceaseless artillery fire.

The horrors of the battlefield were piled up to heights of agony and terror. Living men dwelt among the unburied dead, made their way to the front-lines over heaps of corpses, breathed in the smell of human corruption and had always in their ears the cries of the wounded they could not rescue. They wrote these things in tragic letters—thousands of them—which never reached their homes in Germany, but lay in their captured ditches.

"The number of dead lying about is awful. One stumbles over them."

"The stench of the dead lying round us is unbearable."

"We are no longer men here. We are worse than beasts."

"It is hell let loose."... "It is horrible."... "We've lived in misery."

"If the dear ones at home could see all this perhaps there would be a change. But they are never told."

"The ceaseless roar of the guns is driving us mad."

Poor, pitiful letters, out of their cries of agony one gets to the real truth of war-the "glory" and the "splendor" of it preached by the German philosophers and British Jingoes, who upheld it as the great strengthening tonic for their race, and as the noblest experience of men. Every line these German soldiers wrote might have been written by one of ours; from both sides of the shifting lines there was the same death and the same hell.

Behind the lines the German General Staff, counting up the losses of battalions and divisions who staggered out weakly, performed juggling tricks with what reserves it could lay its hands on, and flung up stray units to relieve the poor wretches in the trenches. Many of those reliefs lost their way in going up, and came up late, already shattered by the shell-fire through which they passed.

"Our position," wrote a German infantry officer, "was, of course, quite different from what we had been told. Our company alone relieved a whole battalion. We had been told we were to relieve a company of fifty men weakened by casualties.

"The men we relieved had no idea where the enemy was, how far off he was, or whether any of our own troops were in front of us. We got no idea of our support position until six o'clock this evening. The English are four hundred yards away, by the windmill over the hill."

One German soldier wrote that the British "seem to relieve their infantry very quickly, while the German commands work on the principle of relieving only in the direst need, and leaving the divisions in as long as possible."

Another wrote that:

"The leadership of the divisions really fell through. For the most part we did not get orders, and the regiment had to manage as best it could. If orders arrived they generally came too late or were dealt out 'from the green table' without knowledge of the conditions in front, so that to carry them out was impossible."

All this was a sign of demoralization, not only among the troops who were doing the fighting and the suffering, but among the organizing generals behind, who were directing the operations. The continual hammer-strokes of the British and French armies on the Somme battlefields strained the German war-machine on the western front almost to breaking-point.

It seemed as though a real debacle might happen, and that they would be forced to effect a general retreat—a withdrawal more or less at ease or a retirement under pressure from the enemy....

But they had luck—astonishing luck. At the very time when the morale of the German soldiers was lowest and when the strain on the High Command was greatest the weather turned in their favor and gave them just the breathing-space they desperately needed. Rain fell heavily in the middle of October, autumn mists prevented airplane activity and artillery-work, and the ground became a quagmire, so that the British troops found it difficult to get up their supplies for a new advance.

The Germans were able in this respite to bring up new divisions, fresh and strong enough to make heavy counter—attacks in the Stuff and Schwaben and Regina trenches, and to hold the lines more securely for a time, while great digging was done farther back at Bapaume and the next line of defense. Successive weeks of bad weather and our own tragic losses checked the impetus of the British and French driving power, and the Germans were able to reorganize and reform.

As I have said, the shock of our offensive reached as far as Germany, and caused a complete reorganization in the system of obtaining reserves of man-power. The process of "combing out," as we call it, was pursued with astounding ruthlessness, and German mothers, already stricken with the loss of their elder sons, raised cries of despair when the youngest born were also seized—boys of eighteen belonging to the 1918 class.

The whole of the 1917 class had joined the depots in March and May of this year, receiving a three months' training before being transferred to the field-recruit depots in June and July. About the middle of July the first large drafts joined their units and made their appearance at the front, and soon after the beginning of our offensive at least half this class was in the front-line regiments. The massacre of the boys had begun.

Then older men, men beyond middle age, who correspond to the French Territorial class, exempted from fighting service and kept on lines of communication, were also called to the front, and whole garrisons of these gray heads were removed from German towns to fill up the ranks.

"The view is held here," wrote a German soldier of the Somme, "that the Higher Command intends gradually to have more and more Landsturm battalions (men of the oldest reserves) trained in trench warfare for a few weeks, as we have been, according to the quality of the men, and thus to secure by degrees a body of troops on which it can count in an emergency."

In the month of November the German High Command believed that the British attacks were definitely at an end, "having broken down," as they claimed, "in mud and blood," but another shock came to them when once more British troops—the 51st Highland Division and the 63d Naval Division—left their trenches, in fog and snow, and captured the strongest fortress position on the enemy's front, at Beaumont Hamel, bringing back over six thousand prisoners. It was after that they began their retreat.

These studies of mine, of what happened on both sides of the shifting lines in the Somme, must be as horrible to read as they were to write. But they are less than the actual truth, for no pen will ever in one book, or in hundreds, give the full record of the individual agony, the broken heart-springs, the soul-shock as well as the shell-shock, of that frightful struggle in which, on one side and the other, two million men were engulfed. Modern civilization was wrecked on those fire-blasted fields, though they led to what we called "Victory." More died there than the flower of our youth and German manhood. The Old Order of the world died there, because many men who came alive out of that conflict were changed, and vowed not to tolerate a system of thought which had led up to such a monstrous massacre of human beings who prayed to the same God, loved the same joys of life, and had no hatred of one another except as it had been lighted and inflamed by their governors, their philosophers, and their newspapers. The German soldier cursed the militarism which had plunged him into that horror. The British soldier cursed the German as the direct cause of all his trouble, but looked back on his side of the lines and saw an evil there which was also his enemy—the evil of a secret diplomacy which juggled with the lives of humble men so that war might be sprung upon them without their knowledge or consent, and the evil of rulers who hated German militarism not because of its wickedness, but because of its strength in rivalry and the evil of a folly in the minds of men which had taught them to regard war as a glorious adventure, and patriotism as the right to dominate other peoples, and liberty as a catch—word of politicians in search of power. After the Somme battles there were many other battles as bloody and terrible, but they only confirmed greater numbers of men in the faith that the old world had been wrong in its "make-up" and wrong in its religion of life. Lip service to Christian ethics was not good enough as an argument for this. Either the heart of the world must be changed by a real obedience to the gospel of Christ or Christianity must be abandoned for a new creed which would give better results between men and nations. There could be no reconciling of bayonet-drill and high explosives with the words "Love one another." Or if bayonet-drill and high-explosive force were to be the rule of life in preparation for another struggle such as this, then at least let men put hypocrisy away and return to the primitive law of the survival of the fittest in a jungle world subservient to the king of beasts. The devotion of military chaplains to the wounded, their valor, their decorations for gallantry under fire, their human comradeship and spiritual sincerity, would not bridge the gulf in the minds of many soldiers between a gospel of love and this argument by bayonet and bomb, gas-shell and high velocity, blunderbuss, club, and trench-shovel. Some time or other, when German militarism acknowledged defeat by the break of its machine or by the revolt of its people—not until then—there must be a new order of things, which would prevent such another massacre in the fair fields of life, and that could come only by a faith in the hearts of many peoples breaking down old barriers of hatred and reaching out to one another in a fellowship of common sense based on common interests, and inspired by an ideal higher than this beast-like rivalry of nations. So thinking men thought and talked. So said the soldier—poets who wrote from the trenches. So said many onlookers. The simple soldier did not talk like that unless he were a Frenchman. Our men only began to talk like that after the war—as many of them are now talking—and the revolt of the spirit, vague but passionate, against the evil that had produced this devil's trap of war, and the German challenge, was subconscious as they sat in their dugouts and crowded in their ditches in the battles of the Somme.

PART SEVEN

THE FIELDS OF ARMAGEDDON

I

During the two years that followed the battles of the Somme I recorded in my daily despatches, republished in book form ("The Struggle in Flanders" and "The Way to Victory"), the narrative of that continuous conflict in which the British forces on the western front were at death-grips with the German monster where now one side and then the other heaved themselves upon their adversary and struggled for the knock-out blow, until at last, after staggering losses on both sides, the enemy was broken to bits in the last combined attack by British, Belgian, French, and American armies. There is no need for me to retell all that history in detail, and I am glad to know that there is nothing I need alter in the record of events which I wrote as they happened, because they have not been falsified by any new evidence; and those detailed descriptions of mine stand true in fact and in the emotion of the hours that passed, while masses of men were slaughtered in the fields of Armageddon.

But now, looking back upon those last two years of the war as an eye-witness of many tragic and heroic things, I see the frightful drama of them as a whole and as one act was related to another, and as the plot which seemed so tangled and confused, led by inevitable stages, not under the control of any field-marshal or chief of staff, to the climax in which empires crashed and exhausted nations looked round upon the ruin which followed defeat and victory. I see also, as in one picture, the colossal scale of that human struggle in that Armageddon of our civilization, which at the time one reckoned only by each day's success or failure, each day's slaughter on that side or the other. One may add up the whole sum according to the bookkeeping of Fate, by double-entry, credit and debit, profit and loss. One may set our attacks in the battles of Flanders against the strength of the German defense, and say our losses of three to one (as Ludendorff reckons them, and as many of us guessed) were in our favor, because we could afford the difference of exchange and the enemy could not put so many human counters into the pool for the final "kitty" in this gamble with life and death. One may balance the German offensive in March of '18 with the weight that was piling up against them by the entry of the Americans. One may also see now, very clearly, the paramount importance of the human factor in this arithmetic of war, the morale of men being of greater influence than generalship, though dependent on it, the spirit of peoples being as vital to success as the mechanical efficiency of the war-machine; and above all, one is now able to observe how each side blundered on in a blind, desperate way, sacrificing masses of human life without a clear vision of the consequences, until at last one side blundered more than another and was lost. It will be impossible to pretend in history that our High Command, or any other, foresaw the thread of plot as it was unraveled to the end, and so arranged its plan that events happened according to design. The events of March, 1918, were not foreseen nor prevented by French or British. The ability of our generals was not imaginative nor inventive, but limited to the piling up of men and munitions, always more men and more munitions, against positions of enormous strength and overcoming obstacles by sheer weight of flesh and blood and high explosives. They were not cunning so far as I could see, nor in the judgment of the men under their command, but simple and straightforward gentlemen who said "once more unto the breach," and sent up new battering-rams by brigades and divisions. There was no evidence that I could find of high directing brains choosing the weakest spot in the enemy's armor and piercing it with a sharp sword, or avoiding a direct assault against the enemy's most formidable positions and leaping upon him from some unguarded way. Perhaps that was impossible in the conditions of modern warfare and the limitations of the British front until the arrival of the tanks, which, for a long time, were wasted in the impassable bogs of Flanders, where their steel skeletons still lie rusting as a proof of heroic efforts vainly used. Possible or not, and rare genius alone could prove it one way or another, it appeared to the onlooker, as well as to the soldier who carried out commands that our method of warfare was to search the map for a place which was strongest in the enemy's lines, most difficult to attack, most powerfully defended, and then after due advertisement, not to take an unfair advantage of the enemy, to launch the assault. That had always been the English way and that was our way in many battles of the great war, which were won (unless they were lost) by the sheer valor of men who at great cost smashed their way through all obstructions.

The Germans, on the whole, showed more original genius in military science, varying their methods of attack and defense according to circumstances, building trenches and dugouts which we never equaled; inventing the concrete blockhouse or "pill-box" for a forward defensive zone thinly held in advance of the main battle zone, in order to lessen their slaughter under the weight of our gun-fire (it cost us dearly for a time); scattering their men in organized shell-craters in order to distract our barrage fire; using the "elastic system of defense" with frightful success against Nivelle's attack in the Champagne; creating the system of assault of "infiltration" which broke the Italian lines at Caporetto in 1917 and ours and the French in 1918. Against all that we may set only our tanks, which in the end led the way to victory, but the German High Command blundered atrociously in all the larger calculations of war, so that they brought about the doom of their empire by a series of acts which would seem deliberate if we had not known that they were merely blind. With a folly that still seems incredible, they took the risk of adding the greatest power in the world—in numbers of men and in potential energy—to their list of enemies at a time when their own man-power was on the wane. With deliberate arrogance they flouted the United States and forced her to declare war. Their temptation, of course, was great. The British naval blockade was causing severe suffering by food shortage to the German people and denying them access to raw material which they needed for the machinery of war.

The submarine campaign, ruthlessly carried out, would and did inflict immense damage upon British and Allied shipping, and was a deadly menace to England. But German calculations were utterly wrong, as Ludendorff in his Memoirs now admits, in estimating the amount of time needed to break her bonds by submarine warfare before America could send over great armies to Europe. The German war lords were wrong again in underestimating the defensive and offensive success of the British navy and mercantile marine against submarine activities. By those miscalculations they lost the war in the long run, and by other errors they made their loss more certain.

One mistake they made was their utter callousness regarding the psychology and temper of their soldiers and civilian population. They put a greater strain upon them than human nature could bear, and by driving their fighting-men into one shambles after another, while they doped their people with false promises which were never fulfilled, they sowed the seeds of revolt and despair which finally launched them into gulfs of ruin. I have read nothing more horrible than the cold-blooded cruelty of Ludendorff's Memoirs, in which, without any attempt at self-excuse, he reveals himself as using the lives of millions of men upon a gambling chance of victory with the hazards weighted against him, as he admits. Writing of January, 1917, he says: "A collapse on the part of Russia was by no means to be contemplated and was, indeed, not reckoned upon by any one... Failing the U-boat campaign we reckoned with the collapse of the Quadruple Alliance during 1917." Yet with that enormous risk visible ahead, Ludendorff continued to play the grand jeu, the great game, and did not advise any surrender of imperial ambitions in order to obtain a peace for his people, and was furious with the Majority party in the Reichstag for preparing a peace resolution. The collapse of Russia inspired him with new hopes of victory in the west, and again he prepared to sacrifice masses of men in the slaughter-fields. But he blundered again, and this time fatally. His time-table was out of gear. The U—boat war had failed. American manhood was pouring into France, and German soldiers on the Russian front had been infected with ideas most dangerous to German discipline and the "will to win." At the end, as at the beginning, the German war lords failed to understand the psychology of human nature as they had failed to understand the spirit of France, of Belgium, of Great Britain, and of America. One of the most important admissions in history is made by Ludendorff when he writes:

"Looking back, I say our decline began clearly with the outbreak of the revolution in Russia. On the one side the government was dominated by the fear that the infection would spread, and on the other by the feeling of their helplessness to instil fresh strength into the masses of the people and to strengthen their warlike ardor, waning as it was through a combination of innumerable circumstances."

So the web of fate was spun, and men who thought they were directing the destiny of the world were merely caught in those woven threads like puppets tied to strings and made to dance. It was the old Dance of Death which has happened before in the folly of mankind.

II

During the German retreat to their Hindenburg line we saw the full ruthlessness of war as never before on the western front, in the laying waste of a beautiful countryside, not by rational fighting, but by carefully organized destruction. Ludendorff claims, quite justly, that it was in accordance with the laws of war. That is true. It is only that our laws of war are not justified by any code of humanity above that of primitive savages. "The decision to retreat," he says, "was not reached without a painful struggle. It implied a confession of weakness that was bound to raise the morale of the enemy and to lower our own. But as it was necessary for military reasons we had no choice. It had to be carried out... The whole movement was a brilliant performance... The retirement proved in a high degree remunerative."

I saw the brilliant performance in its operation. I went into beautiful little towns like Peronne, where the houses were being gutted by smoldering fire, and into hundreds of villages where the enemy had just gone out of them after touching off explosive charges which had made all their cottages collapse like card houses, their roofs spread flat upon their ruins, and their churches, after centuries of worship in them, fall into chaotic heaps of masonry. I wandered through the ruins of old French chateaux, once very stately in their terraced gardens, now a litter of brickwork, broken statuary, and twisted iron—work above open vaults where not even the dead had been left to lie in peace. I saw the little old fruit-trees of French peasants sawn off at the base, and the tall trees along the roadsides stretched out like dead giants to bar our passage. Enormous craters had been blown in the roadways, which had to be bridged for our traffic of men and guns, following hard upon the enemy's retreat.

There was a queer sense of illusion as one traveled through this desolation. At a short distance many of the villages seemed to stand as before the war. One expected to find inhabitants there. But upon close approach one saw that each house was but an empty shell blown out from cellar to roof, and one wandered through the streets of the ruins in a silence that was broken only by the sound of one's own voice or by a few shells crashing into the gutted houses. The enemy was in the next village, or the next but one, with a few field-guns and a rear-guard of machine-gunners.

In most villages, in many of his dugouts, and by contraptions with objects lying amid the litter, he had left "booby traps" to blow our men to bits if they knocked a wire, or stirred an old boot, or picked up a fountain-pen, or walked too often over a board where beneath acid was eating through a metal plate to a high-explosive charge. I little knew when I walked round the tower of the town hall of Bapaume that in another week, with the enemy far away, it would go up in dust and ashes. Only a few of our men were killed or blinded by these monkey-tricks. Our engineers found most of them before they were touched off, but one went down dugouts or into ruined houses with a sense of imminent danger. All through the devastated region one walked with an uncanny feeling of an evil spirit left behind by masses of men whose bodies had gone away. It exuded from scraps of old clothing, it was in the stench of the dugouts and in the ruins they had made.

In some few villages there were living people left behind, some hundreds in Nesle and Roye, and, all told, some thousands. They had been driven in from the other villages burning around them, their own villages, whose devastation they wept to see. I met these people who had lived under German rule and talked with many of them—old women, wrinkled like dried-up apples, young women waxen of skin, hollow-eyed, with sharp cheekbones, old peasant farmers and the gamekeepers of French chateaux, and young boys and girls pinched by years of hunger that was not quite starvation. It was from these people that I learned a good deal about the psychology of German soldiers during the battles of the Somme. They told me of the terror of these men at the increasing fury of our gun-fire, of their desertion and revolt to escape the slaughter, and of their rage against the "Great People" who used them for gun-fodder. Habitually many of them talked of the war as the "Great Swindle." These French civilians hated the Germans in the mass with a cold, deadly hatred. They spoke with shrill passion at the thought of German discipline, fines, punishments, requisitions, which they had suffered in these years. The hope of vengeance was like water to parched throats. Yet I noticed that nearly every one of these people had something good to say about some German soldier who had been billeted with them. "He was a good-natured fellow. He chopped wood for me and gave the children his own bread. He wept when he told me that the village was to be destroyed." Even some of the German officers had deplored this destruction. "The world will have a right to call us barbarians," said one of them in Ham. "But what can we do? We are under orders. If we do not obey we shall be shot. It is the cruelty of the High Command. It is the cruelty of war."

On the whole it seemed they had not misused the women. I heard no tales of actual atrocity, though some of brutal passion. But many women shrugged their shoulders when I questioned them about this and said: "They had no need to use violence in their way of love—making. There were many volunteers."

They rubbed their thumbs and fingers together as though touching money and said, "You understand?"

I understood when I went to a convent in Amiens and saw a crowd of young mothers with flaxen-haired babies, just arrived from the liberated districts. "All those are the children of German fathers," said the old Reverend Mother. "That is the worst tragedy of war. How will God punish all this? Alas! it is the innocent who suffer for the guilty."

Eighteen months later, or thereabouts, I went into a house in Cologne, where a British outpost was on the Hohenzollern bridge. There was a babies' creche in an upper room, and a German lady was tending thirty little ones whose chorus of *"Guten Tag! Guten Tag!"* was like the quacking of ducks.

"After to-morrow there will be no more milk for them," she said.

"And then?" I asked.

"And then many of them will die."

She wept a little. I thought of those other babies in Amiens, and of the old Reverend Mother.

"How will God punish all this? Alas! it is the innocent who suffer for the guilty."

Of those things General Ludendorff does not write in his Memoirs, which deal with the strategy and machinery of war.

III

Sir Douglas Haig was not misled into the error of following up the German retreat, across that devastated country, with masses of men. He sent forward outposts to keep in touch with the German rear-guards and prepared to deliver big blows at the Vimy Ridge and the lines round Arras. This new battle by British troops was dictated by French strategy rather than by ours. General Nivelle, the new generalissimo, was organizing a great offensive in the Champagne and desired the British army to strike first and keep on striking in order to engage and exhaust German divisions until he was ready to launch his own legions. The "secret" of his preparations was known by every officer in the French army and by Hindenburg and his staff, who prepared a new method of defense to meet it. The French officers with whom I talked were supremely confident of success. "We shall go through," they said. "It is certain. Anybody who thinks otherwise is a traitor who betrays his country by the poison of pessimism. Nivelle will deal the death—blow." So spoke an officer of the Chasseurs Alpins, and a friend in the infantry of the line, over a cup of coffee in an estaminet crammed with other French soldiers who were on their way to the Champagne front.

Nivelle did not launch his offensive until April 16th, seven days after the British had captured the heights of Vimy and gone far to the east of Arras. Hindenburg was ready. He adopted his "elastic system of defense," which consisted in withdrawing the main body of his troops beyond the range of the French barrage fire, leaving only a few outposts to camouflage the withdrawal and be sacrificed for the sake of the others (those German outposts must have disliked their martyrdom under orders, and I doubt whether they, poor devils, were exhilarated by the thought of their heroic service). He also withdrew the full power of his artillery beyond the range of French counter-battery work and to such a distance that when it was the German turn to fire the French infantry would be beyond the effective protection of their own guns. They were to be allowed an easy walk through to their death-trap. That is what happened. The French infantry, advancing with masses of black troops in the Colonial Corps in the front-line of assault, all exultant and inspired by a belief in victory, swept through the forward zone of the German defenses, astonished, and then disconcerted by the scarcity of Germans, until an annihilating barrage fire dropped upon them and smashed their human waves. From French officers and nurses I heard appalling tales of this tragedy. The death—wail of the black troops froze the blood of Frenchmen with horror. Their own losses were immense in a bloody shambles. I was told by French officers that their losses on the first day of battle were 150,000 casualties, and these figures were generally believed. They were not so bad as that, though terrible. Semi-official figures state that the operations which lasted from April 16th to April 25th cost France 28,000 killed on the field of battle, 5,000 who died of wounds in hospital, 4,000 prisoners, and 80,000 wounded. General Nivelle's offensive was called off, and French officers who had said, "We shall break through... It is certain," now said: "We came up against a bec de gaz. As you English would say, we 'got it in the neck.' It is a great misfortune."

The battle of Arras, in which the British army was engaged, began on April 9th, an Easter Sunday, when there was a gale of sleet and snow. From ground near the old city of Arras I saw the preliminary bombardment when the Vimy Ridge was blasted by a hurricane of fire and the German lines beyond Arras were tossed up in earth and flame. From one of old Vauban's earthworks outside the walls I saw lines of our men going up in assault beyond the suburbs of Blangy and St.-Laurent to Roclincourt, through a veil of sleet and smoke. Our gun-fire was immense and devastating, and the first blow that fell upon the enemy was overpowering. The Vimy Ridge was captured from end to end by the Canadians on the left and the 51st Division of Highlanders on the right. By the afternoon the entire living German population, more than seven thousand in the tunnels of Vimy, were down below in the valley on our side of the lines, and on the ridge were many of their dead as I saw them afterward horribly mangled by shell-fire in the upheaved earth. The Highland Division, commanded by General Harper—"Uncle Harper," he was called—had done as well as the Canadians, though they had less honor, and took as many prisoners. H.D. was their divisional sign as I saw it stenciled on many ruined walls throughout the war. "Well, General," said a Scottish sergeant, "they don't call us Harper's Duds any more!"... On the right English county troops of the 12th Division, 3d Division, and others, the 15th (Scottish) and the 36th (London) had broken through, deeply and widely, capturing many men and guns after hard fighting round machine-gun redoubts. That night masses of German prisoners suffered terribly from a blizzard in the barbed-wire cages at Etrun, by Arras, where Julius Caesar had his camp for a year in other days of history. They herded together with their bodies bent to the storm, each man sheltering his fellow and giving a little human warmth. All night through a German commandant sat in our Intelligence hut with his head bowed on his breast. Every now and then he said: "It is cold! It is cold!" And our men lay out in the captured ground beyond Arras and on the Vimy Ridge, under harassing fire and machine-gun fire, cold, too, in that wild blizzard, with British dead and German dead in the mangled earth about them.

Ludendorff admits the severity of that defeat.

"The battle near Arras on April 9th formed a bad beginning to the capital fighting during this year.

"April 10th and the succeeding days were critical days. A breach twelve thousand to fifteen thousand yards wide and as much as six thousand yards and more in depth is not a thing to be mended without more ado. It takes a good deal to repair the inordinate wastage of men and guns as well as munitions that results from such a breach. It was the business of the Supreme Command to provide reserves on a large scale. But in view of the troops available, and of the war situation, it was simply not possible to hold a second division in readiness behind each division that might, perhaps, be about to drop out. A day like April 9th upset all calculations. It was a matter of days before a new front could be formed and consolidated. Even after the troops were ultimately in line the issue of the crisis depended, as always in such cases, very materially upon whether the enemy followed up his initial success with a fresh attack and by fresh successes made it difficult for us to create a firm front. In view of the weakening of the line that inevitably resulted, such successes were only too easy to achieve.

"From April 10th onward the English attacked in the breach in great strength, but after all not in the grand manner; they extended their attack on both wings, especially to the southward as far as Bullecourt. On April 11th they gained Monchy, while we during the night before the 12th evacuated the Vimy heights. April 23d and 28th, and also May 3d, were again days of heavy, pitched battle. In between there was some bitter local fighting. The struggle continued, we delivered minor successful counter-attacks, and on the other hand lost ground slightly at various points."

I remember many pictures of that fighting round Arras in the days that followed the first day. I remember the sinister beauty of the city itself, when there was a surging traffic of men and guns through its ruined streets in spite of long-range shells which came crashing into the houses. Our soldiers, in their steel hats and goatskin coats, looked like medieval men-at-arms. The Highlanders who crowded Arras had their pipe-bands there and they played in the Petite Place, and the skirl of the pipes shattered against the gables of old houses. There were tunnels beneath Arras through which our men advanced to the German lines, and I went along them when one line of men was going into battle and another was coming back, wounded, some of them blind, bloody, vomiting with the fumes of gas in their lungs—their steel hats clinking as they groped past one another. In vaults each side of these passages men played cards on barrels, to the light of candles stuck in bottles, or slept until their turn to fight, with gas-masks for their pillows. Outside the Citadel of Arras, built by Vauban under Louis XIV, there were long queues of wounded men taking their turn to the surgeons who were working in a deep crypt with a high-vaulted roof. One day there were three thousand of them, silent, patient, muddy, blood-stained. Blind boys or men with smashed faces swathed in bloody rags groped forward to the dark passage leading to the vault, led by comrades. On the grass outside lay men with leg wounds and stomach wounds. The way past the station to the Arras-Cambrai road was a death-trap for our transport and I saw the bodies of horses and men horribly mangled there. Dead horses were thick on each side of an avenue of trees on the southern side of the city, lying in their blood and bowels. The traffic policeman on "point duty" on the Arras-Cambrai road had an impassive face under his steel helmet, as though in Piccadilly Circus; only turned his head a little at the scream of a shell which plunged through the gable of a corner house above him. There was a Pioneer battalion along the road out to Observatory Ridge, which was a German target. They were mending the road beyond the last trench, through which our men had smashed their way. They were busy with bricks and shovels, only stopping to stare at shells plowing holes in the fields on each side of them. When I came back one morning a number of them lay covered with blankets, as though asleep. They were dead, but their comrades worked on grimly, with no joy of labor in their sweat.

Monchy Hill was the key position, high above the valley of the Scarpe. I saw it first when there was a white village there, hardly touched by fire, and afterward when there was no village. I was in the village below Observatory Ridge on the morning of April 11th when cavalry was massed on that ground, waiting for orders to go into action. The headquarters of the cavalry division was in a ditch covered by planks, and the cavalry generals and their staffs sat huddled together with maps over their knees. "I am afraid the general is busy for the moment," said a young staff-officer on top of the ditch. He looked about the fields and said, "It's very unhealthy here." I agreed with him. The bodies of many young soldiers lay about. Five-point-nines (5.9's) were coming over in a haphazard way. It was no ground for cavalry. But some squadrons of the 10th Hussars, Essex Yeomanry, and the Blues were ordered to take Monchy, and rode up the hill in a flurry of snow and were seen by German gunners and slashed by shrapnel. Most of their horses were killed in the village or outside it, and the men suffered many casualties, including their general—Bulkely Johnson—whose body I saw carried back on a stretcher to the ruin of Thilloy, where crumps were bursting. It is an astonishing thing that two withered old French women stayed in the village all through the fighting. When our troops rode in these women came running forward, frightened and crying "Camarades!" as though in fear of the enemy. When our men surrounded them they were full of joy and held up their scraggy old faces to be kissed by these troopers. Afterward Monchy was filled with a fury of shell-fire and the troopers crawled out from the ruins, leaving the village on the hill to be attacked and captured again by our infantry of the 15th and 37th Divisions, who were also badly hammered.

Heroic folly! The cavalry in reserve below Observatory Hill stood to their horses, staring up at a German airplane which came overhead, careless of our "Archies." The eye of the German pilot must have widened at the sight of that mass of men and horses. He carried back glad tidings to the guns.

One of the cavalry officers spoke to me.

"You look ill."

"No, I'm all right. Only cold."

The officer himself looked worn and haggard after a night in the open.

"Do you think the Germans will get their range as far as this? I'm nervous about the men and the horses. We've been here for hours, and it seems no good."

I did not remind him that the airplane was undoubtedly the herald of long-range shells. They came within a few minutes. Some men and horses were killed. I was with a Highland officer and we took cover in a ditch not more than breast high. Shells were bursting damnably close, scattering us with dirt.

"Let's strike away from the road," said Major Schiach. "They always tape it out."

We struck across country, back to Arras, glad to get there... other men had to stay.

The battles to the east of Arras that went before the capture of Monchy and followed it were hard, nagging actions along the valley of the Scarpe, which formed a glacis, where our men were terribly exposed to machine—gun fire, and suffered heavily day after day, week after week, for no object apparent to our battalion officers and men, who did not know that they were doing team-work for the French. The Londoners of the 56th Division made a record advance through Neuville-Vitasse to Henin and Heninel, and broke a switch-line of the Hindenburg system across the little Cojeul River by Wancourt. There was a fatal attack in the dark on May 3d, when East Kents and Surreys and Londoners saw a gray dawn come, revealing the enemy between them and our main line, and had to hack their way through if they could, There were many who could not, and even divisional generals were embittered by these needless losses and by the hard driving of their men, saying fierce things about our High Command.

Their language was mild compared with that of some of our young officers. I remember one I met near Henin. He was one of a group of three, all gunner officers who were looking about for better gun positions not so clearly visible to the enemy, who was in two little woods—the Bois de Sart and Bois Vert—which stared down upon them like green eyes. Some of their guns had been destroyed, many of their horses killed; some of their men. A few minutes before our meeting a shell had crashed into a bath close to their hut, where men were washing themselves. The explosion filled the bath with blood and bits of flesh. The younger officer stared at me under the tilt forward of his steel hat and said, "Hullo, Gibbs!" I had played chess with him at Groom's Cafe in Fleet Street in days before the war. I went back to his hut and had tea with him, close to that bath, hoping that we should not be cut up with the cake. There were noises "off," as they say in stage directions, which were enormously disconcerting to one's peace of mind, and not very far off. I had heard before some hard words about our generalship and staff-work, but never anything so passionate, so violent, as from that gunner officer. His view of the business was summed up in the word "murder." He raged against the impossible orders sent down from headquarters, against the brutality with which men were left in the line week after week, and against the monstrous, abominable futility of all our so-called strategy. His nerves were in rags, as I could see by the way in which his hand shook when he lighted one cigarette after another. His spirit was in a flame of revolt against the misery of his sleeplessness, filth, and imminent peril of death. Every shell that burst near Henin sent a shudder through him. I stayed an hour in his hut, and then went away toward Neuville-Vitasse with harassing fire following along the way. I looked back many times to the valley, and to the ridges where the enemy lived above it, invisible but deadly. The sun was setting and there was a tawny glamour in the sky, and a mystical beauty over the landscape despite the desert that war had made there, leaving only white ruins and slaughtered trees where once there were good villages with church spires rising out of sheltering woods. The German gunners were doing their evening hate. Crumps were bursting heavily again amid our gun positions.

Heninel was not a choice spot. There were other places of extreme unhealthfulness where our men had fought their way up to the Hindenburg line, or, as the Germans called it, the Siegfried line. Croisille and Cherisy were targets of German guns, and I saw them ravaging among the ruins, and dodged them. But our men, who lived close to these places, stayed there too long to dodge them always. They were inhabitants, not visitors. The Australians settled down in front of Bullecourt, captured it after many desperate fights, which left them with a bitter grudge against tanks which had failed them and some English troops who were held up on the left while they went forward and were slaughtered. The 4th Australian Division lost three thousand men in an experimental attack directed by the Fifth Army. They made their gun emplacements in the Noreuil Valley, the valley of death as they called it, and Australian gunners made little slit trenches and scuttled into them when the Germans ranged on their batteries, blowing gun spokes and wheels and breech-blocks into the air. Queant, the bastion of the Hindenburg line, stared straight down the valley, and it was evil ground, as I knew when I went walking there with another war correspondent and an Australian officer who at a great pace led us round about, amid 5.9's, and debouched a little to see one of our ammunition-dumps exploding like a Brock's Benefit, and chattered brightly under "woolly bears" which made a rending tumult above our heads. I think he enjoyed his afternoon out from staff-work in the headquarters huts. Afterward I was told that he was mad, but I think he was only brave. I hated those hours, but put on the mask that royalty wears when it takes an intelligent interest in factory-work.

The streams of wounded poured down into the casualty clearing stations day by day, week by week, and I saw the crowded Butchers' Shops of war, where busy surgeons lopped at limbs and plugged men's wounds.

Yet in those days, as before and afterward, as at the beginning and as at the end, the spirits of British soldiers kept high unless their bodies were laid low. Between battles they enjoyed their spells of rest behind the lines. In that early summer of '17 there was laughter in Arras, lots of fun in spite of high velocities, the music of massed pipers and brass bands, jolly comradeship in billets with paneled walls upon which perhaps Robespierre's shadow had fallen in the candle-light before the Revolution, when he was the good young man of Arras.

As a guest of the Gordons, of the 15th Division, I listened to the pipers who marched round the table and stood behind the colonel's chair and mine, and played the martial music of Scotland, until something seemed to break in my soul and my ear-drums. I introduced a French friend to the mess, and as a guest of honor he sat next to the colonel, and the eight pipers played behind his chair. He went pale, deadly white, and presently swooned off his chair... and the Gordons thought it the finest tribute to their pipes!

The officers danced reels in stocking feet with challenging cries, Gaelic exhortations, with fine grace and passion, though they were tangled sometimes in the maze... many of them fell in the fields outside or in the bogs of Flanders.

On the western side of Arras there were field sports by London men, and Surreys, Buffs, Sussex, Norfolks, Suffolks, and Devons. They played cricket between their turns in the line, lived in the sunshine of the day, and did not look forward to the morrow. At such times one found no trace of war's agony in their faces or their eyes nor in the quality of their laughter.

My dwelling-place at that time, with other war correspondents, was in an old white chateau between St.-Pol and Hesdin, from which we motored out to the line, Arras way or Vimy way, for those walks in Queer Street. The contrast of our retreat with that Armageddon beyond was profound and bewildering. Behind the old white house were winding walks through little woods beside the stream which Henry crossed on his way to Agincourt; tapestried in early spring with bluebells and daffodils and all the flowers that Ronsard wove into his verse in the springtime of France. Birds sang their love-songs in the thickets. The tits twittered fearfully at the laugh of the jay. All that beauty was like a sharp pain at one's heart after hearing the close tumult of the guns and trudging over the blasted fields of war, in the routine of our task, week by week, month by month.

"This makes for madness," said a friend of mine, a musician surprised to find himself a soldier. "In the morning we see boys with their heads blown off"—that morning beyond the Point du Jour and Thelus we had passed a group of headless boys, and another coming up stared at them with a silly smile and said, "They've copped it all right!" and went on to the same risk; and we had crouched below mounds of earth when shells had scattered dirt over us and scared us horribly, so that we felt a little sick in the stomach—"and in the afternoon we walk through this garden where the birds are singing... There is no sense in it. It's just midsummer madness!"

But only one of us went really mad and tried to cut his throat, and died. One of the best, as I knew him at his best.

IV

The battles of the Third Army beyond Arras petered out and on June 7th there was the battle of Messines and Wytschaete when the Second Army revealed its mastery of organization and detail. It was the beginning of a vastly ambitious scheme to capture the whole line of ridges through Flanders, of which this was the southern hook, and then to liberate the Belgian coast as far inland as Bruges by a combined sea-and-land attack with shoregoing tanks, directed by the Fourth Army. This first blow at the Messines Ridge was completely and wonderfully successful, due to the explosion of seventeen enormous mines under the German positions, followed by an attack "in depth," divisions passing through each other, or "leap-frogging," as it was called, to the final objectives against an enemy demoralized by the earthquake of the explosions.

For two years there had been fierce underground fighting at Hill 60 and elsewhere, when our tunnelers saw the Germans had listened to one another's workings, racing to strike through first to their enemies' galleries and touch off their high-explosive charges. Our miners, aided by the magnificent work of Australian and Canadian tunnelers, had beaten the enemy into sheer terror of their method of fighting and they had abandoned it, believing that we had also. But we did not, as they found to their cost.

I had seen the working of the tunnelers up by Hill 70 and elsewhere. I had gone into the darkness of the tunnels, crouching low, striking my steel hat with sharp, spine-jarring knocks against the low beams overhead, coming into galleries where one could stand upright and walk at ease in electric light, hearing the vibrant hum of great engines, the murmur of men's voices in dark crypts, seeing numbers of men sleeping on bunks in the gloom of caverns close beneath the German lines, and listening through a queer little instrument called a microphone, by which I heard the scuffle of German feet in German galleries a thousand yards away, the dropping of a pick or shovel, the knocking out of German pipes against charcoal stoves. It was by that listening instrument, more perfect than the enemy's, that we had beaten him, and by the grim determination of those underground men of ours, whose skin was the color of the chalk in which they worked, who coughed in the dampness of the caves, and who packed high explosives at the shaft-heads—hundreds of tons of it—for the moment when a button should be touched far away, and an electric current would pass down a wire, and the enemy and his works would be blown into dust.

That moment came at Hill 60 and sixteen other places below the Wytschaete and Messines Ridge at three-thirty on the morning of June 7th, after a quiet night of war, when a few of our batteries had fired in a desultory way and the enemy had sent over some flocks of gas-shells, and before the dawn I heard the cocks crow on Kemmel Hill. I saw the seventeen mines go up, and earth and flame gush out of them as though the fires of hell had risen. A terrible sight, as the work of men against their fellow—creatures... It was the signal for seven hundred and fifty of our heavy guns and two thousand of our field—guns to open fire, and behind a moving wall of bursting shells English, Irish, and New Zealand soldiers moved forward in dense waves. It was almost a "walk-over." Only here and there groups of Germans served their machine-guns to the death. Most of the living were stupefied amid their dead in the upheaved trenches, slashed woods, and deepest dugouts. I walked to the edge of the mine-craters and stared into their great gulfs, wondering how many German bodies had been engulfed there. The following day I walked through Wytschaete Wood to the ruins of the Hospice on the ridge. In 1914 some of our cavalry had passed this way when the Hospice was a big red-brick building with wings and outhouses and a large community of nuns and children. Through my glasses I had often seen its ruins from Kemmel Hill and the Scherpenberg. Now nothing was left but a pile of broken bricks, not very high. Our losses were comparatively small, though some brave men had died, including Major Willie Redmond, whose death in Wytschaete Wood was heard with grief in Ireland.

Ludendorff admits the severity of the blow:

"The moral effect of the explosions was simply staggering... The 7th of June cost us dear, and, owing to the success of the enemy attack, the price we paid was very heavy. Here, too, it was many days before the front was again secure. The British army did not press its advantage; apparently it only intended to improve its position for the launching of the great Flanders offensive. It thereupon resumed operations between the old Arras battlefield and also between La Bassee and Lens. The object of the enemy was to wear us down and distract our attention from Ypres."

That was true. The Canadians made heavy attacks at Lens, some of which I saw from ground beyond Notre Dame de Lorette and the Vimy Ridge and the enemy country by Grenay, when those men besieged a long chain of mining villages which girdled Lens itself, where every house was a machine-gun fort above deep tunnels. I saw them after desperate struggles, covered in clay, parched with thirst, gassed, wounded, but indomitable. Lens was the Troy of the Canadian Corps and the English troops of the First Army, and it was only owing to other battles they were called upon to fight in Flanders that they had to leave it at last uncaptured, for the enemy to escape.

All this was subsidiary to the great offensive in Flanders, with its ambitious objects. But when the battles of Flanders began the year was getting past its middle age, and events on other fronts had upset the strategical plan of Sir Douglas Haig and our High Command. The failure and abandonment of the Nivelle offensive in the Champagne were disastrous to us. It liberated many

German divisions who could be sent up to relieve exhausted divisions in Flanders. Instead of attacking the enemy when he was weakening under assaults elsewhere, we attacked him when all was quiet on the French front. The collapse of Russia was now happening and our policy ought to have been to save men for the tremendous moment of 1918, when we should need all our strength. So it seems certain now, though it is easy to prophesy after the event.

I went along the coast as far as Coxyde and Nieuport and saw secret preparations for the coast offensive. We were building enormous gun emplacements at Malo-les—Bains for long-range naval guns, camouflaged in sand—dunes. Our men were being trained for fighting in the dunes. Our artillery positions were mapped out.

"Three shots to one, sir," said Sir Henry Rawlinson to the King, "that's the stuff to give them!"

But the Germans struck the first blow up there, not of importance to the strategical position, but ghastly to two battalions of the 1st Division, cut off on a spit of land at Lombartzyde and almost annihilated under a fury of fire.

At this time the enemy was developing his use of a new poison-gas—mustard gas—which raised blisters and burned men's bodies where the vapor was condensed into a reddish powder and blinded them for a week or more, if not forever, and turned their lungs to water. I saw hundreds of these cases in the 3rd Canadian casualty clearing station on the coast, and there were thousands all along our front. At Oast Dunkerque, near Nieuport, I had a whiff of it, and was conscious of a burning sensation about the lips and eyelids, and for a week afterward vomited at times, and was scared by queer flutterings of the heart which at night seemed to have but a feeble beat. It was enough to "put the wind up." Our men dreaded the new danger, so mysterious, so stealthy in its approach. It was one of the new plagues of war.

V

The battle of Flanders began round Ypres on July 31st, with a greater intensity of artillery on our side than had ever been seen before in this war in spite of the Somme and Messines, when on big days of battle two thousand guns opened fire on a single corps front. The enemy was strong also in artillery arranged in great groups, often shifting to enfilade our lines of attack. The natural strength of his position along the ridges, which were like a great bony hand outstretched through Flanders, with streams or "beeks," as they are called, flowing in the valleys which ran between the fingers of that clawlike range, were strengthened by chains of little concrete forts or "pill-boxes," as our soldiers called them, so arranged that they could defend one another by enfilade machine-gun fire. These were held by garrisons of machine—gunners of proved resolution, whose duty was to break up our waves of attack until, even if successful in gaining ground, only small bodies of survivors would be in a position to resist the counter-attacks launched by German divisions farther back. The strength of the pill—boxes made of concrete two inches thick resisted everything but the direct hit of heavy shells, and they were not easy targets at long range. The garrisons within them fought often with the utmost courage, even when surrounded, and again and again this method of defense proved terribly effective against the desperate heroic assaults of British infantry.

What our men had suffered in earlier battles was surpassed by what they were now called upon to endure. All the agonies of war which I have attempted to describe were piled up in those fields of Flanders. There was nothing missing in the list of war's abominations. A few days after the battle began the rains began, and hardly ceased for four months. Night after night the skies opened and let down steady torrents, which turned all that country into one great bog of slime. Those little rivers or "beeks," which ran between the knobby fingers of the clawlike range of ridges, were blown out of their channels and slopped over into broad swamps. The hurricanes of artillery fire which our gunners poured upon the enemy positions for twenty miles in depth churned up deep shell-craters which intermingled and made pits which the rains and floods filled to the brim. The only way of walking was by "duck-boards," tracks laid down across the bogs under enemy fire, smashed up day by day, laid down again under cover of darkness. Along a duckboard walk men must march in single file, and if one of our men, heavily laden in his fighting-kit, stumbled on those greasy boards (as all of them stumbled at every few yards) and fell off, he sank up to his knees, often up to his waist, sometimes up to his neck, in mud and water. If he were wounded when he fell, and darkness was about him, he could only cry to God or his pals, for he was helpless otherwise. One of our divisions of Lancashire men—the 66th—took eleven hours in making three miles or so out of Ypres across that ground on their way to attack, and then, in spite of their exhaustion, attacked. Yet week after week, month after month, our masses of men, almost every division in the British army at one time or another, struggled on through that Slough of Despond, capturing ridge after ridge, until the heights at Passchendaele were stormed and won, though even then the Germans clung to Staden and Westroosebeeke when all our efforts came to a dead halt, and that Belgian coast attack was never launched.

Sir Douglas Haig thinks that some of the descriptions of that six months' horror were "exaggerated." As a man who knows something of the value of words, and who saw many of those battle scenes in Flanders, and went out from Ypres many times during those months to the Westhoek Ridge and the Pilkem Ridge, to the Frezenburg and Inverness Copse and Glencourse Wood, and beyond to Polygon Wood and Passchendaele, where his dead lay in the swamps and round the pill-boxes, and where tanks that had wallowed into the mire were shot into scrap-iron by German gun-fire (thirty were knocked out by direct hits on the first day of battle), and where our own guns were being flung up by the harassing fire of heavy shells, I say now that nothing that has been written is more than the pale image of the abomination of those battlefields, and that no pen or brush has yet achieved the picture of that Armageddon in which so many of our men perished.

They were months of ghastly endurance to gunners when batteries sank up to their axles as I saw them often while they fired almost unceasingly for days and nights without sleep, and were living targets of shells which burst about them. They were months of battle in which our men advanced through slime into slime, under the slash of machine-gun bullets, shrapnel, and high explosives, wet to the skin, chilled to the bone, plastered up to the eyes in mud, with a dreadful way back for walking wounded, and but little chance sometimes for wounded who could not walk. The losses in many of these battles amounted almost to annihilation to many battalions, and whole divisions lost as much as 50 per cent of their strength after a few days in action, before they were "relieved." Those were dreadful losses. Napoleon said that no body of men could lose more than 25 per cent of their fighting strength in an action without being broken in spirit. Our men lost double that, and more than double, but kept their courage, though in some cases they lost their hope.

The 55th Division of Lancashire men, in their attacks on a line of pill-boxes called Plum Farm, Schuler Farm, and Square Farm, below the Gravenstafel Spur, lost 3,840 men in casualties out of 6,049. Those were not uncommon losses. They were usual losses. One day's fighting in Flanders (on October 4th) cost the British army ten thousand casualties, and they were considered "light" by the Higher Command in relation to the objects achieved.

General Harper of the 51st (Highland) Division told me that in his opinion the official communiques and the war correspondents' articles gave only one side of the picture of war and were too glowing in their optimism. (I did not tell him that my articles were accused of being black in pessimism, pervading gloom.) "We tell the public," he said, "that an enemy division has been 'shattered.' That is true. But so is mine. One of my brigades has lost eighty-seven officers and two thousand men since the spring." He protested that there was not enough liaison between the fighting-officers and the Higher Command, and could not blame them for their hatred of "the Staff."

The story of the two Irish divisions—the 36th Ulster; and 16th (Nationalist)—in their fighting on August 16th is black in tragedy. They were left in the line for sixteen days before the battle and were shelled and gassed incessantly as they crouched in wet ditches. Every day groups of men were blown to bits, until the ditches were bloody and the living lay by the corpses of their comrades. Every day scores of wounded crawled back through the bogs, if they had the strength to crawl. Before the attack on August 16th the Ulster Division had lost nearly two thousand men. Then they attacked and lost two thousand more, and over one hundred officers. The 16th Division lost as many men before the attack and more officers. The 8th Dublins had been annihilated in holding the line. On the night before the battle hundreds of men were gassed. Then their comrades attacked and lost over two thousand more, and one hundred and sixty—two officers. All the ground below two knolls of earth called Hill 35 and Hill 37, which were defended by German pill-boxes called Pond Farm and Gallipoli, Beck House and Borry Farm, became an Irish shambles. In spite of their dreadful losses the survivors in the Irish battalion went forward to the assault with desperate valor on the morning of August 16th, surrounded the pill-boxes, stormed them through blasts of machine-gun fire, and toward the end of the day small bodies of these men had gained a footing on the objectives which they had been asked to capture, but were then too weak to resist German counter-attacks. The 7th and 8th Royal Irish Fusiliers had been almost exterminated in their efforts to dislodge the enemy from Hill 37. They lost seventeen officers out of twenty-one, and 64 per cent of their men. One company of four officers and one hundred men, ordered to capture the concrete fort known as Borry Farm, at all cost, lost four officers and seventy men. The 9th Dublins lost fifteen officers out of seventeen, and 66 per cent of their men.

The two Irish divisions were broken to bits, and their brigadiers called it murder. They were violent in their denunciation of the Fifth Army for having put their men into the attack after those thirteen days of heavy shelling, and after the battle they complained that they were cast aside like old shoes, no care being taken for the comfort of the men who had survived. No motor-lorries were sent to meet them and bring them down, but they had to tramp back, exhausted and dazed. The remnants of the 16th Division, the poor, despairing remnants, were sent, without rest or baths, straight into the line again, down south.

I found a general opinion among officers and men, not only of the Irish Division, under the command of the Fifth Army, that they had been the victims of atrocious staff-work, tragic in its consequences. From what I saw of some of the Fifth Army staff-officers I was of the same opinion. Some of these young gentlemen, and some of the elderly officers, were arrogant and supercilious without revealing any symptoms of intelligence. If they had wisdom it was deeply camouflaged by an air of inefficiency. If they had knowledge they hid it as a secret of their own. General Gough, commanding the Fifth Army in Flanders, and afterward north and south of St.-Quentin, where the enemy broke through, was extremely courteous, of most amiable character, with a high sense of duty. But in Flanders, if not personally responsible for many tragic happenings, he was badly served by some of his subordinates; and battalion officers and divisional staffs raged against the whole of the Fifth Army organization, or lack of organization, with an extreme passion of speech.

"You must be glad to leave Flanders," I said to a group of officers trekking toward the Cambrai salient.

One of them answered, violently: "God be thanked we are leaving the Fifth Army area!"

In an earlier chapter of this book I have already paid a tribute to the Second Army, and especially to Sir John Harington, its chief of staff. There was a thoroughness of method, a minute attention to detail, a care for the comfort and spirit of the men throughout the Second Army staff which did at least inspire the troops with the belief that whatever they did in the fighting-lines had been prepared, and would be supported, with every possible help that organization could provide. That belief was founded not upon fine words spoken on parade, but by strenuous work, a driving zeal, and the fine intelligence of a chief of staff whose brain was like a high-power engine.

I remember a historic little scene in the Second Army headquarters at Cassel, in a room where many of the great battles had been planned, when Sir John Harington made the dramatic announcement that Sir Herbert Plumer, and he, as General Plumer's chief of staff, had been ordered to Italy—in the middle of a battle—to report on the situation which had become so grave there. He expressed his regret that he should have to leave Flanders without completing all his plans, but was glad that Passchendaele had been captured before his going.

In front of him was the map of the great range from Wytschaete to Staden, and he laid his hand upon it and smiled and said: "I often used to think how much of that range we should get this year. Now it is nearly all ours." He thanked the war correspondents for all their articles, which had been very helpful to the army, and said how glad he had been to have our co-operation.

"It was my ambition," he said, speaking with some emotion, "to make cordial relations between battalion officers and the staff, and to get rid of that criticism (sometimes just) which has been directed against the staff. The Second Army has been able to show the fighting soldiers that the success of a battle depends greatly on efficient staff work, and has inspired them with confidence in the preparations and organization behind the lines."

Yet it seemed to me, in my pessimism, and seems to me still, in my memory of all that ghastly fighting, that the fine mechanism of the Second Army applied to those battles in Flanders was utterly misspent, that after the first heavy rains had fallen the offensive ought to have been abandoned, and that it was a frightful error of judgment to ask masses of men to attack in conditions where they had not a dog's chance of victory, except at a cost which made it of Pyrrhic irony.

Nevertheless, it was wearing the enemy out, as well as our own strength in man-power. He could less afford to lose his one man than we could our three, now that the United States had entered the war. Ludendorff has described the German agony, and days of battle which he calls "terrific," inflicting "enormous loss" upon his armies and increasing his anxiety at the "reduction of our fighting strength."

"Enormous masses of ammunition, the like of which no mortal mind before the war had conceived, were hurled against human beings who lay, eking out but a bare existence, scattered in shell-holes that were deep in slime. The terror of it surpassed even that of the shell-pitted field before Verdun. This was not life; it was agony unspeakable. And out of the universe of slime the attacker wallowed forward, slowly but continually, and in dense masses. Time and again the enemy, struck by the hail of our projectiles in the fore field, collapsed, and our lonely men in the shell-holes breathed again. Then the mass came on. Rifle and machine-gun were beslimed. The struggle was man to man, and—only too often—it was the mass that won.

"What the German soldier accomplished, lived through, and suffered during the Flanders battle will stand in his honor for all time as a brazen monument that he set himself with his own hands on enemy soil!

"The enemy's losses, too, were heavy. When, in the spring of 1918, we occupied the battlefield, it presented a horrible spectacle with its many unburied dead. Their number ran into thousands. Two-thirds of them were enemy dead; one-third were German soldiers who had met here a hero's death.

"And yet the truth must be told; individual units no longer surmounted as before the demoralizing influences of the defensive campaign.

"October 26th and 30th and November 6th and 10th were also days of pitched battle of the heaviest kind. The enemy stormed like a wild bull against the iron wall that kept him at a distance from our U-boat base. He hurled his weight against the Houthulst Wood; he hurled it against Poelcapelle, Passchendaele, Becelaere, Gheluvelt, and Zandvoorde; at very many points he dented the line. It seemed as if he would charge down the wall; but, although a slight tremor passed through its foundation, the wall held. The impressions that I continued to receive were extremely grave. Tactically everything had been done; the fore field was good. Our artillery practice had materially improved. Behind nearly every fighting—division there stood a second, as rear wave. In the third line, too, there were still reserves. We knew that the wear and tear of the enemy's forces was high. But we also knew that the enemy was extraordinarily strong and, what was equally important, possessed extraordinary will-power."

That was the impression of the cold brain directing the machinery of war from German headquarters. More human and more tragic is a letter of an unknown German officer which we found among hundreds of others, telling the same tale, in the mud of the battlefield:

"If it were not for the men who have been spared me on this fierce day and are lying around me, and looking timidly at me, I should shed hot and bitter tears over the terrors that have menaced me during these hours. On the morning of September 18th my dugout containing seventeen men was shot to pieces over our heads. I am the only one who withstood the maddening bombardment of three days and still survives. You cannot imagine the frightful mental torments I have undergone in those few hours. After crawling out through the bleeding remnants of my comrades, and through the smoke and debris, wandering and running in the midst of the raging gun-fire in search of a refuge, I am now awaiting death at any moment. You do not know what Flanders means. Flanders means endless human endurance. Flanders means blood and scraps of human bodies. Flanders means heroic courage and faithfulness even unto death."

To British and to Germans it meant the same.

VI

During the four and a half months of that fighting the war correspondents were billeted in the old town of Cassel, where, perched on a hill which looks over a wide stretch of Flanders, through our glasses we could see the sand-dunes beyond Dunkirk and with the naked eyes the whole vista of the battle-line round Ypres and in the wide curve all the countryside lying between Aire and Hazebrouck and Notre Dame de Lorette. My billet was in a monastery for old priests, on the eastern edge of the town, and at night my window was lighted by distant shell-fire, and I gazed out to a sky of darkness rent by vivid flashes, bursts of red flame, and rockets rising high. The priests used to tap at my door when I came back from the battlefields all muddy, with a slime-plastered face, writing furiously, and an old *padre* used to plague me like that, saying:

"What news? It goes well, eh? Not too well, perhaps! Alas! it is a slaughter on both sides."

"It is all your fault," I said once, chaffingly, to get rid of him. "You do not pray enough."

He grasped my wrist with his skinny old hand.

"Monsieur," he whispered, "after eighty years I nearly lose my faith in God. That is terrible, is it not? Why does not God give us victory? Alas! perhaps we have sinned too much!"

One needed great faith for courage then, and my courage (never much to boast about) ebbed low those days, when I agonized over our losses and saw the suffering of our men and those foul swamps where the bodies of our boys lay in pools of slime, vividly colored by the metallic vapors of high explosives, beside the gashed tree-stumps; and the mangled corpses of Germans who had died outside their pill-boxes; and when I saw dead horses on the roads out of Ypres, and transport drivers dead beside their broken wagons, and officers of ours with the look of doomed men, nerve-shaken, soul-stricken, in captured blockhouses, where I took a nip of whisky with them now and then before they attacked again; and groups of dazed prisoners coming down the tracks through their own harrowing fire; and always, always, streams of wounded by tens of thousands.

There was an old mill-house near Vlamertinghe, beyond Goldfish Chateau, which was made into a casualty clearing station, and scores of times when I passed it I saw it crowded with the "walking wounded," who had trudged down from the fighting-line, taking eleven hours, fourteen hours sometimes, to get so far. They were no longer "cheerful" like the gay lads who came lightly wounded out of earlier battles, glad of life, excited by their luck. They were silent, shivering, stricken men; boys in age, but old and weary in the knowledge of war. The slime of the battlefields had engulfed them. Their clothes were plastered to their bodies. Their faces and hands were coated with that whitish clay. Their steel hats and rifles were caked with it. Their eyes, brooding, were strangely alive in those corpselike figures of mud who huddled round charcoal stoves or sat motionless on wooden forms, waiting for ambulances. Yet they were stark in spirit still.

"Only the mud beat us," they said. Man after man said that.

"We should have gone much farther except for the mud."

Along the Menin road there were wayside dressing stations for wounded, with surgeons at work, and I saw the same scenes there. They were not beyond the danger zone. Doctors and orderlies were killed by long-range shells. Wounded were wounded again or finished off. Some ambulances were blown to bits. A colonel who had been standing in talk with a doctor was killed halfway through a sentence.

There was never a day in which Ypres was not shelled by long-range high velocities which came howling overhead as I heard them scores of times in passing through those ruins with gas-mask at the alert, according to orders, and steel hat strapped on, and a deadly sense of nostalgia because of what was happening in the fields of horror that lay beyond. Yet to the soldier farther up the Menin road Ypres was sanctuary and God's heaven.

The little old town of Cassel on the hill—where once a Duke of York marched up and then marched down again—was beyond shell-range, though the enemy tried to reach it and dropped twelve-inch shells (which make holes deep enough to bury a coach and horses) round its base. There is an inn there—the Hotel du Sauvage—which belongs now to English history, and Scottish and Irish and Welsh and Australian and Canadian. It was the last place along the road to Ypres where men who loved life could get a dinner sitting with their knees below a table-cloth, with candle-light glinting in glasses, while outside the windows the flickering fires of death told them how short might be their tarrying in the good places of the world. This was a good place where the blinds were pulled down by Madame, who understood. Behind the desk was Mademoiselle Suzanne, "a dainty rogue in porcelain," with wonderfully bright eyes and just a little greeting of a smile for any young officer who looked her way trying to get that greeting, because it was ever so long since he had seen a pretty face and might be ever so long again. Sometimes it was a smile met in the mirror against the wall, to which Suzanne looked to touch her curls and see, like the Lady of Shalott, the pictures of life that passed. A man would tilt his chair to get that angle of vision. Outside, on these nights of war, it was often blusterous, very dark, wet with heavy rain. The door opened, and other officers came in with waterproofs sagging round their legs and top-boots muddy to the tags, abashed because they made pools of water on polished boards.

"Pardon, Madame."

"Ca ne fait rien, Monsieur."

There was a klip-klop of horses' hoofs in the yard. I thought of D'Artagnan and the Musketeers who might have ridden into this very yard, strode into this very room, on their way to Dunkirk or Calais. Madame played the piano remarkably well, classical music of all kinds, and any accompaniment to any song. Our young officers sang. Some of them touched the piano with a loving touch and said, "Ye gods, a piano again!" and played old melodies or merry ragtime. Before Passchendaele was taken a Canadian boy brought a fiddle with him, and played last of all, after other tunes, "The Long, Long Trail," which his comrades sang.

"Come and play to us again," said Madame.

"If I come back," said the boy.

He did not come back along the road through Ypres to Cassel.

From the balcony one could see the nightbirds fly. On every moonlight night German raiders were about bombing our camps and villages. One could see just below the hill how the bombs crashed into St.-Marie Capelle and many hamlets where British soldiers lay, and where peasants and children were killed with them. For some strange reason Cassel itself was never bombed.

"We are a nest of spies," said some of the inhabitants, but others had faith in a miraculous statue, and still others in Sir Herbert Plumer.

Once when a big shell burst very close I looked at Mademoiselle Suzanne behind the desk. She did not show fear by the flicker of an eyelid, though officers in the room were startled.

"Vous n'avez pas peur, meme de la mort?" ("You are not afraid, even of death?") I asked.

She shrugged her shoulders.

"Je m'en fiche de la mort!" ("I don't care a damn for death!")

The Hotel du Sauvage was a pleasant rendezvous, but barred for a time to young gentlemen of the air force, who lingered too long there sometimes and were noisy. It was barred to all officers for certain hours of the day without special permits from the A.P.M., who made trouble in granting them. Three Scottish officers rode down into Cassel. They had ridden down from hell-fire to sit at a table covered with a table-cloth, and drink tea in a room again. They were refused permission, and their language to me about the A.P.M. was unprintable. They desired his blood and bones. They raised their hands to heaven to send down wrath upon all skunks dwelling behind the lines in luxury and denying any kind of comfort to fighting-men. They included the P.M. in their rage, and all staff-officers from Cassel to Boulogne, and away back to Whitehall.

To cheer up the war correspondents' mess when we assembled at night after miserable days, and when in the darkness gusts of wind and rain clouted the window-panes and distant gun-fire rumbled, or bombs were falling in near villages, telling of peasant girls killed in their beds and soldiers mangled in wayside burns, we had the company sometimes of an officer (a black-eyed fellow) who told merry little tales of executions and prison happenings at which he assisted in the course of his duty.

I remember one about a young officer sentenced to death for cowardice (there were quite a number of lads like that). He was blindfolded by a gas-mask fixed on the wrong way round, and pinioned, and tied to a post. The firing—party lost their nerve and their shots were wild. The boy was only wounded, and screamed in his mask, and the A.P.M. had to shoot him twice with his revolver before he died.

That was only one of many little anecdotes told by a gentleman who seemed to like his job and to enjoy these reminiscences.

The battles of Flanders ended with the capture of Passchendaele by the Canadians, and that year's fighting on the western front cost us 800,000 casualties, and though we had dealt the enemy heavy blows from which he reeled back, the drain upon our man-power was too great for what was to happen next year, and our men were too sorely tried. For the first time the British army lost its spirit of optimism, and there was a sense of deadly depression among many officers and men with whom I came in touch. They saw no ending of the war, and nothing except continuous slaughter, such as that in Flanders.

Our men were not mythical heroes exalted by the gods above the limitations of nature. They were human beings, with wives and children, or mothers and sisters, whom they desired to see again. They hated this war. Death had no allurement for them, except now and then as an escape from intolerable life under fire. They would have been superhuman if they had not revolted in spirit, though still faithful to discipline, against the foul conditions of warfare in the swamps, where, in spite of all they had, in that four months or so of fighting, achieved the greatest effort of human courage and endurance ever done by masses of men in obedience to command.

VII

At the end of those battles happened that surprising, audacious adventure in the Cambrai salient organized by the Third Army under General Byng, when on November 20, 1917, squadrons of tanks broke through the Hindenburg line, and infantry streamed through the breach, captured hundreds of guns, ten thousand prisoners, many villages and ridges, and gave a monstrous shock to the German High Command.

The audacity of the adventure lay in the poverty of manpower with which it was attempted and supported. The divisions engaged had all been through the grinding mill of Flanders and were tired men. The artillery was made up largely of those batteries which had been axle—deep in Flanders mud. It was clearly understood by General Byng and Gen. Louis Vaughan, his chief of staff, that Sir Douglas Haig could not afford to give them strong reserves to exploit any success they might gain by surprise or to defend the captured ground against certain counter-attacks. It was to be a surprise assault by tanks and infantry, with the hope that the cavalry corps might find its gap at last and sweep round Cambrai before the enemy could recover and reorganize. With other correspondents I saw Gen. Louis Vaughan, who expounded the scheme before it was launched. That charming man, with his professional manner, sweetness of speech, gentleness of voice and gesture, like an Oxford don analyzing the war correspondence of Xenophon, made no secret of the economy with which the operation would have to be made.

"We must cut our coat according to our cloth," he said.

The whole idea was to seize only as much ground as the initial success could gain, and not to press if resistance became strong. It was a gamble, with a chance of luck. The cavalry might do nothing, or score a big triumph. All depended on the surprise of the tanks. If they were discovered before the assault the whole adventure would fail at the start.

They had been brought up secretly by night, four hundred of them, with supply-tanks for ammunition and petrol lying hidden in woods by day. So the artillery and infantry and cavalry had been concentrated also. The enemy believed himself secure in his Hindenburg line, which had been constructed behind broad hedges of barbed wire with such wide ditches that no tank could cross.

How, then, would tanks cross? Ah, that was a little trick which would surprise the Germans mightily. Each tank would advance through the early morning mists with a bridge on its nose. The bridge was really a big "fascine," or bundle of fagots about a yard and a half in diameter, and controlled by a lever and chain from the interior of the tank. Having plowed through the barbed wire and reached the edge of the Hindenburg trench, the tank would drop the fascine into the center of the ditch, stretch out its long body, reach the bundle of fagots, find support on it, and use it as a stepping-stone to the other side. Very simple in idea and effect!

So it happened, and the mists favored us, as I saw on the morning of the attack at a little place called Beaumont, near Villers Pluich. The enemy was completely surprised, caught at breakfast in his dugouts, rounded up in batches. The tanks went away through the breach they had made, with the infantry swarming round them, and captured Havrincourt, Hermies, Ribecourt, Gouzeaucourt, Masnieres, and Marcoing, and a wide stretch of country forming a cup or amphitheater below a series of low ridges south of Bourlon Wood, where the ground rose again.

It was a spectacular battle, such as we had never seen before, and during the following days, when our troops worked up to Bourlon Wood and through the intervening villages of Anneux, Graincourt, Containg, and Fontaine Notre Dame, I saw tanks going into action and cruising about like landships, with cavalry patrols riding over open ground, airplanes flying low over German territory, and masses of infantry beyond all trench-lines, and streams of liberated civilians trudging through the lines from Marcoing. The enemy was demoralized the first day and made only slight resistance. The chief losses of the tanks were due to a German major of artillery who served his own guns and knocked out a baker's dozen of these monsters as they crawled over the Flesquieres Ridge. I saw them lying there with the blood and bones of their pilots and crews within their steel walls. It was a Highland soldier who checked the German major.

"You're a brave man," he said, "but you've got to dee," and ran him through the stomach with his bayonet. It was this check at the Flesquieres Ridge, followed by the breaking of a bridge at Masnieres under the weight of a tank and the holding of a trench-line called the Rumilly switch by a battalion of Germans who raced to it from Cambrai before our men could capture it, which thwarted the plans of the cavalry. Our cavalry generals were in consultation at their headquarters, too far back to take immediate advantage of the situation. They waited for the capture of the Rumilly switch, and held up masses of cavalry whom I saw riding through the village of Ribecourt, with excitement and exaltation, because they thought that at last their chance had come. Finally orders were given to cancel all previous plans to advance. Only one squadron, belonging to the Canadian Fort Garry Horse in General Seely's division, failed to receive the order (their colonel rode after them, but his horse slipped and fell before he caught them up), and it was their day of heroic folly. They rode fast and made their way through a gap in the wire cut by the troopers, and came under rifle and machine-gun fire, which wounded the captain and several men.

The command was carried on by a young lieutenant, who rode with his men until they reached the camouflaged road southeast of the village of Rumilly, where they went through in sections under the fire of the enemy hidden in the banks. Here they came up against a battery of field-guns, one of which fired point-blank at them. They charged the battery, putting the guns out of action and killing some of the gunners. Those who were not destroyed surrendered, and the prisoners were left to be sent back by the supports. The squadron then dealt with the German infantry in the neighborhood. Some of them fled, while some were killed or surrendered. All these operations were done at a gallop under fire from flanking blockhouses. The squadron then slowed down to a walk and took up a position in a sunken road one kilometer east of Rumilly. Darkness crept down upon them, and gradually they were surrounded by German infantry with machine-guns, so that they were in great danger of capture or destruction. Only five of their horses remained unhit, and the lieutenant in command decided that they must endeavor to cut their way through and get back. The horses were stampeded in the direction of the enemy in order to draw the machine-gun fire, and while these riderless horses galloped wildly out of one end of the sunken road, the officer and his surviving troopers escaped from the other end. On the way back they encountered four bodies of the enemy, whom they attacked and routed. On one occasion their escape was due to the cunning of another young lieutenant, who spoke German and held conversations with the enemy in the darkness, deceiving them as to the identity of his force until they were able to take the German troops by surprise and hack a way through. This lieutenant was hit in the face by a bullet, and when he arrived back in Masnieres with his men in advance of the rear-guard he was only able to make his report before falling in a state of collapse.

Other small bodies of cavalry—among them the 8th Dragoons and 5th Hussars—had wild, heroic adventures in the Cambrai salient, where they rode under blasts of machine-gun fire and rounded up prisoners in the ruined villages of Noyelles and Fontaine Notre Dame. Some of them went into the Folie Wood nearby and met seven German officers strolling about the glades, as though no war was on. They took them prisoners, but had to release some of them later, as they could not be bothered with them. Later they came across six ammunition—wagons and destroyed them. In the heart of the wood was one of the German divisional headquarters, and one of our cavalry officers dismounted and approached the cottage stealthily, and looked through the windows. Inside was a party of German officers seated at a table, with beer mugs in front of them, apparently unconscious of any danger near them. Our officer fired his revolver through the windows and then, like a schoolboy who has thrown a stone, ran away as hard as he could and joined his troop. Youthful folly of gallant hearts!

After the enemy's surprise his resistance stiffened and he held the village of Fontaine Notre Dame, and Bourlon Wood, on the hill above, with strong rear-guards. Very quickly, too, he brought new batteries into action, and things became unpleasant in fields and villages where our men, as I saw them on those days, hunted around for souvenirs in German dugouts and found field-glasses, automatic pistols, and other good booty.

It seemed to me that the plan as outlined by Gen. Louis Vaughan, not to exploit success farther than justified by the initial surprise, was abandoned for a time. A brigade of Guards was put in to attack Fontaine Notre Dame, and suffered heavily from machine-gun fire before taking it. The 62d (Yorkshire) Division lost many good men in Bourlon Village and Bourlon Wood, into which the enemy poured gas-shells and high explosives.

Then on November 30th the Germans, under the direction of General von Marwitz, came back upon us with a tiger's pounce, in a surprise attack which we ought to have anticipated. I happened to be on the way to Gouzeaucourt early that morning, and, going through the village of Fins, next to it, I saw men straggling back in some disorder, and gun-teams wedged in a dense traffic moving in what seemed to me the wrong direction.

"I don't know what to do," said a young gunner officer. "My battery has been captured and I can't get into touch with the brigade."

"What has happened?" I asked.

He looked at me in surprise.

"Don't you know? The enemy has broken through."

"Broken through where?"

The gunner officer pointed down the road.

"At the present moment he's in Gouzeaucourt."

I went northward, and saw that places like Hermies and Havrincourt, which had been peaceful spots for a few days, were under heavy fire. Bourlon Wood beyond was a fiery furnace. Hell had broken out again and things looked bad. There was a general packing up of dumps and field hospitals and heavy batteries. In Gouzeaucourt and other places our divisional and brigade headquarters were caught napping. Officers were in their pajamas or in their baths when they heard the snap of machine-gun bullets. I saw the Guards go forward to Gouzeaucourt for a counter-attack. They came along munching apples and whistling, as though on peace maneuvers. Next day, after they had gained back Gouzeaucourt, I saw many of them wounded, lying under tarpaulins, all dirty and bloody.

The Germans had adopted our own way of attack. They had assembled masses of troops secretly, moving them forward by night under the cover of woods, so that our air scouts saw no movement by day. Our line was weakly held along the front—the 55th Division, thinned out by losses, was holding a line of thirteen thousand yards, three times as much as any troops can hold, in safety—and the German storm-troops, after a short, terrific bombardment, broke through to a distance of five miles.

Our tired men, who had gained the first victory, fought heroic rear-guard actions back from Masnieres and Marcoing, and back from Bourlon Wood on the northern side of the salient. They made the enemy pay a high price in blood for the success of his counter-attack, but we lost many thousands of brave fellows, and the joy bells which had rung in London on November 20th became sad and ironical music in the hearts of our disappointed people.

So ended 1917, our black year; and in the spring of 1918, after all the losses of that year, our armies on the western front were threatened by the greatest menace that had ever drawn near to them, and the British Empire was in jeopardy.

VIII

In the autumn of 1917 the Italian disaster of Caporetto had happened, and Sir Herbert Plumer, with his chief of staff, Sir John Harington, and many staff-officers of the Second Army, had, as I have told, been sent to Italy with some of our best divisions, so weakening Sir Douglas Haig's command. At that very time, also, after the bloody losses in Flanders, the French government and General Headquarters brought severe pressure upon the British War Council to take over a greater length of line in France, in order to release some of the older classes of the French army who had been under arms since 1914. We yielded to that pressure and Sir Douglas Haig extended his lines north and south of St.-Quentin, where the Fifth Army, under General Gough, was intrusted with the defense.

I went over all that new ground of ours, out from Noyon to Chaulny and Barisis and the floods of the Oise by La Fere; out from Ham to Holmon Forest and Francilly and the Epine de Dullon, and the Fort de Liez by St.-Quentin; and from Peronne to Hargicourt and Jeancourt and La Verguier. It was a pleasant country, with living trees and green fields not annihilated by shell-fire, though with the naked eye I could see the scarred walls of St.-Quentin cathedral, and the villages near the frontlines had been damaged in the usual way. It was dead quiet there for miles, except for short bursts of harassing fire now and then, and odd shells here and there, and bursts of black shrapnel in the blue sky of mild days.

"Paradise, after Flanders!" said our men, but I knew that there was a great movement of troops westward from Russia, and wondered how long this paradise would last.

I looked about for trench systems, support lines, and did not see them, and wondered what our defense would be if the enemy attacked here in great strength. Our army seemed wonderfully thinned out. There were few men to be seen in our outpost line or in reserve. It was all strangely quiet. Alarmingly quiet.

Yet, pleasant for the time being. I had a brother commanding a battery along the railway line south of St.-Quentin. I went to see him, and we had a picnic meal on a little hill staring straight toward St.-Quentin cathedral. One of his junior officers set the gramophone going. The colonel of the artillery brigade came jogging up on his horse and called out, "Fine morning, and a pretty spot!" The infantry divisions were cheerful. "Like a rest-cure!" they said. They had sports almost within sight of the German lines. I saw a boxing-match in an Irish battalion, and while two fellows hammered each other I glanced away from them to winding, wavy lines of chalk on the opposite hillsides, and wondered what was happening behind them in that quietude.

"What do you think about this German offensive?" I asked the general of a London division (General Gorringe of the 47th) standing on a wagon and watching a tug-of—war. From that place also we could see the German positions.

"G. H. Q. has got the wind-up," he said. "It is all bluff."

General Hall, temporarily commanding the Irish Division, was of the same opinion, and took some pains to explain the folly of thinking the Germans would attack. Yet day after day, week after week, the Intelligence reports were full of evidence of immense movements of troops westward, of intensive training of German divisions in back areas, of new hospitals, ammunition-dumps, airplanes, battery positions. There was overwhelming evidence as to the enemy's intentions. Intelligence officers took me on one side and said: "England ought to know. The people ought to be prepared. All this is very serious. We shall be 'up against it.'" G.H.Q. was convinced. On February 23d the war correspondents published articles summarizing the evidence, pointing out the gravity of the menace, and they were passed by the censorship. But England was not scared. Dances were in full swing in London. Little ladies laughed as usual, light-hearted. Flanders had made no difference to national optimism, though the hospitals were crowded with blind and maimed and shell-shocked.

"I am skeptical of the German offensive" said Mr. Bonar Law.

Nobody believed the war correspondents. Nobody ever did believe us, though some of us wrote the truth from first to last as far as the facts of war go apart from deeper psychology, and a naked realism of horrors and losses, and criticism of facts, which did not come within our liberty of the pen.

They were strange months for me. I felt that I was in possession, as indeed I was, of a terrible secret which might lead to the ending of the world—our world, as we knew it—with our liberties and power. For weeks I had been pledged to say no word about it, to write not a word about it, and it was like being haunted by a specter all day long. One laughed, but the specter echoed one's laughter and said, "Wait!" The mild sunshine of those spring days was pleasant to one's spirit in the woods above La Fere, and in fields where machine-guns chattered a little, while overhead our airplanes dodged German "Archies." But the specter chilled one's blood at the reminder of vast masses of field-gray men drawing nearer to our lines in overwhelming numbers. I motored to many parts of the front, and my companion sometimes was a little Frenchman who had lost a leg in the war—D'Artagnan with a wooden peg, most valiant, most gay. Along the way he recited the poems of Ronsard. At the journey's end one day he sang old French chansons, in an English mess, within gunshot of the German lines. He climbed up a tree and gazed at the German positions, and made sketches while he hummed little tunes and said between them, "Ah, les sacres Boches!.. . If only I could fight again!"

I remember a pleasant dinner in the old town of Noyon, in a little restaurant where two pretty girls waited. They had come from Paris with their parents to start this business, now that Noyon was safe. (Safe, O Lord!) And everything was very dainty and clean. At dinner that night there was a hostile air raid overhead. Bombs crashed. But the girls were brave. One of them volunteered to go with an officer across the square to show him the way to the A.P.M., from where he had to get a pass to stay for dinner. Shrapnel bullets were whipping the flagstones of the Grande Place, from anti-aircraft guns. The officer wore his steel helmet. The girl was going out without any hat above her braided hair. We did not let her go, and the officer had another guide. One night I brought my brother to the place from his battery near St. Quentin. We dined well, slept well.

"Noyon is a good spot," he said. "I shall come here again when you give me a lift."

A few days later my brother was firing at masses of Germans with open sights, and the British army was in a full-tide retreat, and the junior officer who had played his gramophone was dead, with other officers and men of that battery. When I next passed through Noyon shells were falling into it, and later I saw it in ruins, with the glory of the Romanesque cathedral sadly scarred. I have ofttimes wondered what happened to the little family in the old hotel.

So March 21st came, as we knew it would come, even to the very date, and Ludendorff played his trump cards and the great game.

Before that date I had an interview with General Gough, commanding the Fifth Army. He pulled out his maps, showed his method of forward redoubts beyond the main battle zone, and in a quiet, amiable way spoke some words which froze my blood.

"We may have to give ground," he said, "if the enemy attacks in strength. We may have to fall back to our main battle zone. That will not matter very much. It is possible that we may have to go farther back. Our real line of defense is the Somme. It will be nothing like a tragedy if we hold that. If we lose the crossings of the Somme it will, of course, be serious. But not a tragedy even then. It will only be tragic if we lose Amiens, and we must not do that."

"The crossings of the Somme... Amiens!"

Such a thought had never entered my imagination. General Gough had suggested terrible possibilities.

All but the worst happened. In my despatches, reprinted in book form with explanatory prefaces, I have told in full detail the meaning and measure of the British retreat, when forty-eight of our divisions were attacked by one hundred and fourteen German divisions and fell back fighting stubborn rear-guard actions which at last brought the enemy to a dead halt outside Amiens and along the River Ancre northward from Albert, where afterward in a northern attack the enemy under Prince Rupprecht of Bavaria broke through the Portuguese between Givenchy and Festubert, where our wings held, drove up to Bailleul, which was burned to the ground, and caused us to abandon all the ridges of Flanders which had been gained at such great cost, and fall back to the edge of Ypres. In this book I need not narrate all this history again.

They were evil days for us. The German offensive was conducted with masterly skill, according to the new method of "infiltration" which had been tried against Italy with great success in the autumn of '17 at Caporetto.

It consisted in a penetration of our lines by wedges of machine-gunners constantly reinforced and working inward so that our men, attacked frontally after terrific bombardment, found themselves under flanking fire on their right and left and in danger of being cut off. Taking advantage of a dense fog, for which they had waited according to meteorological forecast, the Germans had easily made their way between our forward redoubts on the Fifth Army front, where our garrisons held out for a long time, completely surrounded, and penetrated our inner battle zone. Through the gaps they made they came in masses at a great pace with immense machine—gun strength and light artillery. On the Third Army front where penetrations were made, notably near Bullecourt between the 6th and 51st Divisions, the whole of our army machine was upset for a time like a watch with a broken mainspring and loose wheels. Staffs lost touch with fighting units. Communications were broken down. Orders were given but not received. After enormous losses of men and guns, our heavy artillery was choking the roads of escape, while our rear-guards fought for time rather than for ground. The crossings of the Somme were lost too easily. In the confusion and tumult of those days some of our men, being human, were demoralized and panic-stricken, and gave ground which might have been longer held. But on the whole, and in the mass, there was no panic, and a most grim valor of men who fought for days and nights without sleep; fought when they were almost surrounded or quite surrounded, and until few of them remained to hold any kind of line. Fortunately the Germans were unable to drag their heavy guns over the desert they had made a year before in their own retreat, and at the end of a week their pace slackened and they halted, in exhaustion.

I went into the swirl of our retreat day after day up by Guiscard and Hum; then, as the line moved back, by Peronne and Bapaume, and at last on a dreadful day by the windmill at Pozieres, our old heroic fighting-ground, where once again after many battles the enemy was in Courcelette and High Wood and Delville Wood, and, as I saw by going to the right through Albert, driving hard up to Mametz and Montauban. That meant the loss of all the old Somme battlefields, and that struck a chill in one's heart. But what I marveled at always was the absence of panic, the fatalistic acceptance of the turn of fortune's wheel by many officers and men, and the refusal of corps and divisional staffs to give way to despair in those days of tragedy and crisis.

The northern attack was in many ways worse to bear and worse to see. The menace to the coast was frightful when the enemy struck up to Bailleul and captured Kemmel Hill from a French regiment which had come up to relieve some of our exhausted and unsupported men. All through this country between Estaires and Merville, to Steenwerck, Metern, and Bailleul, thousands of civilians had been living on the edge of the battlefields, believing themselves safe behind our lines. Now the line had slipped and they were caught by German shell-fire and German guns, and after nearly four years of war had to abandon their homes like the first fugitives. I saw old women coming down lanes where 5.9's were bursting and where our gunners were getting into action. I saw young mothers packing their babies and their bundles into perambulators while shells came hurtling over the thatched roofs of their cottages. I stood on the Mont des Chats looking down upon a wide sweep of battle, and saw many little farmsteads on fire and Bailleul one torch of flame and smoke.

There was an old monastery on the Mont des Chats which had been in the midst of a cavalry battle in October of 1914, when Prince Max of Hesse, the Kaiser's cousin, was mortally wounded by a shot from one of our troopers. He was carried into the cell of the old prior, who watched over him in his dying hours when he spoke of his family and friends. Then his body was borne down the hill at night and buried secretly by a parish priest; and when the Kaiser wrote to the Pope, desiring to know the whereabouts of his cousin's grave, the priest to whom his message was conveyed said, "Tell the Kaiser he shall know when the German armies have departed from Belgium and when reparation has been made for all their evil deeds." It was the prior who told me that story and who described to me how the British cavalry had forged their way up the hill. He showed me the scars of bullets on the walls and the windows from which the monks looked out upon the battle.

"All that is a wonderful memory," said the prior. "Thanks to the English, we are safe and beyond the range of German shells."

I thought of his words that day I climbed the hill to see the sweep of battle beyond. The monastery was no longer beyond the range of German shells. An eight—inch shell had just smashed into the prior's parlor. Others had opened gaps in the high roofs and walls. The monks had fled by order of the prior, who stayed behind, like the captain of a sinking ship. His corridors resounded to the tramp of army boots. The Ulster gunners had made their headquarters in the refectory, but did not stay there long. A few days later the monastery was a ruin.

From many little villages caught by the oncoming tide of war our soldiers helped the people to escape in lorries or on gun-wagons. They did not weep, nor say much, but were wonderfully brave. I remember a little family in Robecq whom I packed into my car when shells began to fall among the houses. A pretty girl, with a little invalid brother in her arms, and a mother by her side, pointed the way to a cottage in a wood some miles away. She was gay and smiling when she said, "Au revoir et merci!" A few days later the cottage and the wood were behind the German lines.

The northern defense, by the 55th Lancashires, 51st Highlanders (who had been all through the Somme retreat), the 25th Division of Cheshires, Wiltshires and Lancashire Fusiliers, and the 9th Scottish Division, and others, who fought "with their backs to the wall," as Sir Douglas Haig demanded of them, without reliefs, until they were worn thin, was heroic and tragic in its ordeal, until Foch sent up his cavalry (I saw them riding in clouds of dust and heard the panting of their horses), followed by divisions of blue men in hundreds of blue lorries tearing up the roads, and forming a strong blue line behind our thin brown line. Prince Rupprecht of Bavaria had twenty-six fresh divisions in reserve, but had to hold them until other plans were developed—the Crown Prince's plan against the French, and the attack on Arras.

The defense of Arras by the 3d and 56th Divisions—the Iron Division and the London Division on the left, and by the 15th Division and Guards on the right, saved the center of our line and all our line. We had a breathing—space while heavy blows fell against the French and against three British divisions who had been sent to hold "a quiet sector" on their right. The Germans drove across the Chemin des Dames, struck right and left, terrific blows, beat the French back, reached the Marne again, and threatened Paris.

Foch waited to strike. The genius of Foch was that he waited until the last minute of safety, taking immense risks in order to be certain of his counter-stroke. For a time he had to dissipate his reserves, but he gathered them together again. As quick as the blue men had come up behind our lines they were withdrawn again. Three of our divisions went with them, the 51st Highlanders and 15th Scottish, and the 48th English. The flower of the French army, the veterans of many battles, was massed behind the Marne, and at Chateau Thierry the American marines and infantry were given their first big job to do. What happened all the world knows. The Crown Prince's army was attacked on both flanks and in the center, and was sent reeling back to escape complete annihilation.

IX

Ludendorff's great offensive had failed and had turned to ruin. Some of the twenty-six fresh divisions under Rupprecht of Bavaria were put into the melting-pot to save the Crown Prince. The British army, with its gaps filled up by 300,000 new drafts from England, the young brothers of the elder brothers who had gone before, was ready to strike again, and on August 8th the Canadians and Australians north and south of the Somme, led by many tanks, broke the enemy's line beyond Amiens and slowly but surely rolled it back with enormous losses.

For the first time in the war the cavalry had their chance of pursuit, and made full use of it, rounding up great batches of prisoners, capturing batteries of heavy and light guns, and fighting in many actions.

"August 8th," writes Ludendorff, "was the black day of the German army in the history of this war."

He describes from the German point of view what I and others have described from the British point of view, and the general narrative is the same—a succession of hammer-blows by the British armies, which broke not only the German war-machine, but the German spirit. It was a marvelous feat when the 19th Division and the Welsh waded at dusk across the foul waters of the River Ancre, under the heights of Thiepval, assembled under the guns of the enemy up there, and then, wet to their skins, and in small numbers compared with the strength of the enemy, stormed the huge ridges from both sides, and hurled the enemy back from what he thought was an impregnable position, and followed him day by day, taking thousands of prisoners and smashing his rear-guard defenses one by one.

The most decisive battle of the British front in the "come-back," after our days of retreat, was when with the gallant help of American troops of the 27th New York Division our men of the English Midlands, the 46th Division, and others, broke the main Hindenburg line along the St.-Quentin Canal. That canal was sixty feet wide, with steep cliffs rising sheer to a wonderful system of German machine-gun redoubts and tunneled defenses, between the villages of Bellicourt and Bellinglis. It seemed to me an impossible place to assault and capture. If the enemy could not hold that line they could hold nothing. In a dense fog on Sunday morning, September 30th, our men, with the Americans and Australians in support, went down to the canal-bank, waded across where the water was shallow, swam across in life-belts where it was deep, or got across somehow and anyhow, under blasts of machine-gun fire, by rafts and plank bridges. A few hours after the beginning of the battle they were far out beyond the German side of the canal, with masses of prisoners in their hands. The Americans on the left of the attack, where the canal goes below ground, showed superb and reckless gallantry (they forgot, however, to "mop up" behind them, so that the enemy came out of his tunnels and the Australians had to cut their way through), and that evening I met their escorts with droves of captured Germans. They had helped to break the last defensive system of the enemy opposite the British front, and after that our troops fought through open country on the way to victory.

I saw many of the scenes which led up to Mons and Le Cateau and afterward to the Rhine. Something of the horror of war passed when the enemy drew back slowly in retreat from the lands he had invaded, and we liberated great cities like Lille and Roubaix and Tourcoing, and scores of towns and villages where the people had been waiting for us so long, and now wept with joy to see us. The entry into Lille was unforgetable, when old men and women and girls and boys and little children crowded round us and kissed our hands. So it was in other places. Yet not all the horror had passed. In Courtrai, in St.-Amand by Valenciennes, in Bohain, and other villages, the enemy's shell-fire and poison-gas killed and injured many of the people who had been under the German yoke so long and now thought they were safe. Hospitals were filled with women gasping for breath, with gas-fumes in their lungs, and with dying children. In Valenciennes the cellars were flooded when I walked there on its day of capture, so that when shells began to fall the people could not go down to shelter. Some of them did not try to go down. At an open window sat an old veteran of 1870 with his medal on his breast, and with his daughter and granddaughter on each side of his chair. He called out, "Merci! Merci!" when English soldiers passed, and when I stopped a moment clasped my hands through the window and could not speak for the tears which fell down his white and withered cheeks. A few dead Germans lay about the streets, and in Maubeuge on the day before the armistice I saw the last dead German of the war in that part of the line. He lay stretched outside the railway station into which many shells had crashed. It was as though he had walked from his own comrades toward our line before a bullet caught him.

Ludendorff writes of the broken morale of the German troops, and of how his men surrendered to single troopers of ours, while whole detachments gave themselves up to tanks. "Retiring troops," he wrote, "greeted one particular division (the cavalry) that was going up fresh and gallantly to the attack, with shouts of 'Blacklegs!' and 'War-prolongers!'" That is true. When the Germans left Bohain they shouted out to the French girls: "The English are coming. Bravo! The war will soon be over!" On a day in September, when British troops broke the Drocourt-Queant line, I saw the Second German Guards coming along in batches, like companies, and after they had been put in barbed-wire inclosures they laughed and clapped at the sight of other crowds of comrades coming down as prisoners. I thought then, "Something has broken in the German spirit." For the first time the end seemed very near.

Yet the German rear-guards fought stubbornly in many places, especially in the last battles round Cambrai, where, on the north, the Canadian corps had to fight desperately, and suffered heavy and bitter losses under machine-gun fire, while on the south our naval division and others were badly cut up.

General Currie, whom I saw during those days, was anxious and disheartened. He was losing more men in machine-gun actions round Cambrai than in bigger battles. I watched those actions from Bourlon Wood, saw the last German railway train steam out of the town, and went into the city early on the morning of its capture, when there was a roaring fire in the heart of it and the Canadians were routing out the last Germans from their hiding-places.

The British army could not have gone on much farther after November 11th, when the armistice brought us to a halt. For three months our troops had fought incessantly, storming many villages strongly garrisoned with machine-gunners, crossing many canals under heavy fire, and losing many comrades all along the way. The pace could not have been kept up. There is a limit even to the valor of British troops, and for a time we had reached that limit. There were not many divisions who could have staggered on to new attacks without rest and relief. But they had broken the German armies against them by a succession of hammer-strokes astounding in their rapidity and in their continuity, which I need not here describe in detail, because in my despatches, now in book form, I have narrated that history as I was a witness of it day by day.

Elsewhere the French and Americans had done their part with steady, driving pressure. The illimitable reserves of Americans, and their fighting quality, which triumphed over a faulty organization of transport and supplies, left the German High Command without hope even for a final gamble.

Before them the German troops were in revolt, at last, against the bloody, futile sacrifice of their manhood and people. A blinding light had come to them, revealing the criminality of their war lords in this "Great Swindle" against their race. It was defeat and agony which enlightened them, as most people—even ourselves—are enlightened only by suffering and disillusionment, and never by successes.

X

After the armistice I went with our troops to the Rhine, and entered Cologne with them. That was the most fantastic adventure of all in four and a half years of strange and terrible adventures. To me there was no wild exultation in the thought of being in Cologne with our conquering army. The thought of all the losses on the way, and of all the futility of this strife, smote at one's heart. What fools the Germans had been, what tragic fools! What a mad villainy there had been among rival dynasties and powers and politicians and peoples to lead to this massacre! What had any one gained out of it all? Nothing except ruin. Nothing except great death and poverty and remorse and revolt.

The German people received us humbly. They were eager to show us courtesy and submission. It was a chance for our young Junkers, for the Prussian in the hearts of young pups of ours, who could play the petty tyrant, shout at German waiters, refuse to pay their bills, bully shopkeepers, insult unoffending citizens. A few young staff-officers behaved like that, disgustingly. The officers of fighting battalions and the men were very different. It was a strange study in psychology to watch them. Here they were among the "Huns." The men they passed in the streets and sat with in the restaurants had been in German uniforms a few weeks before, or a few days. They were "the enemy," the men they had tried to kill, the men who had tried to kill them. They had actually fought against them in the same places. At the Domhof Hotel I overheard a conversation between a young waiter and three of our cavalry officers. They had been in the same fight in the village of Noyelles, near Cambrai, a tiny place of ruin, where they had crouched under machine-gun fire. The waiter drew a diagram on the table-cloth. "I was just there." The three cavalry officers laughed. "Extraordinary! We were a few yards away." They chatted with the waiter as though he were an old acquaintance who had played against them in a famous football-match. They did not try to kill him with a table-knife. He did not put poison in the soup.

That young waiter had served in a hotel in Manchester, where he had served a friend of mine, to whom he now expressed his opinion on the folly of the war, and the criminality of his war lords, and things in general. Among these last he uttered an epigram which I remember for its brutal simplicity. It was when a staff-officer of ours, rather the worse for wine, had been making a scene with the head waiter, bullying him in a strident voice.

"Some English gentlemen are swine," said the young waiter. "But all German gentlemen are swine."

Some of our officers and men billeted in houses outside Cologne or across the Rhine endeavored to stand on distant terms with the "Huns." But it was impossible to be discourteous when the old lady of the house brought them an early cup of coffee before breakfast, warmed their boots before the kitchen fire, said, "God be praised, the war is over." For English soldiers, anything like hostility was ridiculous in the presence of German boys and girls who swarmed round their horses and guns, kissed their hands, brought them little pictures and gifts.

"Kids are kids," said a sergeant-major. "I don't want to cut their throats! Queer, ain't it?"

Many of the "kids" looked half starved. Our men gave them bread and biscuit and bully beef. In Cologne the people seemed pleased to see British soldiers. There was no sense of humiliation. No agony of grief at this foreign occupation. Was it lack of pride, cringing—or a profound relief that the river of blood had ceased to flow and even a sense of protection against the revolutionary mob which had looted their houses before our entry? Almost every family had lost one son. Some of them two, three, even five sons, in that orgy of slaughter. They had paid a dreadful price for pride. Their ambition had been drowned in blood.

In the restaurants orchestras played gay music. Once I heard them playing old English melodies, and I sickened a little at that. That was going too far! I looked round the Cafe Bauer—a strange scene after four and a half years Hun-hating. English soldiers were chatting with Germans, clinking beer mugs with them. The Germans lifted their hats to English "Tommies"; our men, Canadian and English, said "Cheerio!" to German soldiers in uniforms without shoulder-straps or buttons. English people still talking of Huns, demanding vengeance, the maintenance of the blockade, would have become hysterical if they had come suddenly to this German cafe before the signing of peace.

Long before peace was signed at Versailles it had been made on the Rhine. Stronger than the hate of war was human nature. Face to face, British soldiers found that every German had two eyes, a nose, and a mouth, in spite of being a "Hun." As ecclesiastics would say when not roused to patriotic fury, they had been made "in the image of God." There were pleasant-spoken women in the shops and in the farmhouses. Blue-eyed girls with flaxen pigtails courtesied very prettily to English officers. They were clean. Their houses were clean, more spotless even than English homes. When soldiers turned on a tap they found water came out of it. Wonderful! The sanitary arrangements were good. Servants were hard—working and dutiful. There was something, after all, in German Kultur. At night the children said their prayer to the Christian God. Most of them were Catholics, and very pious.

"They seem good people," said English soldiers.

At night, in the streets of Cologne, were women not so good. Shameless women, though daintily dressed and comely. British soldiers—English, Scottish, and Canadian—grinned back at their laughing eyes, entered into converse with them, found they could all speak English, went down side-streets with them to narrow-fronted houses. There were squalid scenes when the A.P.M. raided these houses and broke up an entente cordiale that was flagrant and scandalous.

Astonishing climax to the drama of war! No general orders could stop fraternization before peace was signed. Human nature asserted itself against all artificial restrictions and false passion. Friends of mine who had been violent in their hatred of all Germans became thoughtful, and said: "Of course there are exceptions," and, "The innocent must not suffer for the guilty," and, "We can afford to be a little generous now."

But the innocent were made to suffer for the guilty and we were not generous. We maintained the blockade, and German children starved, and German mothers weakened, and German girls swooned in the tram-cars, and German babies died. Ludendorff did not starve or die. Neither did Hindenburg, nor any German war lord, nor any profiteer. Down the streets of Cologne came people of the rich middle classes, who gorged themselves on buns and cakes for afternoon tea. They were cakes of ersatz flour with ersatz cream, and not very healthy or nutritious, though very expensive. But in the side-streets, among the working—women, there was, as I found, the wolf of hunger standing with open jaws by every doorway. It was not actual starvation, but what the Germans call unternahrung (under-nourishment), producing rickety children, consumptive girls, and men out of whom vitality had gone They stinted and scraped on miserable substitutes, and never had enough to eat. Yet they were the people who for two years at least had denounced the war, had sent up petitions for peace, and had written to their men in the trenches about the Great Swindle and the Gilded Ones. They were powerless, as some of them told me, because of the secret police and martial law. What could they do against the government, with all their men away at the front? They were treated like pigs, like dirt. They could only suffer and pray. They had a little hope that in the future, if France and England were not too hard, they might pay back for the guilt of their war lords and see a new Germany arise out of its ruin, freed from militarism and with greater liberties. So humble people talked to us when I went among them with a friend who spoke good German, better than my elementary knowledge. I believed in their sincerity, which had come through suffering, though I believed that newspaper editors, many people in the official classes, and the old military caste were still implacable in hatred and unrepentant.

The German people deserved punishment for their share in the guilt of war. They had been punished by frightful losses of life, by a multitude of cripples, by the ruin of their Empire. When they told me of their hunger I could not forget the hungry wives and children of France and Belgium, who had been captives in their own land behind German lines, nor our prisoners who had been starved, until many of them died. When I walked through German villages and pitied the women who yearned for their men, still prisoners in our hands, nearly a year after the armistice, and long after peace (a cruelty which shamed us, I think), I remembered hundreds of French villages broken into dust by German gun-fire, burned by incendiary shells, and that vast desert of the battlefields in France and Belgium which never in our time will regain its life as a place of human habitation. When Germans said, "Our industry is ruined," "Our trade is killed," I thought of the factories in Lille and many towns from which all machinery had been taken or in which all machinery had been broken. I thought of the thousand crimes of their war, the agony of millions of people upon whose liberties they had trampled and upon whose necks they had imposed a brutal yoke. Yet even with all those memories of tragic scenes which in this book are but lightly sketched, I hoped that the peace we should impose would not be one of vengeance, by which the innocent would pay for the sins of the guilty, the children for their fathers' lust, the women for their war lords, the soldiers who hated war for those who drove them to the shambles; but that this peace should in justice and mercy lead the working-people of Europe out of the misery in which all were plunged, and by a policy no higher than common sense, but as high as that, establish a new phase of civilization in which military force would be reduced to the limits of safety for European peoples eager to end the folly of war and get back to work.

I hoped too much. There was no such peace.

PART EIGHT

FOR WHAT MEN DIED

I

In this book I have written in a blunt way some episodes of the war as I observed them, and gained first-hand knowledge of them in their daily traffic. I have not painted the picture blacker than it was, nor selected gruesome morsels and joined them together to make a jig-saw puzzle for ghoulish delight. Unlike Henri Barbusse, who, in his dreadful book Le Feu, gave the unrelieved blackness of this human drama, I have here and in other books shown the light as well as the shade in which our men lived, the gaiety as well as the fear they had, the exultation as well as the agony of battle, the spiritual ardor of boys as well as the brutality of the task that was theirs. I have tried to set down as many aspects of the war's psychology as I could find in my remembrance of these years, without exaggeration or false emphasis, so that out of their confusion, even out of their contradiction, the real truth of the adventure might be seen as it touched the souls of men.

Yet when one strives to sum up the evidence and reach definite conclusions about the motives which led men of the warring nations to kill one another year after year in those fields of slaughter, the ideals for which so many millions of men laid down their lives, and the effect of those years of carnage upon the philosophy of this present world of men, there is no clear line of thought or conviction.

It is difficult at least to forecast the changes that will be produced by this experience in the social structure of civilized peoples, and in their relations to one another though it is certain, even now, that out of the passion of the war a new era in the world's history is being born. The ideas of vast masses of people have been revolutionized by the thoughts that were stirred up in them during those years of intense suffering. No system of government designed by men afraid of the new ideas will have power to kill them, though they may throttle them for a time. For good or ill, I know not which, the ideas germinated in trenches and dugouts, in towns under shell—fire or bomb-fire, in hearts stricken by personal tragedy or world-agony, will prevail over the old order which dominated the nations of Europe, and the old philosophy of political and social governance will be challenged and perhaps overthrown. If the new ideas are thwarted by reactionary rulers endeavoring to jerk the world back to its old-fashioned discipline under their authority, there will be anarchy reaching to the heights of terror in more countries than those where anarchy now prevails. If by fear or by wisdom the new ideas are allowed to gain their ground gradually, a revolution will be accomplished without anarchy. But in any case, for good or ill, a revolution will happen. It has happened in the sense that already there is no resemblance between this Europe after-the-war and that Europe-before-the-war, in the mental attitude of the masses toward the problems of life. In every country there are individuals, men and women, who are going about as though what had happened had made no difference, and as though, after a period of restlessness, the people will "settle down" to the old style of things. They are merely sleep-walkers. There are others who see clearly enough that they cannot govern or dupe the people with old spell-words, and they are struggling desperately to think out new words which may help them to regain their power over simple minds. The old gangs are organizing a new system of defense, building a new kind of Hindenburg line behind which they are dumping their political ammunition. But their Hindenburg line is not impregnable. The angry murmur of the mob—highly organized, disciplined, passionate, trained to fight, is already approaching the outer bastions.

In Russia the mob is in possession, wiping the blood out of their eyes after the nightmare of anarchy, encompassed by forces of the old regime, and not knowing yet whether its victory is won or how to shape the new order that must follow chaos.

In Germany there is only the psychology of stunned people, broken for a time in body and spirit, after stupendous efforts and bloody losses which led to ruin and the complete destruction of their old pride, philosophy, and power. The revolution that has happened there is strange and rather pitiful. It was not caused by the will—power of the people, but by a cessation of will-power. They did not overthrow their ruling dynasty, their tyrants. The tyrants fled, and the people were not angry, nor sorry, nor fierce, nor glad. They were stupefied. Members of the old order joined hands with those of the people's parties, out to evolve a republic with new ideals based upon the people's will and inspired by the people's passion. The Germans, after the armistice and after the peace, had no passion, as they had no will. They were in a state of coma. The "knock-out blow" had happened to them, and they were incapable of action. They just ceased from action. They had been betrayed to this ruin by their military and political rulers, but they had not vitality enough to demand vengeance on those men. The extent of their ruin was so great that it annihilated anger, political passion, pride, all emotion except that of despair. How could they save something out of the remnants of the power that had been theirs? How could they keep alive, feed their women and children, pay their monstrous debts? They had lost their faith as well as their war. Nothing that they had believed was true. They had believed in their invincible armies—and the armies had bled to death and broken. They had believed in the supreme military genius of their war lords, and the war lords, blunderers as well as criminals, had led them to the abyss and dropped them over. They had believed in the divine mission of the German people as a civilizing force, and now they were despised by all other peoples as a brutal and barbarous race, in spite of German music, German folk-songs, German art, German sentiment. They had been abandoned by God, by the protecting hand of the *altes gutes Deutsches Gottes* to whom many had prayed for comfort and help in those years of war, in Protestant churches and Catholic churches, with deep piety and childlike faith. What sins had they done that they should be abandoned by God? The invasion of Belgium? That, they argued, was a tragic necessity. Atrocities? Those were (they believed) the inventions of their enemies. There had been stern things done, terrible things, but according to the laws of war. *Francs-tireurs* had been shot. That was war. Hostages had been shot. It was to save German lives from slaughter by civilians. Individual brutalities, yes. There were brutes in all armies. The U-boat war? It was (said the German patriot) to break a blockade that was starving millions of German children to slow death, condemning millions to consumption, rickets, all manner of disease. Nurse Cavell? She pleaded guilty to a crime that was punishable, as she knew, by death. She was a brave woman who took her risk open-eyed, and was judged according to the justice of war, which is very cruel. Poison-gas? Why not, said German soldiers, when to be gassed was less terrible than to be blown to bits by high explosives? They had been the first to use that new method of destruction, as the English were the first to use tanks, terrible also in their destructiveness. Germany was guilty of this war, had provoked it against peaceful peoples? No! A thousand times no. They had been, said the troubled soul of Germany, encompassed with enemies. They had plotted to close her in. Russia was a huge menace. France had entered into alliance with Russia, and was waiting her chance to grab at Alsace-Lorraine. Italy was ready for betrayal. England hated the power of Germany and was in secret alliance with France and Russia. Germany had struck to save herself. "It was a war of self-defense, to save the Fatherland."

The German people still clung desperately to those ideas after the armistice, as I found in Cologne and other towns, and as friends of mine who had visited Berlin told me after peace was signed. The Germans refused to believe in accusations of atrocity. They knew that some of these stories had been faked by hostile propaganda, and, knowing that, as we know, they thought all were false. They said "Lies-lies-lies!"—and made counter—charges against the Russians and Poles. They could not bring themselves to believe that their sons and brothers had been more brutal than the laws of war allow, and what brutality they had done was imposed upon them by ruthless discipline. But they deplored the war, and the common people, ex-soldiers and civilians, cursed the rich and governing classes who had made profit out of it, and had continued it when they might have made peace with honor. That was their accusation against their leaders—that and the ruthless, bloody way in which their men had been hurled into the furnace on a gambler's chance of victory, while they were duped by faked promises of victory.

When not put upon their defense by accusations against the whole Fatherland, the German people, as far as I could tell by talking with a few of them, and by those letters which fell into our hands, revolted in spirit against the monstrous futility and idiocy of the war, and were convinced in their souls that its origin lay in the greed and pride of the governing classes of all nations, who had used men's bodies as counters in a devil's game. That view was expressed in the signboards put above the parapet, "We're all fools: let's all go home"; and in that letter by the woman who wrote:

"For the poor here it is terrible, and yet the rich, the gilded ones, the bloated aristocrats, gobble up everything in front of our very eyes... All soldiers—friend and foe—ought to throw down their weapons and go on strike, so that this war, which enslaves the people more than ever, may cease."

It is that view, terrible in its simplicity, which may cause a more passionate revolution in Germany when the people awaken from their stupor. It was that view which led to the Russian Revolution and to Bolshevism. It is the suspicion which is creeping into the brains of British working-men and making them threaten to strike against any adventure of war, like that in Russia, which seems to them (unless proved otherwise) on behalf of the "gilded ones" and for the enslavement of the peoples.

Not to face that truth is to deny the passionate convictions of masses of men in Europe. That is one key to the heart of the revolutionary movement which is surging beneath the surface of our European state. It is a the belief of many brooding minds that almost as great as the direct guilt of the German war lords was the guilt of the whole political society of Europe, whose secret diplomacy (unrevealed to the peoples) was based upon hatred and fear and rivalry, in play for imperial power and the world's markets, as common folk play dominoes for penny points, and risking the lives of common folk in a gamble for enormous stakes of territory, imperial prestige, the personal vanity of politicians, the vast private gain of trusts and profiteers. To keep the living counters quiet, to make them jump into the pool of their own free will at the word "Go," the statesmen, diplomats, trusts, and profiteers debauch the name of patriotism, raise the watchword of liberty, and play upon the ignorance of the mob easily, skillfully, by inciting them to race hatred, by inflaming the brute-passion in them, and by concocting a terrible mixture of false idealism and self-interest, so that simple minds quick to respond to sentiment, as well as those quick to hear the call of the beast, rally shoulder to shoulder and march to the battlegrounds under the spell of that potion. Some go with a noble sense of sacrifice, some with blood-lust in their hearts, most with the herd-instinct following the lead, little knowing that they are but the pawns of a game which is being played behind closed doors by the great gamblers in the courts and Foreign Offices, and committee-rooms, and counting-houses, of the political casinos in Europe.

I have heard the expression of this view from soldiers during the war and since the war, at street-corners, in tram-cars, and in conversations with railway men, mechanics, policemen, and others who were soldiers a year ago, or stay-at-homes, thinking hard over the meaning of the war. I am certain that millions of men are thinking these things, because I found the track of those common thoughts, crude, simple, dangerous, among Canadian soldiers crossing the Atlantic, in Canadian towns, and in the United States, as I had begun to see the trail of them far back in the early days of the war when I moved among French soldiers, Belgian soldiers, and our own men.

My own belief is not so simple as that. I do not divorce all peoples from their governments as victims of a subtle tyranny devised by statesmen and diplomats of diabolical cunning, and by financial magnates ready to exploit human life for greater gains. I see the evil which led to the crime of the war and to the crimes of the peace with deep-spread roots to the very foundation of human society. The fear of statesmen, upon which all international relations were based, was in the hearts of peoples. France was afraid of Germany and screwed up her military service, her war preparations, to the limit of national endurance, the majority of the people of France accepting the burden as inevitable and right. Because of her fear of Germany France made her alliance with Russian Czardom, her entente cordiale with Imperial England, and the French people poured their money into Russian loans as a life insurance against the German menace. French statesmen knew that their diplomacy was supported by the majority of the people by their ignorance as well as by their knowledge.

So it was in Germany. The spell-words of the German war lords expressed the popular sentiment of the German people, which was largely influenced by the fear of Russia in alliance with France, by fear and envy of the British Empire and England's sea-power, and by the faith that Germany must break through that hostile combination at all costs in order to fulfil the high destiny which was marked out for her, as she thought, by the genius and industry of her people. The greed of the "bloated aristocrats" was only on a bigger scale than the greed of the small shopkeepers. The desire to capture new markets belonged not only to statesmen, but to commercial travelers. The German peasant believed as much in the might of the German armies as Hindenburg and Ludendorff. The brutality of German generals was not worse than that of the *Unteroffizier* or the foreman of works.

In England there was no traditional hatred of Germany, but for some years distrust and suspicions, which had been vented in the newspapers, with taunts and challenges, stinging the pride of Germans and playing into the hands of the Junker caste.

Our war psychology was different from that of our allies because of our island position and our faith in seapower which had made us immune from the fear of invasion. It took some time to awaken the people to a sense of real peril and of personal menace to their hearths and homes. To the very end masses of English folk believed that we were fighting for the rescue of other peoples—Belgian, French, Serbian, Rumanian—and not for the continuance of our imperial power.

The official propaganda, the words and actions of British statesmen, did actually express the conscious and subconscious psychology of the multitude. The call to the old watchwords of national pride and imperial might thrilled the soul of a people of proud tradition in sea—battles and land-battles. Appeals for the rescue of "the little nations" struck old chords of chivalry and sentiment—though with a strange lack of logic and sincerity Irish demand for self-government was unheeded. Base passions as well as noble instincts were stirred easily. Greedy was the appetite of the mob for atrocity tales. The more revolting they were the quicker they were swallowed. The foul absurdity of the "corpse-factory" was not rejected any more than the tale of the "crucified Canadian" (disproved by our own G.H.Q.) or the cutting off of children's hands and women's breasts, for which I could find no evidence from the only British ambulances working in the districts where such horrors were reported. Spy-mania flourished in mean streets, German music was banned in English drawing-rooms. Preachers and professors denied any quality of virtue or genius to German poets, philosophers, scientists, or scholars. A critical weighing of evidence was regarded as pro-Germanism and lack of patriotism. Truth was delivered bound to passion. Hatred at home, inspired largely by feminine hysteria and official propaganda, reached such heights that when fighting-men came back on leave their refusal to say much against their enemy, their straightforward assertions that Fritz was not so black as he was painted, that he fought bravely, died gamely, and in the prison-camps was well-mannered, decent, industrious, good-natured, were heard with shocked silence by mothers and sisters who could only excuse this absence of hate on the score of war-weariness.

II

The people of all countries were deeply involved in the general blood-guiltiness of Europe. They made no passionate appeal in the name of Christ or in the name of humanity for the cessation of the slaughter of boys and the suicide of nations and for a reconciliation of peoples upon terms of some more reasonable argument than that of high explosives. Peace proposals from the Pope, from Germany, from Austria, were rejected with fierce denunciation, most passionate scorn, as "peace plots" and "peace traps," not without the terrible logic of the vicious circle, because, indeed, there was no sincerity of renunciation in some of those offers of peace, and the powers hostile to us were simply trying our strength and our weakness in order to make their own kind of peace which should be that of conquest. The gamblers, playing the game of "poker," with crowns and armies as their stakes, were upheld generally by the peoples, who would not abate one point of pride, one fraction of hate, one claim of vengeance, though all Europe should fall in ruin and the last legions of boys be massacred. There was no call from people to people across the frontiers of hostility: "Let us end this homicidal mania! Let us get back to sanity and save our younger sons. Let us hand over to justice those who will continue the slaughter of our youth!" There was no forgiveness, no generous instinct, no large-hearted common sense in any combatant nation of Europe. Like wolves they had their teeth in one another's throats, and would not let go, though all bloody and exhausted, until one should fall at the last gasp, to be mangled by the others. Yet in each nation, even in Germany, there were men and women who saw the folly of the war and the crime of it, and desired to end it by some act of renunciation and repentance, and by some uplifting of the people's spirit to vault the frontiers of hatred and the barbed wire which hedged in patriotism. Some of them were put in prison. Most of them saw the impossibility of counteracting the forces of insanity which had made the world mad, and kept silent, hiding their thoughts and brooding over them. The leaders of the nations continued to use mob-passion as their argument and justification, excited it anew when its fires burned low, focused it upon definite objectives, and gave it a sense of righteousness by the high-sounding watchwords of liberty, justice, honor, and retribution. Each side proclaimed Christ as its captain and invoked the blessing and aid of the God of Christendom, though Germans were allied with Turks and France was full of black and yellow men. The German people did not try to avert their ruin by denouncing the criminal acts of their war lords nor by deploring the cruelties they had committed. The Allies did not help them to do so, because of their lust for bloody vengeance and their desire for the spoils of victory. The peoples shared the blame of their rulers because they were not nobler than their rulers. They cannot now plead ignorance or betrayal by false ideals which duped them, because character does not depend on knowledge, and it was the character of European peoples which failed in the crisis of the world's fate, so that they followed the call-back of the beast in the jungle rather than the voice of the Crucified One whom they pretended to adore.

III

The character of European peoples failed in common sense and in Christian charity. It did not fail in courage to endure great agonies, to suffer death largely, to be obedient to the old tradition of patriotism and to the stoic spirit of old fighting races.

In courage I do not think there was much difference between the chief combatants. The Germans, as a race, were wonderfully brave until their spirit was broken by the sure knowledge of defeat and by lack of food. Many times through all those years they marched shoulder to shoulder, obedient to discipline, to certain death, as I saw them on the Somme, like martyrs. They marched for their Fatherland, inspired by the spirit of the German race, as it had entered their souls by the memory of old German songs, old heroic ballads, their German home life, their German women, their love of little old towns on hillsides or in valleys, by all the meaning to them of that word Germany, which is like the name of England to us—who is fool enough to think otherwise?—and fought often, a thousand times, to the death, as I saw their bodies heaped in the fields of the Somme and round their pill-boxes in Flanders and in the last phase of the war behind the Hindenburg line round their broken batteries on the way of Mons and Le Cateau. The German people endured years of semi-starvation and a drain of blood greater than any other fighting people—two million dead—before they lost all vitality, hope, and pride and made their abject surrender. At the beginning they were out for conquest, inspired by arrogance and pride. Before the end they fought desperately to defend the Fatherland from the doom which cast its black shadow on them as it drew near. They were brave, those Germans, whatever the brutality of individual men and the cold-blooded cruelty of their commanders.

The courage of France is to me like an old heroic song, stirring the heart. It was medieval in its complete adherence to the faith of valor and its spirit of sacrifice for La Patrie. If patriotism were enough as the gospel of life—Nurse Cavell did not think so—France as a nation was perfect in that faith. Her people had no doubt as to their duty. It was to defend their sacred soil from the enemy which had invaded it. It was to hurl the brutes back from the fair fields they had ravaged and despoiled. It was to liberate their brothers and sisters from the outrageous tyranny of the German yoke in the captured country. It was to seek vengeance for bloody, foul, and abominable deeds.

In the first days of the war France was struck by heavy blows which sent her armies reeling back in retreat, but before the first battle of the Marne, when her peril was greatest, when Paris seemed doomed, the spirit of the French soldiers rose to a supreme act of faith—which was fulfilled when Foch attacked in the center, when Manoury struck on the enemy's flank and hundreds of thousands of young Frenchmen hurled themselves, reckless of life, upon the monster which faltered and then fled behind the shelter of the Aisne. With bloodshot eyes and parched throats and swollen tongues, blind with sweat and blood, mad with the heat and fury of attack, the French soldiers fought through that first battle of the Marne and saved France from defeat and despair.

After that, year after year, they flung themselves against the German defense and died in heaps, or held their lines, as at Verdun, against colossal onslaught, until the dead lay in masses. But the living said, "They shall not pass!" and kept their word.

The people of France—above all, the women of France—behind the lines, were the equals of the fighting-men in valor. They fought with despair, through many black months, and did not yield. They did the work of their men in the fields, and knew that many of them—the sons or brothers or lovers or husbands—would never return for the harvest-time, but did not cry to have them back until the enemy should be thrust out of France. Behind the German line, under German rule, the French people, prisoners in their own land, suffered most in spirit, but were proud and patient in endurance.

"Why don't your people give in?" asked a German officer of a woman in Nesle. "France is bleeding to death."

"We shall go on for two years, or three years, or four, or five, and in the end we shall smash you," said the woman who told me this.

The German officer stared at her and said, "You people are wonderful!"

Yes, they were wonderful, the French, and their hatred of the Germans, their desire for vengeance, complete and terrible, at all cost of life, even though France should bleed to death and die after victory, is to be understood in the heights and depths of its hatred and in the passion of its love for France and liberty. When I think of France I am tempted to see no greater thing than such patriotism as that to justify the gospel of hate against such an enemy, to uphold vengeance as a sweet virtue. Yet if I did so I should deny the truth that has been revealed to many men and women by the agony of the war—that if civilization may continue patriotism is "not enough," that international hatred will produce other wars worse than this, in which civilization will be submerged, and that vengeance, even for dreadful crimes, cannot be taken of a nation without punishing the innocent more than the guilty, so that out of its cruelty and injustice new fires of hatred are lighted, the demand for vengeance passes to the other side, and the devil finds another vicious circle in which to trap the souls of men and "catch 'em all alive O!"

To deny that would also be a denial of the faith with which millions of young Frenchmen rushed to the colors in the first days of the war. It was they who said, "This is a war to end war." They told me so. It was they who said: "German militarism must be killed so that all militarism shall be abolished. This is a war for liberty." So soldiers of France spoke to me on a night when

Paris was mobilized and the tragedy began. It is a Frenchman—Henri Barbusse—who, in spite of the German invasion, the outrages against his people, the agony of France, has the courage to say that all peoples in Europe were involved in the guilt of that war because of their adherence to that old barbaric creed of brute force and the superstitious servitude of their souls to symbols of national pride based upon military tradition. He even denounces the salute to the flag, instinctive and sacred in the heart of every Frenchman, as a fetish worship in which the narrow bigotry of national arrogance is raised above the rights of the common masses of men. He draws no distinction between a war of defense and a war of aggression, because attack is the best means of defense, and all peoples who go to war dupe themselves into the belief that they do so in defense of their liberties, and rights, and power, and property. Germany attacked France first because she was ready first and sure of her strength. France would have attacked Germany first to get back Alsace-Lorraine, to wipe out 1870, if she also had been ready and sure of her strength. The political philosophy on both sides of the Rhine was the same. It was based on military power and rivalry of secret alliances and imperial ambitions. The large-hearted internationalism of Jean Jaures, who with all his limitations was a great Frenchman, patriot, and idealist, had failed among his own people and in Germany, and the assassin's bullet was his reward for the adventure of his soul to lift civilization above the level of the old jungle law and to save France from the massacre which happened.

In war France was wonderful, most heroic in sacrifice, most splendid in valor. In her dictated peace, which was ours also, her leaders were betrayed by the very evil which millions of young Frenchmen had gone out to kill at the sacrifice of their own lives. Militarism was exalted in France above the ruins of German militarism. It was a peace of vengeance which punished the innocent more than the guilty, the babe at the breast more than the Junker in his Schloss, the poor working-woman more than the war lord, the peasant who had been driven to the shambles more than Sixt von Arnim or Rupprecht of Bavaria, or Ludendorff, or Hindenburg. It is a peace that can only be maintained by the power of artillery and by the conscription of every French boy who shall be trained for the next "war of defense" (twenty years hence, thirty years hence), when Germany is strong again—stronger than France because of her population, stronger then, enormously, than France, in relative numbers of able-bodied men than in August, 1914. So if that philosophy continue—and I do not think it will—the old fear will be re-established, the old burdens of armament will be piled up anew, the people of France will be weighed down as before under a military regime stifling their liberty of thought and action, wasting the best years of their boyhood in barracks, seeking protective alliances, buying allies at great cost, establishing the old spy system, the old diplomacy, the old squalid ways of inter—national politics, based as before on fear and force. Marshal Foch was a fine soldier. Clemenceau was a strong Minister of

War. There was no man great enough in France to see beyond the passing triumph of military victory and by supreme generosity of soul to lift their enemy out of the dirt of their despair, so that the new German Republic should arise from the ruins of the Empire, remorseful of their deeds in France and Belgium, with all their rage directed against their ancient tyranny, and with a new-born spirit of democratic liberty reaching across the old frontiers.

Is that the foolish dream of the sentimentalist? No, more than that; for the German people, after their agony, were ready to respond to generous dealing, pitiful in their need of it, and there is enough sentiment in German hearts—the most sentimental people in Europe—to rise with a surge of emotion to a new gospel of atonement if their old enemies had offered a chance of grace. France has not won the war by her terms of peace nor safeguarded her frontiers for more than a few uncertain years. By harking back to the old philosophy of militarism she has re-established peril amid a people drained of blood and deeply in debt. Her support of reactionary forces in Russia is to establish a government which will guarantee the interest on French loans and organize a new military regime in alliance with France and England. Meanwhile France looks to the United States and British people to protect her from the next war, when Germany shall be strong again. She is playing the militarist role without the strength to sustain it.

IV

What of England?... Looking back at the immense effort of the British people in the war, our high sum of sacrifice in blood and treasure, and the patient courage of our fighting-men, the world must, and does, indeed, acknowledge that the old stoic virtue of our race was called out by this supreme challenge, and stood the strain. The traditions of a thousand years of history filled with war and travail and adventure, by which old fighting races had blended with different strains of blood and temper—Roman, Celtic, Saxon, Danish, Norman-survived in the fiber of our modern youth, country-bred or city-bred, in spite of the weakening influences of slumdom, vicious environment, ill-nourishment, clerkship, and sedentary life. The Londoner was a good soldier. The Liverpools and Manchesters were hard and tough in attack and defense. The South Country battalions of Devons and Dorsets, Sussex and Somersets, were not behindhand in ways of death. The Scots had not lost their fire and passion, but were terrible in their onslaught. The Irish battalions, with recruiting cut off at the base, fought with their old gallantry, until there were few to answer the last roll-call. The Welsh dragon encircled Mametz Wood, devoured the "Cockchafers" on Pilkem Ridge, and was hard on the trail of the Black Eagle in the last offensive. The Australians and Canadians had all the British quality of courage and the benefit of a harder physique, gained by outdoor life and unweakened ancestry. In the mass, apart from neurotic types here and there among officers and men, the stock was true and strong. The spirit of a seafaring race which has the salt in its blood from Land's End to John o' Groat's and back again to Wapping had not been destroyed, but answered the ruffle of Drake's drum and, with simplicity and gravity in royal navy and in merchant marine, swept the highways of the seas, hunted worse monsters than any fabulous creatures of the deep, and shirked no dread adventure in the storms and darkness of a spacious hell. The men who went to Zeebrugge were the true sons of those who fought the Spanish Armada and singed the King o' Spain's beard in Cadiz harbor. The victors of the Jutland battle were better men than Nelson's (the scourings of the prisons and the sweepings of the press-gang) and not less brave in frightful hours. Without the service of the British seamen the war would have been lost for France and Italy and Belgium, and all of us.

The flower of our youth went out to France and Flanders, to Egypt, Palestine, Gallipoli, Mesopotamia, and Saloniki, and it was a fine flower of gallant boyhood, clean, for the most part eager, not brutal except by intensive training, simple in minds and hearts, chivalrous in instinct, without hatred, adventurous, laughter-loving, and dutiful. That is God's truth, in spite of vice-rotted, criminal, degenerate, and brutal fellows in many battalions, as in all crowds of men.

In millions of words during the years of war I recorded the bravery of our troops on the western front, their patience, their cheerfulness, suffering, and agony; yet with all those words describing day by day the incidents of their life in war I did not exaggerate the splendor of their stoic spirit or the measure of their sacrifice. The heroes of mythology were but paltry figures compared with those who, in the great war, went forward to the roaring devils of modern gun-fire, dwelt amid high explosives more dreadful than dragons, breathed in the fumes of poison-gas more foul than the breath of Medusa, watched and slept above mine-craters which upheaved the hell-fire of Pluto, and defied thunderbolts more certain in death-dealing blows than those of Jove.

Something there was in the spirit of our men which led them to endure these things without revolt—ideals higher than the selfish motives of life. They did not fight for greed or glory, not for conquest, nor for vengeance. Hatred was not the inspiration of the mass of them, for I am certain that except in hours when men "see red" there was no direct hatred of the men in the opposite trenches, but, on the other hand, a queer sense of fellow—feeling, a humorous sympathy for "old Fritz," who was in the same bloody mess as themselves. Our generals, it is true, hated the Germans. "I should like one week in Cologne," one of them told me, before there seemed ever a chance of getting there, "and I would let my men loose in the streets and turn a blind eye to anything they liked to do."

Some of our officers were inspired by a bitter, unrelenting hate.

"If I had a thousand Germans in a row," one of them said to me, "I would cut all their throats, and enjoy the job."

But that was not the mentality of the men in the ranks, except those who were murderers by nature and pleasure. They gave their cigarettes to prisoners and filled their water-bottles and chatted in a friendly way with any German who spoke a little English, as I have seen them time and time again on days of battle, in the fields of battle. There were exceptions to this treatment, but even the Australians and the Scots, who were most fierce in battle, giving no quarter sometimes, treated their prisoners with humanity when they were bundled back. Hatred was not the motive which made our men endure all things. It was rather, as I have said, a refusal in their souls to be beaten in manhood by all the devils of war, by all its terrors, or by its beastliness, and at the back of all the thought that the old country was "up against it" and that they were there to avert the evil.

Young soldiers of ours, not only of officer rank, but of "other ranks," as they were called, were inspired at the beginning, and some of them to the end, with a simple, boyish idealism. They saw no other causes of war than German brutality. The enemy to them was the monster who had to be destroyed lest the world and its beauty should perish—and that was true so long as the individual German, who loathed the war, obeyed the discipline of the herd-leaders and did not revolt against the natural laws which, when the war had once started, bade him die in defense of his own Fatherland. Many of those boys of ours made a dedication of their lives upon the altar of sacrifice, believing that by this service and this sacrifice they would help the victory of civilization over barbarism, and of Christian morality over the devil's law. They believed that they were fighting to dethrone militarism, to insure the happiness and liberties of civilized peoples, and were sure of the gratitude of their nation should they not have the fate to fall upon the field of honor, but go home blind or helpless.

I have read many letters from boys now dead in which they express that faith.

"Do not grieve for me," wrote one of them, "for I shall be proud to die for my country's sake."

"I am happy," wrote another (I quote the tenor of his letters), "because, though I hate war, I feel that this is the war to end war. We are the last victims of this way of argument. By smashing the German war-machine we shall prove for all time the criminal folly of militarism and Junkerdom."

There were young idealists like that, and they were to be envied for their faith, which they brought with them from public schools and from humble homes where they had read old books and heard old watchwords. I think, at the beginning of the war there were many like that. But as it continued year after year doubts crept in, dreadful suspicions of truth more complex than the old simplicity, a sense of revolt against sacrifice unequally shared and devoted to a purpose which was not that for which they had been called to fight.

They had been told that they were fighting for liberty. But their first lesson was the utter loss of individual liberty under a discipline which made the private soldier no more than a number. They were ordered about like galley—slaves, herded about like cattle, treated individually and in the mass with utter disregard of their comfort and well-being. Often, as I know, they were detrained at rail-heads in the wind and rain and by ghastly errors of staff-work kept waiting for their food until they were weak and famished. In the base camps men of one battalion were drafted into other battalions, where they lost their old comrades and were unfamiliar with the speech and habits of a crowd belonging to different counties, the Sussex men going to a Manchester regiment, the Yorkshire men being drafted to a Surrey unit. By R.T.O.'s and A.M.L.O.'s and camp commandments and town majors and staff pups men were bullied and bundled about, not like human beings, but like dumb beasts, and in a thousand ways injustice, petty tyranny, hard work, degrading punishments for trivial offenses, struck at their souls and made the name of personal liberty a mockery. From their own individuality they argued to broader issues. Was this war for liberty? Were the masses of men on either side fighting with free will as free men? Those Germans—were they not under discipline, each man of them, forced to fight whether they liked it or not? Compelled to go forward to sacrifice, with machine-guns behind them to shoot them down if they revolted against their slave-drivers? What liberty had they to follow their conscience or their judgment—"Theirs not to reason why, theirs but to do and die"—like all soldiers in all armies. Was it not rather that the masses of men engaged in slaughter were serving the purpose of powers above them, rival powers, greedy for one another's markets, covetous of one another's wealth, and callous of the lives of humble men? Surely if the leaders of the warring nations were put together for even a week in some such place as Hooge, or the Hohenzollern redoubt, afflicted by the usual harassing fire, poison-gas, mine explosions, lice, rats, and the stench of rotting corpses, with the certainty of death or dismemberment at the week-end, they would settle the business and come to terms before the week was out. I heard that proposition put forward many times by young officers of ours, and as an argument against their own sacrifice they found it unanswerable.

V

The condition and psychology of their own country as they read about it in the Paris Daily Mail, which was first to come into their billets, filled some of these young men with distress and disgust, strengthened into rage when they went home on leave. The deliberate falsification of news (the truth of which they heard from private channels) made them discredit the whole presentation of our case and state. They said, "Propaganda!" with a sharp note of scorn. The breezy optimism of public men, preachers, and journalists, never downcast by black news, never agonized by the slaughter in these fields, minimizing horrors and loss and misery, crowing over the enemy, prophesying early victory which did not come, accepting all the destruction of manhood (while they stayed safe) as a necessary and inevitable "misfortune," had a depressing effect on men who knew they were doomed to die, in the law of averages, if the war went on. "Damn their optimism!" said some of our officers. "It's too easy for those behind the lines. It is only we who have the right of optimism. It's we who have to do the dirty work! They seem to think we like the job! What are they doing to bring the end nearer?"

The frightful suspicion entered the heads of some of our men (some of those I knew) that at home people liked the war and were not anxious to end it, and did not care a jot for the sufferings of the soldiers. Many of them came back from seven days' leave fuming and sullen. Everybody was having a good time. Munition-workers were earning wonderful wages and spending them on gramophones, pianos, furs, and the "pictures." Everybody was gadding about in a state of joyous exultation. The painted flapper was making herself sick with the sweets of life after office hours in government employ, where she did little work for a lot of pocket-money. The society girl was dancing bare-legged for "war charities," pushing into bazaars for the "poor, dear wounded," getting her pictures into the papers as a "notable warworker," married for the third time in three years; the middle-class cousin was driving staff-officers to Whitehall, young gentlemen of the Air Service to Hendon, junior secretaries to their luncheon. Millions of girls were in some kind of fancy dress with buttons and shoulder—straps, breeches and puttees, and they seemed to be making a game of the war and enjoying it thoroughly. Oxford dons were harvesting, and proud of their prowess with the pitchfork—behold their patriotism!—while the boys were being blown to bits on the Yser Canal. Miners were striking for more wages, factory hands were downing tools for fewer hours at higher pay, the government was paying any price for any labor—while Tommy Atkins drew his one-and-twopence and made a little go a long way in a wayside estaminet before jogging up the Menin road to have his head blown off. The government had created a world of parasites and placemen housed in enormous hotels, where they were engaged at large salaries upon mysterious unproductive labors which seemed to have no result in front-line trenches. Government contractors were growing fat on the life of war, amassing vast fortunes, juggling with excess profits, battening upon the flesh and blood of boyhood in the fighting-lines. These old men, these fat men, were breathing out fire and fury against the Hun, and vowing by all their gods that they would see their last son die in the last ditch rather than agree to any peace except that of destruction. There were "fug committees" (it was Lord Kitchener's word) at the War Office, the Board of Trade, the Foreign Office, the Home Office, the Ministry of Munitions, the Ministry of Information, where officials on enormous salaries smoked cigars of costly brands and decided how to spend vast sums of public money on "organization" which made no difference to the man stifling his cough below the parapet in a wet fog of Flanders, staring across No Man's Land for the beginning of a German attack.

In all classes of people there was an epidemic of dancing, jazzing, card-playing, theater-going. They were keeping their spirits up wonderfully. Too well for men slouching about the streets of London on leave, and wondering at all this gaiety, and thinking back to the things they had seen and forward to the things they would have to do. People at home, it seemed, were not much interested in the life of the trenches; anyhow, they could not understand. The soldier listened to excited tales of air raids. A bomb had fallen in the next street. The windows had been broken. Many people had been killed in a house somewhere in Hackney. It was frightful. The Germans were devils. They ought to be torn to pieces, every one of them. The soldier on leave saw crowds of people taking shelter in underground railways, working—men among them, sturdy lads, panic-stricken. But for his own wife and children he had an evil sense of satisfaction in these sights. It would do them good. They would know what war meant—just a little. They would not be so easy in their damned optimism. An air raid? Lord God, did they know what a German barrage was like? Did they guess how men walked day after day through harassing fire to the trenches? Did they have any faint idea of life in a sector where men stood, slept, ate, worked, under the fire of eight-inch shells, five-point—nines, trench-mortars, rifle-grenades, machine-gun bullets, snipers, to say nothing of poison-gas, long-range fire on the billets in small farmsteads, and on every moonlight night air raids above wooden hutments so closely crowded into a small space that hardly a bomb could fall without killing a group of men.

"Oh, but you have your dugouts!" said a careless little lady.

The soldier smiled.

It was no use talking. The people did not want to hear the tragic side of things. Bairnsfather's "Ole Bill" seemed to them to typify the spirit of the fighting-man... "'Alf a mo', Kaiser!"...

The British soldier was gay and careless of death—always. Shell-fire meant nothing to him. If he were killed—well, after all, what else could he expect? Wasn't that what he was out for? The twice-married girl knew a charming boy in the air force. He had made love to her even before Charlie was "done in." These dear boys were so greedy for love. She could not refuse them, poor darlings! Of course they had all got to die for liberty, and that sort of thing. It was very sad. A terrible thing—war!... Perhaps she had better give up dancing for a week, until Charlie had been put into the casualty lists.

"What are we fighting for?" asked officers back from leave, turning over the pages of the Sketch and Tatler, with pictures of race-meetings, strike-meetings, bare—backed beauties at war bazaars, and portraits of profiteers in the latest honors list. "Are we going to die for these swine? These parasites and prostitutes? Is this the war for noble ideals, liberty, Christianity, and civilization? To hell with all this filth! The world has gone mad and we are the victims of insanity."

Some of them said that below all that froth there were deep and quiet waters in England. They thought of the anguish of their own wives and mothers, their noble patience, their uncomplaining courage, their spiritual faith in the purpose of the war. Perhaps at the heart England was true and clean and pitiful. Perhaps, after, all, many people at home were suffering more than the fighting-men, in agony of spirit. It was unwise to let bitterness poison their brains. Anyhow, they had to go on. How long, how long, O Lord?

"How long is it going to last?" asked the London Rangers of their chaplain. He lied to them and said another three months. Always he had absolute knowledge that the war would end three months later. That was certain. "Courage!" he said. "Courage to the end of the last lap!"

Most of the long-service men were dead and gone long before the last lap came. It was only the new boys who went as far as victory. He asked permission of the general to withdraw nineteen of them from the line to instruct them for Communion. They were among the best soldiers, and not afraid of the ridicule of their fellows because of their religious zeal. The chaplain's main purpose was to save their lives, for a while, and give them a good time and spiritual comfort. They had their good time. Three weeks later came the German attack on Arras and they were all killed. Every man of them.

The chaplain, an Anglican, found it hard to reconcile Christianity with such a war as this, but he did not camouflage the teachings of the Master he tried to serve. He preached to his men the gospel of love and forgiveness of enemies. It was reported to the general, who sent for him.

"Look here, I can't let you go preaching 'soft stuff' to my men. I can't allow all that nonsense about love. My job is to teach them to hate. You must either cooperate with me or go."

The chaplain refused to change his faith or his teaching, and the general thought better of his intervention.

For all chaplains it was difficult. Simple souls were bewildered by the conflict between the spirit of Christianity and the spirit of war. Many of them—officers as well as men—were blasphemous in their scorn of "parson stuff," some of them frightfully ironical.

A friend of mine watched two chaplains passing by. One of them was a tall man with a crown and star on his shoulder-strap.

"I wonder," said my friend, with false simplicity, "whether Jesus Christ would have been a lieutenant—colonel?"

On the other hand, many men found help in religion, and sought its comfort with a spiritual craving. They did not argue about Christian ethics and modern warfare. Close to death in the midst of tragedy, conscious in a strange way of their own spiritual being and of a spirituality present among masses of men above the muck of war, the stench of corruption, and fear of bodily extinction, they groped out toward God. They searched for some divine wisdom greater than the folly of the world, for a divine aid which would help them to greater courage. The spirit of God seemed to come to them across No Man's Land with pity and comradeship. Catholic soldiers had a simpler, stronger faith than men of Protestant denominations, whose faith depended more on ethical arguments and intellectual reasonings. Catholic chaplains had an easier task. Leaving aside all argument, they heard the confessions of the soldiers, gave them absolution for their sins, said mass for them in wayside barns, administered the sacraments, held the cross to their lips when they fell mortally wounded, anointed them when the surgeon's knife was at work, called the names of Jesus and Mary into dying ears. There was no need of argument here. The old faith which has survived many wars, many plagues, and the old wickedness of men was still full of consolation to those who accepted it as little children, and by their own agony hoped for favor from the Man of Sorrows who was hanged upon a cross, and found a mother-love in the vision of Mary, which came to them when they were in fear and pain and the struggle of death. The padre had a definite job to do in the trenches and for that reason was allowed more liberty in the line than other chaplains. Battalion officers, surgeons, and nurses were patient with mysterious rites which they did not understand, but which gave comfort, as they saw, to wounded men; and the heroism with which many of those priests worked under fire, careless of their own lives, exalted by spiritual fervor, yet for the most part human and humble and large-hearted and tolerant, aroused a general admiration throughout the army. Many of the Protestant clergy were equally devoted, but they were handicapped by having to rely more upon providing physical comforts for the men than upon spiritual acts, such as anointing and absolution, which were accepted without question by Catholic soldiers.

Yet the Catholic Church, certain of its faith, and all other churches claiming that they teach the gospel of Christ, have been challenged to explain their attitude during the war and the relation of their teaching to the world-tragedy, the Great Crime, which has happened. It will not be easy for them to do so. They will have to explain how it is that German bishops, priests, pastors, and flocks, undoubtedly sincere in their professions of faith, deeply pious, as our soldiers saw in Cologne, and fervent in their devotion to the sacraments on their side of the fighting-line, as the Irish Catholics on our side, were able to reconcile this piety with their war of aggression. The faith of the Austrian Catholics must be explained in relation to their crimes, if they were criminal, as we say they were, in leading the way to this war by their ultimatum to Serbia. If Christianity has no restraining influence upon the brutal instincts of those who profess and follow its faith, then surely it is time the world abandoned so ineffective a creed and turned to other laws likely to have more influence on human relationships. That, brutally, is the argument of the thinking world against the clergy of all nations who all claimed to be acting according to the justice of God and the spirit of Christ. It is a powerful argument, for the simple mind, rejecting casuistry, cuts straight to the appalling contrast between Christian profession and Christian practice, and says: "Here, in this war, there was no conflict between one faith and another, but a murderous death-struggle between many nations holding the same faith, preaching the same gospel, and claiming the same God as their protector. Let us seek some better truth than that hypocrisy! Let us, if need be, in honesty, get back to the savage worship of national gods, the Ju-ju of the tribe."

My own belief is that the war was no proof against the Christian faith, but rather is a revelation that we are as desperately in need of the spirit of Christ as at any time in the history of mankind. But I think the clergy of all nations, apart from a heroic and saintly few, subordinated their faith, which is a gospel of charity, to national limitations. They were patriots before they were priests, and their patriotism was sometimes as limited, as narrow, as fierce, and as bloodthirsty as that of the people who looked to them for truth and light. They were often fiercer, narrower, and more desirous of vengeance than the soldiers who fought, because it is now a known truth that the soldiers, German and Austrian, French and Italian and British, were sick of the unending slaughter long before the ending of the war, and would have made a peace more fair than that which now prevails if it had been put to the common vote in the trenches; whereas the Archbishop of Canterbury, the Archbishop of Cologne, and the clergy who spoke from many pulpits in many nations, under the Cross of Christ, still stoked up the fires of hate and urged the armies to go on fighting "in the cause of justice," "for the defense of the Fatherland," "for Christian righteousness," to the bitter end. Those words are painful to write, but as I am writing this book for truth's sake, at all cost, I let them stand....

VI

The entire aspect of the war was changed by the Russian Revolution, followed by the collapse of the Russian armies and the Peace of Brest-Litovsk, when for the first time the world heard the strange word "Bolshevism," and knew not what it meant.

The Russian armies had fought bravely in the first years of the war, with an Oriental disregard of death. Under generals in German pay, betrayed by a widespread net of anarchy and corruption so villainous that arms and armaments sent out from England had to be bribed on their way from one official to another, and never reached the front, so foul in callousness of human life that soldiers were put into the fighting-line without rifle or ammunition, these Russian peasants flung themselves not once, but many times, against the finest troops of Germany, with no more than naked bayonets against powerful artillery and the scythe of machine-gun fire, and died like sheep in the slaughter-houses of Chicago. Is it a wonder that at the last they revolted against this immolation, turned round upon their tyrants, and said: "You are the enemy. It is you that we will destroy"?

By this new revelation they forgot their hatred of Germans. They said: "You are our brothers; we have no hatred against you. We do not want to kill you. Why should you kill us? We are all of us the slaves of bloodthirsty castes, who use our flesh for their ambitions. Do not shoot us, brothers, but join hands against the common tyranny which enslaves our peoples." They went forward with outstretched hands, and were shot, down like rabbits by some Germans, and by others were not shot, because German soldiers gaped, wide-eyed, at this new gospel, as it seemed, and said: "They speak words of truth. Why should we kill one another?"

The German war lords ordered a forward movement, threatened their own men with death if they fraternized with Russians, and dictated their terms of peace on the old lines of military conquest. But as Ludendorff has confessed, and as we now know from other evidence, many German soldiers were "infected" with Bolshevism and lost their fighting spirit.

Russia was already in anarchy. Constitutional government had been replaced by the soviets and by committees of soldiers and workmen. Kerensky had fled. Lenin and Trotzky were the Marat and Danton of the Revolution, and decreed the Reign of Terror. Tales of appalling atrocity, some true, some false (no one can tell how true or how false), came through to France and England. It was certain that the whole fabric of society in Russia had dissolved in the wildest anarchy the world has seen in modern times, and that the Bolshevik gospel of "brotherhood" with humanity was, at least, rudely "interrupted" by wholesale murder within its own boundaries.

One other thing was certain. Having been relieved of the Russian menace, Germany was free to withdraw her armies on that front and use all her striking force in the west. It should have cautioned our generals to save their men for the greatest menace that had confronted them. But without caution they fought the battles of 1917, in Flanders, as I have told.

In 1917 and in the first half of 1918 there seemed no ending to the war by military means. Even many of our generals who had been so breezy in their optimism believed now that the end must come by diplomatic means—a "peace by understanding." I had private talks with men in high command, who acknowledged that the way must be found, and the British mind prepared for negotiations, because there must come a limit to the drain of blood on each side. It was to one man in the world that many men in all armies looked for a way out of this frightful impasse.

President Wilson had raised new hope among many men who otherwise were hopeless. He not only spoke high words, but defined the meanings of them. His definition of liberty seemed sound and true, promising the self-determination of peoples. His offer to the German people to deal generously with them if they overthrew their tyranny raised no quarrel among British soldiers. His hope of a new diplomacy, based upon "open covenants openly arrived at," seemed to cut at the root of the old evil in Europe by which the fate of peoples had been in the hands of the few. His Fourteen Points set out clearly and squarely a just basis of peace. His advocacy of a League of Nations held out a vision of a new world by which the great and small democracies should be united by a common pledge to preserve peace and submit their differences to a supreme court of arbitration. Here at last was a leader of the world, with a clear call to the nobility in men rather than to their base passions, a gospel which would raise civilization from the depths into which it had fallen, and a practical remedy for that suicidal mania which was exhausting the combatant nations.

I think there were many millions of men on each side of the fighting-line who thanked God because President Wilson had come with a wisdom greater than the folly which was ours to lead the way to an honorable peace and a new order of nations. I was one of them... Months passed, and there was continual fighting, continued slaughter, and no sign that ideas would prevail over force. The Germans launched their great offensive, broke through the British lines, and afterward through the French lines, and there were held and checked long enough for our reserves to be flung across the Channel—300,000 boys from England and Scotland, who had been held in hand as the last counters for the pool. The American army came in tidal waves across the Atlantic, flooded our back areas, reached the edge of the battlefields, were a new guaranty of strength. Their divisions passed mostly to the French front. With them, and with his own men, magnificent in courage still, and some of ours, Foch had his army of reserve, and struck.

So the war ended, after all, by military force, and by military victory greater than had seemed imaginable or possible six months before.

In the peace terms that followed there was but little trace of those splendid ideas which had been proclaimed by President Wilson. On one point after another he weakened, and was beaten by the old militarism which sat enthroned in the council-chamber, with its foot on the neck of the enemy. The "self-determination of peoples" was a hollow phrase signifying nothing. Open covenants openly arrived at were mocked by the closed doors of the

Conference. When at last the terms were published their merciless severity, their disregard of racial boundaries, their creation of hatreds and vendettas which would lead, as sure as the sun should rise, to new warfare, staggered humanity, not only in Germany and Austria, but in every country of the world, where at least minorities of people had hoped for some nobler vision of the world's needs, and for some healing remedy for the evils which had massacred its youth. The League of Nations, which had seemed to promise so well, was hedged round by limitations which made it look bleak and barren. Still it was peace, and the rivers of blood had ceased to flow, and the men were coming home again... Home again!

VII

The men came home in a queer mood, startling to those who had not watched them "out there," and to those who welcomed peace with flags. Even before their homecoming, which was delayed week after week, month after month, unless they were lucky young miners out for the victory push and back again quickly, strange things began to happen in France and Flanders, Egypt and Palestine. Men who had been long patient became suddenly impatient. Men who had obeyed all discipline broke into disobedience bordering on mutiny. They elected spokesmen to represent their grievances, like trade-unionists. They "answered back" to their officers in such large bodies, with such threatening anger, that it was impossible to give them "Field Punishment Number One," or any other number, especially as their battalion officers sympathized mainly with their point of view. They demanded demobilization according to their terms of service, which was for "the duration of the war." They protested against the gross inequalities of selection by which men of short service were sent home before those who had been out in 1914, 1915, 1916. They demanded justness, fair play, and denounced red tape and official lies. "We want to go home!" was their shout on parade. A serious business, subversive of discipline.

Similar explosions were happening in England. Bodies of men broke camp at Folkestone and other camps, demonstrated before town halls, demanded to speak with mayors, generals, any old fellows who were in authority, and refused to embark for France until they had definite pledges that they would receive demobilization papers without delay. Whitehall, the sacred portals of the War Office, the holy ground of the Horse Guards' Parade, were invaded by bodies of men who had commandeered ambulances and lorries and had made long journeys from their depots. They, too, demanded demobilization. They refused to be drafted out for service to India, Egypt, Archangel, or anywhere. They had "done their bit," according to their contract. It was for the War Office to fulfil its pledges. "Justice" was the word on their lips, and it was a word which put the wind up (as soldiers say) any staff-officers and officials who had not studied the laws of justice as they concern private soldiers, and who had dealt with them after the armistice and after the peace as they had dealt with them before—as numbers, counters to be shifted here and there according to the needs of the High Command. What was this strange word "justice" on soldiers' lips?... Red tape squirmed and writhed about the business of demobilization. Orders were made, communicated to the men, canceled even at the railway gates. Promises were made and broken. Conscripts were drafted off to India, Egypt, Mesopotamia, Archangel, against their will and contrary to pledge. Men on far fronts, years absent from their wives and homes, were left to stay there, fever-stricken, yearning for home, despairing. And while the old war was not yet cold in its grave we prepared for a new war against Bolshevik Russia, arranging for the spending of more millions, the sacrifice of more boys of ours, not openly, with the consent of the people, but on the sly, with a fine art of camouflage.

The purpose of the new war seemed to many men who had fought for "liberty" an outrage against the "self—determination of peoples" which had been the fundamental promise of the League of Nations, and a blatant hypocrisy on the part of a nation which denied self—government to Ireland. The ostensible object of our intervention in Russia was to liberate the Russian masses from "the bloody tyranny of the Bolsheviks," but this ardor for the liberty of Russia had not been manifest during the reign of Czardom and grand dukes when there were massacres of mobs in Moscow, bloody Sundays in St. Petersburg, pogroms in Riga, floggings of men and girls in many prisons, and when free speech, liberal ideas, and democratic uprisings had been smashed by Cossack knout and by the torture of Siberian exile.

Anyhow, many people believed that it was none of our business to suppress the Russian Revolution or to punish the leaders of it, and it was suspected by British working-men that the real motive behind our action was not a noble enthusiasm for liberty, but an endeavor to establish a reactionary government in Russia in order to crush a philosophy of life more dangerous to the old order in Europe than high explosives, and to get back the gold that had been poured into Russia by England and France. By a strange paradox of history, French journalists, forgetting their own Revolution, the cruelties of Robespierre and Marat, the September Massacres, the torture of Marie Antoinette in the Tuileries, the guillotining of many fair women of France, and after 1870 the terrors of the Commune, were most horrified by the anarchy in Russia, and most fierce in denunciation of the bloody struggle by which a people made mad by long oppression and infernal tyrannies strove to gain the liberties of life.

Thousands of British soldiers newly come from war in France were sullenly determined that they would not be dragged off to the new adventure. They were not alone. As Lord Rothermere pointed out, a French regiment mutinied on hearing a mere unfounded report that it was being sent to the Black Sea.

The United States and Japan were withdrawing. Only a few of our men, disillusioned by the ways of peace, missing the old comradeship of the ranks, restless, purposeless, not happy at home, seeing no prospect of good employment, said: "Hell!... Why not the army again, and Archangel, or any old where?" and volunteered for Mr. Winston Churchill's little war.

After the trouble of demobilization came peace pageants and celebrations and flag-wavings. But all was not right with the spirit of the men who came back. Something was wrong. They put on civilian clothes again, looked to their mothers and wives very much like the young men who had gone to business in the peaceful days before the August of '14. But they had not come back the same men. Something had altered in them. They were subject to queer moods, queer tempers, fits of profound depression alternating with a restless desire for pleasure. Many of them were easily moved to passion when they lost control of themselves. Many were bitter in their speech, violent in opinion, frightening. For some time, while they drew their unemployment pensions, they did not make any effort to get work for the future. They said: "That can wait. I've done my bit. The country can keep me for a while. I helped to save it... Let's go to the 'movies.'" They were listless when not excited by some "show." Something seemed to have snapped in them; their will-power. A quiet day at home did not appeal to them.

"Are you tired of me?" said the young wife, wistfully. "Aren't you glad to be home?"

"It's a dull sort of life," said some of them.

The boys, unmarried, hung about street-corners, searched for their pals, formed clubs where they smoked incessantly, and talked in an aimless way.

Then began the search for work. Boys without training looked for jobs with wages high enough to give them a margin for amusement, after the cost of living decently had been reckoned on the scale of high prices, mounting higher and higher. Not so easy as they had expected. The girls were clinging to their jobs, would not let go of the pocket-money which they had spent on frocks. Employers favored girl labor, found it efficient and, on the whole, cheap. Young soldiers who had been very skilled with machine-guns, trench-mortars, hand-grenades, found that they were classed with the ranks of unskilled labor in civil life. That was not good enough. They had fought for their country. They had served England. Now they wanted good jobs with short hours and good wages. They meant to get them. And meanwhile prices were rising in the shops. Suits of clothes, boots, food, anything, were at double and treble the price of pre-war days. The profiteers were rampant. They were out to bleed the men who had been fighting. They were defrauding the public with sheer, undisguised robbery, and the government did nothing to check them. England, they thought, was rotten all through.

Who cared for the men who had risked their lives and bore on their bodies the scars of war? The pensions doled out to blinded soldiers would not keep them alive. The consumptives, the gassed, the paralyzed, were forgotten in institutions where they lay hidden from the public eye. Before the war had been over six months "our heroes," "our brave boys in the trenches" were without preference in the struggle for existence.

Employers of labor gave them no special consideration. In many offices they were told bluntly (as I know) that they had "wasted" three or four years in the army and could not be of the same value as boys just out of school. The officer class was hardest hit in that way. They had gone straight from the public schools and universities to the army. They had been lieutenants, captains, and majors in the air force, or infantry battalions, or tanks, or trench-mortars, and they had drawn good pay, which was their pocket-money. Now they were at a loose end, hating the idea of office-work, but ready to knuckle down to any kind of decent job with some prospect ahead. What kind of job? What knowledge had they of use in civil life? None. They scanned advertisements, answered likely invitations, were turned down by elderly men who said: "I've had two hundred applications. And none of you young gentlemen from the army are fit to be my office-boy." They were the same elderly men who had said: "We'll fight to the last ditch. If I had six sons I would sacrifice them all in the cause of liberty and justice."

Elderly officers who had lost their businesses for their country's sake, who with a noble devotion had given up everything to "do their bit," paced the streets searching for work, and were shown out of every office where they applied for a post. I know one officer of good family and distinguished service who hawked round a subscription—book to private houses. It took him more courage than he had needed under shell-fire to ring the bell and ask to see "the lady of the house." He thanked God every time the maid handed back his card and said, "Not at home." On the first week's work he was four pounds out of pocket... Here and there an elderly officer blew out his brains. Another sucked a rubber tube fastened to the gas-jet... It would have been better if they had fallen on the field of honor.

Where was the nation's gratitude for the men who had fought and died, or fought and lived? Was it for this reward in peace that nearly a million of our men gave up their lives? That question is not my question. It is the question that was asked by millions of men in England in the months that followed the armistice, and it was answered in their own brains by a bitterness and indignation out of which may be lit the fires of the revolutionary spirit.

At street-corners, in tramway cars, in tea-shops where young men talked at the table next to mine I listened to conversations not meant for my ears, which made me hear in imagination and afar off (yet not very far, perhaps) the dreadful rumble of revolution, the violence of mobs led by fanatics. It was the talk, mostly, of demobilized soldiers. They asked one another, "What did we fight for?" and then other questions such as, "Wasn't this a war for liberty?" or, "We fought for the land, didn't we? Then why shouldn't we share the land?" Or, "Why should we be bled white by profiteers?"

They mentioned the government, and then laughed in a scornful way.

"The government," said one man, "is a conspiracy against the people. All its power is used to protect those who grow fat on big jobs, big trusts, big contracts. It used us to smash the German Empire in order to strengthen and enlarge the British Empire for the sake of those who grab the oil-wells, the gold fields, the minerals, and the markets of the world."

VIII

Out of such talk revolution is born, and revolution will not be averted by pretending that such words are not being spoken and that such thoughts are not seething among our working-classes. It will only be averted by cutting at the root of public suspicion, by cleansing our political state of its corruption and folly, and by a clear, strong call of noble-minded men to a new way of life in which a great people believing in the honor and honesty of its leadership and in fair reward for good labor shall face a period of poverty with courage, and co-operate unselfishly for the good of the commonwealth, inspired by a sense of fellowship with the workers of other nations. We have a long way to go and many storms to weather before we reach that state, if, by any grace that is in us, and above us, we reach it.

For there are disease and insanity in our present state, due to the travail of the war and the education of the war. The daily newspapers for many months have been filled with the record of dreadful crimes, of violence and passion. Most of them have been done by soldiers or ex-soldiers. The attack on the police station at Epsom, the destruction of the town hall at Luton, revealed a brutality of passion, a murderous instinct, which have been manifested again and again in other riots and street rows and solitary crimes. Those last are the worst because they are not inspired by a sense of injustice, however false, or any mob passion, but by homicidal mania and secret lust. The many murders of young women, the outrages upon little girls, the violent robberies that have happened since the demobilizing of the armies have appalled decent—minded people. They cannot understand the cause of this epidemic after a period when there was less crime than usual.

The cause is easy to understand. It is caused by the discipline and training of modern warfare. Our armies, as all armies, established an intensive culture of brutality. They were schools of slaughter. It was the duty of officers like Col. Ronald Campbell—"O.C. Bayonets" (a delightful man)—to inspire blood-lust in the brains of gentle boys who instinctively disliked butcher's work. By an ingenious system of psychology he played upon their nature, calling out the primitive barbarism which has been overlaid by civilized restraints, liberating the brute which has been long chained up by law and the social code of gentle life, but lurks always in the secret lairs of the human heart. It is difficult when the brute has been unchained, for the purpose of killing Germans, to get it into the collar again with a cry of, "Down, dog, down!" Generals, as I have told, were against the "soft stuff" preached by parsons, who were not quite militarized, though army chaplains. They demanded the gospel of hate, not that of love. But hate, when it dominates the psychology of men, is not restricted to one objective, such as a body of men behind barbed wire. It is a spreading poison. It envenoms the whole mind. Like jealousy.

It is the green-eyed monster which doth mock

The meat it feeds on.

Our men, living in holes in the earth like ape-men, were taught the ancient code of the jungle law, to track down human beasts in No Man's Land, to jump upon their bodies in the trenches, to kill quickly, silently, in a raid, to drop a hand-grenade down a dugout crowded with men, blowing their bodies to bits, to lie patiently for hours in a shell-hole for a sniping shot at any head which showed, to bludgeon their enemy to death or spit him on a bit of steel, to get at his throat if need be with nails and teeth. The code of the ape-man is bad for some temperaments. It is apt to become a habit of mind. It may surge up again when there are no Germans present, but some old woman behind an open till, or some policeman with a bull's-eye lantern and a truncheon, or in a street riot where fellow-citizens are for the time being "the enemy."

Death, their own or other people's, does not mean very much to some who, in the trenches, sat within a few yards of stinking corpses, knowing that the next shell might make such of them. Life was cheap in war. Is it not cheap in peace?...

The discipline of military life is mainly an imposed discipline—mechanical, and enforced in the last resort not by reason, but by field punishment or by a firing platoon. Whereas many men were made brisk and alert by discipline and saw the need of it for the general good, others were always in secret rebellion against its restraints of the individual will, and as soon as they were liberated broke away from it as slaves from their chains, and did not substitute self-discipline for that which had weighed heavy on them. With all its discipline, army life was full of lounging, hanging about, waste of time, waiting for things to happen. It was an irresponsible life for the rank and file. Food was brought to them, clothes were given to them, entertainments were provided behind the line, sports organized, their day ordered by high powers. There was no need to think for themselves, to act for themselves. They moved in herds dependent on their leaders. That, too, was a bad training for the individualism of civil life. It tended to destroy personal initiative and willpower. Another evil of the abnormal life of war sowed the seeds of insanity in the brains of men not strong enough to resist it. Sexually they were starved. For months they lived out of the sight and presence of women. But they came back into villages or towns where they were tempted by any poor slut who winked at them and infected them with illness. Men went to hospital with venereal disease in appalling numbers. Boys were ruined and poisoned for life. Future generations will pay the price of war not only in poverty and by the loss of the unborn children of the boys who died, but by an enfeebled stock and the heritage of insanity.

The Prime Minister said one day, "The world is suffering from shell-shock." That was true. But it suffered also from the symptoms of all that illness which comes from syphilis, whose breeding-ground is war.

The majority of our men were clean-living and clean—hearted fellows who struggled to come unscathed in soul from most of the horrors of war. They resisted the education of brutality and were not envenomed by the gospel of hate. Out of the dark depths of their experience they looked up to the light, and had visions of some better law of life than that which led to the world-tragedy. It would be a foul libel on many of them to besmirch their honor by a general accusation of lowered morality and brutal tendencies. Something in the spirit of our race and in the quality of our home life kept great numbers of them sound, chivalrous, generous-hearted, in spite of the frightful influences of degradation bearing down upon them out of the conditions of modern warfare. But the weak men, the vicious, the murderous, the primitive, were overwhelmed by these influences, and all that was base in them was intensified, and their passions were unleashed, with what result we have seen, and shall see, to our sorrow and the nation's peril.

The nation was in great peril after this war, and that peril will not pass in our lifetime except by heroic remedies. We won victory in the field and at the cost of our own ruin. We smashed Germany and Austria and Turkey, but the structure of our own wealth and industry was shattered, and the very foundations of our power were shaken and sapped. Nine months after the armistice Great Britain was spending at the rate of £2,000,000 a day in excess of her revenue. She was burdened with a national debt which had risen from 645 millions in 1914 to 7,800 millions in 1919. The pre-war expenditure of £200,000,000 per annum on the navy, army, and civil service pensions and interest on national debt had risen to 750 millions.

Our exports were dwindling down, owing to decreased output, so that foreign exchanges were rising against us and the American dollar was increasing in value as our proud old sovereign was losing its ancient standard. So that for all imports from the United States we were paying higher prices, which rose every time the rate of exchange dropped against us. The slaughter of 900,000 men of ours, the disablement of many more than that, had depleted our ranks of labor, and there was a paralysis of all our industry, owing to the dislocation of its machinery for purposes of war, the soaring cost of raw material, the crippling effect of high taxation, the rise in wages to meet high prices, and the lethargy of the workers. Ruin, immense, engulfing, annihilating to our strength as a nation and as an empire, stares us brutally in the eyes at the time I write this book, and I find no consolation in the thought that other nations in Europe, including the German people, are in the same desperate plight, or worse.

IX

The nation, so far, has not found a remedy for the evil that has overtaken us. Rather in a kind of madness that is not without a strange splendor, like a ship that goes down with drums beating and banners flying, we are racing toward the rocks. At this time, when we are sorely stricken and in dire poverty and debt, we have extended the responsibilities of empire and of world—power as though we had illimitable wealth. Our sphere of influence includes Persia, Thibet, Arabia, Palestine, Egypt—a vast part of the Mohammedan world. Yet if any part of our possessions were to break into revolt or raise a "holy war" against us, we should be hard pressed for men to uphold our power and prestige, and our treasury would be called upon in vain for gold. After the war which was to crush militarism the air force alone proposed an annual expenditure of more than twice as much money as the whole cost of the army before the war. While the armaments of the German people, whom we defeated in the war against militarism, are restricted to a few warships and a navy of 100,000 men at a cost reckoned as £10,000,000 a year, we are threatened with a naval and military program costing £300,000,000 a year. Was it for this our men fought? Was it to establish a new imperialism upheld by the power of guns that 900,000 boys of ours died in the war of liberation? I know it was otherwise. There are people at the street-corners who know; and in the tram-cars and factories and little houses in mean streets where there are empty chairs and the portraits of dead boys.

It will go hard with the government of England if it plays a grandiose drama before hostile spectators who refuse to take part in it. It will go hard with the nation, for it will be engulfed in anarchy.

At the present time, in this August of 1919, when I write these words, five years after another August, this England of ours, this England which I love because its history is in my soul and its blood is in my body, and I have seen the glory of its spirit, is sick, nigh unto death. Only great physicians may heal it, and its old vitality struggling against disease, and its old sanity against insanity. Our Empire is greater now in spaciousness than ever before, but our strength to hold it has ebbed low because of much death, and a strain too long endured, and strangling debts. The workman is tired and has slackened in his work. In his scheme of life he desires more luxury than our poverty affords. He wants higher wages, shorter hours, and less output—reasonable desires in our state before the war, unreasonable now because the cost of the war has put them beyond human possibility. He wants low prices with high wages and less work. It is false arithmetic and its falsity will be proved by a tremendous crash.

Some crash must come, tragic and shocking to our social structure. I see no escape from that, and only the hope that in that crisis the very shock of it will restore the mental balance of the nation and that all classes will combine under leaders of unselfish purpose, and fine vision, eager for evolution and not revolution, for peace and not for blood, for Christian charity and not for hatred, for civilization and not for anarchy, to reshape the conditions of our social life and give us a new working order, with more equality of labor and reward, duty and sacrifice, liberty and discipline of the soul, combining the virtue of patriotism with a generous spirit to other peoples across the old frontiers of hate. That is the hope but not the certainty.

It is only by that hope that one may look back upon the war with anything but despair. All the lives of those boys whom I saw go marching up the roads of France and Flanders to the fields of death, so splendid, so lovely in their youth, will have been laid down in vain if by their sacrifice the world is not uplifted to some plane a little higher than the barbarity which was let loose in Europe. They will have been betrayed if the agony they suffered is forgotten and "the war to end war" leads to preparations for new, more monstrous conflict.

Or is war the law of human life? Is there something more powerful than kaisers and castes which drives masses of men against other masses in death-struggles which they do not understand? Are we really poor beasts in the jungle, striving by tooth and claw, high velocity and poison-gas, for the survival of the fittest in an endless conflict? If that is so, then God mocks at us. Or, rather, if that is so, there is no God such as we men may love, with love for men.

The world will not accept that message of despair; and millions of men to-day who went through the agony of the war are inspired by the humble belief that humanity may be cured of its cruelty and stupidity, and that a brotherhood of peoples more powerful than a League of Nations may be founded in the world after its present sickness and out of the conflict of its anarchy.

That is the new vision which leads men on, and if we can make one step that way it will be better than that backward fall which civilization took when Germany played the devil and led us all into the jungle. The devil in Germany had to be killed. There was no other way, except by helping the Germans to kill it before it mastered them. Now let us exorcise our own devils and get back to kindness toward all men of good will. That also is the only way to heal the heart of the world and our own state. Let us seek the beauty of life and

God's truth somehow, remembering the boys who died too soon, and all the falsity and hatred of these past five years. By blood and passion there will be no healing. We have seen too much blood. We want to wipe it out of our eyes and souls. Let us have Peace.